D1038103

# GRAND TOUR
## A to Z
### The Capitals of Europe

0      Miles     300

FINLAND

HELSINKI

RWAY

SLO

SWEDEN

STOCKHOLM

*Baltic Sea*

COPENHAGEN

BERLIN

EAST GERMANY

POLAND

U. S. S. R.

MANY

CZECHOSLOVAKIA

DANUBE R.

VIENNA

AUSTRIA

HUNGARY

HTENSTEIN

ADUZ

ROMANIA

*Black Sea*

YUGOSLAVIA

DANUBE R.

BULGARIA

ISTANBUL

ITALY

*Adriatic Sea*

ROME

ALBANIA

T U R K E Y

GREECE

ATHENS

palacios

# Grand Tour A to Z: The Capitals of Europe

## Robert S. Kane's A to Z Travel Guides

Grand Tour A to Z: The Capitals of Europe

Eastern Europe A to Z

South Pacific A to Z

Canada A to Z

Asia A to Z

South America A to Z

Africa A to Z

# Grand Tour A to Z: The Capitals of Europe

## Robert S. Kane

DOUBLEDAY & COMPANY, INC., GARDEN CITY, NEW YORK

Research Editor: Max Drechsler
Endpaper Map: Rafael Palacios

"The Grand Tour: Eighteenth-Century Style" is
adapted from an article by Robert S. Kane that appeared in *Cue* magazine, May 16, 1970, and is reprinted by permission of Cue Publishing Company.
ISBN: 0-385-00441-9
Library of Congress Catalog Card Number 72-79401

For Billie and Ty

For Billie and TV

# Contents

viii

# *Foreword*

This is a book of the latter-day Grand Tour: of Europe's capitals, great and small, eminent and lesser, insular and mainland, familiar, and even—to some, I suspect—questionable, at least insofar as their eligibility for inclusion within these covers.

I have written *Grand Tour A to Z* for the traveler who is hopelessly in love with Europe, as a result of previous experience, or who is convinced he or she will be, given an opportunity. It is as much for the neophyte first-timer as for the veteran returnee anxious for new destinations in the capitals he has already visited, or for new capitals not yet inspected. It is about things we cross the Atlantic to find in Europe, much more than about things we encounter in Europe that are not all that distinctive from what we know at home.

Although all of the A to Z books are subjective and personal, this is probably more so than the others. I have employed the luxury of selectivity in this seventh volume more than in the other six, writing principally about what has interested me, to the exclusion of what I have been indifferent to, or disliked, or considered relatively insignificant. The on-location research for the book has extended over a period that I hesitate admitting approaches the quarter-century mark—of visits and repeated revisits. I was wandering about Europe a full decade before researching and writing *Africa A to Z*, the first of the series, and

I have never stopped: there have been frequent journeys in between work on the volumes dealing with South America, Asia, Canada, the South Pacific, and Eastern Europe. I suppose these have been motivated, to a great extent, because I have considered (and here I am hardly alone) that when all is said and done, the capitals of Western Europe are the roots of our culture; they have the answers, if any places do, to what Western life is all about, and why we live as we do, for better or for worse.

Ever since I was a student at England's Southampton University, when Professor Alexander Farquharson and his wife Dorothea dragged my fellow students and me on field trips to churches and villages and palaces and museums all over Hampshire and Wiltshire, I have been an inveterate sightseer . . . and sampler of foreign foods and wines . . . and shopper or at least browser in foreign shops and markets . . . and theater-, opera-, and concertgoer . . . and in between, relaxer in cafes, preferably sidewalk. This book reflects these interests. I don't think you will find more than half a dozen nightclubs in the text. But I have had to discipline myself to be selective as I have been, when it comes to stumbled-upon churches and townhouses-turned-art-repositories, and atmospheric places in which to eat and drink, or listen to concerts or watch operas and plays.

And so, if your idea of the Grand Tour at all coincides with mine, I hope you will join me. We may not come home as well rounded as the Grand Tourists of two centuries back, but it will not have been for want of trying, for I have dipped into background on each of the capitals, so as to relate their past—highlights of history, memorable personalities, cultural accomplishments—to the way they come through to us today. And in any event, we can be sure that our journey, albeit shorter than the prototypes, will have been a good deal more comfortable, and hopefully, quite as much fun.

*Robert S. Kane*

# Grand Tour A to Z:
## The Capitals of Europe

# The Grand Tour
## Eighteenth=Century Style

It was the eighteenth-century English who started it all, and it's the English who continue intrigued with its beginnings, to the point where they've come up with no less than three contemporary volumes on the Grand Tour, two with that very title. The latest is written by Christopher Hibbert (Putnam, and evocatively illustrated). It was preceded by a couple of seasons by Geoffrey Trease's also-illustrated volume (Holt, Rinehart & Winston). The third is probably the most splendidly designed and sumptuously illustrated book that I'll ever have in my library: *The Age of the Grand Tour* (Crown), with a perceptive introductory essay on early grand-tourists by Anthony Burgess, an appraisal of the continental art of their era by Francis Haskell, and contributions from tourists themselves (ranging from James Fenimore Cooper to Edward Gibbon).

But just how grand were these early grand tours? Not very. Take packing for starters. Here are just a very few of one guidebook writer's "things most requisite" (1797): "a cot, so constructed that it may be transformed into a sofa-bed; two leather sheets, a traveling chamber-lock (easily fixed upon any door in less than five minutes), a pocket-knife to eat with, a medicine chest, double-soled shoes and boots . . . oil of lavender (to drive away fleas from hotel beds), letters of recommendation to all our Ministers on the Continent."

There were, as well, some valuable gentleman's rules of the road, such as: "If traveling by sea, keep clear of the sailors who are sure to be covered with vermin, and take off your spurs; otherwise they will be stolen while you are being sick . . . Always have something to eat with you, both as a means of assuaging your own hunger and of keeping off starving dogs." And readers were warned never to take out money before strangers, there being "a great many villains on the roads."

Red tape was tiresome, too. Each authority preferred to supply the traveler with its own passport . . . John Evelyn, for example, "presented a Dutch passport at Antwerp, wisely keeping in his pocket another one granted him by the Spaniards, in which the States of Holland were named as rebels. Later, going from Padua to Milan (then held by Spain), he obtained a 'passport of extraordinary length and magnificence' from the Spanish ambassador." And money: "Tuscany alone used the sequin, the scudo, the livre and the paul. And until the unification of Italy, the tourist had to cope with three kinds of lira . . ."

Accommodation, far more often than not, was appalling. The English, then as now, rarely had good to say of French hoteliers, other than, occasionally, their tables. "The landlords, hostesses, and servants of the inns upon the road have not the least dash of complaisance in their behavior to strangers," an Englishman reported in 1763. ". . . In general, you are served with the most mortifying indifference, at the very time they are laying schemes for fleecing you of your money." The rural Germans came off less well, and even in Italy—always the ultimate goal—public places were often unsavory in all the major cities save Florence, even then beloved of the English.

Handicaps and horrors notwithstanding, tours were of long duration (often a year or two or three), for the whole idea was to achieve status upon return to the motherland as a result of having broadened one's horizons. One guidebook made 117 suggestions for questions to be asked of the locals at each destination. And travel then was more work than play: "Upon arrival, the tourist must not only make an effort to perfect his mastery of the language, but to learn all he can about the history, geography, trade, climate, crops, minerals, food, clothes, fauna, flora, politics, laws, art and military fortifications of the district. On entering a strange town, he should at once ascend the highest steeple to gain a good view of it and pick out the buildings worthy of further inspection."

Or, as another observer put it: "Unless the German or Englishman is willing to submit, however remotely, to the influence of the South, there is always the danger of his relapsing into coarseness at best, at worst brutishness. That is why, in the most enlightened phases of Northern history, no man could be considered cultivated if he had not gone out to enage the art, philosophy and manners of the Latin countries." And so the young man of the North— generally accompanied by servant and/or tutor, less frequently by feminine companions—at times nearly killed himself mucking about Europe in cramped, snail-slow, horse-drawn conveyances, acquiring the veneer which only continental travel was believed to be able to impart—until the early decades of the nineteenth century. Two things happened then to change the pattern of travel. The first was the railroad. The second was a project of a part-time Baptist minister who, in 1841, was inspired to book a whole train to carry his flock from Leicester to Loughborough for a meeting. What he wrought was group travel—the Package, if you will. He was, of course, Thomas Cook.

# Today's Grand Tour: the Preliminaries

### ... AS ROLLING OFF A LOG

It's true: travel to Western Europe *is* as easy as rolling off a log. Of all the areas of the globe, only the Caribbean is as effortless and as red-tape-free for visiting Americans. Western European countries have long, long since abandoned asking for any documents but a valid passport and a smallpox vaccination certificate from United States citizens on purely touristic missions. Pick a tour or go on your own. Go by ship or by plane or by a combination of the two. Get about within Europe by air or by train or by car—or some of each. Stay for a couple of weeks, or for a couple of months. Make yours a Grand Tour, going from London all the way to Istanbul. Or confine yourself to but one capital—Paris or Rome or Dublin—or a cluster in a geographical area, say Amsterdam, Brussels, and Luxembourg. And seasons: Europe is all-year-round holiday territory. The summer months offer the advantage of warm weather, but the disadvantages of crowds of fellow Americans who can vacation at no other times—including students; and of vacationing Europeans, as well, along with *their* students. Spring and autumn are traditionally fine seasons, but winter—when every capital is at its peak, with music and plays and ballet and all the locals at home enjoying themselves—is when the wise traveler goes. And not only to ski.

Here are some suggestions on preparations.


FIRST STEP:

OBTAINING A U. S. PASSPORT


A U.S. passport is valid for five years, but cannot be renewed. Instead, a new passport must be applied for. The charge for a passport is twelve dollars. For your *first* passport, you will need, aside from the twelve bucks, a pair of passport pictures (head-on —no profiles, 2½ inches to three inches square, with a white background, and, yes, you may smile), a birth or baptismal certificate or a notarized affidavit of your birth vouched for by a relative or someone who has known you from way back. For *successive* passports—any after the first—the expired passport will take the place of the birth or baptismal certificate or notarized affidavit of your birth, and a personal appearance is not required when applying. Passports may be obtained at Department of State passport offices in New York, Miami, San Francisco, Washington, D.C., Boston, Seattle, Los Angeles, Chicago, New Orleans, Honolulu, Philadelphia, and San Diego, or, in other cities, at the office of the clerk of a federal court; and, if the government's experiment continues a success, at some three thousand state courts and post offices in some eight hundred cities in all fifty states. Allow two weeks, although your passport may arrive in the mail sooner than that. If you are in a whiz-bang of a hurry, say so when applying; frequently, the authorities will try to speed things up for you. It should go without saying that your passport is one hell of an important document. Upon receipt of it, fill in your name, full address, and next of kin on the inside front cover. And keep the passport with you—*not packed in a suitcase*—while you're traveling. In case of loss, theft, or destruction, perish the thought, notify, or have your hotel notify, local police, and immediately get in touch with the nearest United States embassy or consulate, or the Passport Office, Department of State, Washington, D.C.

### INOCULATIONS AND HEALTH

All that's suggested is a valid smallpox vaccination; it should be not less than eight days nor more than three years old, and should be validated by one's local board of health, or a regional office of the United States Public Health Service. Have it inscribed on the yellow booklet known as the "International Certificates of Vaccination as Approved by the World Health Organization"; these are issued by the U. S. Public Health Service, often via airlines and travel agencies. A physician's letterhead will suffice, instead, but the yellow booklets are passport-size and I find it convenient to staple mine in the inside back cover of my passport. (If you live in or around New York, or will be departing from New York, you may be vaccinated—and get inoculations against a number of other diseases—at the Life Extension Institute, 11 East 44th Street, second floor, anytime between 9 A.M. and 4 P.M., Monday through Friday, without appointment, and for a fee of five dollars. The institute is authorized to validate vaccination certificates, which saves one the bother of taking or mailing the form to a municipal health department or the Public Health Service.)

If you have a hidden medical problem, consider wearing the nonprofit Medic Alert Foundation's emblem or tag. It is of value to persons with diabetes, epilepsy, a heart condition, of any one of a number of allergies, including the common allergy to penicillin. Here's how it works: On the front of the emblems are engraved the words "Medic Alert" around the staff of Aesculapius, the internationally recognized medical symbol. On the reverse are engraved the wearer's problem, his identification number and the phone number of Medic Alert headquarters in the United States. This number is available to physicians, nurses, law-enforcement, and other authorized personnel on a collect-call basis at any hour, from any place in the world. Through the Foundation's computerized file, vital information on a member can be relayed in seconds. Lifetime memberships, costing seven dollars, are available from Medic Alert, Turlock, California 95380.

Keeping fit as one travels need be no problem whatsoever. To start, water is potable throughout most all of Western Europe, including all of its capitals. Be as merry as you like everywhere, of course, but eat and drink in moderation, get a good night's sleep at least five nights out of seven (sightseeing can be enervating), and you'll not come in contact with whatever it is you'd like to call the indisposition that can befall one in any new place in any country.

## CLIMATE

Most of Europe's capitals are temperate-zone, with the same four seasons most Americans are accustomed to. A minority of the more southerly capitals enjoy milder Mediterranean climates. The chapters on the various cities break down climate, season by season, so you'll have a fair idea of the kind of weather to expect. Let me repeat here what I said earlier: Go to the European capitals at any and all seasons of the year. Each has its lure, most definitely including winter—which is surprisingly milder in the capitals than one might imagine.

## PACKING SIMPLIFIED

The what-to-pack bugaboo need not be that at all. International air travelers, by now accustomed to forty-four-pound (economy and tourist classes) and sixty-six-pound (first class) limitations have learned that the best rule is: Easy does it. Wash-and-wear garments, with percentages of such fibers as dacron, which preclude frequent pressing, are, of course, the easiest to care for. Laundry is never a problem; every hotel will do it quickly and well. Extra-speedy service—for which there is, of course, a surcharge—is generally available; if the laundry is turned in before breakfast it is back in one's room at dinnertime, with luck. (In this regard, a kudo to Hilton Hotels International, for pioneering with a no-surcharge policy for same-day laundry.)

The "travel light" policy hinges on acceptance of the fact that it is not necessary to appear in a smashing new costume every day of the week. When moving about, one sees people for periods often so brief that they're not able to note the variety of one's dress, even if they're so inclined. Quantities of each item of clothing depend, of course, on individual stubbornness, as well as baggage allowances for air travelers; those traveling on ships are of course unrestricted in this regard, and they will want to include dress clothes for evening wear (including—in first class, at least—dinner jackets for men). (Notes on local clothing conditions, city by city, are included in the chapters following.)

**Both men and women** will want to take sunglasses, an extra pair of eyeglasses, and a copy of the prescription (for wearers of glasses); some Band-Aids, adhesive tape, and gauze; a roll of Scotch Tape (it has innumerable uses on a trip), an envelope of rubber bands and paper clips—also valuable at the most unexpected times; a few packs of Chiclets and/or Life Savers—for the occasional small aircraft whose crews do not serve them, on take-off or landing; a half-dozen of the cheapest ball-point pens—they are occasionally lost when filling in landing cards, customs forms, etc.; a tiny scissors, several plastic bags—of inestimable convenience all along the way; a pocket-size flashlight; small foreign-language dictionaries for travelers who think they will bother to use them; printed or engraved personal or business cards; a plastic bottle of aspirin; an antidiarrhea preparation (paregoric is effective, although some physicians prescribe codeine —which doubles as an emergency pain-killer—while others prefer Lomotil); also worth packing are an antihistamine (for allergies or rashes that may develop), antibiotics, and sleeping pills for overnight flights. Photographers will want, aside from their cameras and equipment, as much film as they think they may use; most common types can be replenished en route; names and addresses of friends of friends to contact; and, it goes without saying, this book! It's not at all necessary to carry soap; a single cake is more than enough, for virtually every hotel provides it; it can be easily filched, in case of dire need, from aircraft washrooms, or, for that matter, purchased everywhere.

A basic **woman's wardrobe**—and here I am indebted to Jane Chapin, the well-traveled, well-dressed head of Adventures Unlimited, at Abercrombie & Fitch, in New York—would include: a lightweight wool travel suit, and/or a wool jumper to be worn with long-sleeved cuffed blouses in drip-dry fabrics, and a coat-length jacket and matching pleated skirt; a couple of non-crush knit dresses that can, as Mrs. Chapin puts it, be "dressed up or down," with accessories, and possibly with matching jacket or coat for cooler climes; a pants outfit for dressy occasions (so long, of course, as these are in style) or a cocktail dress or two; a casual play-outfit or two if resorts are on the itinerary; lingerie and stockings, housecoat and slippers, both as lightweight as possible; a cardigan sweater and/or jersey-type stole for coolish evenings; sport shoes for sightseeing, preferably with closed toes; a pair of dressy shoes and cocktail sandals, these latter for wear with pants, if they are part of the wardrobe; a topcoat (preferably waterproof so that it can double as a raincoat), a crushable hat for those diehard hat-wearers remaining; a bathing suit in its own plastic bag; cosmetic and toilet requisites, and if you please, a wig.

A **man's wardrobe,** based upon my experience, should include a dark (gray or navy blue), medium- or summer-weight knit or dacron-and-wool suit which is appropriate for both day and evening wear; a knit or dacron-and-wool blazer or cord-type cotton-and-dacron sport jacket; a pair of gray knit dacron-and-wool medium- or summer-weight slacks, for wear with the blazer and sport jacket and with several short-sleeved sport shirts, as well as at least one long-sleeved sport shirt; a pair of khaki or chino slacks, convenient for excursions; a supply of regular long-sleeved shirts (wash-and-wear fabrics are handy) which may double as sport shirts; a good choice of ties—there being no better or lighter-in-weight variety-adders for the suit and sport-jacket combinations; a pair of wash-and-wear pajamas (wash them in the morning and they're dry in the evening); a raincoat with detachable wool liner which will serve also as topcoat and bathrobe; socks, underwear, and handkerchiefs; a hat, if you wear one; two pairs of comfortable shoes (one may be loafers and thereby double as bedroom slippers); a swimsuit in its own plastic bag, so that it may be packed when wet; two sweaters—one pullover and one turtleneck light enough in weight to be worn under the blazer; and, of course, a toilet kit—the contents of which can easily be replenished in any city. If the itinerary is a winter one, add a winter-weight worsted suit (it need not be overly heavy), a muffler and gloves. And replace the lighter-weight garments above, with winter counterparts, omitting the swimsuit.

### CUSTOMS: SIGNPOSTS OF SOVEREIGNTY

**In Europe:** Customs counters continue to be regarded by virtually every nation as signposts of sovereignty. The result is that we continue to be considered smugglers, or worse, until proven otherwise.

Withal, it is a formality at most, almost always in Western Europe. Still, one does well to regard customs inspectors with the respect they expect as officials of their governments; to speak only when spoken to (other than a "Good morning" or "Good evening"), to have necessary documents in hand, and to be candid as regards cameras, tape recorders, cigarettes, and liquor. A carton or two of cigarettes (or fifty cigars or a pound of pipe tobacco) and a bottle of liquor are usually allowable, and there's no problem with film for personal use, particularly if (where there are prodigious amounts) each packet is partially opened.

**Returning to the United States:** The current limit on duty-free purchases is one hundred dollars, allowable once every thirty days, providing you have been out of the country at least forty-eight hours. (If you haven't, you're allowed a big, fat ten-dollar exemption.)

Worth noting: You may ship, *duty-free,* without having to declare them, and *not* counting as part of your hundred-dollar allowance, gifts or parcels not exceeding a total value of ten dollars, so long as they are not liquor, perfume, or tobacco. Send *as many as you like* from wherever you like, but not more than one parcel per day *to the same recipient.* Mark each such package "GIFT—TOURIST PURCHASE—VALUE UNDER TEN DOLLARS." Remember, too, that *antiques,* duly certified to be at least one hundred years old, are admitted duty-free, and do not count as part of the hundred-dollar quota; neither do *paintings, sculptures,* and other *works of art,* of any date, if certified as original; it is advisable that certification from the seller or other authority, as to their authenticity, accompany them. Also exempt from duty, but as a part of the hundred-dollar quota: one quart of liquor. And —this is important—there is no restriction on how much one may bring in above the one-hundred-dollar limit so long as the duty is paid; on many articles the duty is surprisingly moderate.

### EMBASSIES

There are United States embassies in all of the Western European capitals (save Vaduz, inasmuch as Liechtenstein's foreign affairs are handled by Switzerland). They are very often among the handsomest embassies in town, and in the fanciest neighborhoods. By and large, they rank in looks and location with those of Britain and France. We have embassies in fine old buildings (as in Paris) and in unconventional new ones, which some of

our best architects have designed (as in London). Often on the
Fourth of July, our ambassadors invite whatever Americans happen to be in town for some sort of Independence Day celebration,
depending upon the current state of the embassy's entertainment
budget. The rest of the year our embassy folks aren't particularly
interested in messing with us, unless we have serious problems of
a nontouristic nature, like losing our passports, or being arrested,
or—perish the thought—having our travelers checks stolen. With
the exception of a party or two to which I have been invited
with press colleagues, I haven't been near an embassy, in any
part of the world, in many years. Still, if you need help, have
no hesitancy in asking for it; it's one of the reasons we pay
taxes. Our State Department appears, sadly, to have lost a good
deal of its prestige in recent years, but its embassies still function,
and the caliber of many, if not all, of the personnel is high. It
should be remembered that in no overseas post is the life as
depicted in Hollywood; foreign service has more than its share of
frustration, as well as the manifold problems—educational, domestic, health, child-rearing—that come of residence in a strange
land.


### CURRENCY

Travelers checks are recommended for the bulk of one's funds.
Take a good many in ten-dollar denominations. Credit cards—
Diners Club and American Express particularly—are acceptable
all over Europe, for charging at hotels, restaurants, and countless shops. Carry along, too, about twenty-five or thirty one-dol-
lar bills. These are negotiable for purchases of drinks on many
international flights, and also come in handy for last-minute use,
just before leaving a country, when it would be inconvenient to
cash a travelers check. If you like, stock up at banks or foreign-
currency dealers with a few dollars' worth of the currency of the
countries you will be visiting. It can be handy for the initial

ride from airport to town. But don't worry if you haven't so prepared yourself. Invariably, banks are open at all hours in virtually all the important European airports. You may change money at them after going through customs and just before hopping into a cab or bus for town. When you do change money, at airport banks, hotel cashiers, or wherever, *insist* upon some *small*-denomination bills and some *small* change. Cashiers in Europe, as on every continent, are loath to dispense much-needed low-value notes and coins, for the simple reason that it requires a little more effort.

## TIPPING

Tipping is rarely the problem first-time travelers think it may be. Still, tips on tipping are never out of order, and they will be found, capital by capital, in the succeeding chapters.

## A WORD ABOUT CONCIERGES

They have a desk of their own in virtually any hotel of size— quite separate from that of the reception clerks. Their badge is a pair of crossed keys. They are called concierges in non-English-speaking countries, hall porters where English is the principal language. They have their own professional organization, the Clefs d'or International. And, when they are good, they are wizards, and valued friends of the traveler. Of course, they keep your room key for you and take care of postage for your cards, letters, and packages (which they'll have wrapped and shipped for you). But that is just routine. You may use your concierge to call you a cab in hotels where they do not congregate out front, to book you on reserved-seat trains, planes, city sightseeing tours, or to hire guides for you; get you theater, opera, concert, ballet, or sports tickets; order your favorite newspapers sent up each

morning with your breakfast, even taking your order for that
breakfast the night before, on your way upstairs; take care of re-
pairs on your camera, watch, eyeglasses, shoes, or business equipment; advise on restaurants, shops, barbers and hairdressers,
physicians and dentists, stenographers, currently popular discos
and other after-dark diversions, including those suitable (and not
suitable) for women traveling alone. Now, neither I nor the concierge guarantees that you're going to approve wholeheartedly of
whatever it is he recommends. But he is—or damned well should
be—an experienced jack-of-all-trades, and he is there to be of
service, tipped by you, of course (on your departure), but invariably well worth every penny, franc, krona, lira, mark, or
schilling.

### SIGHTSEEING AND GUIDES

Every capital has travel agencies that offer either guided group
tours or individual escort. Often, however, sightseeing is included
on tours arranged by one's home travel agent, prior to departure
from the United States—in which case there's no problem whatsoever. Taxi drivers can serve as good guides, provided they speak
your language. Self-drive and chauffeur-driven cars may be hired
everywhere; in the cities where I believe chauffeur-driven cars
are to be preferred, I so indicate. Everywhere, regardless of how
extensive one's guided tours, additional shoe-leather expeditions
are absolutely essential, if one is to know a city. The guided
tours hit only the highlights—and not even the major ones, in
many cases. Too often, one *drives past* rather than stops for an
interior inspection. Stay long enough, if possible, to poke about on
your own; there are more than enough specific, tested suggestions
for so doing in each chapter following. Never underestimate the
value of relaxation on a park bench or at a cafe table, nor of
the friends of friends you've been asked to look up—particularly
if they are citizens of the country you're visiting. Americans,

while often eminently worth meeting and knowing, are found in
great quantities at home.

## MAIL

If your itinerary is planned in advance, have letters addressed
to you, care of your hotels, along the way. American Express
offices—frequently used by itinerant youngsters who have no idea
of where they will be next week and are in no hurry—are fine,
but they are closed evenings, part of each weekend, and on
certain holidays, whereas hotels never close. Even if you should
end up in a different hotel than the one on your itinerary, you
may always hop over to it and pick up whatever mail awaits you.
Correspondents should allow five or six days air mail (even a
week, to play it safe) for a letter to reach you in a Western European capital. Have your correspondents mark your letters "Hold
for Arrival"; with these instructions, there's no problem if your
mail checks in before you do. Air letters or *aerogrammes* are
purchasable in post offices—both American and European—and
are cheaper than regular air mail, but may contain no enclosures.

## LANGUAGE

If you plan way, way ahead, and have a little cash lying
around, take a language course in the language of one of the
countries where you will be spending some time. Language fluency
is a great tool when traveling. Remember, though, in the case of
Western Europe, that English is the sole or principal language
of England, Wales, Scotland, and Ireland, and that the overwhelming majority of Danes, Dutchmen, and Norwegians speak
English astonishingly well. In every other capital, a good deal of
English is spoken. The language situation, capital by capital,
is discussed in subsequent chapters.

### PLANNING YOUR GRAND TOUR

*"The wise traveler, the self-indulgent and the happy one, is he
who never looks at his timetable and hides his watch."*
                                            —JOHN MASON BROWN

How much is budgeted for your Grand Tour? How much time
do you have? Is this your first or third or eleventh trip to Europe?
Would you like it to be easy and relaxing, taking in museums
and old houses and churches and markets you had not gotten
to before? Or is it to be a kind of introductory survey, with bits
and pieces of everything, to prepare you for subsequent, more
specialized journeys? These are the basic questions of the pre-
planning stage.

**Three types of trips:** What must be decided next is the degree
of effort you yourself want to put into the details of the trip. There
are three major types of journeys: (1) *independent* travel, in
which you purchase your own transportation tickets, book your
own hotels, arrange for your own sightseeing—either in advance,
or as you go along; (2) *group* travel, on a package tour purchased in advance from a travel agency; (3) *individual* travel,
but by means of a travel agent's *prearranged individual itinerary,*
with some or all arrangements—transportation, hotels, sightseeing
—made for you prior to departure. There are advantages to all
three. The solitary traveler might enjoy the companionship af-
forded by group tours. The student on a tight budget, or the
veteran traveler who knows the ropes, might enjoy free-lancing
his trip as he goes along. Many travelers prefer the third-men-
tioned procedure, whereby a travel agent tailors the basic arrangements—transportation and hotels, for example—to the
traveler's order, and the traveler himself proceeds unescorted but
with the assurance that his major requirements are taken care
of, and with the advantage that he's going where he wants, for

as long as he wants. (If desired, and at slight extra cost, he can be met upon arrival at each point by his travel agent's local representatives.)

**Selecting a travel agent:** American travel agents know Europe better than any other part of the world, the Caribbean, Mexico, and Israel possibly excepted. Still, it is as important as ever to secure the services of a travel agent who is reputable and efficient (members of ASTA—the American Society of Travel Agents —are invariably good bets), and who is as personally well acquainted as he can be with the capitals you want to visit.

**Air Fares:** The member airlines of IATA—International Air Transport Association—meet every year to set fares. The advent of the jumbo jets in the seventies, and a concurrent economic recession, have occasioned a variety of special fare packages and one round of changes after another. The packages can be very good bargains *if* they are for the period of time you prefer and *if* they take you where you would like to go, *with the facilities you would like to have.* Regular-fare tickets, in contrast, are valid for an entire year, and include certain stopover privileges at no extra cost. (You must inquire of your travel agent as to specifically which stopovers are allowed with whatever ticket you buy.) Additionally, these tickets have no limitations whatsoever; you may fly at any hour of the day, any day of the week, and any season of the year. Regular-fare tickets are either economy class or first class, the latter much more costly, of course. Every traveler should fly transatlantic first class at least once. All of the score-plus airlines crossing the Atlantic compete to make theirs the most luxurious first-class passage of the lot. In all cases, though, the aisles are wider, the seats are bigger and more comfortable, and are only two-abreast; there is more leg room, the cabin service is more personal and the food more elaborate (served on fine china rather than plastic, with complimentary cocktails, dinner or luncheon wines, and after-meal drinks). In great contrast are the charter flights; with these you must suit your convenience to that of the departure dates of the flight, whereas with the scheduled carriers, there is a flight departing, as per the timetable, empty or full, to be available if and when you want it. That, of course, is why scheduled airlines cost so much more money to operate. Hopefully, there will be a market for both types of airlines for a long time to come.

Fares, as I have noted, change frequently. To give you an idea of the regular, one-year-validity economy-class peak-season fares, I include these—subject to change, of course—for the three major European capitals.

London    $590
Paris     $636
Rome      $746

First-class fares remain the same year round, and are, for the same cities—subject to change—London $842; Paris, $888; Rome, $1036.

**Airlines serving Europe:** More than a score of airlines cross the Atlantic from United States and Canadian points to the Western European capitals. In looking over the list I see that I have flown every single airline, save one. (That's TAP, if you're wondering.) Each is good in its own way, reflecting the characteristics —both strengths and eccentricities—of the country it represents. The equipment on all is similar, of course. It's the service that varies, along with the food and the drinks.

The airlines include: *Air Canada, Air France, Air-India, Alitalia, British Overseas Airways Corporation (BOAC), Finnair, Irish International Airlines, Icelandic Airlines, Iberia Airlines, Japan Air Lines, KLM Royal Dutch Airlines, Lufthansa German Airlines, Olympic Airlines, Pakistan International Airlines, Pan American World Airways, Qantas Airlines, Scandinavian Airlines System, Sabena Belgian World Airlines, Swissair, TAP,* and *Trans World Airlines (TWA).*

**To Europe by Sea:** It is sad but a fact that scheduled passenger transatlantic steamship service is a near-victim of the air age. A tiny minority of something like 2 percent of transatlantic travelers are today ship travelers; a couple of decades back, almost the opposite was the case. Cruises—Caribbean, Mediterranean, Pacific, 'round-the-world—are saving the passenger liner, but the transatlantic runs have become skeletal. It is rather depressing. Those of us who love ships had for long hoped against hope that there would always be room for both the airplane and the passenger liner—the one offering speed, the other luxury and relaxation no other way obtainable. One bright point: *air-sea combinations* still attract quite a few travelers; fly one way, sail the other; it is worth discussing with your travel agent. Meanwhile here are some ships that I particularly like that are still making transatlantic crossings: *Cunard Line* (British)—the sleek, beautiful *Queen Elizabeth 2; French Line*—the very handsome, very Gallic *France; Holland America Cruises: Nieuw Amsterdam*— a *grande dame* splendidly updated and skillfully and charmingly operated; *Rotterdam*—HAC's flagship—newer but no less agreeable than the *Nieuw Amsterdam, Hapag-Lloyd: Europa*—German elegance, service, and cuisine afloat. *Italian Line:* a quartet of modern, well-run, ever-so-congenial vessels—*Cristoforo Colombo, Leonardo da Vinci, Michelangelo,* and *Raffaelo; Norwegian-American Line:* the popular *Sagajord,* flagship of the Norwegian fleet; *Swedish-American Line:* two perennial favorites, the *Gripsholm* and the *Kungsholm,* both of which offer *luxe* facilities and fine Swedish service and cuisine; and *Royal Viking Line*'s new-as-tomorrow beauties, most especially the spectacular *Royal Viking Star.*

**Motoring in Europe:** Every capital has a number of rent-a-car firms. To drive in Europe, you need a driving license issued by an American state, and—for some countries—an international driving license; *Information:* local auto clubs, or International Division, American Automobile Association, 750 Third Avenue, New York 10017. Think through in advance the purchase of a car abroad, for shipment to the United States; it can be complicated. Your travel agent should be able to advise you, or direct you to a source that can.

**European trains:** The passenger train has never stopped playing

a vital role on the European transportation scene. Unlike the
United States, where it almost expired before the national Amtrak
organization attempted to revive it with a pitifully minimal budget,
the trains in Europe are government-operated and generously
budgeted. Maintenance is, by and large, excellent. Staffs are
professional, multilingual (which they must be, as so many trains
are international), and helpful. There are not as many baggage
porters in stations as there once were, but they still exist. Sleeping
cars (*Wagons-Lits*) are comfortable, and often the ideal solution
for getting from one distant town to another; although they
cost extra, they take the place of a hotel room. There are two
classes of train travel, first and second; the difference is in the
thickness of seat upholstery and the number of passengers per
compartment. First is recommended for a trip of any length,
unless you are on a very tight budget. It is also recommended
that you reserve your first-class seats, *particularly in Italy,*
whose trains are the most crowded in Western Europe. (Hotel
concierges can do this for you. They can also book you Wagons-
Lits space, but you may do these things yourself at railroad
stations or through travel agents.) Most trains have dining
cars, and sometimes buffet-snack cars in addition or in place of
the regular restaurant cars. There is often more than one meal
sitting; stewards come through in advance taking bookings, and
handing out seating tickets. Refreshment vendors often make
the rounds of cars, and are frequently to be seen on station
platforms en route. Europeans, particularly those traveling in
second class, are great believers in taking nourishment with them
—just in case. You may do the same—chocolate is always good
to have along, should restaurant facilities fail to materialize as
scheduled. So are fruit, bread, and cheese, or packaged sandwiches.

Particularly worth noting is the crack streamliner system of the
Trans-Europe Express, whose trains connect a hundred major cities. TEE serves many of the capitals, and is train travel at its most
comfortable (the cars are American-style—all seats face in the

same direction and there are no compartments). Restaurant service is excellent. Note that it is first-class only, and that all seats must be reserved in advance.

*Eurailpass* is worth being acquainted with if you plan extensive train travel through the Continent. It is a great bargain, but it can only be purchased in North or South America *before you depart*— from travel agents and offices of the representatives of the various European railroads. It is simply a pass that covers unlimited first-class travel by train in thirteen continental countries, for twenty-one-day, one-month, two-month, or three-month periods. (To give you an idea of cost, the twenty-one-day Eurailpass is $110, the one-month pass, $140—subject to change, of course.) It is valid in Austria, Belgium, Denmark, France, Germany, Holland, Italy, Luxembourg, Norway, Portugal, Spain, Sweden, and Switzerland—but not Britain or Ireland. A smiliar pass, for train travel in the British Isles, is available through British Railways, and its representatives. Eurailpass is easy to use; I can tell you from experience; it comes in its own plastic wallet with a convenient little map of the routes on which it is valid, and you just show it to gate attendants and conductors. It does not, of course, guarantee a reserved seat when such is desired, nor Wagons-Lits sleeping accommodation, either. Cheaper Student-Railpasses, using second-class accommodations, are available for bona fide scholars.

**Hotel rates:** Unless otherwise specified, the selected hotels I have suggested in this book are either first-class or de luxe. In virtually every capital, I have also recommended moderate-category hotels. In all cases, all rooms have private bath unless otherwise noted. Hotels can be booked by travel agents, in much the same way as one buys transportation and sightseeing from agents. Travel agents are, of course, familiar with current hotel rates; they vary season to season, year to year. But you may also book your own rooms; simply write air mail to the hotels that interest you, asking for a confirmation, whether or not a deposit is required, and, if you like, the hotel's brochure and its tariff card.

# *Amsterdam and The Hague*

Why both Amsterdam *and* The Hague for this book on Europe's capitals? I could do no other. Amsterdam, with its splendid if rarely inhabited Royal Palace, and a church next door where monarchs are inaugurated, is the official capital of the Netherlands. The Hague, though, is where the government's work gets done, where the diplomats accredited to the Crown live, and where there are several royal palaces—all, like their bigger counterpart in Amsterdam, rarely used. The Dutch royal family is unique in that for the most part it lives in neither capital nor seat of government, but away from the people, in the quiet countryside.

But then the Dutch royal family is in other ways unique. Its name—Orange-Nassau—is foreign, the "Orange" being a French province, the "Nassau" being German. It entered the Dutch scene in the early sixteenth century, when it inherited a considerable portion of the Netherlands and its William of Orange went to take possession, initiating the country's struggle for freedom from the Inquisition-mad government of the fanatic Spaniard Philip II, himself the inheritor of the Netherlands from his papa, Charles V, the Hapsburg emperor.

**Ousting the Spaniards:** Now William of Orange—whom you may remember as William the Silent—was no stranger either to Philip, whom he had served as a diplomat, or to his father, of whom he was a special favorite. But he didn't like what was

happening to his newfound country or its peoples, and he raised
an army that was successful in driving the Spaniards out, in
1576. By the time he died of an assassin's wounds, he had been
four times married—No. 3 was a French princess who was a
runaway nun—and he had been proclaimed Count of Holland
and Zeeland. What resulted was the independent Republic of
the United Netherlands, with its governors (for most if not all of
its history) princes of Orange instead of commoners. William
may have been silent but he was surely the most memorable of
the Oranges, save one: a descendant-prince named William III—
who pulled off the neat trick of becoming king of a foreign
country (England, of course, which he co-ruled with his English
wife, Mary) at a time when his family had not yet ruled their
*own* country as monarchs.

The Dutch republic may have been rather oddball, what with
the descendants of German nobility mostly serving as its hered-
itary heads. But it constituted the era, as any Dutchman will
tell you today, of Holland's Golden Age. Amsterdam became
one of the centers of the world. Dutch explorers and mariners
sailed their tiny ships all over the globe. (If you grew up in
Albany, New York, as I did, you had it drummed into your
head, in the sixth grade, that Henry Hudson sailed his *Half
Moon* up the Hudson, reaching the site of what is now Albany
on September 19, 1609; within a decade Albany—then called
Fort Orange, after the name of the princes' house—came into
being, the oldest continuous settlement of the original thirteen
states, with the Hudson River itself long called Riviere Vanden
Verst Mauritius, or River of Prince Maurice, after the descendant
of William of Orange who was then the Dutch Republic's *stad-
holder,* or governor. Another Dutch settlement—New Amsterdam—at the mouth of the river, became rather prominent; the
English later renamed it New York. Still other Dutch ships went
to the Caribbean (Willemstad, the capital of Curaçao, remains
Dutch Colonial in façade), to Surinam on the northern coast of

South America, and in distant Asia to what is now the Republic
of Indonesia, but had been for centuries the Dutch East Indies.

**Golden Age:** At home, the republican Dutch achieved an enviable reputation as the most tolerant people in Europe. They
welcomed the diamond traders and other mercantile experts from
Antwerp, which remained under Spanish control. And they opened
their doors to religious refugees, as well—French Huguenots and
the Jews from Portugal and Spain, whom Philip II was persecuting.
(Until World War II, Amsterdam's Jewish community was one of
the most important in Europe.) All of these newcomers brought
Holland skills and talents and ideas. Dutch commerce became the
marvel of Europe. A substantial middle class—which to this day
is a hallmark of Holland—developed, and in so doing it created a
market for the great art and architecture and artisanship that lure
us to Dutch shores several centuries later. (Holland, we might
mention at this point, is the name of two provinces—North and
South—of the modern Netherlands; in modern times we call the
entire country Holland quite as often as we use the official designation, the Netherlands.) The cities developed, not only as
*entrepôts* for the conduct of commerce, with the extremes of
nobility and royalty at one end, and impoverished masses at the
other, but as the attractive, eminently livable, solidly bourgeois
communities most of whose cores are happily little changed today.
The central area of Amsterdam of which we are so fond is
largely an achievement of this Golden Era.

The Hague started out, in the thirteenth century, as the site of a
hunting lodge of the counts of Holland. Indeed, one of The
Hague's two Dutch names—Gravenhaage—means the count's
wood. A castle replaced the lodge, a town came to surround the
castle, and later the United Republic took to holding the sessions of
its States General—the name the Dutch Parliament retains—in
The Hague, with the *stadholders* making it their residence.

The early eighteenth century saw the decline of the great Golden
Era. The Orange princes had been in and out of the stadholder-
ship, and before the century was out, the French-founded Batavian

Republic was in, only to be followed, some years later, by a
monarchy of Napoleon's devising, in which his brother Louis
was made king. Louis surprised everyone, both his subjects and
his brother. They had all expected him to be nothing more than
a rubber stamp for Paris. But he attempted to reshape a Netherlands for the Netherlanders, to the point where Napoleon would
have none of it, booted him off his throne, and took over himself
in 1810, annexing the Netherlands to France.

**At last—a reigning monarchy:** The Congress of Vienna brought
Holland, at long last, its first Dutch king. The Congress united
the northern and southern Netherlands (read Holland and Belgium), making The Hague and Brussels co-capitals. But it didn't
work. The Belgians revolted and formed their own kingdom, and
the Dutch kings (that same Orange-Nassau dynasty that had
provided the earlier princes) continued on as sovereigns of the area
that had been the United Republic. They included a trio of
unexciting Williams—I, II, and III, with Wilhelmina following.
The long reign of that no-nonsense lady embraced the two World
Wars. Holland remained neutral during the first and attempted a
similar policy in the second. But the Nazis invaded in May 1940
without warning, quickly overcame Dutch resistance and almost
completely destroyed the venerable port city of Rotterdam, to the
point where it is a new city today.

Wilhelmina, her family and government, set up exile headquarters in England and Canada, while Dutch forces fought
alongside the Allies abroad; at home, the Dutch underground
so thwarted the Nazis that they retaliated with mass executions
and the deportation—to concentration camp ovens—of 104,000
of the 112,000 Dutch Jews. (The fate of many Dutch Jews is
nowhere better brought home than in the Amsterdam house of
young Anne Frank and her family.) The waning years of the war
were particularly cruel to Holland. In September 1944 the Dutch
people united to rise against their captors in the premature con-
viction that Allied landings at nearby ports would lead to their
immediate liberation. But only the extreme north of the country

was freed; the rest suffered ferocious Nazi reprisals, mass starvation among these. In May 1945, with the demise of the German cause, Queen Wilhelmina and the cabinet in exile returned. Post-World War II recovery (marked by Holland originally uniting for economic purpose with neighboring Luxembourg and Belgium into the Benelux Union, which was the nucleus of the Common Market) was miraculously successful. The old Dutch colony of the East Indies became Indonesia, and the New World colonies— Surinam and the Netherlands Antilles—became component parts of a modernized kingdom.

**Juliana succeeds Wilhelmina:** Old Queen Wilhelmina abdicated —and why not, after a strenuous, event-packed half-century reign? —in 1948, to be succeeded by her daughter Juliana. The kingdom is destined to be ruled by still another queen (the third in a row), because Queen Juliana and her enterprising German-born husband, Prince Bernhard—are the parents of four daughters. The eldest and the heir to the throne is Princess Beatrix. She and her husband (German-born, like her father) have a son. Beatrix's sisters are the Princesses Irene (also married), Margriet, and Maria Christina.

But lest the reader be under the impression that today's Holland is a fairyland kingdom, it should be pointed out that this is the same Holland of radical *provo* demonstrators, of inventive engineers who continue to enlarge the kingdom's territory by creating land out of the sea, of result-producing governments that are invariably coalitions of a maze of disparate political parties (they total twenty-eight), and of a Roman Catholic community (there are almost as many Catholics in Holland as Protestants) that is at the forefront of the worldwide movement for change within the Catholic Church.

# *Amsterdam*

## TO SEE

**Lay of the land:** Although the nineteenth century saw business-minded modernists raze far too much of Amsterdam's old façade, we must be grateful for the substantial core that remains, and also for the endeavors of the city's Municipal Monument Office, which has decreed—and listed—more than fifty-five hundred structures as monuments, and has helped to restore well over a thousand of them. The central city, in large part, is seventeenth- and eighteenth-century, to the extent that contemporary vistas—with people's clothes (not faces!) changed, and some electric wires, neon signs, and modern vehicles deleted—are frequently as they were a few centuries ago. Central Amsterdam embraces an area that is largely ringed by a series of dams that are almost concentric half-circles. But let us start at what for many visitors is the beginning: the Central Station. It is an immense late-nineteenth-century building that is situated near the oddly named Ij River. A major thoroughfare known as *Damrak* connects the station with the principal square of the town, known simply as *The Dam,* with its major landmarks the Royal Palace and, just behind, the spires of the so-called New Church, in which Dutch sovereigns are inaugurated. The main shopping street leads off The Dam. For most of the day (from 11:00 A.M. onward) it is happily off-limits to motor vehicles. A onetime cattle path, it is called *Kalverstraat,* or Calves' Street. It connects The Dam with the *Muntplein,* or Mint Square, the landmark of which is a tower which, for a brief dark period in Holland's history, had to coin some desperately needed currency. The Muntplein is but a few minutes' stroll down the street called *Reguliersbreestraat* to a hotel-cafe-*boîte*-bordered square called

*Rembrandtsplein.* On one side of the Muntplein is the *Amstel River,* for which the city is named; and on another side is one of the four principal canals. As you continue walking into town from this area, you pass one canal after the other. It is worth remembering their sequence. I have my own system. The first is *Singel* (think of one, the first); the next three are in alphabetical order: *Herengracht* (H), *Kaizersgracht* (K), and finally *Prinsengracht* (P). Going farther into the city, beyond the canal network, one comes to *Leidseplein* (a busy after-dark area not unlike the earlier-mentioned Rembrandtsplein), with its landmark, the Municipal Theater. Beyond is *Museumplein,* with the Riksmuseum, Municipal Museum, Van Gogh Museum, Concertgebouw Concert Hall, and—nearby—P. C. Hoofstraat, with the city's smartest shops.

As for the *main canals,* Herengracht has the loveliest *houses* (particularly in the choice area between Leidsestraat and Vijzelgracht). Kaizersgracht follows, with Prinsengracht a by no means inconsequential No. 3, and Singel an interesting mix of churches, warehouses, and residences. Prinsengracht's houses were traditionally those of the lower-middle and middle-middle classes, and many of them today are handsomely maintained. Kaizersgracht's standouts include No. 123 (the House with the Heads, the heads being half a dozen Roman busts on the façade of this brick, gabled mansion); the Kooimans House at No. 125, and Nos. 778 through 786—a row of five beautifully matched structures. Herengracht has even more beauties of note: the Mayor's Mansion at No. 502, the eighteenth-century structure that houses the Wallet-Holthuysen Museum, at No. 605; No. 465, with its Louis XIV façade, and the pair of early seventeenth-century warehouses at Nos. 43 and 45.

Visible everywhere is Amsterdam's coat of arms, surely the most easily identifiable in Europe, with its three X-shaped St. Andrew's crosses on a red-and-black shield above the Dutch words for "Heroic, Resolute, Compassionate"—officially added by decree of Queen Wilhelmina in 1947, in recognition of the citizens' bravery during the Nazi occupation of World War II.

**Requisite attractions:** The *Royal Palace,* the Renaissance structure that dominates The Dam, started life in the mid-seventeenth
century as the City Hall, and might still be, if Napoleon's brother
Louis, when he became king in the early nineteenth century, had
not opted it for himself. It has been the Royal Palace ever since,
even though it is rarely inhabited (a couple of weeks at most
per year) by the Royal Family, who live mainly at their country
palace at Soestdijk (near Utrecht) although they also have palaces
in The Hague, their official home. There is a good deal of marble
sculpture in the Amsterdam palace, particularly in the main
reception room, the Burgerzaal; there is also considerable Dutch
painting of the period of the building's construction, though none
of it is the work of Golden Age masters. *Rembrandt's House,*
Nos. 4–6 Jodenbreestraat, is an early structure where the master
lived from 1639 until 1658. It is full of Rembrandtiana—including
sketches and etchings. But don't look for paintings; you'll find
them at the Rijksmuseum. *The Beguinage* (entrance on Spui) is
old Amsterdam at its most serene: an inner courtyard in the
heart of town surrounded by a clutch of originally medieval
houses (some façades have been altered in the succeeding centuries) and a church that is now English Presbyterian. Beguinages
were named for their inhabitants (beguines, or lay nuns). *Anne
Frank's house,* at No. 263 Prinsengracht is where the young
Jewish girl and her family hid from the Nazis during the war, or at
least until 1944, when they were found. As most of the world
knows, all but Anne's father were exterminated in concentration
camps. Most moving, at least to me, are the movie fan-magazine
photos Anne had affixed to the wall of her attic bedroom—
Shirley Temple, Norma Shearer, David Niven, Deanna Durbin,
and Garbo among them. *Waterlooplein* is the square in a quarter
that had been heavily Jewish before World War II, and near
which are the city's two most handsome Jewish houses of worship—the seventeenth-century *German* and *Portuguese synagogues,*
the latter quite as splendid as ever, towering above the surrounding

buildings, and still with its original brass chandeliers. The square itself is the site of Amsterdam's flea market, and is surrounded by the neoclassic mid-nineteenth-century *Church of Moses and Aaron* (Roman Catholic), some seventeenth-century warehouses, and a one-time poorhouse that is such a gem of mid-seventeenth-century architecture that it has been honored by the Architects' Academy, which has its headquarters within.

Amsterdam's old churches are surely among its chief treasures. *The New Church (Nieuw Kerk)*, which, like other similarly named churches in Europe was new some centuries ago, is a capacious late-Gothic pile, with unusual clustered columns and the tombs of a number of celebrated Hollanders. All of the kingdom's sovereigns—from William I in 1814 through Juliana in 1948—have been sworn in at the New Church. *The Old Church (Oude Kerk)* embraces several centuries, from the fourteenth to the seventeenth. Its masterwork is a sixteenth-century spire, but the immense Gothic windows are splendid, too, and so are the seventeenth-century pulpit and chancel screen. Rembrandt's wife, Saskia, is buried within, along with other noted Dutchmen, including the New York patroon Kilaen van Rensselaer. There are, as well, the *quartet of churches named for the points of the compass.* They are *Noorderkerk, Zuiderkerk, Oesterkerk,* and *Wester-kerk*—all Reformation-era landmarks, but if one must choose, the choice should be *Westerkerk.* Its massiveness (it is the biggest Protestant church in town) does not detract from its gracefulness. Its telescopelike spire, the highest in town, is lovelier than any other in a city of lovely towers. The interior is breathtaking—a superb sixteenth-century organ with an unusual clock above it, and a series of those sumptuously simple brass chandeliers that are a high point of Dutch Renaissance décor. There is, as well, the tomb of Rembrandt.

*Museums* deserve time in Amsterdam. *The Rijksmuseum,* or national museum, in its enormous late-nineteenth-century home on the Museumplein, is one of the most skimmed-over such

institutions in Europe. People rush in to see Rembrandt's *Night
Watch* in much the same way as they flit into the Louvre to see
the *Mona Lisa*. Relax. Give yourself half a day, or two half-days,
for that matter. (Three would do even better.) Go first to the
enormous Main Hall on the first floor (that means up one flight)
and buy the excellently organized *Guide to the Rijksmuseum*.
The paintings you want first to see are, naturally enough, those
of the Dutch Renaissance, on the same first floor. Here are
Rembrandt, Hals, van Ruysdael, de Keyser, van Ostade, Bols,
Maes, de Hooch, and Steen, to name some. Note, though, that
the Rijksmuseum has great foreign paintings, as well—Renaissance masters and those of later eras. And it is particularly rich
in applied arts from the Middle Ages through the last century, with
the Golden Age of Holland a highlight. Exhibits run from dolls'
houses through liturgical objects. There are period rooms, silver,
ceramics (there is a noted Blue Delft collection), and tapestries.
Still another oft-missed section has to do with Dutch national
history, with exhibits of flags, weapons, costumes, ship models,
and historically important paintings. A final treat is the Asian
collection—things from throughout the Far East, with the most
special those from Indonesia, collected during the long centuries
that that country was a Dutch colony. The *Amsterdam Historical
Museum* is one of the city's newest, ingeniously housed in one
of its oldest buildings. The site is the fifteenth-century Convent
of St. Lucia, which had seen service from the sixteenth century
until the mid-twentieth, as the Amsterdam Municipal Orphanage.
In 1969, when it became apparent that the Historical Museum
was becoming cramped in the ancient Weigh House, preparations
were begun for the transformation of the venerable heart-of-town
orphanage, which is entered from Kalverstraat, the busy main
shopping thoroughfare. The exhibits—paintings, prints, maps, all
manner of Amsterdamiana—are housed in the quadrangular-
shaped structure, the cafe in the big courtyard understandably
busy with Amsterdammers taking coffee breaks. The Rijksmuseum

has two Museumplein neighbors. One is the *Stedelijk,* or *Municipal Museum,* whose specialty is modern art, dealing with contemporary including applied arts—houseware, furniture, and architecture. But the paintings are the thing; they include works of Matisse, Chagall, Picasso, Monet, Dubuffet; Americans such as Rauschenberg, de Kooning and Pollack are exhibited, too. The newest of the trio of museums, the *Van Gogh Museum,* is devoted to the world-famous collection of some two-hundred Van Goghs that heretofore had been exhibited at the Stedelijk Museum. The late-nineteenth-century Dutch master's work is imaginatively spread among paintings by contemporaries whom he had known in Paris, like Toulouse-Lautrec and Gaugin, and there are as well exhibits, letters, drawings, and the like relating to the tragic, far-too-short life of the tormented albeit prolific genius who died by his own hand at the age of thirty-nine, hardly known in his lifetime. The *Wollet Holthuysen Museum* at No. 605 Herengracht is a splendid "double" (meaning extra-wide) mansion dating to the seventeenth century and is full of sumptuously furnished period rooms, the contents of which range from the sixteenth to the nineteenth centuries, with a good deal from the eighteenth. These interiors are among the finest in the Netherlands open to the public. *The Theater Museum,* at No. 168 Herengracht, is another old house turned exhibit hall, and theater buffs will love it. The collections tell the story of Dutch theater over a long period. *The Maritime Museum,* at 57 Cornelius Schuytstraat, has to do with matters nautical of a nation with an exceptional nautical tradition—old globes, maps, prints, ship models, atlases, and mariners' instruments. *Ons Lieve Heer op Solder* ("Our Lord in the Attic") at 40 Oude Zijds Voorburwal, is an Amsterdam oddity: a Roman Catholic chapel stretching across the top floor of three joined canal houses, the lower floors of which are handsomely furnished. The upstairs chapel dates from the seventeenth-century Reformation period, when to be Catholic was out—but only sort of—and this form of semisecret worship was winked at by the authorities.

TO WATCH

*The Concertgebouw* is the name both of the capacious concert
hall at Museumplein (built in 1888 to house the Amsterdam
Symphony, which was formed shortly thereafter) and of the
orchestra itself. The orchestra gained an international reputation
during the half-century conductorship of Wilhelm Mengelberg,
which terminated after World War II. Bernard Haitink assumed
the orchestra's baton in 1959, and rapidly achieved a global
reputation. Music critic Harold Schonberg wrote in the New York
*Times* upon the occasion of the orchestra's 1971 appearance at
Carnegie Hall: "The Concertgebouw is still one of the great
orchestras, precise and powerful, capable of huge but disciplined
bursts of sound as well as of ethereal tenderness." The *Municipal
Theater,* or *Stadsschouwburg,* on Leidseplein, is the city's chief
venue for opera, plays, and ballet of high caliber. The *Holland
Festival* takes place annually, usually from mid-June to mid-July,
and usually in Amsterdam, The Hague, and other locales, as well.
*Nightclubs* are about as they are everywhere, expensive and
according to formula; there are smaller, more intimate—and admittedly more relaxing and enjoyable—*bar-lounges,* with piano or
some other sort of music. There are *discos,* which remain more
popular than they appear to be in the United States. There are
*gay clubs, bars, and hotels.* (The Netherlands has the most progressive legislation in this area of any country in the world, and it
has not hurt intra-European tourist traffic on weekends, holidays,
and in summer, particularly from the United Kingdom and Germany.) The Rembrandtsplein and the Seamen's District is *ladies-
of-the-night territory*—A.Y.O.R., needless to say. For the current
favorites in all these areas, ask your hotel concierge; gay and
exclusively Lesbian bars can be located by means of directories
sold in bookshops, or through the world-famous membership
clubs, the C.O.C. and D.O.K. And there are the *movies*—always

shown in their original sound track, with Dutch-printed subtitles, so that if they are imports from a country whose language you know, you have no comprehension problem.

### TO STAY

The Dutch are not among Europe's best hoteliers. They tend occasionally to slough over things. They can be abrupt in their dealings with guests—not nasty, mind you, but abrupt and quick, lacking the finesse of, say, their Swiss or French or Belgian counterparts. You have the feeling, often, that they are overworked and tired. On the other hand, there can be perfectly delightful surprise situations, when hotel personnel can be gracious and kind and charming, and can make you feel as though you were the most important guest ever. There seems to be no rhyme or reason as to the category of hotel in which you find good, well-trained personnel—some of the better ones, but not all; some of the cheaper ones, but not all.

Here are some hotels in Amsterdam that I like: the *Amstel* is a late-nineteenth-century hostelry that is one of the still-grand grand hotels. The lobby is enormous, several stories high, and very elaborate. The rooms are updated period pieces that are a joy to look at, look out of (particularly if you are on the Amstel River side), and to live in. The restaurant is superlative, and there are as well a grill, bar-lounge, and in fine weather a riverbank terrace cafe. This is a link in the Grand Metropolitan chain, the big British firm whose properties range all the way from Monte Carlo's Metropole to New York's Royal Manhattan. And service is skilled, if not always as smiling as it might be. There is only one drawback, and that is that the location is not quite central; still, one can walk—not drive—to the heart of town in ten or fifteen minutes, and there can be no disputing that this is one of Europe's great ones.

The *Hotel de l'Europe* (Nos. 2–4 Nieuwe Doelenstraat) has

everything going for it: in an inspired, central, in-the-heart-of-things location, it's a structure that began as a fifteenth-century fortress, knew succeeding centuries as an inn, and in the late nineteenth century was converted to its present design, except that it has been modernized frequently ever since. The plumbing, in other words, is new; the ambience is quietly traditional, the guest and public rooms handsome (these include one of the best restaurants in town plus a congenial bar-lounge and a snack bar), and the management and staff are professional in the best sense. And the views from the rooms: most all afford panoramas of the busy Muntplein and the Amstel River. If you have read other chapters of this book, you know that I do not normally recommend hotels that are well away from the center of things. I am making two exceptions in the case of Amsterdam, because this city does not have so many top-category hotels that these can be overlooked. They are both in attractive residential neighborhoods of the city that are a ten-minute taxi ride or a somewhat longer tram ride from downtown. The first is the *Amsterdam Hilton,* which ever since I knew it shortly after it went up in the early sixties has been a favorite of mine. It constitutes Dutch Modern architecture and design at their very best—substantial and functional, to be sure, but at the same time distinctive, inviting, and conveying an atmosphere of warmth and cordiality. It is expertly managed; you know, after a stay, that Hilton International knows what training and service are all about. It has a full range of facilities, even sightseeing boats that depart from its own pier on the canal at its back door. And its hundred-room garden wing opened in 1972. The other residential-area hotel that I want you to know about is the *Apollo,* the crackerjack British Trust Houses-Forte chain's Amsterdam property, and another stellar example of Dutch Modern, but newer and with a completely different look than the mellower Amsterdam Hilton. With its main building crescent-shaped, and like the Hilton, canalside, and a more conventionally designed annex tower alongside, the Apollo comprises a slew of restaurants, bars, and cafes, even

including a waterfront terrace for warm-weather drinks and snacks.
The guest rooms are the first I have encountered *anywhere* with
electric pants pressers. How about *that?* Moving closer to town,
there is the moderate-tab *Centraal* on Leidesbosje, near the
Leidseplein. This is an interesting Bauhaus-era structure with a
spotless, efficient air about it—intelligently refurbished, with a
good restaurant-grill-bar, indoor pool, and a preponderant majority of its cheerful and functional rooms with bath. Depending
upon what you think about prisons, you may or may not want
a room with a view of the Amsterdam jail. Even more central
than the Centraal is the relatively recent *Alexander Hotel*—
fifty rooms, all with bath or shower, in the building housing
Dikker & Thijs Restaurant, and under the same ownership.
The rooms are attractive, the location (No. 444 Prinsengracht)
ideal, and aside from the restaurant (about which more later),
there are, as well a ground-floor coffee shop, a delicatessen that specializes in food gifts and ships them, and next door, still another
related restaurant in an atmospheric eighteenth-century warehouse. There are two hotels I would call to your attention on the
Rembrandtsplein. I prefer the nice, old-fashioned, plain-as-a-
Dutch-wooden-shoe *Schiller.* By no means all rooms have baths,
but there are a pair of restaurants in addition to an animated
on-the-square cafe, and there is a very cozy feeling to the place.
Across the square is the modern *Caransa*—very, *very* fancy, with
a décor that could do with considerable toning down. All rooms,
though, are equipped with TV and radio, service bar, refrigerator,
ice water tap and, though Amsterdam rarely needs it, air conditioning—not to mention full baths. There is an assortment of
restaurants and bars. The *Port van Cleve* Restaurant is such an
Amsterdam institution that the hotel of which it is a part often
gets short shrift. But it is a pleasant, middle-level hotel—hardly
elaborate, but comfortable, elderly, and well located next to the
main post office, and just behind the New Church, with the Royal
Palace on The Dam square just steps beyond. *The Polen* is
another middle-level oldie (it occupies a substantial late-nine-

teenth-century building), with a super situation. It is just steps away from The Dam, with one entrance on the Kalverstraat (the main shopping street that connects The Dam with the Muntplein), and with the other entrance on Rokin, the thoroughfare that parallels Kalverstraat. Many rooms have bath, and there are both restaurant and cafe—the latter a capacious, traditional-style place much frequented by locals. Amsterdam is a chock-a-block full of hotels occupying old canal houses; sometimes they extend into several adjacent structures. There are rarely elevators, and the stairways are often so narrow that all furniture must be moved to the upper floors by means of outdoor cranes and the windows. Additionally, there are relatively few private baths, these being difficult to install in quantity, in these old structures. One that I particularly like is the *Ambassade,* at Herengracht 341. The house it occupies is a beauty, the public rooms (including a crystal-chandeliered, antique-furnished parlor) more like those of an affluent family; 90 percent of the thirty-four rooms (no two are alike) have private bath (an astonishingly high proportion for a canal house-hotel), and the management—Mr. Van der Veldon and his sister, Mrs. Kempers—is at once congenial and professional. Considerably simpler, if bigger, is the *Familiehotel Ardina,* Nos. 268–280–284 Keizersgracht. As its address indicates, it occupies a trio of houses, all of them venerable, but updated. Mind, though, that very few rooms have full private facilities. There's a breakfast room, and a tearoom-bar that features, as the multigraphed menu charmingly puts it, "cold and hot drinks and snacks served by color-TV and candlelight." I liked the Woldendorf family management, and I was pretty impressed, as I entered to inspect the place, to have to stand aside while the front stoop was being hand scrubbed with soap and water.

## TO EAT (AND DRINK)

Dutch food is about as subtle as a crowbar. It tends to be
solid and plain, and a great deal of it is eaten; of Europeans
only the Irish consume more calories (3450) per day than the
Dutch (3240). But the Dutch, to their great credit, have allowed
themselves to be occasionally influenced gastronomically by their
Belgian neighbors to the south, who in turn derive the best of
their cuisine from the next-door French. Still, the local repertoire
is limited. Few cow-filled countries come up, for example, with
so relatively few cheeses; Edam and Gouda are just about it.
They are delicious cheeses, to be sure, but one might wish for
more variety. The local national drinks are *genever*—never to be
confused with Anglo-American-type gin (the "old" types being
more oily and stronger-tasting than the "young") and the very
good beer, Amstel and Heineken being the leading brands. The
thick pea soup (Erwtensoep) is a cold-weather favorite. Breakfast,
in hotels at least, embraces a couple of species of not very tasty
bread and/or rolls, a slice or two of cheese, a boiled egg, and
coffee. The national lunch is the *Hollandse Koffietafel,* which
might unkindly be described as a truncated *smorgasbord*—sausage,
cheese, bread, a warm dish, and dessert, to be sure, but rarely
with the flair or drama of the Swedes' *smorgasbord* or the Danes'
*koltbord.* Dinner, for most Dutch, is meat, potatoes, and gravy,
with a pudding-type dessert. *Hutspot,* or hodgepodge, dishes (cas-
serole-type meat-potato-vegetable combinations) can be good.
Herring is the favorite seafood, and in May, when the fleet comes
in with the first catch of the season, alfresco stands appear everywhere; the Dutch take the fishes whole and poof! swallow them,
in one fell swoop, tails going down first. The Dutch bake a lot.
Usually their bread and rolls are no better than the supermarket
varieties of the same found in the United States. But they are
good at thin, *crêpe*like pancakes (*flensjes*) and the American-

English word, cookies, came through their settlers on our shores
from their *koejkies.* There are sandwich—or *broodje*—shops everywhere for quick if unexciting snacks. And there are Indonesian
restaurants with the interesting cuisine of the former Dutch colony,
the usual meal being *rijstaffel,* or rice table—rice served with a
great variety of savory dishes.

Amsterdam's best restaurants are in hotels. The dining room
of the *Amstel,* with its red damask draperies, off-white walls,
and crystal chandeliers extending from a high ceiling is, surely,
the most elegant eatery in town, with high-caliber food to match.
The menu is extensive, and largely French in both style and
execution. The service is impeccably correct, but at the same time
congenial. (Frequently in expensive Dutch restaurants the waiters
take themselves and their work so seriously that they turn sour-
puss.) Aside from the à la carte, there is a menu du jour, prix
fixe, at lunch and dinner, that is reasonable and invariably excellent. And there is, as well, an additional card with the eight or
ten special dishes of the day. About on the same high level is the
*Restaurant Excelsior in the Hotel de l'Europe*—handsome period
décor, picture windows overlooking the Amstel and Muntplein, an
extensive à la carte—classic French style and very good indeed;
and a variety of daily specials. The same hotel's *Relais de l'Europe*
is a smart, informal place—counter as well as tables—with both
hot dishes and sandwiches. The *Amsterdam Hilton's Diamond
Restaurant* is still another example of hotel leadership in the food
field; it is handsome and with an interesting international menu.
Good, too, is its *New Amsterdam Grill*—particularly if one
yearns for a Stateside steak; they're flown from America, as
they are for similar restaurants in the Paris and Brussels Hiltons.
The *Dikker & Thijs* complex is a mixed bag. The restaurant with
the D & T name is up a flight, expensive, and traditional both as
regards menu and surroundings. The food is safe—good, to be
sure, but unexciting. The street-level *Café du Centre* is coffee-
shop-convenient, and the adjoining and atmospheric *Prinsenkeller*
is more down-home Dutchy—and good. The *Port Van Cleve,* like

Dikker & Thijs, attached to a hotel, is something everyone visits in Amsterdam on one trip or other. The specialty is steaks in a variety of shapes, styles, and sizes. Your waiter places the order by shouting it into the kitchen, as his illiterate predecessors— several generations removed—did, and it comes to you numbered, to what advantage no one seems to know. You will want to try at least one typical Indonesian restaurant. *Djawa*, upstairs at No. 18 Kortekleidse Dwaarsstraat, off Leidseplein, is among the best; the *rijstaffel* is first-rate, and the Indonesian staff gracious and welcoming. *Dorrius*, No. 338 Nieuwe Zijds Voorburgwal, has been around for some eighty years; the locals like it because it offers good Dutch and Continental dishes and the value is sound. *Oester Bar*, No. 10 Leidseplein, serves all kinds of seafood, not only oysters; there are two dining rooms; downstairs is more casual than upstairs. *Nacht Restaurant*, No. 26 Reguliersgracht, opens at 10:00 P.M., when a lot of other places are shutting up; the menu is not-bad Continental. Of the snack-and-drink-type places, *Abraham Kef*, No. 192 Marnixstraat, is good; it features wine and cheese. *Continental Bodega*, No. 246 Lijnbaasgracht, is a sherry-snack spot, with an attractive clientele that keeps it fairly busy. *Bols Tavern and Crêperie* serves the Dutch-made Bols genever and liqueurs, and anything else you might want to quench your thirst, along with Dutch cheeses and thin pancakes. *Pieper*, No. 424 Pinsengracht, is a pleasant bar with a pleasant clientele in a fine old house, and with good snacks. The bar-lounge of the venerable *Doelen Hotel* on Nieuwe Doelenstraat is out of a seventeenth-century painting, with oriental rugs serving as tablecloths, in traditional style, and lovely canal views from the windows. *Papaneiland*, No. 2 Prinsengracht, is in a seventeenth-century house whose ace-in-the-hole—quite literally—is a tunnel that runs into the basement of a church across the canal. And last, two outdoor cafes to watch animated Amsterdam pass in review: that of the *American Hotel* near Leidseplein, where fellow customers are likely to be interested in the arts and theater, and that of the *Schiller Hotel* on the Rembrandtsplein.

TO BUY

The Netherlands is paydirt for the cutesy-pie-type of souvenir shopper. There are tiny wooden shoes and tiny Delft-type windmills and tiny Dutch-girl and Dutch-boy dolls *ad nauseam.* Chocolate, everywhere obtainable, makes a good gift; Van Houten and Droste are the leading brands, and the round boxes of pastilles— especially the semisweet ones—put out by Droste are always appreciated back home (at least by me!). The cheeses—Edam and Gouda—are good, too. Delftware is so copied that you find yourself not wanting to see blue-and-white pottery with windmill designs for some time after leaving Holland. Still, some of the real stuff can be attractive and valued. Royal Leerdam is the best of the Dutch glass and crystal firms, but no longer approaches that of the Scandinavian countries. I am told that diamonds are good buys, but it is my feeling that not many visitors are in the market for them; if you are, ask your hotel concierge to direct you to a reliable dealer. There are some handicrafts, but few that will bowl you over—still, some nice things. The Dutch have taken to designing clothes in recent years; some of their stuff—both male and female—is very smart. Last, the antiques shops are still full of antiques, more so than are their counterparts in a number of other European capitals. Start out in the biggest and best *department store, De Bijenkorf* (The Beehive) on The Dam. Give its main floor (which includes a snack bar and gift sections) a once-over, and the upper floors (clothing, furniture, housewares) a glance, too. Then proceed down Kalverstraat, the main shopping street, which is for pedestrians only every day after 11:00 A.M. Actually, the pedestrians are more interesting than the wares of most of the Kalverstraat shops. But you might want to look inside *Maison de Bonneterie,* a woman's clothing store which—with its crystal chandeliers—is one of the most attractive of the city's emporia. Take a look, also, at the No. 2 department

store, *Vroom & Dreesman,* and at *Snop,* men's and women's
clothing. You will want to check *Focke & Meltzer,* also on
Kalverstraat. I know of no other china and glassware shop in
Europe that makes its merchandise look less attractive, nor which
has less discernment in what it chooses to sell. Holland's Royal
Leerdam crystal and Delftware are there, along with stuff from all
over Europe. The nearby *St. Lucienshop,* No. 18 St. Luciensteeg,
though under the same ownership, is far less tacky. It is, as a
matter of fact, quite attractive, and so are some of its varied
wares—silver, porcelain, tin, enamelware, and the like. Delft is
also on sale at the retail shop of *De Porceleyne Fles* (the manufacturers) on the Muntplein. I would then move along toward
Leidsestraat, checking its shops—many are a cut above those of
Kalverstraat. Your next destinations should be *P. C. Hoofstraat,*
which is to Amsterdam what the Faubourg St.-Honoré is to Paris,
Bond Street to London, and Madison Avenue to New York.
Consider *antiques* at *Paul Rutten, J. C. Kermer, C. Simon,* and
*H. Schlichte Bergen; antique prints and etchings* at *A. van der
Meer;* take a look inside the striking black-and-white butcher
shop of *Heijenbrock* and pop into its adjoining *Belegdebroodjes*
shop for sandwiches and coffee; see contemporary furniture at
*Crawford;* contemporary jewelry at Aragne; women's *haute cou-
ture* at *Edgar Vos;* the men's clothes and accessories at
*Kostermans* (on Van Baerlestraat, just off P. C. Hoofstraat);
books at *Boonacker;* and food delicacies and wines at *Warmolts.*
Have a look at the *antiques shops on Spiegelgracht and neighboring Nieuwe Spiegelstraat*—including *Tilla & Coorengel; Huise de
Hoop; Smit Vaness;* and—for old Delft and Chinese export porcelain—*A. Aronson.* I have saved what is surely the most beautiful
shop in town for last: the Spiegelgracht location of the firm of
*A. van der Meer* (also located on P. C. Hoofstraat), No. 3
Speigelgracht, is one of Amsterdam's finest canal houses—elegant
gray brick with white trim, on the outside, and sumptuously
furnished within; I don't know whether you'll be able to afford

them or not, but the wares for sale are paintings of the seventeenth-century Dutch school.

## The Hague

### TO SEE

**Lay of the Land:** If The Hague is one of the most serene cities of Europe, it is also one of the most beautiful. Although its major monument is essentially and originally medieval, its dominant feeling is of the eighteenth century, rather than the seventeenth, which typifies larger, more vibrant Amsterdam. Like other seats of government where the business of government is a major business, there is a strange lack of the spontaneity which other cities with more diverse mixes of endeavor seem to have. Not even the cosmopolitan influx of diplomats—the Netherlands exchanges embassies or legations with several-score countries—seems to add color or flair, because the diplomats tend to stay largely among themselves, mixing socially with their own countrymen or, at best, with *other* diplomats in the other embassies. But no matter. Walk about, sightsee, relax in the cafes, enjoy the restful charm of the place. *The Binnenhof*—the remarkable complex that is the center of the Dutch Government—is the town's pre-eminent landmark, and is easily located, for it borders on a lake called the Hofjliver. To the north, along *Kneuter Dijk,* is the eye-filling part of town in and about the splendid green known as *Lange Voorhout.* This largely eighteenth-century square has, among other monuments, one of The Hague's three royal palaces, a relatively small mid-eighteenth-century house that is locked up 364 of the year's 365 days. The 365th is when the Queen opens Parliament. She comes in from the country to stay overnight and to ride from her little palace to the Binnenhof. The Lange Voorhout area is full of equally handsome houses; it is A-1 walking territory.

Retrace your steps via the *Kneuter Dijk* to the *Hofjliver,* continuing southward past the Binnenhof complex onto the *Hof Weg* (the street's changed name) and down to the first thoroughfare that intersects it. This is variously known as *Lange Poten, Spui Straat,* and *Vlaming Straat,* and is the core of the city's shopping area. Still continuing south, Hof Weg changes its name to *Spui,* and the next major intersection is the thoroughfare variously known as *Grote Markt Straat* and *Kalvermarkt;* it is a part of the shopping area.

**Choice destinations:** Head first for the *Binnenhof.* This is where The Hague had its beginnings nearly eight centuries ago, when a count of Holland built a hunting lodge into a moated castle, and 'ere long a village sprouted to serve the needs of the court. And so it went. The thirteenth century saw Count Floris V build the Ridderzaal, or Hall of Knights, which remains the most spectacular part of the Binnenhof. Its vaulted, beamed ceiling, reminiscent of a ship's hull, is almost ninety feet high. The hall had its start as a setting for banquets and receptions. It was altered architecturally, and there was a period when it became a kind of indoor market, with stalls for the sale of books, paintings, and textiles. As recently as 1878 the government was using it to store records. In 1894, though, a restoration was begun again. It was completed in 1904, just in time for Queen Wilhelmina to open Parliament under its roof. Every year since, the two houses of the Parliament have gathered in the Ridderzaal for a joint opening by the sovereign, on the third Tuesday of September, after a procession through the town—from the earlier-mentioned Paleis Voorhout, with troops, military bands, mounted soldiers, and police following behind the royal coach. There is more to the Binnenhof: the Rolzaal, a longtime justice court which has been authentically restored; the De Lairesse Room, with Renaissance paintings and décor; the Treves and Staten chambers—elaborately decorated meeting rooms; and the halls of the two houses of Parliament, or States General, as it is called—that of the First Chamber, whose seventy-five members are elected by the legislative councils of the eleven provinces, and that of the Second or Lower Chamber, with 150 members. Outstanding *churches* in The Hague include the Renaissance *Kloosterkerk* on Lange Voorhout, and the much larger, much older *Grote Kerk* (also known as St. Jacobskerk), the magnificent fifteenth-century cathedral with a recently restored spire. The *Peace Palace* is the Andrew Carnegie-funded neo-Renaissance structure (from the turn of the century, when heavy-handed décor was in vogue) that is the home of the International Court of Justice, the permanent Court of Habituation, and the Academy of International Law; open for guided tours. *Madurodam* is a miniature Dutch city, built in astonishing detail. Sections of it come to the KLM office on New York's Fifth Avenue every Christmas; children of all ages love it.

Then there are the *museums.* The *Mauritshuis,* next door to the Binnenhof, occupies a honey of a seventeenth-century mansion, which was the home of a prince named, not unsurprisingly, Maurits, who served as governor of Brazil during the brief period that it went from Portuguese to Dutch hands. Since the time when Holland was under Napoleonic rule, the house has been an art gallery, housing the superb collection of the stadtholders of the Netherlands. There are bigger collections in Europe, but few choicer. To be seen are works of Van der Weyden, Memling, David, the Holbeins, Jordaens, Rubens, Brueghel, and a number of choice Rembrandts and Steens. The *Gemeentemuseum,* or Municipal Museum, is justifiably noted for its superlative Mondrians, but it has other modern Dutch and foreign works as well, and a first-rate department of contemporary applied arts, whose special shows are the talk of the museum world. The *Museum Bredius* occupies an absolute treasure of a mid-seventeenth-century house—you pull the original doorpull to be admitted. The collection is that of a one-time curator of the Mauritshuis, whose will stipulated that the contents must stay as they were when he died, in 1952. The house is handsomely furnished, and among the paintings are Rembrandts, Van Ostades, and Steens, not to mention a number of others of the Dutch Renaissance school; not all are familiar, but many are superb. This is one of the finest small museums in Europe. The *Kostummuseum* occupies a lovely seventeenth-century house at 14 Lange Vijverberg. The clothes are mostly from the succeeding two centuries, all imaginatively displayed. The locals will probably insist that you see the *Panorama Mesdag,* an 1880 painting (they bill it as the world's largest) of Scheveningen in the latter part of the nineteenth century. Well, it only takes a few minutes. But do not confuse the *Panorama* with the *Museum Mesdag,* a nice old house turned into a cheerless repository of dreary nineteenth-century paintings.

*Scheveningen* is at once a suburb of The Hague and Holland's premier North Sea resort. Given the climate of the area, it is not surprising that most Dutchmen prefer heading for southerly climes, where they can be virtually assured of really hot sunshine, during the course of summer holidays. But you might be surprised at how many Dutchmen continue to jam Scheveningen in season. Its core is the Strandweg, a boulevard that separates beach from town. There are a number of hotels and guesthouses, and the major attraction is an amusement pier of the kind northern Europeans like so much. It juts into the sea and embraces a variety of restaurants, snack bars, shops, and even something called a "Wild West City," the authenticity of which not even the most chauvinistic locals vouch for. Scheveningen is pleasant enough in fine weather. You may or may not be up to the waters of the North Sea for swimming, but strolls along the Strandweg are good ways to become acquainted with the locals.

TO WATCH

The *Koningklijke Schouwburg* is the handsome eighteenth-century Royal Theater; its stage is home to both ballet and theater. If you don't want to see a play in Dutch, cross your fingers that there will be some ballet during your visit, as the theater is a beauty. The *Netherlands Congress Center* is a modern convention complex built so that The Hague could draw some of the congress business away from Amsterdam. It includes a concert hall, theater, recital hall, and two cinemas; concierges can advise on schedules of symphony concerts, musical comedies, and other entertainment. Keep the *Circustheater* in mind, too; despite its name it is the site of frequent opera, ballet, and concerts.

## TO STAY

The Hague's Old Faithful for generations had been the *Hotel des Indes,* a beautiful eighteenth-century house on the Lange Voorhout, just across from the little Royal Palace. When I last stayed at Des Indes, service had begun to deteriorate, and work was still needed on some of the bedrooms. Shortly thereafter, the hotel changed hands. I hope that means its standards will once again be what they were, for there are few small hotels in any major European city that occupy such fine premises. The public rooms—lobby, restaurant, bar, basement grill—are handsome, and to have a front bedroom with a view of the square is to have a happy Hague holiday—assuming, of course, that the hotel is being run well. The elderly *Central*—and central it is, indeed—has been stylishly refurbished, from stem to stern. All of its rooms now have bath or shower; there are two good restaurants, and a bar-lounge as well. Very pleasant. The also-central *Park Hotel* is not as up to date as the Central; it remains a downtown leader, though; and its restaurant, of which more later, is one of the best in the Netherlands. The *Wittebrug* is well away from the center of town, in an attractive country setting near Scheveningen. It is relatively modern, but its interiors are traditional in style. The public rooms are spacious and smart; so are the restaurant and cocktail lounge, the latter the only modern-décor room in the hotel. But the bedrooms are the Wittebrug's glory; virtually no two are alike, all are sumptuous and have baths as luxurious as one is likely to encounter in Europe. There are gardens without,

and a restful, resortlike ambience within. But you have to want
to be away from town. Not far beyond, in the thick of things on
the beach at Scheveningen, is the venerable *Kurhaus,* an immense
nineteenth-century pile that appears to go on for miles, in the
manner of the oldies on the seacoasts of England and Belgium.
Management appears to be doing its best to keep the place
up, not always as well as one would like. But credit must be
given for keeping this *grande dame* open at all. The seaview
bedrooms in good repair are pleasant (look before you book), as
are the dining room and bar-lounge, and the special treat that is
the outdoor terrace cafe just above the beach. And the elaborate,
high-ceilinged ballroom-banquet hall-meeting room called the
Kursaal is a must-see period piece.

## TO EAT (AND DRINK)

The *Queen's Garden Restaurant* of the Park Hotel, despite its
overfussy décor (lace tablecloths *on top* of satin tablecloths—to
give you an idea) and a waiter staff that takes its work so seriously
that one sees nary a smile, albeit a good deal of perspiration, is
one of the best restaurants in the kingdom. The menu is classic
French, the food is skillfully prepared, the wine list extensive,
and a meal a remembered experience. *'T Goude Hooft*—the
Golden Head—is a two-story, typically Dutch establishment with
a cafe downstairs and the restaurant proper above. The menu is
Dutch-Continental, and good; prices are moderate. The Central
Hotel's *House of Lords,* dignified in its neo-Renaissance décor, is
an invariably reliable place for Continental-Dutch cuisine; *Postil-
jon,* in the heart of town on Lange Poten, is good for a quick
lunch or a late-hour snack; there's counter service, and the place
never closes.

## TO BUY

For commentary on the shopping scene generally, refer back to the "To Buy" section for Amsterdam, where, of course, there are considerably more and bigger shops. The Hague has branches of major department stores like De Bijenkorf (there's a super supermarket on the fourth floor) and Vroom & Dreesman, to name two. Wander about the central shopping area, if you have time. If not, worry not, if Amsterdam is also on your itinerary.

### BOTH CITIES: TO NOTE

**Access:** Schiphol serves as the kingdom's international airport, and quite an airport it is: sleekly good-looking, intelligently designed, and convenience-filled. One of the most popular air destinations in Europe, it is served by a slew of airlines, transatlantic and otherwise, including beautifully run KLM Royal Dutch Airlines, which connects a number of North American points with Schiphol and has extensive additional routes on every continent. Amsterdam is but six quick miles distant; airport buses into town are very cheap, and taxis are moderate. The Hague, though more distant from the airport, is joined to it by regular and inexpensive airport buses as well as taxis. The Hague is about thirty-five miles from Amsterdam; train service between the two is excellent, comfortable (trains designated "D"—hardly to be confused with similarly identified conveyances in the New York City subway system —are particularly comfortable and worth the minor surcharge), and frequent, with several runs per hour. Indeed, train service linking both cities with the rest of Holland, and all of Europe, is excellent. Each city has more than its share of car-hire (with or without driver), sightseeing bus tours (generally well done), sightseeing boat tours in Amsterdam, and public transport, with the conductors (*and* all of your helpful fellow passengers) invariably English-speaking. Taxis are not hailable; you pick them up at taxi ranks or you or your hotel concierge phone for them. The tip is theoretically included in the metered fare in Amsterdam, though not The Hague. The flat terrain in both towns makes central-area walking effortless and a pleasure, assuming you have your collapsible umbrella with you as protection—or at the very least, insurance from the frequent moisture in the air. Which brings us to **Climate:** One does well to be prepared for a bit of rain at almost any time, although I do not mean to say that there cannot be brilliantly dry and sunny spells in the spring and summer. Winters surprise with their mildness, averaging in the thirties December through February, going on to the low forties in November and March. Spring and autumn (April to May and September to October) are high-forties and low-fifties months. And the summer (June, July, and August) averages in the sixties, occasionally the low seventies (although I have been caught off guard with eightyish heat waves; they come seldom). **Clothes:** Dutch cities—Amsterdam more than The Hague—are as full of informal places as are larger cities like London and New York. The younger Dutch are quite as partial to mod clothes as are the British, and I would say that Dutchmen's hair is collectively the longest and fullest on the Continent, exceeded in all of Europe only by that of the gents in Britain. Still, it is worth remembering that the better and more conventional places in this most solidly bourgeois of bourgeois countries expect one to look reasonably square—tie and jacket, that is—after dark. **Currency:** The guilder, also known as the florin. It is divided into one hundred cents, which look like miniature American pennies. **Tipping:** Service is invariably included in restaurant, cafe, and hotel bills, so there is no need to tip additionally, though you might give the concierge a guilder or two per day if he's done anything special for you. Give bellhops and baggage porters half a guilder per bag. In Amsterdam, the taxi drivers' tips are included in the meter readings; in The Hague, tip cabbies 15 percent. **Business hours:**

Shops, usually, are open from 8:30 or 9:00 A.M. to 5:30 or 6:00 P.M. including Saturday. Note, though, that many—usually the major ones—are closed Monday morning; others, Wednesday afternoons. In season (May to September) most shops at Scheveningen, the beach resort adjacent to The Hague, are usually open from 9:00 A.M. to 9:00 P.M. **Language:** Dutch (which the Dutch call *Hollands*) is the national language. A major marvel of the Netherlands, though, is the English-language fluency of virtually the entire populace. It is difficult to find even a kindergartener who would not be able to direct you in English (assuming, of course, that the tyke knew the location of what you were looking for). Of Europeans whose native tongue is not English, only the Danes and Norwegians rank with the Dutch in this matter. And it is not only English that the Dutch speak so well; they are also whizzes at French, and in recent years—the horrors of the Nazi World War II occupation a generation behind them—they have again begun to speak German, which is closely related to their own language. **Local literature:** *Amsterdam This Week* is available to guests gratis in most hotels; similar giveaways are to be found in The Hague. The bookshops are full of handsomely illustrated books on Amsterdam, although there is not, unfortunately, a good deal available on The Hague. **Further information:** Netherlands National Tourist Office, 576 Fifth Avenue, New York; 681 Market Street, San Francisco; Royal Trust Tower, Toronto; Amsterdam Tourist Office (VVV), 5 Rokin, Amsterdam, The Netherlands; The Hague/Scheveningen Tourist Office (VVV), 38 Parkstraat, The Hague, The Netherlands.

# *Athens*

Nobody gives Athens the credit it deserves for solving its gaposis problem so successfully. Nobody even thinks much about Athens' gaposis problem. But one must, on a first visit. Surely it is worth recalling that until Greece became a sovereign monarchy, in the 1830s, the entire town consisted only of the ruined Acropolis on its own eminence, and the little community—now known as Plaka—directly beneath it.

When one considers the turmoil that Greece has known in the past century and a half—the plot is one gigantic political soap opera—it is to its great credit that modern Athens has managed to become such an agreeable, stimulating city. The story goes, just to give you an idea of what the place was like, that the young German prince hired to be the first king, determined the site of his palace (it is now the Parliament, which has been put out of business by the ruling colonels) by setting out great chunks of raw meat at a number of locales; the one chosen—today's Constitution Square—attracted the fewest bugs and maggots, and thus was the winner.

**Ancient beginnings:** That is not the image we have of Athens. What we think of is the ancient city-state that reached its zenith in the fifth century before Christ. Its people were the first ever to conceive the historical sense, to look upon solving mankind's problems realistically and practically rather than solely through gods and deities. Greek civilization did not, of course, begin in Athens. Two European archaeologists—a German, Heinrich Schliemann, and an Englishman, Sir Arthur Evans—discovered as recently as the late nineteenth century that the Hellenic culture had its start on the island of Crete as long ago as 1400 B.C. The Cretans organized democratic city-states, in which they brought art and artisanship—painting, exquisitely thin pottery, metalwork —to a high level, and architecture as well. The Cretan culture was later transferred to the mainland, during the chaotic Dark Age (1000–800 B.C.) about which Homer wrote—for the ages—in his *Odyssey* and *Iliad*. Sparta was the earliest of the leading city-states (those same Dorians who gave their names to Doric columns founded it), and its way of life was what we would now call spartan—the adjective that was Sparta's immortal gift to later eras.

Athens was founded later by the Ionians (they, too, gave *their* name to a type of column). Although it began as a semi-absolute monarchy, it gradually saw power transferred from the kings to the nobles, from the nobles to the emerging merchant class, and finally—after the grim period known in the history books as the Age of Tyrants—into representative democracy.

**Instant refresher course:** And now for a back-to-school respite. Here are some ancient Greek names and expressions worth re-familiarizing yourself with.

*Draco:* gathered all the existing laws, copied them—for the first time—into the Draconian Code, and woe to those who disobeyed (621 B.C.). *Draconian,* even today according to the dictionary, is something "dangerously severe, harsh."

*Solon:* the Great Reformer, in matters both political and economic; gave democracy to the Athenian in the street (638–558 B.C.), and his very name to the ages; a "solon," according to Webster, is "a wise man."

*Ostraka:* the practice of negative voting, whereby citizens wrote on small bits of pottery (*ostraka*) and dropped into urns the names of politicos they did *not* like; those receiving enough such ballots were *ostracized*—ousted from Athens for a minimum of a decade.

*Pericles* (500–429 B.C.): Mr. Big of Athenian democracy, who introduced a paid civil service and public welfare system, among other things.

*Zeus:* chief god, symbolized by the thunderbolts he hurled down to earth from high on Mt. Olympus; *Hera:* his wife and goddess of fertility; *Apollo:* the sun god; *Aphrodite:* goddess of love; *Athena:* goddess of Athens.

*Pythagoras* (c. 500 B.C.): the philosopher who believed that the universe was based on numbers and governed by a basic system of mathematics.

*Socrates* (496–399 B.C.): the ambulatory streetcorner speech-maker who was the founder of modern philosophy—even though his fellow Athenians sentenced him to death by the drinking of hemlock, for impiety and corrupting the morals of youth.

*Plato* (427–347 B.C.): a pupil of Socrates, best known for his political treatise, *The Republic.*

*Aristotle* (384–322 B.C.): he was, in turn, a pupil of Plato; one of the reasons Alexander the Great was supposed to have been so brilliant is that he was a pupil of Aristotle, who wrote about every then-existing area of knowledge, from ethics to physics, and put together the first encyclopedia.

*Hippocrates* (460–377 B.C.): the first great medical man; every Western physician still takes his oath.

*Praxiteles:* one of the greats among sculptors.

*Sappho:* a name to remember among the poets.

*Aeschylus, Sophocles, Aristophanes,* and *Euripides:* the top dramatists, and moreover the first dramatists; plays as we know them today were their inventions.

*Demosthenes:* the orator who learned his art by speaking with stones in his mouth.

*Herodotus* and *Thucydides:* they pioneered as both students and writers of history.

It was not to last. Philip of Macedonia and later his genius son, Alexander, spread Greek culture as far away as India, and did it before Alexander died in his thirties. But Greece was weakened, and in the second century after Christ the Romans took it over as a kind of backwater of their empire, the while accepting the richness of the Hellenic culture. Athens sent many teachers to Rome. That same Greek culture was the basis of the Byzantine Empire, of which it became a provincial capital, later passing a part of the medieval era under rule by French and, successively, the Spaniards, Albanians, Venetians, and Florentines.

**The Turkish centuries and the modern kingdom:** Then came the middle of the fifteenth century—the year 1458. The Turks took the Acropolis and—except for a brief period of Venetian rule—kept it for four centuries. (It was in the seventeenth century, when the Turks were defending the city from another Venetian attack, that powder, having been stored by Turkish troops in the Parthenon, of all places, exploded and blew that building's roof to bits.) Only in the nineteenth century did the Greeks begin to assert themselves in a new nationalism, fighting for their independence under a pair of brothers named Ypsilanti, whose name was later given to a city in Michigan. That was in 1821; in succeeding years European help came to the freedom fighters, most dramatically in the person of Lord Byron, the English poet-adventurer who personally joined the troops and lost his life among them in 1824.

Later, for a brief period, there was a Greek republic headed by a onetime Russian foreign minister (European politics were nothing if not odd at that period). A civil war brought the republic to an early end, and in 1832 the European powers determined that Greece would start again as a monarchy. They chose the king—one Prince Otto of Bavaria. As King Othon he turned out to be a nasty piece of goods; his subjects didn't like him. Out he went in 1862, and in came another to sit upon the throne. Although the Russian president and the German king hadn't done

too well, this new import—a Danish prince dubbed King George
I—hung on for a substantial period.

The history of modern Greece is best chronologically capsulized.
King Othon was dethroned. King George I was assassinated.
King Constantine I was expelled after a reign of four years and
later returned to the throne, only to leave it finally, by abdicating.
King Alexander had a three-year reign, ended by his natural
death. King George II first became king in 1922 but was expelled
in 1923 to make way for a republic that lasted until he regained
the throne in 1935, coincident with the rise of the Metaxas dictatorship. He was out again in 1944, during which time a regency
replaced him, until he was recalled. He died in 1947 and was succeeded by his brother, Paul I, who died in 1964, to be succeeded
by his son, Constantine II. Constantine, whose pretty wife is the
former Princess Anne Marie of the very same Danish dynasty
from which the Greek royal house descends, fled to Rome, and exile, after an abortive countercoup, following the 1967 military coup
d'etat that overthrew the constitutional democratic government.

World War II was a cruel time for Greece. Although the Greeks
bravely repulsed the Italians' invasion through Albania in 1940,
the Germans besieged Greece in 1941, occupying it until 1944,
after which time domestic Greek communists and royalists fought
a bloody civil war that went on until 1950. It was concluded only
after the United States—putting into effect the Truman Doctrine—
sent some three hundred million dollars in military and economic
aid as well as military advisers. From that time until the piously
moralistic colonels took over in 1967, Greece enjoyed a sus-
tained albeit imperfect period of representative government. The
colonels—their leader George Papadopoulos, is premier—took
over to protect the country from the advent of a communist
government, which many Greeks believe was not at all imminent,
considering the overwhelming aversion to communism built up
over the long years of the civil war, and the fierce individualism
that typifies the Greek personality.

**The repressive colonels:** The colonels' repressive fascist government has imprisoned a large number of political opponents. The Greece they govern has seen a deprivation of civil liberties, a censored press (there were more than 120 dailies, where there are now only about 60), and antipathy from groups ranging from the Strasbourg-based Council of Europe to the educated, intellectual, and upper-income classes of Greece itself. The United States wisely withheld military aid from the time the coup took power until 1970, by which time it reverted to its traditional pro-dictatorship foreign policy, and not only resumed aid, but sent Greek-descended Vice President Spiro Agnew on a highly bally-hooed visit that gave the junta a measure of the respectability illegal governments invariably crave. Greeks abroad, like actress Melina Mercouri, and Lady Fleming, the elderly Greek-born widow of the English inventor of penicillin, led an anti-colonels opposition with a wide following of friends of Greece around the world, who would like to see it return to democracy before the dictators become too entrenched. It appears, though, that the support of powerful Uncle Sam is helping to keep the colonels on the scene.

### TO SEE

**Lay of the land:** The *Acropolis,* with its magnificent ruined Parthenon, dominates Athens geographically, architecturally, historically, and spiritually, if you will. Beneath it is *Plaka,* the section of town next oldest after the Acropolis and all that there was of inhabited Athens for many centuries, until the advent of the modern monarchy impelled the building of a proper city in the nineteenth century. There are two principal squares downtown, the more important of which is known as *Syntagma* or *Constitution Square.* Its landmark is the Tomb of the Unknown Soldier, and directly behind it the earlier-mentioned Parliament, now in disuse and originally built as the first royal palace by King Othon. A handsome park known as Ethnikos Kipos, or *National Garden,*

lies directly behind Parliament. Also bordering the park—from
another side—is the Royal Palace, deserted when its occupants
went into Roman exile, but still guarded (as is Parliament)
by the Evzone troops in their traditional skirted uniforms and
tasseled shoes. Another avenue leads from Constitution Square
and, as *Queen Sofia Avenue,* passes smart apartment houses
and major museums before reaching the best specimen of
modern architecture in town—the dominantly marble Athens Hilton. Return now to Constitution Square. It is linked with the other
principal downtown square of *Omonia* by the lengthy commercial
thoroughfare *Stadiou Street.* Running parallel with Stadiou is
another principal shopping street called *Venizelou.* Off in the
northeast corner of town is *Mount Lykavittos,* with a funicular
leading to little St. George's Chapel at its summit. The view from
on high is of the town, Acropolis, and beyond—the port city of
Piraeus and the sea.

An interesting *introductory walk* would be through the core
of town from, say, the Royal Palace past Parliament and the
cafes and hotels of Constitution Square, down Stadiou Street or
parallel Venizelou Avenue to vibrant Omonia Square (it contrasts
greatly with the more subdued, not very amusing Constitution
Square). Plaka is after-dark walking territory: Except for shops
it does not unshutter until then; its shops and cafes are mostly
evening-only places. The *bathing beaches* outside of town—including Kalamaki, adjacent to the airport, and somewhat more
distant Glyfada—are destinations in summer, along with the
crescent-shaped yacht-studded harbor of Piraeus, for alfresco dinners at a waterfront restaurant.

**Choice destinations:** The *Acropolis,* when I first visited it on a
hot August afternoon in the early 1950s, was populated with
perhaps a couple of dozen additional visitors besides myself. On
my most recent visit, on a hot August afternoon in the early 1970s,
the place was a mob scene. It was much harder to visualize
what the place must have been like when Athens was at its
Golden Age of splendor during the time of Pericles in the fifth

century B.C. The complex is dominated by the Parthenon, the marble temple appropriately built at its highest point, that is considered to be the masterwork of ancient Greek architecture. There are six Doric columns at either of its short ends, and seventeen along each of the long sides. Much of the building is gone now. (The roof, as I mentioned earlier, was blown off when powder —stored within by the Turks—exploded during a seventeenth-century siege by the Venetians.) Missing, too, is the sanctuary where stood the immense statue of Athena, the helmeted goddess of wisdom, who was simultaneously patron of peace and of war, ruler of storms, and protectress of Athens. The *Parthenon* was built for Athena—a virgin goddess who emerged from the forehead of Zeus after he had swallowed her mother, Metis; you sometimes hear Athena called Nike, and also (after she had been adopted by the Romans) Minerva. The *Erectheum* is the Ionic-design temple with one of its porticos occupied by half a dozen columns that are actually statues (caryatids, they are called) of lovely ladies, one of which is a fake; the original was carted away by Lord Elgin in the last century and, along with other fragments from the Parthenon, reposes in the British Museum in London; the lot is known as the Elgin Marbles, and the Greeks still want them back where they belong. There are other shrines on the Acropolis, and there is as well the *Acropolis Museum;* it is full of sculpture, all of it from the Acropolis. In the area of the ancient Agora, or market place, one finds the *Theseion,* a one-time temple that saw service in later centuries as a Greek Orthodox Church and as a museum; it is in remarkably good shape. Nearby is the *Stoa of Attalus,* an ingeniously designed complex of shops comprising two levels ringed by 134 Doric and Ionic columns, that is now a museum housing objects excavated in the Agora area. *Hadrian's Arch,* though named for a noted Roman emperor, was built by Athenians in the first century A.D. as a tribute to a favorite emperor.

*Byzantine Athens* is best seen on visits to the gemlike cross-shaped churches of that era, with their splendid mosaics and

frescoes. There is one problem in this respect, though: they are
locked more often than not. You must be prepared for disap-
pointments. *Aghios Eleftherios* is unusual in that it is of white
marble instead of the more typical brick or stone used for these
churches; it is typically tiny. *Ayii Apostoli,* near the earlier mentioned Theseion, is interesting—and remarkable—principally because of its great age; it was built about the year 1000, making
it the oldest church in town. *Aghios Nicodemos* on Philhellinon
Street is the biggest of the group; the exterior is still original, although the interior, while still impressive, was restored in 1855
when the Russian community took over the building for its place
of worship. *Daphni* is the loveliest of the group, worth every
drachma of the five-mile taxi ride from town. It consists of a
masterful eleventh-century church with mosaics that are the best
of their type in the area, and of the remains of a monastery twice
as old as the church. Note the painted interior of the dome. The
*Greek Orthodox Cathedral,* though put up in the mid-nineteenth
century and hardly beautiful, qualifies as Byzantine because it is,
for the most part, constructed with bricks, stones, and other materials that came from more than seventy churches that had been
destroyed by the Turks in earlier years.

   **Museums,** in a city with the antiquity of Athens, are as requisite
as the Empire State Building in New York. I have already recommended the *Acropolis Museum* at the Acropolis and the
*Agora Museum* in the Stoa of Attalus; but the No. 1 undisputed
can't-miss of the lot is the *National Archaeological Museum.* It is
on Patission Street, and if you walk to it from Omonia Square, it
is entirely likely that you will mistake the also neoclassic Poly-
technic Institute for it; never mind, you won't be the first to do
so, and the students on the campus will be glad to practice their
English to move you down the street to your destination. The
museum is a great square pile embracing some three-dozen galleries flanking four inner courtyards. The contents are from
throughout Greece. The bulk of the exhibits are sculpture, of
course—magnificent friezes and pediments of temples with com-

plex scenes of classical life; demurely draped ladies, handsome nude males, smiling youngsters, goddesses like Athena, gods like Poseidon, wrestlers and runners, slaves and sphinxes. And there is the added magnificence of the Mycenean Room, with the goldwork of that era; the death mask of Agamemnon is the stunner of the lot. The *Byzantine Museum,* certainly No. 2 in importance, contains what is surely the finest collection of *ikons*—these being the religious paintings of the Greek Orthodox Church—to be seen anywhere outside of the Soviet Union, rich in the scarlet and gold hues that typify them; they include a fifteenth-century painting of St. George (with spear but no dragon), an oddie of an ikon called *Love* portraying angels in the mouths of great fish (one playing a fiddle, the other a tambourine), and another painting, *The Lamentation,* of Christ descended from the Cross; they are but a trio of the greats in the collection. The *Benaki Museum* is a charmer. Occupying the onetime townhouse of its rich bene- factor, Antony Benaki, its exhibits mostly—but not entirely— comprise the treasures he himself collected over a period of several decades, before he died in 1954. Although there are foreign objects (Chinese porcelain, and arts and crafts from nearby Mediterranean cultures), the big news at the Benaki is the sumptuous Greek collections—old manuscripts, superb ceramics, jewelry and other gold and silver objects, folk costumes and em- broideries, and some exceptional ikons, including a sixteenth- century Cretan one—a Madonna and Child flanked by a pair of angels and framed with portraits of saints. The *National Picture Gallery,* newest of the Athens museums, is opposite the Athens Hilton and occupies a striking pavilion. Its subject matter is Greek painting, contemporary and otherwise. I looked through it to see if there might be a painting of El Greco in the land of his birth. Sure enough, I found *Angels' Concert* by Domenicos Theotocopoulos. The proper Greek name is not considered either overlong or difficult of pronunciation on home ground. The *Na- tional Historic Museum* occupies the building that served as the first Parliament. The collections tell the story of modern Greece and include the Crown Jewels. The *Piraeus Archaeological Museum* displays local relics, including statuary of great beauty from this town that dates back some forty-five hundred years.

## TO WATCH

Warm-weather months bring outdoor presentations of dance, music, and classical drama, in conjunction with the annual Athens Festival, usually at the splendidly restored *Theater of Herodes Atticus*. There is *Son et Lumière*, (or Sound and Light, if you prefer) on the hill called *Pynx*, with its ancient associations; it's quite a show on a clear, starlit night. There are theater and dance performances in other locales, alfresco in summer; that goes for movies; they step outdoors in the warm weather too, sort of like a drive-in without cars. In winter there is an opera and theater season as well, with the former at the *Lyriki Skene Theater*.

## TO STAY

Greeks can be more likable than efficient. Their own brand of hospitality is so winning that you usually don't mind when minor things go wrong. And there *are* well-run places. Athens has several top-rank hotels that would hold their own in any capital. The *Athens Hilton,* for example. Architecturally, as I mentioned earlier, it comes off as quite the handsomest modern building in town. It is beautifully sited, on an avenue facing toward town, the Acropolis, Piraeus, and the sea; the view from front-side rooms is inspired. The rooms themselves are honeys—modern, with Greek touches. I don't know of any other contemporary hotel that uses marble (usually it looks gaudy) to better effect and with more style. The immense lobby is a beauty. There is a variety—typically Hilton-imaginative—of places to dine, dance, and drink. And there is the added advantage of a super swimming pool, hardly to be despised during siesta of a summer sightseeing day, or at day's end. The *King George,* on Constitution Square (and *not* to be confused with the nearby, misnamed King's Palace) is a traditional-ambience, period-style hotel in a fully air-conditioned modern building. The public rooms are mostly Louis XVI style, and have great éclat. The bedrooms and suites, in a variety of shapes and sizes, are lovely and luxurious, with superb views of the Acropolis from the terraced front ones; also, restaurants, cafe, bar —all of the same *luxe* caliber as the hotel itself. The *Grand Bretagne,* next-door neighbor to the King George, is older, bigger, and while right up there with the best of them, without the elegance of its quieter next-door neighbor. The Grand Bretagne has a bustling ambience—there's always an agreeable perk to the lobby, full air conditioning, and good-to-excellent rooms and suites. Going down a category from luxe to first-class, there's the *Amalia,* just off Constitution Square, facing the National Garden. It is spiffy-modern, and all rooms have bath and air conditioning; there are spacious public rooms and a nice restaurant and a bar. The *Athenée Palace* is fifties-modern, in contrast to the late sixties of the Amalia. It is heart-of-downtown on Kolocotroni Square at Stadiou Street, with a two-story-high lobby, good-looking restaurant, and bar; all rooms have bath and air conditioning; some have mini-terraces and Acropolis vistas. The whole place has a nice dignity about it. The modern *Arethusa,* at Mitropoleos Street 6–8, is bright and shiny, fully air conditioned, and with baths in all its rooms; the location is downtown and convenient. The quite modern, centrally located *Astor* (16 Karageorgi Servias Street) has smallish bedrooms (all with bath) but a super terrace-with-a-view restaurant to compensate. The even more moderate-category *Hotel Omonia* is on agreeably frenetic Omonia Square, the less-fancy of the town's two main plazas. It's good value: All rooms have bath, and there's a restaurant and bar.

### TO EAT (AND DRINK)

The word is robust. Greek cooking is direct and uncomplicated. There is a near-passion for fresh ingredients. Most Greeks, if they could afford them, might accustom themselves to the convenience of a refrigerator, for short-term storage of perishables, but *never freezers,* the concept of which would be entirely anathema; the idea is to buy it *just* before you cook or serve it. The cuisine revolves around lamb—roast whole baby lamb, roast leg of lamb, lamb chops, lamb stewed in a variety of ways, and *souvlakia*—the skewer-grilled lamb often sold in sandwiches at street stands, and edging up to pizza in newfound American popularity. *Moussaka,* the Greeks' most-noted casserole dish, is a baked blend of eggplant (a favorite vegetable), lamb, and a cheese sauce. Fish and seafood are good, particularly the *babounia* (that's Greek for red mullet), the lobster, and, yes, the octopus. Of the soups, my all-time, every-time favorite is avogolemono—the egg-lemon classic. Like all Mediterranean peoples, the Greeks understand salads, and have respect for the beauty of a simply dressed tomato or cucumber, or a plate of chicory tossed with oil and vinegar. (If you are offered *taramosalata,* accept; it's a delicious cod-roe concoction.) And those oil-cured black olives: only the Italians and the Turks prepare them as well. Of course, you know the pungent, crumbly goat-milk cheese called *feta,* but there are other species—*manouri* and *graviera,* for example. (The Greeks also attempt foreign-type cheeses; one restaurant menu features in delightfully phonetic Greek English, *Rock For;* when you say these things aloud, you understand them.) Pastries are honey-sweet, often with the tissue-thin *philo*-type dough of Turkey and the Middle East; the Greeks prefer to eat them more in cafes than at dessert, when fresh fruit, cheese, and bread are more typical. The bread, when it is coarse-textured and darkish, can be very good indeed. Bakers are everybody's friend in Greece, particularly in the villages, where housewives still take their meats to be roasted in their bakers' ovens. A meal is concluded with tiny cups of the strong, thick coffee (specify sweet, semi-sweet, or black when ordering) that all the world knows as Turkish; needless to say, in this country one identifies it as Greek, or runs risks. (I am not going to get into the question of the extent to which Greek food is derived from the Turkish, except only to note that Greece was Turkish-occupied for so many centuries that culinary influence would seem to have been inevitable. Turkish cooking is the more sophisticated of the two, probably because the Turks, with their incredibly lavish imperial court and a privileged aristocracy to complement it, had much more of an opportunity to create a more elaborate cuisine.)

Greek wine is as unpretentious as Greek food. There is no complicated ritual of vintages and years and charts. The best wines are white, and they are either resinated (*retsina,* in Greek) or *aretsinto*—which is how most non-Greeks prefer to drink them. Popular nonresinated whites by the bottle include Minos and Pallini. But don't hesitate to ask for waiters' recommendations. There is no stigma attached to the consumption of water, as in certain other European lands. (It is, for example, automatically served in cafes, with coffee.) In Athens, it is perfectly safe to drink from the tap; you needn't bother with the bottled stuff. The great Greek apéritif is *ouzo,* the Hellenic counterpart of the Turks' *raki,* and a cousin of the French *anisette,* with its distinctive anise flavor. It is cheap, delicious, and invariably taken in a tall glass splashed with water—which immediately clouds it up—and cooled with ice cubes. The Greeks are big brandy drinkers, too; you will have heard of their Metaxa brand; it is widely exported. Beer (Fix is a popular label) is good, too.

Simplicity is the keynote of most restaurants. and, indeed, of their printed menus. In recent years, menus in many places have been printed in both Greek and a distinctive menu-species of English. Beans may appear as "beens," baby lamb as "baby lamp," vegetable as "vegg-table," peaches as "poaches," cake as "caik," and sweets as "suits." Somewhat complex warnings are issued: "Drinks and fruits without food is overcharged with 45%." And cheery admonitions like this are not uncommon: "For your complaints call the Manager or the Police." Service can be erratic, and in crowded places, slow. It is rarely if ever unkind, or, heaven forbid, impersonal. The point I make is that a meal is considered by the Greeks to be an enjoyable experience. If I had time for but one first-class meal of Greek specialties it would be at the *Taverna* of the *Athena Hilton*. Hilton International has very wisely taken the very best of Greece—typical décor, typical foods, typical wines, and a super chef and staff—and combined the lot into what is the all-round best of its category. There are other places to eat in the hotel for non-Greek foods—a kicky pizzeria (that also serves a few pasta dishes), for example; a big open-late coffee shop, and a rooftop supper club-disco with a continental menu. But the Taverna is the genuine Greek article. Plaka, the venerable quarter directly beneath the Acropolis, has a Times Square air about it during the warm-weather months; tourists from absolutely everywhere mingle with the locals on its steep, narrow streets. There are *tavernas* all over the place, and every Greek—or visitor of more than twenty-four hours—will recommend his favorites. In summer they are mostly outdoors; there is not always much sidewalk space left for pedestrians, and you can amble about and have a look at the food, staff, and clientele before making a choice. My favorite Plaka *taverna* has a location that is strategic—you watch the world go by as you dine, the prices are moderate, as they are throughout the district, and the fare is well prepared. The name is *Old Man Moria. Xynou* is another Plaka possibility, while in winter (and winter only) there is *Zaffaris,* quartered in an atmospheric old Plaka house.

Now then, if meals at the Hilton Taverna and Plaka are requisites, so is a lunch or dinner along the Turkolimono waterfront area of the port city of Piraeus. Coumoundourou Street, facing the harbor, is lined with restaurants, a number of them very good. My recommendation is *Canaris,* at No. 50. You select your entrée—the lobsters are first-rate, but so is the *bar-bounia*—from the refrigerator inside, and then take a table across the street, directly on the water. Everything—appetizers, entrées, salads—is delicious; the service is delightful. There are two additional hotel restaurants that I like; both are rooftop-high and with fine Acropolis views. The *Tudor Grill* of the *King George Hotel* is English only in its décor. The menu is international, and always with Greek specialties. (The lamb stew, for example, is excellent, and so is the Greek salad.) The *Roof Garden* of the *Astor Hotel* is plain as an old shoe, and jam-packed at lunch with Athenians who appreciate an inexpensive restaurant with a million-drachmae Acropolis view. The *dolma*—the typical stuffed grape-leaves appetizer—is very good, as are the grills, both fish and meat. *Costoyiannis,* 37 Zaini Street, is good, Greek, and inexpensive. Easy-to-find *Corfu,* 6 Kriezotou Street (on Constitution Square) has a typical menu and is invariably reliable. You might not expect jelly doughnuts in Athens, but they are among the excellent nibblies at a little stand-up cafe (good for sustenance while on shopping expeditions) called *Pinci,* on Voukourestiou Street, in the heart of downtown. Smarter sit-down cafes (Athens' answer to those on the Champs-Elysée) are nearby: *Foca* and *Zonar's,* on Venizelou Avenue, just off Constitution Square. If you want to join mobs of locals and visitors for corny late-night carousing in Plaka, two of the fairly durable biggies, with entertainment (*bizouki* players and singers and heaven knows what all else) are *Mostrou* and *Vrahos.* Remember, though, that a lot of *bazouki* activity transfers in summer to both the seaside resorts and Piraeus: *Stork,* in Glyfada, is among the smarter of these.

TO BUY

Greece still is a land of isolated tiny villages—thousands of them—where the tradition of making things by hand persists. There are, as a result, fine handicrafts to be obtained. But there is also a great deal of gaudy junk. Tacky curio shops abound in downtown Athens, one little different from the next. The good stuff, though, is worth seeking out—hand-woven rugs and textiles, embroidered work, copperware and trays, bowls, coffee services; jewelry—both fine (very fine!) and costume, and a variety of other objects made from natural materials, utilizing traditional designs. *Their Majesties' Fund*—dating from way before the time when Their Majesties went into exile—is the craft organization that has fostered and promoted the craft industry in villages. The main shop is at 24 Voukourestiou Street, and there is a branch at the Athens Hilton. The big specialty—and you should go to the main shop if it interests you—is carpets. Not only the inexpensive shaggy all-wool *flokates* (these come in natural and in colors), but much more interesting hand-made carpets of traditional design that are embroidered, knotted, or tapestry-woven. The sizes, colors, and designs vary, but the motifs are usually small-design abstracts. They are expensive, but they are also works of art. Their Majesties' Fund also sells a range of less-expensive crafts—ranging from embroideries to copper coffee services. Standards of design, taste, and quality are high. But double-check whatever arrangements you make for shipping. I had two purchases shipped on a recent visit. One arrived, but the other didn't, and almost a year later, the Fund had still not agreed to end its "inquiries" to the post office and simply send me a replacement for the original purchase. *Aporon,* 13 Voukourestiou Street, translates as *Indigent Women's Institution,* and is a nonprofit charitable organization. Most of what's on sale is in the textile line— embroidered linen tablecloths and placemats, blouses, handbags, cushions, and the like, workmanship is first-rate, prices fair. The *Royal Hellenic School of Embroidery and Lace* maintain a retail outlet at 17 Voukourestiou Street (children's dresses, baby clothes, placemats and tablecloths); everything is hand done, and beautiful; custom orders, too. *Ilias Lalaounis* is a jeweler with his own design staff and factory. The stuff is mostly 18- or 22-karat gold and it is high style and elegant. There are rings, bracelets, necklaces, brooches, watches, and a special group of reproductions of the Mycenaean gold in the National Archaeological Museum; two shops: 6 University Avenue and the Athens Hilton. *Men's shoes* turn out to be a Greek bargain—smartly designed, of good quality, and cheap. *Petrides* has several shops, one at 48 Stadiou Street. *Mati*, 20 Voukourestiou Street, is a smallish but unusually good source of handicrafts, costume jewelry, the odd antique. There's not a piece of junk in the whole shop; prices are high, along with the quality. *Filimon*, 5 Koumbari Street, two doors from the Benaki Museum (upstairs), is one of Athens' leading *haute couture* designers—not wild, but with a sure style sense, and with all of his clothes made from interesting Greek materials; dresses from about a hundred dollars. *Martinos*, 50 Pandrossou Street, is surely the most remarkable antiques shop in town. If you've time for but one, this should be it. Chock-a-block full—main floor and basement—of all manner of old and elderly things: Greek, Turkish, Western European, valuable and otherwise, beautiful and ugly. The china and silver are noteworthy. *E. M. Vitali and E. Gazarossian*, 58 Pandrossou Street, is crammed with a wide variety of things. *Patrikiadis*, 64 Pandrossou Street, is still another mixed bag: old coins, terra cotta, jewelry, silver. By now you will have deduced that Pandrossou is a street of antiques shops. In the old part of town, at the entrance to Plaka, it is an Athens requisite, shopper or not. Remember, though, to bargain everywhere (and not only on the shops of this street) and to beware of ikons. Fakes—well-done fakes—abound. They're often so good that only specialists can detect them; postcard reproductions of the ikons in the Byzantine and Benaki museums are much more sensible. Which leads me to the *Benaki Museum Shop*. It sells exceptionally well-made reproductions of antique rings and bracelets in gold, silver, and gold plate—and very reasonably. Christmas cards of ikons and other objects in the collection are good values, too, and are cheaper than comparable ones in U.S. museums. And—but *only* on Sunday—there is the *flea market*, in the Monastiraki quarter, near the Cathedral, whose shops are complemented on Sundays with the diverse wares of countless sidewalk vendors.

## TO NOTE

**Access:** From the United States, there is direct air service, via Paris and/or Rome, by TWA and Olympic, the Onassis-owned Greek national carrier that also operates an extensive domestic service. There is frequent intra-European service connecting Athens and other destinations in Europe, and other continents, as well. Coming from the west, air's best—certainly quickest. Taxi from airport to town; fares are bargains. The *Orient Express* and other trans-Europe trains serve Athens from the west but also connect with Ankara and Istanbul in neighboring Turkey. Good domestic trains are few. There is long-distance bus service, and of course you may drive, given enough time, fortitude, and zest for adventure. Within town, taxis are so cheap (they're metered) that it rarely pays to bother with public transport. There are reasonably priced bus sightseeing tours. **Climate:** The nonsummer seasons are mild. Spring (April and May) averages in the sixties, and is an ideal time to be in Greece. Autumn (late September into early November) is similar. Winter (late November through March) is mostly low-fifties and high-forties weather, although January and February can be in the low forties. Be prepared for the kind of heat prevalent in so many parts of the United States during summer, particularly July and August, when it averages in the eighties, at least during the day. Nights cool off very nicely. Summer is dry, but there can be occasional moisture during the rest of the year. **Clothes:** Especially during the warm-weather months, casual, except after dark in the relatively few dressy places. Most Greeks are not especially fashion-conscious, except insofar as the colonels tell them to be, as, for example, the early junta edict against long male hair (even on the heads of foreign visitors); that was deemed bad for the tourist business and has

long since been rescinded. **Currency:** The drachma. **Tipping:**
Even though a 15% service charge is usually added to restaurant
bills, leave 5–10% extra (on the *plate*) for the waiter, and a small
amount (on the *table*) for the busboy. Tip moderately for hotel—
and other—services. **Language:** Greek—modern Greek, of course.
And that includes the alphabet. If you learned your alpha-beta-
gamma-delta in college, brush up. Knowing even the capital letters
will help you read street and other signs (as for those tricky lower-
case letters, they are there to test us—and most of us fail misera-
bly). Recent years have seen an appreciable increase in the language fluency of Athenians. Many—in hotels, restaurants, cafes,
shops, transport terminals—speak some English. French is a popular foreign language, too; it was the principal foreign language of
educated Greeks before World War II. **Local literature:** Depending upon how they conform to the whims of the colonels—who
shut down papers they don't like—there are several English-language dailies usually available. *This Week in Athens,* given away
in the hotels, is well edited. Picture and local guide books of varying quality and worth are on sale in shops, museums, and at monuments. **Further information:** Greek National Tourist Office, 610
Fifth Avenue, New York; 627 West Sixth Street, Los Angeles;
National Tourist Organization of Greece, 4 Stadiou Street, Athens, Greece.

# Berlin

The capital of Germany between the wars and of Prussia for earlier centuries, Berlin today is half capital of absolutely nothing, the other half of the communist state of which it is a geographical part. It is heady Dietrich-bittersweet, today's Berlin. It is Everyman's Europe. The oldsters who remember-it-when weep when they return. The middlers who grew up with Hitler and goose-stepping Nazis in newsreels—and later in war—pinch themselves, so incredulous does it still seem, the moment their taxi pulls away from Tempelhof Airport. The youngsters, who may or may not have seen Helmut Dantine on "The Late Show" but who have certainly had some academic exposure to the city, find themselves in an Instant History classroom.

And all at once. There it is: the Berlin of the arrogant Prussian kaisers. The Berlin of the Isherwood-Weil Time between the Wars, the preposterous, terrifying Hitlerian Berlin, the ravaged Berlin of the World War II bombers, the contemporary this-very-minute Berlin, an almost diabolical gift of the Cold War, arbitrarily chopped in two, with its grotesque Wall separating capitalist from communist, East from West, Berliner from Berliner.

**Electors to kaisers:** Berlin has had the same name it knows today for eight centuries. One of its most auspicious dates was 1415, when one Frederick of Hohenzollern became the Elector of Brandenburg, the first of a long line of royal rulers for whom Berlin would be home until the First World War—just half a millennium later. The religious-inspired Thirty Years' War, in the mid-seventeenth century, spread from what is now Czechoslovakia, where it began, to a Berlin that it nearly leveled. The war brought remarkable modernity, though, in the reigns that followed. Elector Frederick William introduced the novelty of a civil service. His successor, Elector Frederick II, was no longer content with his title ("electors" were rulers who had the additional privilege of helping select the Holy Roman emperors), styled himself "king," and erected the still-standing Charlottenburg Palace for his queen, Sophie Charlotte. Frederick II, the king we know as Frederick the Great, ascended the throne upon the death of his militaristic and peculiar father, Frederick William I, in 1740. Frederick the Great's title was deserved. Eccentric and homosexual he may have been. But he was, as well, a genius as a militarist (his long-time antagonist was the Hapsburgs' Maria Theresa, in neighboring Vienna), a prolific poet and writer, an intellectual who was a great friend of Voltaire, a man with sophisticated taste in matters of art and architecture (he built the still-visitable Sans Souci and Neues Palais at Potsdam, and also drastically altered, added to, and improved upon, his grandfather's Charlottenburg). The splendid décor style he fostered still bears his name— Frederician Rococo. (It is a pity that his antagonist, Maria Theresa, had not such good taste in palaces. Her Schoenbrunn is no Neues Palais.) Frederick was as well the Prussian king (*Der alte Fritz* —Good old Fred—they called him) who was to be more beloved of his people than any who followed.

William I ascended the throne in 1861, and it was during his reign that all of the German states got together to form modern Germany (this was the era of the strong-willed Bismarck), with a consequent change in kingly title. William became the first *Deutscher kaiser,* or emperor, of the new *reich,* and Germany —indeed, Europe—remained at peace for a record period— until 1914, when it fought the Allied Powers in World War I, suffered devastating defeat, and with its empire disembodied, started life anew as the Weimar Republic.

**The Weimar years—and Hitler:** The Weimar period was Germany's first attempt at democracy. It may not have been the best time in its history to attempt a new form of government, for there was dissatisfaction with the terms of the Versailles Treaty settling the war, there was severe inflation, and heavy unemployment. Oddly, during this period when Berlin was the focal point of an economic and political nadir, it experienced an intellectual renaissance.

These were the years of Max Reinhardt's emergence as a theater great, of Dietrich in classics like *The Blue Angel,* of film directors like Ernst Lubitsch, and of composer-writers like Bertold Brecht, with his *Threepenny Opera.* The poets and writers published. The artists painted. The cafe life was the talk of Europe. But it all came to naught. Or almost.

Austrian-born Adolf Hitler became chancellor of the republic in 1933 and before long assumed dictatorial powers. The Germany he had envisioned in his book, *Mein Kampf,* came to be. Every facet of German life had to conform with the oppressive, repressive Nazi tenets. The weak, ineffectual Weimar Republic had been transformed into one of the most horrendous police states the world has ever known, with anti-Semitism and an expansionist, militarist foreign policy its major credos. By the end of the Hitler-triggered World War II in 1945, six million Jews had died in Nazi concentration camps, much of Europe—including much of Germany and of its capital—was destroyed, Hitler and his mistress, Eva Braun, had committed suicide in Berlin, and Germany had surrendered. The Allied Powers divided Germany into eastern and western sectors—and did likewise with its capital.

In 1948 and 1949, the Allies kept West Berlin alive with a remarkable airlift, their answer to Soviet efforts to isolate the city from the West. In the following decade, so many residents of East Berlin had escaped into West Berlin that the government of East German President Walter Ulbricht (who retired in 1971) erected a heavily guarded wall to keep his people in their own part of the city.

**Occupied Berlin:** In late 1971 the four occupying powers—the Soviet Union, Britain, France, and the United States—got together to work out a new quadripartite agreement on Berlin's *modus vivendi.* The Soviets agreed in writing to allow West Berlin to continue to exist as a Western outpost 110 miles within East Germany's borders, and agreed also to cease harassment so long as the Westerners agreed to cut down excessive political demonstrations. The agreement put it this way: "There shall be no use or threat of force in the area. . . . Disputes shall be settled solely by peaceful means. . . . The Four Governments agree that, irrespective of the differences in legal views the situation which has developed in the area . . . shall not be changed unilaterally."

And so the two Berlins continue to coexist. While East Berlin has had the help of its Soviet mentors in rebuilding over the years, West Berlin has had heavy injections of capital from West Germany and the West generally, to keep it solvent as a showplace of democracy within the geographical confines of a communist state. Most West Germans continue to hope (theoretically, if not practically) for the day when Berlin will again be their capital (the President of West Germany has an official residence in Berlin, and that country's currency is legal tender in West Berlin), and many of them are lured to its good universities and the job opportunities presented in its heavily subsidized economy. Not all stay, though. West Berlin, with all its advantages and amenities, remains an island in not particularly calm waters. The Wall and what it represents can at times be more formidable than even those on the free side would like.

TO SEE

**Lay of the land:** Berlin is not a beautiful city. It may be said that a city heavily damaged in World War II could not possibly be beautiful today. But that is presupposing that contemporary architects are unable to create beauty. I won't buy that. Berlin might have been handsome with other planners and architects in charge of rebuilding it. But it isn't. One takes it as it is: an unlovely city that is not without pockets of interest.

The principal thoroughfare—a street of small shops and large stores, cafes and restaurants, hotels and *boîtes*—is the Kurfurstendamm—long, wide, and with its landmark the ruined tower of the turn-of-century *Kaiser Wilhelm Memorial Church*. The church has wisely been left in ruins intentionally—as a reminder of the tragedy of World War II; adjoining it is a contrastingly modern church, the most interesting aspect of which is a series of striking stained-glass windows.

There are a number of requisite destinations. *The Wall* is best taken in from Potsdamer Platz, which was, in pre-World War II days, what Times Square is to New York and Piccadilly Circus to London. The massive ruined oblong hulk you'll see is all that's left of the old Kempinsky which, during its prime, housed ten restaurants and cabarets, each with a theme and décor of its own —a Vienna coffee house, for example, a Chinese tea garden, a "Wild West USA" saloon, and of course a dance hall with an all-girl band. The *Reichstag,* a massive, graceless, late-nineteenth-century pile that could not have been beautiful even in its youth, and was horrendous during the long years it lay in ruins, has now been restored; you may have a look inside if you like. The *Congress Hall* is nineteen-fifties-modern, daring when it went up —and a gift of the United States. The far more interesting *Hansa Quarter* is an apartment house complex whose various buildings were designed by the architectural greats of a number of European countries; there are specimens of the work of France's Le Corbusier and Finland's Alvar Aalto, among others. The *Schoneberg Town Hall* is on a *platz* named for John F. Kennedy, for it was on the steps of that hall that the late President gave his widely remembered *"Ich bin ein Berliner"* speech. The *Brandenburg Gate* is a long-familiar Berlin landmark—an eighteenth-century neoclassic archway that is somehow still standing, and on the border between East and West Berlin (it is just over the line in the eastern sector) at that.

**Choice destinations:** *Philharmonie,* the home of the Berlin Philharmonic, whose principal conductor is Herbert von Karajan, is not only the finest work of contemporary architecture in Berlin, it is as well one of the few truly superior modern-design concert halls in the world. You must not let its unconventional exterior throw you. It is the interior you want to see, and if there are no Philharmonic concerts scheduled during your visit, get inside by means of the regularly conducted tours. The interior arrangement is completely unsymmetrical. The designer began with a hall of tremendous height and grouped his twenty-two hundred seats in blocks, both above and below the platform on which the orchestra performs, which gives the effect of being tucked in between the maze of seating areas. The foyer areas—promenade section and cafe—is equally as understated, inspired, and striking. *Charlottenburg Palace* had its beginnings with Elector Frederick II in 1701, but Frederick the Great made additions in the elegant, silver-rococo style he so liked, later in the century. The palace was badly damaged in World War II, and it has taken a couple of decades to effect even a partial restoration. The *Royal Apartments* are not completely restored, but a number of important rooms are again as they once were; these include some of the quarters of Frederick the Great, in a wing he added to the place—his study, library, and a waiting room. (The so-called Great Gallery, which was the masterwork of Frederick's designer, Knobelsdorff, was the finest room of the palace, but has not yet been restored.) There are a number of earlier rooms of Frederick I, as well, in the main palace building. *Bellevue Palace,* more modest than Charlottenburg, but nonetheless an eye-filling late-eighteenth-century structure, now serves as the Berlin home of the President of West Germany, whenever he happens to wing into town. The rest of the time—which is most of the time—it is happily open to visitors. The interiors are period style and attractive. *Pfaaueninsel Castle* is an oddball on an island in the Havel River; it, too, is eighteenth-century, and you must not let the exterior put you off; it is *supposed* to look like a ruin. That's the way Frederick William II wanted it, when he built it for his mistress. The interior is something else again, and there are peacocks in the garden. *Tegel Palace* is a onetime royal hunting lodge later occupied by the family that included the same Alexander von Humboldt, for whom the Humboldt Current is named; it's elaborately decorated.

*Museums* are mostly excellent. Let's start with the most disappointing and go upward, as regards quality. The *National Gallery* is a pedestrian oblong of a late-sixties building designed by Ludwig Mies van der Rohe, which might charitably be described as a minor work of that gifted architect. The contents, taken from the museum's former home in the Orangerie of Charlottenburg, include far too many middling nineteenth-century works and far too few Impressionists. Even newer, but far more worth one's time, is the *Ethnological Museum.* This is a handsome 1971 building that is a part of the Dahlem museum complex, and houses a collection embracing ancient America, the South Pacific, and Asia. *Dahlem* is especially strong on paintings—medieval through the eighteenth century. There is an entire gallery of Durer, and other Germans—like Cranach and Holbein—are well represented, too. So are Dutch, Flemish, and Italian schools. Till Riemenschneider, the greatest of the German sculptors in wood, is well represented in the medieval sculpture section. The extraordinarily rich *Egyptian Museum* is housed in a fine old house opposite the main entrance to Charlottenburg Palace. Its admittedly magnificent head of Queen Nefertiti is so touted by the Berliners in their tourist promotion that you would think there wasn't another piece of good art to be seen in the city. Across the street, in the palace proper, is the *Museum of Decorative Art* (*Kunstgewarbemuseum*)—nothing like that of Copenhagen or Paris, to be sure, but with many fine things, including the treasure of the long-important noble house of Guelph, consisting of religious objects of gold and silver. *Grunewald Castle* is Berlin's oldest—a 1542 hunting lodge in what used to be the sticks. It is now beautifully furnished with Renaissance pieces, but doubles as a museum—and a very good one—of paintings by such masters as the Cranachs, younger and elder, Rubens, and Bol. If you go in the winter, as I did, wear your snuggies; there's no heat.

*East Berlin's* long-famous avenue, *Unter den Linden,* will have been noted by you, if you had a look at the Brandenburg Gate from the West Berlin side; it is Unter den Linden's terminus, with the Spree River at its other end. *Friedrichstrasse,* another main East Berlin street, runs perpendicular with it. Both of these thoroughfares—along with Karl-Marx Allee—are good walking territory in this part of town, parts of which were rebuilt during the Stalin era, and therefore are lined with the ugly Stalin ginger-bread skyscrapers of the kind one sees in Moscow. Still other areas are post-Stalin and more aesthetically pleasing, with build-ings of the inoffensive if rarely exciting International Modern school. There are still some lovely old pre-Berlin monuments, like the *Deutsche Staatsoper* (almost completely rebuilt as Fred-erick the Great's architect, Knobelsdorff, designed it in 1743); the early-nineteenth-century *Humboldt University;* and the Renais-sance-era *St. Mary's Church* (still used as a place of worship). Some of Berlin's best art remained in East Berlin after the war. The *museums,* therefore, have a lot to show. The *Pergamon Museum* is the most spectacular, for it houses the block-long ancient Greek altar that gave the museum its name. There are other exhibits of the classic era, and from Asia. The *Bode Mu-seum* contains one of the great world collections of medieval German wood sculpture. There are, as well, exceptional Egyptian and Byzantine departments. The *Altes* (*Old*) *Museum* is in a charmer of an early-nineteenth-century building recently restored, and with contemporary art as its subject matter. The *Zeughaus* is a one-time arsenal of baroque vintage that now houses the East German *Historical Museum,* with its social-uplift exhibits.

TO WATCH

Both Germanies believe in culture, quite literally with a capital
"K," and both have generously subsidized the performing arts.
There are plentiful diversions in this area in both sectors of town.
Take West Berlin, to start. The earlier-described *Philharmonie* is
the home of the high-caliber Berlin Philharmonic, whose principal
conductor is Herbert von Karajan. The Berlin Radio Symphony,
another excellent orchestra, is conducted by Lorin Maazel and
plays at the *Haus des Rundfunks*. The Berlin State Opera is one of
the best in Germany—a country of excellent opera companies,
and performs in the handsome post-World War II *Deutsche Oper*
—far more conventional in design than the Philharmonic, but still
a looker. *Theatre des Westens* specializes in musicals and operettas. The *Schiller Theater* is West Berlin's No. 1 legit theater; plays
are, of course, acted in German, but you may want to go—if you
are a theater buff—even if you don't understand German, because
productions, including sets and costumes, are of high standard.
Only because West Berliners consider their *night life* the greatest
thing since Kleenex do I go into that subject at this point. The
town is full of cabarets, bars, dancings, and what all. I took some
in on recent visits—on your behalf—and found the *New Eden* dull
but fancy; the *Eden Playboy* distinguished by a floor show
utilizing a pool of water; the *Big Eden* mobbed with teens; the
*Daily Girl Club* (sic) with a prosaic show that included a stripper
with a whip, but no particular preponderance of "daily girls";
the *Red Rose,* with a show similar to that of the Daily Girl, minus
the whip; and an establishment known as the *Cir-Bar-Club Nau-
tique,* which is a disco, and then some. There are lots more, and
there are also lots better ways to spend your deutschmarks. *East
Berlin's Deutsche Staatsoper* should be a requisite; see any performance you can of opera and/or ballet. The rebuilt house,
originally dating to Frederick the Great, is a beauty, and so is the

company. Consider also the modern *Komische Oper,* for operettas, certain operas, and some ballet. The *Friedrichstadt* is for vaudeville, or variety, as it is called in Europe. You may buy East Berlin tickets in advance of performances without going through East German customs to get them, by taking the subway from West Berlin (S-Bahn) to Friedrichstrasse Station, where there is a theater ticket office on Platform B; in East Berlin proper, tickets are sold at the Tourist Office on Alexanderplatz.

### TO STAY

The Germans are among Europe's best hoteliers, and there are good examples of their style of innkeeping in Berlin. The town's top two are both operated by American chains, Inter•-Continental and Hilton. The *Kempinski*—Inter•Continental operated—though housed in a modern post-World War II plant, is a spiritual descendant of the earlier-described pre-World War II Kempinski wine-dine enterprises on the now-grim Potsdamer Platz. It has a perfect Kurfurstendamm location. There's a big, traditional-style lobby, off which lead lounges for tea, coffee, or drinks (and later, dancing), and there are a variety of restaurants. The bedrooms are good-looking; singles have shower (cheaper) or bath; doubles all have bath. And the management is Inter•-Continental A-1. The *Berlin Hilton,* a couple of blocks off the Kurfurstendamm, just beyond the zoo, on Budapesterstrasse, is a striking skyscraper with a landmark of a checkerboard-pattern façade, high-ceilinged lobby, zippy Hilton service-with-a-smile, and locales to eat and drink all over the place. Guest rooms have either bath or shower, with the latter cheaper; they're all air-conditioned. The *Palace,* in the Europa Center complex on Kurfurstendamm, is a modern beauty, decorated in traditional style, with the emphasis on style—and very high style at that. All bedrooms have baths, and the singles are particularly spacious. There are a pair of restaurants and a bar. To go from luxe to first-class:

The *Schweitzerhof*—not surprisingly, with that name—is Swiss-operated, and spiffy—with a Budapesterstrasse location almost opposite the Hilton and the zoo, attractive rooms, all with shower or bath, two restaurants, bar, and spacious public areas. The *President* has a no-nonsense, Scandinavian Modern look to it, good-size rooms (particularly the singles) all with shower or bath; cafe and bar; and sauna and sun terrace on the roof. The location, An der Urania 16, is not as central as the earlier-mentioned hotels. The *Berliner,* Kurfurstenstrasse 62, is also a bit away from the Kurfurstendamm, but it's well run and sets one of the best tables in town. Rooms have either shower or bath.

## TO EAT (AND DRINK)

German food is the Continent's most maligned—at least in the United States, thanks to the prevalence of Bavarian-type restaurants in our cities that are often little more than beer halls serving sauerkraut and sausage. I am not about to write an essay on German food. Suffice it to say that at its best—particularly in the north—it is sophisticated and tremendously varied. The Germans prepare their favorite meats—veal, pork, and beef—in a multitude of ways, *schnitzels* being but a single category in the veal department. Fish, both fresh and salt water, are often cooked with finesse. Poultry—chicken, of course, but especially goose and duck—are dealt with masterfully. Vegetables are rarely overcooked. (Salads are far too much of a composite for my taste, but no matter.) No people anywhere, in any country, surpass the Germans as bakers, and by that I mean of bread and rolls, of cakes and tortes, and of delicate pastries. Nor does any other country produce better beer. It was, after all, German brewmasters who came to the United States to get us started with our brewing industry, and the same happened in the case of Japan— now another producer of fine brews. The white wines of Germany —Rhines and Reislings and Moselles—are among the finest to be obtained. Coffee in Germany is excellent; the Germans drink quantities of it and are just as fussy about it as are Americans.

All that said, let me now admit that it is very easy to get a bad meal in Berlin. The town abounds in mediocre-to-poor restaurants and tourist traps, many of them chintzily run by get-rich-quick operators out to make a fast mark. Quite possibly the very best restaurant in Berlin is the *Grill* of the *Hotel Berlin*. The menu is classic German all the way—appetizers, soups, fish and seafood, grills, and game and specialties including Kalbsmedaillon Hotel Berlin—escallop of veal prepared with veal swetbread, diced bacon, onion, mushrooms, artichoke bottoms and olives. *Conti Stuben* is a seafood house in an especially imaginative nautical setting. A specialty is pike soup—a traditional Berlin dish. Entrées range from lobster to sole, and service is professional. The *Grill* of the *Kempinsky Hotel* is a major Berlin gathering place; excellent German dishes and broiled entrées from the big copper-hooded grill; smooth service. The *Golden West* is the Berlin Hilton's newest restaurant; steaks flown in from the United States are among the lures. *Tessiner Stuben,* Bleibtreustrasse 33, is a congenial, good-looker of a place, with a German-Swiss menu; moderate. The *Seehof Hotel Restaurant* is an atmospheric room in an interesting hostelry that overlooks Lake Lietzen, away from the city center. The bar is equally attractive, and in summer, dinner is served at the pool-terrace, overlooking the lake. *Hardy en der Oper* is understandably popular for postopera nourishment. The *Bou Bou* is another late-hours place worth knowing about; good soups and snacks. The Kurfurstendamm is lined with cafes for pastry, snacks, coffee, and drinks. They are all similar, and rarely is the service other than indifferent. Best bets are *Kranzler,* part of a quality German chain, and that of the *Kempinsky Hotel.*

TO BUY

The most distinctive Berlin purchase would be a china service
or a portion of same, from *Stattliche Porzellan-Manufaktur,* the
venerable State Porcelain Factory that has been around for a
couple of centuries, and still turns out lovely traditional-design
china. The address is Wegelystrasse 1; check the seconds, and
sometimes even the third-quality pieces; they are much cheaper
and often perfectly serviceable. Packing, shipping. *KaDeWe,* Tauentzienstrasse 21, is Berlin's major department store. It is without
the style and polish of department stores in other major cities, but
browse around to get an over-all idea of what is available in this
city. German leather goods are of good quality—handbags, men's
and women's wallets, passport cases, even luggage. *Gold-Pfeil,*
Tauentzienstrasse 16 and in the *Europa Center,* has a good
selection. I don't have any other specific suggestions, other than
that you wander the Kurfurstendamm and streets leading from
it; the shops are well stocked, but the merchandise is so similar to
what we have at home that there's little point in buying it. Still,
you may find a bibelot here, or a trinket there, that will appeal.

TO NOTE

**Access:** Air is the quickest and easiest. By terms of the Allied-
Soviet agreements on Berlin, Lufthansa, the crack West German
carrier, is not permitted to fly into West Berlin; only airlines of
the Allied Powers may serve its right-in-town Tempelhof Airport:
namely Air France, British European Airways, and our own Pan
Am. I have flown all three of them in and out of Berlin; all do a
good job. Coming from the United States, you may fly Lufthansa
direct to West Germany and make immediate connections for a
flight to Berlin. There is particularly frequent service from Ham-

burg, but bear in mind that Pan Am runs what amounts to a separate domestic German airline with flights connecting Berlin with a number of West German cities, and that BEA and Air France have additional services, including flights from London and Paris, respectively. Once arrived at Tempelhof you are a cheap ten-minute taxi ride from your hotel. Flying is not the only means of access. There is modern bus service from major West German cities, and good roads from West Germany through East Germany into Berlin; comfortable trains, too. All you need for any of these surface means of transport, in addition to your passport, is an East German transit visa, which East German authorities issue without difficulty at frontier crossing stations. All of the foregoing is for West Berlin, although what I have said about surface transport applies to East Berlin as well. Let me add, though, that East Berlin has its own airport—Schoenfeld, by name. It is served by the East German international airline, Interflug, which flies its Soviet-made aircraft to points throughout Western as well as Eastern Europe, and also by the carriers of other communist countries. If you are coming to Berlin from the east, Schoenfeld is a convenient means of entry; there is airport-arranged transportation into West Berlin, and there are taxis. Within West Berlin there is a modern public transport system, including a subway that also serves East Berlin, and metered taxis. There are varied bus tours of West Berlin, as well as tours of East Berlin, emanating from West Berlin, on which the West Berlin bus drivers—by special arrangement—are allowed to drive into East Berlin but not, heaven forbid, the guides, who change at Checkpoint Charlie. A bus tour of East Berlin—they are of half-day duration—is at best an abbreviated introduction; it should be followed up with individual inspection; hotel concierges can explain the ways and means of the moment for individual travel into East Berlin. There are also one-day bus tours out of West Berlin to Potsdam and Sans Souci in East Germany; these are recommended. There are, in addition, East German tours of all of East Germany, which is not the subject of this book. (See

*Eastern Europe A to Z.*) **Climate:** There are rarely extremes. Winters (November through March) average in the thirties, but can dip to the twenties and be very raw indeed. Spring (mid-forties through mid-fifties) can be pleasant. Summer (June, July, and August) is mid-sixties and low seventies, with the occasional sizzler. And autumn is much like spring. **Clothes:** Berlin has not the clothes sense of more stylish cities like Munich or Hamburg. The young people wear what they like; otherwise, dress is relatively conservative, with jacket and tie for the Opera, the relatively few good restaurants, and the jumble of night clubs, if, indeed, they are your bag. **Currency:** The very same Deutsche mark (DM) that is the legal tender of West Germany is likewise for West Berlin. The mark is divided into one hundred pfennigs. East Berlin uses the mark of the German Democratic Republic; it is at par with its West German counterpart. Excursionists from West to East Berlin must declare the currency on their person at Checkpoint Charlie, and exchange a minimum of five West marks for five East marks, all of which must be spent in the eastern sector of town (unless on a bus tour). The simplest way to handle this is to leave most of your West German (and other) money at your hotel; it's easy enough to spend five marks in the course of an excursion. **Tipping:** Hotels, restaurants, and cafes usually add a service charge of 10 to 15 percent to bills. There is no need to tip additionally, except in the case of bellhops, who average half a mark a bag (as do airport baggage porters), and concierges who have extended themselves to help you especially. You will meet the same impossible, leechlike lady washroom attendants in Berlin that are a part of the landscape of all West Germany. It is impossible to escape without giving them their ransom—20 pfennigs is the minimum or they'll chase you down the corridor. Tip taxi drivers 10 percent. Hat-check girls in restaurants and night spots are tipped as elsewhere, but at the opera and in theaters, coat-checking is obligatory for both sexes, and the fees are set. **Language:** Berliners have their own German dialect, but of course speak proper German with German-speaking visitors; they also speak a lot of English and French. **Further information:** Verkehrsamt Berlin (Official West Berlin Tourist Office), Fasanenstrasse 7–8, West Berlin, Germany; German National Tourist Office, 500 Fifth Avenue, New York; 11 South LaSalle Street, Chicago; 323 Geary Street, San Francisco; Place Bonaventure, Montreal. Reiseburo der Deutschen Demokratischen Republic (Travel Bureau of the German Democratic Republic), Friderichstrasse 110/112, East Berlin, Germany.

# Berne

There are bigger and grander capitals than Berne; none that I
know of, though, is more immediately likable. The Bernese have
kept pace with the times, expanding their millennium-old city beyond its medieval confines. But they have never attempted the
pretentious.

What you realize when you consider Berne is the almost fierce
pride that the various towns and cantons of Switzerland maintain. Capital though Berne may be, it is nowhere in Switzerland
more apparent that this country is a *con*federation; nothing more
centrist would ever do, and Berne is a good example of why that
is so. Berne was for long a powerful city-state, with considerable
territory and influence beyond its borders. It had its start, though,
as little more than a barracks put up by a memorably named
noble of German origin—Berchtold V of Zahringen—who was
ruling the area on behalf of the Burgundians, themselves clients
of the Holy Roman Emperor. The year was 1191, and the Bernese
have researched matters so thoroughly that they know the name
of Berchtold's builder (it was Cuno of Bubenberg), that he
built at first in wood, using the oak trees in the region, later adding a city wall and the still-standing clock tower, which formed
the town's main gate. Within decades—by which time the town
had been accorded the honor of becoming a Free Imperial City
of the Holy Roman Empire—the first coat of arms made its ap-

pearance with—you guessed it—a bear as the focal point, and the name Berne written out. Bernese legend decrees that the name Berne (in local dialect pronounced "Barn") was given the city by Berchtold himself after a hunt in a nearby forest where his first trophy was a bear.

**Medieval greatness:** The succeeding medieval centuries saw Berne expand, with new walls, new quarters, and new towers. Much of the city, though, was built of wood, and a 1405 fire razed virtually everything except the old foundations, on which rebuilding took place, this time with sandstone. The sixteenth and seventeenth centuries saw another major renewal; indeed, many of the still-used structures in the core of the town (on the peninsula formed by the Aare River) date from that time.

But the city grew in power as it did in size, all the while fighting whenever necessary to preserve its sovereignty. In 1339 it was victor in a decisive battle against the Burgundian nobles, remaining free so that soon after, in 1353, it was able to join the Swiss Confederation. Berne's Golden Age extended from the early sixteenth century until the end of the eighteenth, during which time it amassed considerable territory along Lake Geneva. Indeed, historic credit for the inclusion of these French-speaking cantons in the Swiss Confederation is given to Berne.

The French invasion of 1798 was disastrous for Berne; it lost much of its prestige and territory. In the post-Napoleonic Switzerland that emerged in 1815, a chastened Berne found itself with almost all of its territory ceded to two newly formed cantons. In 1848, though, with the creation of the modern Swiss Confederation, Berne was selected as the site of the first federal Parliament and, as such, the capital. Switzerland's traditional neutrality—guaranteed by the Congress of Vienna in 1815 and never violated since then—has made it possible for Berne, like its sister Swiss cities, to develop and expand. Still, Old Berne, despite the development of modern business and commerce, has remained Old Berne. Its streets, bordered by what the Bernese call *lauben* (arcades built into the façades of the houses on either side) remain as they have been for centuries. No house may be built or renovated without the arcade being built into the ground floor, and no façade is okayed that does not conform to the style of the adjacent buildings. There are today some seventy embassies and legations in this city, which has a population of but about two hundred thousand, not to mention the international headquarters of organizations like the Universal Postal Union, the International Telecommunication Union, and the International Copyright Union.

**Chocolate and government:** There are factories and industries (Berne is a big chocolate town). But the major business of the city is government, which, like so much in this country, is uniquely Swiss. Instead of a strong single executive, the executive authority is vested in the Federal Council, composed of seven councilors. They are elected to four-year terms by the members of the Parliament, or Federal Assembly. The Assembly not only selects the council; from among the seven serving on it, it elects a president —which is the closest Switzerland comes to having a chief of state.

The Assembly is bicameral. The bigger of the two houses is the National Council, which approximates the U. S. House of Representatives, with two hundred members elected for four-year terms. The smaller, upper house (the Council of States) is similar to the United States Senate; it has forty-four members, two from each of the cantons. Politically, the government has been a coalition of major parties for many years. Another Swiss twist is the unusual powers reserved for the cantons; they have considerably more leeway than American states, at least as much as the Canadian provinces. The newest twist, though, is feminine voices in the halls of government. It was, to be sure, a long time coming. In 1959, despite urging by the Federal Council and Assembly in Berne, a national referendum giving women the vote in federal elections was defeated. But in 1970 the suffragettes were victorious; the male monopoly that had been in effect since the year 1291 was broken. In the 1971 elections, not only did women vote, but eleven of them won seats in Parliament—ten in the lower house and one in the upper Council of States. The first day of the Parliamentary session in 1971 in Berne's heavy-domed Bundesrat saw bouquets of white and red carnations—the Swiss national colors—on the desks of each distaff member. Women's Lib or no, the ladies loved 'em.

TO SEE

**Lay of the land:** The first thing to do in Berne is to head for the city's Official Tourist Office at Bundesgasse 20 and pick up their town map; it's one of the best such, of any European capital. (And the tourist office is one of the best such of any European capital, as well.) Bundesgasse 20, the site of the tourist office, is just a few blocks from the Central Railway Station (Hauptbahnhof), which is as good a place as any to orient oneself from. The station faces Bahnhofplatz, and diagonally across from it is the tall-spired baroque *Holy Ghost Church* (*Heiliggeist Kirch*). The front of this church faces on the city's *main street,* which goes by a series of names. At this point it is the *Spitalgasse;* going toward the interior of the fingerlike area delineated by the waters of the Aare River, it runs first into *Barenplatz* (which converges into *Bundesplatz,* named for the domed Federal Parliament you can see if you look to the right). Continuing, it becomes *Marktgasse,* until it reaches *Theaterplatz* and the Bernese landmark that is the Clock Tower. The name then changes to *Kramgasse,* for another long block, at the end of which you look left to see the almost Venetian Gothic Town Hall, and you look right to see the high spire of the Cathedral, or *Munster.* Continue down the main street (it is now called *Gerechtigkeitsgasse* for another long block, at the end of which you see a pair of bridges crossing the river. You want the bridge to your right; at its terminus you'll find yourself above the municipal *bear pits.* You may return to the center of town as you came or, for variety, along one of the streets that parallel the main street, or along either riverbank. But the main street is worth a return journey if only for a more careful look at the *medieval fountains* that grace the center of the thoroughfare. They were all erected about 1550 not only to beautify the town but to serve as memorials to its heroes and to commemorate its most noted historic events. As you amble along, you'll pass fountains honoring the guild of runners, who were the bearers of official messages to foreign parts; the founding duke, Berchtold, the guild of musicians; the Bible's Moses, with the Ten Commandments; the revered marksmen of ancient Berne. There is even a fountain whose subject is a rather ferocious child-eater; its function was to frighten rash little boys who had fallen into the city moat (which had been at the point where the statue still stands) and warn them to be careful.

And there are the *historic towers,* as well. The Kafigturm, or Prison Tower, is some seven hundred years old, but the Clock Tower, or Zeitglocken, is the very same mentioned earlier in this chapter: the one, only, and original. Although it has some sixteenth-century embellishment, it dates all the way back to the twelfth century. There remain the houses lining the streets of the old town; they are mostly the very same seventeenth-century ones mentioned in the introduction to this chapter.

By making use of their also-venerable arcades, one can go from one part of town to the other—I have done so—and remain dry as toast.

**Choice destinations:** The fountains, towers, arcades, and bear pit aside, there is a good deal else awaiting the visitor to Berne. The *Cathedral* is a superb Late Gothic structure (only the three-hundred-foot spire—finished in 1893—is modern). Its interior is reward in itself architecturally, but the stained-glass windows are also noteworthy, and there is a fine view of town and river valley from the terrace outside. The *Town Hall,* or Rathaus, looks like it might have been transported from Venice. It is a small but handsome Gothic building—originally fifteenth-century—and I urge you to try to have a look at the Council Chamber within, even though there are no regular open hours. The *Parliament,* whose squarish, high, and not particularly graceful dome serves as a landmark in one's walks, is a modern building with vaguely Renaissance lines. The public is welcome, but only on guided tours, which are given on a fairly rigid schedule. A highlight is the great mural in the lower chamber. It is no lovelier, though, than the view of the river valley and the Alps beyond, which one gains from the Parliament Building terrace around the back.

There are a number of good *museums.* They are all relatively central and can be reached on foot. Divide them into two groups. The first—and most important—is in a class by itself, not only because of its location, but because of its contents. It is the *Kunst,* or *Art, Museum.* The collection is choice, with the big treat a group of two-score Paul Klee oils, and considerably more of the prolific Berne-born modernist who, though he did most of his work in the Germany of the twenties, returned to Berne for his last years; he died in 1940. There is a whole gallery of another Swiss painter of note, the somewhat earlier Fernand Hodler. Swiss work of the medieval and Renaissance periods is well represented, too. There are some great old masters. Fra Angelico's luminescent *Virgin and Child* is in itself worthy of a journey to Berne, but there are even more modern French works—Picasso, Braque, Dérain, and Léger, to name but a few. Then cross over to the other side of town and take in the other museums. The *Bernese Historical Museum* is housed in a late-nineteenth-century version of a Renaissance palace, with what must surely be the steepest and longest stairway in continental Europe—and no elevators. But Swiss food is so good that you find yourself glad to have the exercise, and the exhibits are displayed from the basement all the way to what is not *quite* but *seems* like an attic, so Alpine is the ascent. I enjoy the period rooms—from peasant to palace in theme—but there are tapestries and goldwork and jewelry and paintings and heaven knows what all—caches of treasures from the city's many centuries. Dioramas indeed, you say. But the Bernese *Natural History Museum* is going to make you into a diorama buff even if no other similar in-

stitution has ever succeeded in so doing. Nowhere else have I seen
such displays of animals. I came out a convert, so enthused that
I went up the street to still another museum—a building housing
two small museums. The *Swiss Postal Museum*—the biggest in
the world, I am told, and I believe the Swiss if they say so—is
one of these. There are stamps and stamps and stamps, and if you
don't get dizzy looking at too many, you appreciate the beauty
of their design. The outer museum on the same premises is devoted to *Swiss Alpinism*—all you ever want to know (unless you're
a climber) about the development of Alpinism, its lore, par-
aphernalia, and the like, with climbers' impedimenta ranging from
snowshoes to ski poles, and all manner of maps and scale models.

## TO WATCH

Evenings offer agreeable diversion. An impressive hall known
as the *Casino,* is, in real life, a concert house. The Berne
Symphony and other groups play there. The handsome *Municipal Theater* (*Stadttheater*) on the Kornhausplatz is home to
opera, operetta, and plays—usually, of course, in German. There
are a number of other legitimate theaters, as well. An establishment known as the *Kursaal* offers entertainment, dancing, and
even has a gambling room. Another local institution is a mon-
strous and rather depressing cellar establishment that is at once a
restaurant-dance hall-cabaret. It is called the *Kornhauskeller.*

## TO STAY

The reputation of the Swiss as the world's greatest hoteliers
appears to be taking so many of them to so many distant parts
that there are not always enough to mind the store at home.
When I checked in at a Berne hotel not long ago the reception
clerk proved to be a displaced Dane, and from the lack of

warmth in his welcome, a dispirited one. Employment is so full in Switzerland that there are something like half a million foreigners at work in the country, many of them, of course, in hotels and restaurants, so that traditional Swiss service is no longer as traditional or as Swiss as the Swiss—let alone their guests—would like it. Still, standards remain high; Swiss know-how in the hotel field remains unsurpassed.

Bernese bliss, for me at least, is a valley-view room in the *Bellevue Palace Hotel.* Next door to Parliament, and with the same magnificent situation, the Bellevue Palace is the epitome of the de luxe Swiss hotel. The lobby is enormous and high-ceilinged. So is the dining room, with its view of town and Aare Valley and Alps. So are the outdoor dining terrace and the intimate bar (a sort of second home to MPs). Even the more moderate-priced downstairs restaurants are capacious. The bedrooms, mostly in Louis XV style, are impeccably maintained. You push the button for room service or the maid and poof! at your service! Trailing behind—mainly because service tends not to be as smiling—is the *Schweitzerhof Hotel,* just opposite the Central Station. Its lures—and they are considerable—are priceless collections of antiques, paintings, sculpture, and other objects. They line the corridors of each of the hotel's several floors (somehow or other, they are not stolen), and more of them are used to decorate what are some of the most beautiful hotel bedrooms and suites (no two alike, of course) extant. There is an ever-busy bar, and there are a couple of restaurants, one of them exceptional. And the *Guten Morgen* breakfast trays—white linen and china with red-rooster décor—just have to be the perkiest you'll ever be served. In no other country does one find better moderate-category hotels than Switzerland; Berne offers excellent examples. The *Savoy* on Neuengasse, near the Central Station, has been handsomely refurbished—zingy lobby, bright-as-a-button bedrooms, appetite-producing restaurant. The *Bristol,* though without a proper restaurant (it serves a brunch-type breakfast included in the room rate, until 11:00 A.M. daily) is one of the best-looking

hotels in town; the Globus Department Store people, its owners
have decorated it in a variety of bold plaids against dramatic white
backgrounds. The *Baren,* next door to the Bristol, is smaller, and
without its high-style décor. But the rooms are inviting, and so
is the restaurant. The *Stadthof* is a gem: immaculate, smallish,
charming, and with a cozy bar and good restaurant.

### TO EAT

The cuisine of Switzerland represents an infusion of cultures,
with dishes derivative of French, German, and Italian cooking,
to which is added the so-called International cuisine of the hotel
dining rooms, brought to a peak unsurpassed elsewhere. Fondue is
probably as typically Swiss a dish as there is, and certainly
the most celebrated abroad. It is melted cheese laced with white
wine and kirsch, and a bit of garlic and spices. Half the fun is in
the eating. The dish is contained in a boiling pot placed in the
center of the table. Each diner takes a special long-handled
fondue fork, affixes a cube of white bread to its tines, and then
dips the bread into the hot cheese sauce. But mind: If you
should be so unlucky as to allow the chunk of bread to fall off
the fork, tradition decrees that you must stand your party to the
next round of good, dry Swiss white wine. Fondue Bourguignonne
is a variation; in it cubes of steak replace the cubes of bread; they
are quick-fried on a fork immersed in a pot of boiling oil and
then dipped into a variety of savory sauces. Raclette, another
national dish, also has a cheese base. A wheel of raclette cheese
or a portion thereof is toasted on one side and then, while hot
and melting, scraped onto a plate, combined with a boiled potato
left in its jacket, along with tangy pickles, and eaten at once,
while still hot, and before the melted cheese hardens. The favorite
Swiss meat is veal—*geschnitzeltes* is a good way to ask for it;
it is cubed and then prepared in a typical mushroom-cream sauce.
The sausages are good, too. So is beef, conveniently served or as

*bundnerfleisch*—paper-thin beef slices that have been air-dried and that are served either as snacks or, often, as an hors d'oeuvre course before lunch or dinner in restaurants. *Berne Platte,* named for the capital city, is a Swiss variation of France's *choucroute garni* (sauerkraut topped with pork chops, ham, bacon, sausages, and sometimes—if you're not careful—pigs' feet). Surely the most irresistible Swiss dish is *rösti.* To call this masterwork a variation of fried potatoes is simply not to do it justice. The potatoes for *rösti* are first boiled, then cut into dice, next fried, and finally baked, with the result an almost pancakelike mound, with a crisp brown crust, served piping hot. Swiss chocolate is unsurpassed. One of the first factories to make it was set up by Philippe Suchard in Berne in 1815. Rudolphe Lindt, another famous chocolate name, opened his first factory just below the cathedral in Berne. Tobler chocolate is another famous Berne manufacture. Swiss cheeses are worth knowing, too. The kind we call "Swiss" in the United States, and which virtually every country has copied from the Swiss, is Emmenthaler on home ground. Gruyere, though similar, comes in smaller wheels and has fewer holes. Others you might want to try are Appenzeller, Glarus, and Sap Sago, not to mention Raclette, which you'll have if you order the cheese dish by that name.

The Swiss do not, with their limited vineyard land, produce a great deal of wine. Their reds are not distinguished, but the whites—of which they export a fair amount—can be very pleasant indeed. Johannisberg is the most globally noted, of course, but there are others very worth knowing, L'Ovaille in particular. The Swiss drink a great deal of beer, too—their own (not always as good as the German, Dutch, and Danish brews) and imported, as well.

I mentioned earlier that the Schweitzerhof Hotel has two good restaurants. One of them, the *Grill,* is superlative, among the best in Switzerland. It is smallish, intimate, smart, expensive, and with first-rate food. The beautiful restaurant of the *Bellevue Palace,* with its view of the Aare Valley, the town, and the

Bernese Alps beyond, is as recommendable as the hotel itself.
(Substitute the outdoor terrace in good weather.) The set-menu
luncheons and dinners are delicious, masterfully served, and good
value. *Frohsinn,* Munstergasse 52, is very Bernese, very animated,
very good, and moderate in price. *Della Casa,* Schauplatzgasse
16, is another Bernese-style place that the locals and MPs from
the country over frequent, and with good reason; moderate-priced
and good. *Le Mazor,* Barentplatz 5, is inexpensive and as good
a place as any to sample raclette or fondue. *Confisseries*—for
coffee, tea, pastry, or a snack—include *Meyer,* Marktgasse 31,
and *Ryser,* Spitalgasse 29, as well as the second-floor tearoom-
cafe in *Loeb's* department store. Better *bar-lounges*—with piano
music, usually—include *Due Theater,* Theaterplatz 7; *Pery-Bar,*
Zeughausgasse 3, and those of such hotels as the *Bellevue Palace*
and *Schweitzerhof.*

## TO BUY

You may say you're not going to buy a watch in Switzerland,
but of course you will. And maybe not only one. And maybe
a traveling alarm and a desk clock and . . . well, have a look
and you won't be able to resist. Nowhere in the world do watches
*seem* more beautiful. And nowhere else do there appear to be
such large selections of smartly styled watches. With discount
houses in the United States and their frequently fantastic prices,
and with the plethora of duty-free shops in airports and vacation
spots the world over, I am not about to tell you how much less
you will pay for a Swiss watch on home soil. But believe me, you
can't go wrong; spend as little as you want. For thirty-five or
forty dollars you can have a handsome watch. You may also
spend three or four hundred—or more. There are novelty travel
alarms for five or ten bucks. And all sorts of gimmicky, amusing novelty pieces. Just make sure, if it's a proper watch, that
the one-year guarantee is enclosed, along with the list of ad-

dresses of U.S. repair shops. *Gubelin,* Bahhofplatz 11, next door to the Schweitzerhof Hotel entrance, has a super selection in a setting of great luxe, and with a knowledgeable staff. *Türler,* at Marktgasse 27, is very good, too. After watches, Swiss handicrafts—or at least some Swiss handicrafts—rate consideration. The best store in Berne is *Swiss Crafthouse (Oberlander Heimatwerk)*, Kramgasse 61. It's the Berne retail outlet of a commendable nonprofit organization whose aim is to foster the continuation of the handicraft traditions. Take your time looking around. You'll find woodenware, linens, and textiles in all shapes and sizes and functions, pottery and ceramics, copperware, wickerwork, stuffed animals, egg and tea cosies, and unusual costume jewelry. The staff ladies are glad to explain what everything is, and where and how it's made; and they ship. *Loeb* is one of the top department stores—modern, attractive, worth combing all three floors and the Schauplatzgasse annex, which has the grocery department. *Globus,* Spitalgasse 17–21, is another department store. The *Public Market* on Tuesday and Saturday mornings is a special treat. *Gaffner,* Marktgasse 61, and *Meystra,* Spitalgasse 14, are for chocolates—Tobler and Lindt are leading brands (they are, actually, everywhere available). *Franz Carl Weber,* Marktgasse 52–44, is the Berne branch of a national chain of toy stores for shoppers of all ages; Swiss toys, if you don't know them, are inventive and whimsical.

TO NOTE

**Access:** Coming from the United States, the most direct route would be a Swissair flight from New York to Zurich, thence a connecting fight to Berne, which has a small but efficient airport, quite close to town. The train situation is excellent, as where is it not anywhere in Switzerland? Schedules are frequent, with trains coming from north, south, east, and west; particularly popular is the Trans-Europe Express's *Rheingold* (with its sleek ob-

servation car), which passes through Berne on its Amsterdam–
Geneva route. Within town there is modern public transport, with
conductors frequently English-speaking, and of course there are
taxis. Central Berne is relatively compact and easy to get about
in, though. You'll find yourself walking everywhere, and enjoying it. Both chauffeur-driven and self-drive cars are for hire, and
the sightseeing tours of town and environs are good buys and
well conducted. **Climate:** Pick any season; chances are it will be
pleasant. Berne winters are as bracing as those elsewhere in
Switzerland—snowy, of course, with temperatures averaging in
the low thirties, from December through March, the latter part
of which may be warmer. April and May are nippy spring
months—about fifty; summer (June through August is pleasantly
mild and sunny, in the high sixties and low seventies, but invariably cool in the evening. It dips to the fifties in September,
with autumn (October and November) in the forties. Rain is a
distinct possibility, here and there, during the nonwinter months.
**Clothes:** For country excursions and city sightseeing during the
day, informal comfort is the ticket. After dark, in better places, the
Bernese like to dress up a bit. **Currency:** The Rock of Gibraltar-
like Swiss franc. **Tipping:** Hotels add 15 percent if you've
stayed less than three days, less if longer, so that additional
tips are not necessary except—in the case of hotels—for bellhops or baggage porters, who expect a franc a bag and, if you
like, half that per night for chambermaids who have done a
tiptop job. Most restaurants and cafes also add the 15 percent
service charge; you need tip nothing additional except perhaps
for the few coins that would round out your bill upward, but only
if you were happy with the service. Tip taxi drivers no more than
15 percent. **Language:** Berne is in the heart of the German-
speaking sector of Switzerland, but among themselves its people
—like all German-speaking Swiss—speak a mysterious tongue
called Schweitzerdeutsch, which is German-based, of course, but
no one but the Swiss attempt to speak or understand it. With German-speaking visitors, the Bernese speak perfect German; signs,

newspapers, menus, public notices, books, magazines, and the like are also in German, rather than the dialect. Besides German (spoken by some 75 percent of the people), Switzerland has three other official languages: French, spoken by 20 percent; Italian, spoken by 4 percent; and Romansch, spoken by 10 percent. About 10 percent of Berne's citizens are basically French-speaking, but many other Bernese also speak French and/or Italian, not to mention English, which is very widely used. Never fear, you will communicate. **Further information:** Swiss National Tourist Office, 608 Fifth Avenue, New York; 661 Market Street, San Francisco; Official Tourist Office of the City of Berne, Bundegasse 20, Berne, Switzerland. **Business hours:** Shops open early, usually at 8:00 A.M., close for lunch from about noon to 1:30 P.M., and remain open again until 6:00 or 6:30 P.M.

# *Bonn*

Like it or not, Bonn is a Western European capital, and that's why it rates a chapter in this book. I'm not at all sure that I like it—it is, in my experience, the coldest, least friendly city I have visited anywhere in Germany, north, south, east, or west; but there are facets of it that are of considerable interest, not the least of which is how it came to be the capital of West Germany.

The story you used to hear is that when World War II was over, and the longtime capital of Berlin was found to be plop in the middle of East Germany and under four-power occupation, West German Chancellor Konrad Adenauer—who had a house in the neighborhood of Bonn and had been a mayor of nearby Cologne —banged his first on a table and said, simply but firmly, "Bonn it will be!" But Paul Zurnieden, in the book *Bonn: Federal Capital*, says that it wasn't that melodramatic, that at the time the selection was made Adenauer was not yet chancellor, and that there were other reasons for the German Parliamentary Council's close vote on May 10, 1949. On that day, Bonn got thirty-three of the council's votes, and Frankfurt, twenty-nine. What helped swing the votes to Bonn was the Berlin bloc's votes. They voted for relatively obscure Bonn rather than for bigtime Frankfurt because they feared that if Frankfurt won, it would remain the capital permanently, even after that day—sometime in the future—when the two Germanies are again one. This was not only because of

Frankfurt's size and prestige but for its historical eminence as well, it having been the place where German kaisers were crowned, and the longtime capital of old German Federation.

**University town to capital:** And so Bonn, which had been heavily bombed during World War II, and which had looked forward only to the day when it could resume its role as a provincial university center, found itself the seat of government of a vanquished Axis power about which the whole world was curious. It had never before known such attention.

What it may have lacked in eminence it made up for in age. Bonn goes back a thousand years to the time of the Romans who, in the middle of the first century A.D., set up a garrison called Castra Bonnensia. It lasted four centuries, and its successor, after an interval, was an early Christian community called the Cassius Foundation. The foundation became popular as a place of pilgrimage and gradually attracted commerce, to the point where the *Vicus Bonnensis* came to be considered the earliest version of the present city. Later centuries saw the Electors of nearby Cologne involve themselves in the growing, by-then-fortified Bonn. Twice in the fourteenth century the Bonn cathedral, or *minster,* was the site of coronations, and it then came to serve as a residence of the archbishops and Electors of Cologne.

The Renaissance was an era of dramatic ups and downs, both temporal and spiritual; more than once the town was razed and rebuilt. Its golden period came in the eighteenth century, an era that saw the construction of buildings that remain Bonn's best monuments. The founding of the present university came a century later, by which time Bonn had become part of Prussia. The following century saw the city prosper to the point where, in the late 1800s, rich merchants and industrialists were attracted to it—they liked the bucolic, riverfront setting—and built the great houses that came to stand the town in such good stead when the post-World War II government needed residences for such latter-day eminences as the Federal President and the Federal Chancellor.

**Prosperity and insecurity:** Fully a third of the town was destroyed by World War II air raids. But with the designation as capital after the war, a new prosperity engulfed the city. The German people have never quite accepted the indignity of such an obscure town becoming their capital. But this did not stop construction that was necessary to house government departments. Civil servants from all over the country moved to their new capital. According to my count there are 111 diplomatic and consular missions in the city, ranging from *Athiopien* (Ethiopia) to *Zypern* (Cyprus). The interaction of such a mixed group of people, representing every major faith, race, and culture of the globe, often results in a cosmopolitan community, particularly in an already intellectually oriented place like Bonn, with its respected university. But none of this seems to have had much effect. To at least one visitor, this is quite the dullest capital in Europe. If things were not more lively in earlier days, I can well appreciate why Beethoven—native son No. 1—escaped to Vienna at the age of twenty-two. The poor chap was probably bored silly.

TO SEE

**Lay of the land:** Bonn straddles the west bank of the Rhine, extending from north to south. The heart of town, with the baroque old quarter, university, and the pedestrians-only shopping area in and around *Bonngasse,* is in the vicinity of the *Kennedy Bridge* (Kennedybrucke). Leading south, roughly paralleling the river, is the wide *Adenauerallee,* along which are a number of important public and semipublic structures. Adenauerallee leads to the new and pitifully tacky shopping-office building-hotel complex called the *Bonn Center,* and the somewhat older area of government ministries known as *Tulpenfeld.* The largely residential *Bad Godesberg* area, is a few minutes' drive south, Cologne is to the north, and a number of Bonn suburbs are across the river.

The charming part of town is the central area, with its remaining baroque monuments. These include the onetime *Elector's Palace,* which is now (and has been for a long time) the main building of the *University of Bonn;* the *Poppelsdorf Palace,* now a part of the university and linked with it by means of the lovely *Poppelsdorfer Allee;* the *Kreuzberg Church,* with its unusual altar in the form of a stairway, the work of the great Balthasar Neumann; the lovely *Town Hall,* on the triangular *Munsterplatz,* with a stairway that has served as a podium for such contemporary speakers as John F. Kennedy, Charles de Gaulle, and Queen Elizabeth II; and the streets in the neighborhood of the Town Hall, and the houses bordering them, including that at *Bonngasse* 20, where on December 17, 1770, Ludwig van Beethoven was born. Within are the composer's bedroom, his last grand piano, and his stringed instruments, and room after room of Beethoveniana. Still another house-*cum*-museum is that of the poet-publicist *Ernst Moritz Arndt* on Adenauerallee. It dates from 1819, and is full of paintings of that era and of Biedermeier furniture.

The earlier-mentioned *cathedral* is a Romanesque-Gothic gem with a pleasing cloister. Even more unusual is the two-story twelfth-century church at suburban *Schwarz-Rheindorf,* with the upper part for the higher clergy, the lower for the lower—and perfectly splendid frescoes on the walls.

There are some very good *museums.* The *Academic Art Gallery (Akademisches Kunstmuseum)* has an exceptional collection of Roman and Greek pottery and sculpture. The scope of the *Rhenish State Museum (Rheinisches Landesmuseum)* is the culture and art of the Rhineland from prehistoric man to the current era, with the Roman medieval collections especially exciting, and a fine group of Old Dutch Rhenish masters, too. The *Municipal Art Collection (Stadtische Kunstammlungen Bonn)* is very big on German art of this century—with the works of such painters as August Macks and Max Ernst, going right through to contemporary younger painters like Willi Baumeister and Otto Piene. The *Folklore Museum* in the old main building of the university has a choice collection of works from the South Pacific, Africa, Asia, and South America. And even if rocks and minerals are not your scene, and you might want to pop into the *Museum of Minerals,* if only because it is located in Poppelsdorf Palace. The river-front *Parliament,* (*Bundeshaus*) is a onetime teacher's college that is open to the public only when sessions are not being held. The former private mansions housing the top two government officials (*Palais Schaumburg* for the Chancellor, *Villa Hammer-schmidt* for the President) are not open to the public, al-though it is possible to see the baroque structure known as the *Redoute,* in nearby Bad Godesberg, where the government holds a lot of its parties, mostly for diplomats, many of whom live in and about Bad Godesberg.

<br>

TO WATCH

There are a pair of modern theaters, both worthwhile: the immense *Beethovenhalle* and the smaller but architecturally more interesting *Municipal Theater.*

<br>

TO STAY

I don't know of another European capital—East or West—with such a sorry hotel situation as Bonn. Ambience, graciousness, style, pizazz—all are absent. German hoteliers, who are today among Europe's best, must have something against this town. At any rate, my choice is the one-hundred-room riverfront *Konigs-hof.* It dates to 1966 in its present form, but has a century-old history. All rooms have bath, of course; there is a riverfront terrace cafe in summer, an agreeable restaurant, bar-lounge, and other amenities. The location is at once attractive and con-venient, with the heart of town just a few minutes' walk away. In case you are tempted—because of the otherwise good reputation of the chain of which it is a part—be advised that at least one ex-customer of the *Steigenberger-Bonn* would never go near it again. It's new, clean, and functional, to be sure. But I found the service so inept as to be almost laughable, and the non-central location, in the dreary new Bonn Center complex, depressing.

### TO EAT

German food is among Europe's least appreciated cuisines. I discuss it in the chapter on Berlin. Head down the road a piece to Bad Godesberg and the *Haus Maternus,* a restaurant in an attractive old house (the garden is a delight of a summer evening) with a perfectly splendid traditional North German menu—particularly strong on veal dishes, game in season, poultry, and seafood, with those beautiful-to-behold (and taste) appetizers and desserts at which the Germans excel when they are cooking seriously. Snacks, coffee, pastry, quickie meals? Our old friend, *Kranzler,* the very same from Berlin, Frankfurt, Cologne, and Dusseldorf—has an outpost in Bad Godesberg in the heart of things on Theaterplatz. And back in Bonn, *Im Stiefel* is a reasonably priced old wine restaurant/pub that can be agreeable.

### TO BUY

Offhand, I can't think of anything distinctive. But stroll about the pedestrians-only shopping area on Bonngasse and see for yourself.

TO NOTE

**Access:** Bonn and its big neighbor, Cologne, share an international airport, whose major occupant is Lufthansa, the West German carrier that is one of of the great global airlines. Bonn is served by trains of the also first-rate German Federal Railroads. You must often change trains at Cologne for the remaining short run to Bonn; make sure you get the right train or you may find yourself going in the opposite direction and have to backtrack. Cologne Station, for some reason or other, lends itself to making errors of this sort. Motoring? West Germany's highways are as celebrated—and as extensive, wide, and car-clogged—as those of the United States. There are, as well, the fabled Rhine River steamers. Bonn is a port of call, although nearby Cologne is the traditional starting point for cruises. **Getting about:** Bonn is not as small in area as you might imagine from its image abroad. You cannot walk everywhere, and will need either a car (rental services are available) or use taxis or public transport. **Climate:** Northern Europe north-temperate, which means relatively mild but damp winters, which can be very raw; warm but rarely sizzling-hot summers; in-between springs and autumns. **Clothes:** Because this city is a diplomat/bureaucrat-populated seat of government, after-dark attire tends to be conservative; jacket and tie, of course, for daytime business or official visits. **Currency:** The unit of currency is the Deutsche mark (DM), divided into one hundred pfennigs. **Tipping:** A service charge of 10 or 15 percent is added to hotel, restaurant, and cafe bills, so that additional tips are not necessary. Tips are expected by taxi drivers (10 percent) and bellhops (50 pfennigs per bag). Railway station porters get 80 pfennigs per bag as a fee, and expect a tip of about 50 pfennigs additional. The most tip-happy of Germans—indeed, of all Europeans—are the women who seat themselves before public washrooms with nasty expressions on their faces, and who practically pounce if you attempt a getaway without paying tribute. (They are particularly odious in airports, where they seem to delight in preying upon transit passengers, who haven't a mark or pfennig to their name, and it would seem that with the unemployment rate so low, the German airport authorities could fire all these leechlike ladies without upsetting the economy.) The minimum ransom is 20 pfennigs. **Language:** German, of course. But the proportion of English-speaking Germans is very high—nothing like Denmark, Norway, or the Netherlands, but still very high. Lots of French-speakers, too. **Local literature:** *Bonn Information* is published twice monthly as a hotel giveaway, but only in the German language. **Further information:** German National Tourist Office, 500 Fifth Avenue, New York; 11 South LaSalle Street, Chicago; 323 Geary Street, San Francisco; Place Bonaventure, Montreal. Bonn Municipal Tourist Office, Bahnhof, Bahnhofstrasse 22, Bonn, West Germany.

*Brussels*

Brussels suffers from an identity problem. Of course, its own people know who they are. But so often the rest of us don't. Not to the point, at least, where we do them and their city justice. Not in the manner of the outsider knowing quite how British London is, or how Italian Rome is, or how Dutch Amsterdam is.

This odd state of affairs has certainly not come about because of Belgian backwardness, for this is one of the richest and most go-getting of countries; nor because of Belgian bashfulness; the Bruxelloise, bright as a button and convincingly loquacious in at least two languages, are always glad to explain, if we would but ask, and so are the efficient government information authorities. Certainly the country is not without contemporary eminence. Brussels is, after all, the only capital extant where representatives of foreign governments are accredited to three distinct entities—the Belgian Crown, the European Community, or Common Market, and the North Atlantic Treaty Organization. And no one can say that we are not clear about this city because it is out of the way, for if Brussels is not the heart of Europe, no city is.

**Complex beginnings:** No, I think the reason lies in the extraordinary complexity of the background not only of Brussels but of Belgium. What other Western country was not popularly called by its present name during the entire modern era, until as relatively recently as the latter part of the eighteenth century? "Belgium"

is a modernization of Belgica, an ancient Roman province inhabited by a people known as the Belgae, whom Julius Caesar
conquered nearly twenty-one hundred years ago. Caesar was not
unique in wanting to control this people, whose land—nice and
flat and unjagged, so that armies could traverse it with relative
ease—lay between the power zones of the Gallic and Germanic
peoples. The Franks occupied the area in the fifth century. Charlemagne added it to his empire in the eighth century. It became
part of Lotharingia—now, who remembers Lotharingia?—in the
ninth, and of Lorraine, after that.

The twelfth century saw what is now Belgium take shape as a
quartet of political entities: Brabant (of which Brussels was the
center), Luxembourg (now the name of a Belgian province *and*
of a neighboring sovereign country), Liège, and Hainaut, or
Flanders. With this political sophistication came material wealth,
thanks to a burgeoning wool industry. Brussels acquired a reputation for luxury and levity which, vicissitudes notwithstanding, it
has not lost to this day. The Duke of Burgundy took over the area
in the sixteenth century, and later Ghent-born Charles V, the
Holy Roman Emperor, made Brussels the seat of the governors of
the low countries, which passed from Burgundian to Spanish, and
later Austrian hands.

**Post-Napoleon years:** But that was not all. After the French
Revolution, Brussels found itself a part of Napoleon's empire.
(Napoleon, it will be remembered, met his Waterloo in Belgium;
the battlefield of that name is an excursion-ride away from Brussels.) In 1815, the Congress of Vienna passed it from France to
the Kingdom of the Netherlands, with Brussels and The Hague
co-capitals. The Belgians would have none of it. The performance
of a particularly patriotic opera at the Théatre de la Monnaie,
still the national opera house, impelled them to demonstrate
against the Dutch regime in 1830, and their revolt became the
revolution that brought them independence.

And, at long last, a name, identity, and national government of
their very own. Republics were still not all that popular, and

as people were wont to do even in later decades (the Norwegians, for example), the Belgians chose a foreigner as their first modern king. He was the first of the three Leopolds, the most interesting of the nation's monarchs. This Leopold No. 1 hailed from Saxe-Coburg, one of the relatively obscure German duchies that have long since gone with the wind. Leopold's brother was Ernest I, who was not only the Duke of Saxe-Coburg but the daddy of a marriageable young man named Albert.

**The Belgian Leopolds:** Uncle Leopold (who was to be called the Uncle of Europe because of a proclivity at royal matchmaking) played a major role in bringing about the marriage of his nephew Albert to his niece, Queen Victoria, which was possible because Leopold's wife was an aunt of Victoria. The point is that the influence of this first Belgian king—at matchmaking, negotiation, and secret diplomacy—gave him considerably more importance in the affairs of the Continent than the size of his realm might have indicated.

The second Leopold was quite as important, if hardly as endearing. He is remembered as the Congo King. With the collaboration of an American named Henry M. Stanley—who was himself to gain celebrity—he organized something called the International Association for the Exploration and Civilization of the Congo. That was in 1876. In 1885, the Berlin Conference that took it upon itself to divide Africa among the major European powers, awarded the Congo Free State, as it was called, not to Belgium or the Belgian government, but to Leopold II *himself*. He used it to build up an astonishing fortune directly and through concessions, with forced labor—frequently exacted by methods of barbarous cruelty—of the Congolese as the basis for his wealth. Tales of Leopold's horrendous Congo methods developed into an international scandal, to the point where he was forced to turn his personal possession over to the Belgian Government to administer as a colony. That it did—immensely profitably, to be sure, if not wisely—until 1960, when the Congo became independent and was the scene of domestic turmoil for several ensuing years; after achieving sovereignty it understandably changed the name of its capital from Leopoldville to Kinshasa, and in 1971, to erase even more completely its bitter colonial past, it changed its national name from Congo to Zaïre, even renaming the Stanley Pool (called after Leopold's original partner).

**Belgium and the World Wars:** If the Belgians were the Congo's oppressors, World War I was once again to see Belgium oppressed. The Germans occupied it—and harshly, even as Belgian troops fought against them on French soil. But World War II was even more disastrous. The Nazis, despite earlier guarantees of respect for Belgian neutrality, attacked, invaded, and occupied in 1940. This was during the reign of the third Leopold, who surrendered unconditionally, even though his cabinet continued to wage war on Germany from London. The German occupation was far more oppressive than it had been during the First World War. Hundreds upon hundreds of thousands were shipped to Germany to work as slave laborers. American and British forces, helped by a valiant Belgian underground, liberated the country in September 1944. But the unsuccessful Nazi counteroffensive of the Battle of the Bulge, that winter, caused Belgium even more destruction.

Postwar recovery was an absolute marvel; the drama of the third Leopold played itself out during the early postwar years. Because he surrendered unconditionally to the Nazis in 1940, even though his government chose to fight on in exile, he opened himself up to accusations of treason from Liberals and Socialists. He remained in Belgium, at his suburban palace in Laeken, as a prisoner of war, refusing to rule even as a puppet under the Germans; in 1941 Leopold, a widower since Queen Astrid (a Swedish princess) had died in an auto crash, married a commoner who later became styled the Princess of Rethy. In 1944 his captors shipped him off to Germany, where he was released by the Allies in 1945, to live in Swiss exile while a brother acted as regent. Not for half a decade, though, was his fate resolved. Even though a majority of the people voted for him to resume the throne, demonstrations by the Socialists and Liberals impelled him to decide upon abdication. His elder son, Baudouin, born in 1930, succeeded him in 1951, visited the United States shortly thereafter (I will never forget how well he handled himself at what surely must have been the most informal press conference he had ever known, at New York's Overseas Press Club), and in 1960 married a Spaniard who reigns with him as Queen Fabiola. The king's popular brother, Prince Albert, keeps busy representing his country in various endeavors, not least among them tourism.

**Commercial genius:** During all of these many centuries that it has been fought over, becoming the territory of first one power, then another, Belgium developed an absolute genius at trade and commerce, building up heavy industry, and even—despite its small, congested area—a thriving agriculture. Brussels itself came to reflect the success of its burghers, and during neither of this century's World Wars was it damaged. Indeed, it has only itself to blame for whatever of the old it razes to make way for the new. There appears to be no end in sight, with the imminent completion of a world trade center—to be called Manhattan, at that—soon to rival that of New York's world trade center.

Belgium's apparently interminable *bête noire* is its language situation. The price it pays for the genius with which it has melded Latin and Germanic peoples is endless bickering over the languages they speak. The way it breaks down is that the Flemings, or Dutch-related people, comprise more than half the population, and occupy, roughly, the northern half of the kingdom. The Walloons, who are French-speaking, constitute less than half of the Belgian populace and live in the south. (Brussels, though within Flanders, has a French-speaking majority, though both languages are official there; all street signs and official notices are bilingual.) Making both French and Flemish (which is a dialect of Dutch) official languages has never been quite enough. So in 1970, the old 1830 Constitution was amended, giving autonomous cultural and economic powers to Flanders, Wallonia, and the city of Brussels, the concept being a compromise between federalism and centralism. It was having somewhat tough sledding in its early years. But Brussels continues to go about its business. The complexities of its country notwithstanding, it remains host to the Common Market, to NATO, and to countless visitors bent solely upon pleasure in a city they will surely enjoy even if they do not completely understand it.

TO SEE

**Lay of the land:** At first glance, Brussels seems neither fish nor fowl: a mishmash of the architecture of an era or two, too many. What it wants, to be appreciated, is to be inspected on foot, particularly in its central sector, for old Brussels is a magnetic place, with pockets of Gothic and Renaissance and baroque beauty in its narrow streets, and little parklets and formal squares, and public buildings, not to mention markets, cafes, bakery shops, and restaurants that make for some of the most delicious pauses in all Europe. You need a good map to help you get about. The best I have been able to find was one given me by the Brussels Hilton; I've also used the one issued by the Commissariat General au Tourisme, which I don't think is quite as good.

Best starting point for orientation is the *Central Railway Station/Sabena Air Terminal.* This is a good focal point, from which you can walk to most areas of interest. Just a few minutes distant—by any of a number of routes, one being the *Rue de la Madeleine*—you are at the *Grand' Place,* about which more later. This originally Renaissance square is dominated by the slender tower of the Town Hall, which is worth retaining as a landmark. From the Grand' Place, one can take one of several very short routes of a couple of blocks—via the *Rue du Beurre* or the *Rue du Marché Aux Herbes,* for example—to the *Place de la Bourse,* which is the site of the *Bourse,* or *Stock Exchange* —a not-unimportant institution in as rich a city as Brussels, and from which one gains the major commercial thoroughfare known as *Boulevard Anspach.* From this point, walk north up the Boulevard Anspach to the major square that is the biggest and busiest in town, the *Place de Brouckère.* On the other side of the Place de Brouckère, the Boulevard Anspach becomes *Boulevard Adolph Max,* continuing to another square—the *Place Rogier,* with the *Gare du Nord,* or *North Station,* beyond. The area roughly between the Grand' Place and the Place de Brouckère is Brussels' major shopping district. It is known, generally, as downtown, or the lower town, and has been traditionally the bailiwick of the merchants and businessmen and the municipal government. A higher part of the city—uptown—has traditionally been the seat of the crown and the better residential areas. One may easily walk between the two, in which territory there is much of interest. Uptown's major landmark is the towering *Palais de Justice,* which is just a hop and a skip from the easily remembered *Boulevard de Waterloo*—a principal uptown thoroughfare. To go from the Grand' Place to the Palais de Justice makes for a pleasant walk. From the Grand' Place one would walk up the Rue de la Madeleine to the modern *Beaux Arts Concert Hall's* complex, continuing up the *Rue des Sols* to the *Place du Musée,* which is only a short block or so from the Royal Palace and the *Parc de Bruxelles,* which separates it from the Parliament. The Place du Musée is separated from the neoclassic *Place Royale* by the Ancient Arts Museum. One crosses the Place Royale, continuing on the curvy *Rue de Namur* to the *Rue des Petits Carmes,* which leads to the monstrously massive Palais de Justice, with the *Boulevard Waterloo* just beyond, at the intersection of the *Avenue Louise,* worth remembering because it is uptown's main shopping street, and, as such, the smartest in town.

**Choice destinations:** Now, to take things more slowly. You are going to want to lead off with the *Grand' Place,* and with good reason. Although it was rebuilt after Louis XIV's forces destroyed much of it in 1695, it dates back to the twelfth century. What one sees today, though, is one of the great Late Renaissance corners of Europe, blessedly cleared of autos—which had made it appear to be Europe's most elegant parking lot—by a 1972 civic edict, as a result of a campaign by the English-language Brussels *Bulletin.* The *Town Hall* dominates, and it is by no means to be admired only from without. Go right in and have a look around, for there are brilliant Brussels tapestries and some fine paintings embellishing floor after floor of reception and public rooms, including the Wedding Chamber. The Maison du Roi (about which more later in the museums section) occupies another side of the square, and the guild houses complete its façade. The *Mannekin-Pis,* the tiny bit of seventeenth-century sculpture that is to Brussels what the Little Mermaid is to Copenhagen, is not far from the Grand' Place, along a touristically well-trod route along which the souvenir shops increase in quantity and vulgarity the closer one gets to the statue. The *Galeries St. Hubert* are a nineteenth-century Brussels Valentine—still quite as charming as they were many decades ago when fashionable Brussels promenaded past their shops. The two-chamber *Parliament,* in the handsome eighteenth-century Palais de la Nation (which had been the seat of the Supreme Council of the old Duchy of Brabant) is eminently inspectable, with the Senate the more eye-filling of the chambers. Although it is open only during a part of each summer season, the Royal Palace—built by Leopold II in the late nineteenth century in Louis XVI style—should most certainly be on one's inspection schedule. The throne room alone, with its array of immense crystal chandeliers, makes a visit worthwhile. (Although the King has an office here he and his family live in another palace in the suburb of Laeken.) *St. Michael's Cathedral* is Brussels' architectural surprise package. (The Grand' Place, after all, is usually not a surprise.) It is an exquisite Gothic masterwork; the choir is thirteenth-century, the nave fourteenth and fifteenth, the towers fifteenth. The Dukes of Brabant are buried in the chapels, and the stained-glass windows were a gift of no less a personage than Charles V.

But Brussels has a number of visit-worthy *churches.* These in-

clude *Notre Dame des Victoires* (No. 2 after the Cathedral), a
treasure from the fourteenth century; *Notre Dame de la Cha-
pelle*—and not only because Peter Breugel the Elder is buried
there; the adjacent Chapels of *St. Anne* (baroque) and *La Madeleine* (Gothic), *Notre Dame de Bon Secours* (baroque), *Notre
Dame aux Riches-Claires* (Renaissance), and *St.-Jean Baptiste*
(baroque).

There are, aside from the earlier-mentioned Parc de Bruxelles,
some additional charmers. The *Place des Martyrs*—dedicated to
the heroes of the Revolution of 1830, which brought the country
independence—is neoclassic and quietly relaxing. And the two
Sablon squares are both lovely. The *Place du Grand Sablon* is
distinguished by a central fountain, with antiques dealers all about.
The *Place du Petit Sablon* is more unusual, with statues of four
dozen medieval merchants' guilds lining it. The *Palais de Justice*
is so monumentally ugly that you might want to go inside (the
idea, apparently, was to exceed the excesses of both ancient
Greece *and* ancient Rome); there are enough courtrooms, surely,
to last Brussels into the twenty-second century, no matter how
criminal-ridden the city may ever become.

Brussels has some super museums; I would like to recommend
a few. But before you get bogged down at those in town, take
a taxi or Tram No. 44 out to the green suburb of Tervuren and
the *Royal Museum of Central Africa*. After you see it you have to
admit that Leopold II could not have been all bad, for he established this collection. It is housed in a park of its own in a huge
neoclassic, early-twentieth-century building. Buy an English-language guide book and map and head for the rooms marked Congolese Art, Ethnography (Congo) and Ethnography (Africa). The
exhibits in these constitute some of the finest one can see on any
continent, Africa included.

The *Musée Communal de Bruxelles* is housed in the Maison du
Roi, the beautiful building opposite the *Town Hall* on the Grand'
Place, and I would like to have a quarter for every Grand' Place
visitor who doesn't bother to go inside. What awaits is a feast of

riches, including the Saluces *rétable,* or altar piece; eighteenth-century furniture and decorations in the Caryatid Room; venerable documents relating to the history of the town, in St. Michael's Room; the Lace Room—to get an idea of what really fine Brussels lace was all about (in contrast to so much of the souveniry stuff sold today); the Dutch Regime and 1830 Revolution rooms, for graphic pictures of what impelled the revolution and how it transpired; the Nineteenth-Century Room for the Brussels of Leopold I and Leopold II, and for many, the treat of the museum; a whole room full of costumes for our friend, the Mannekin-Pis (the first was offered in the late seventeenth century and they have never stopped coming). The *Musée d'Art Ancien* (Museum of Ancient Art) is Brussels' Old Masters gallery: Roger van der Weyden's great *Pietà* (is there a greater *Pietà?*); and *Portrait of Jean de Coimbre;* Memling's *Martyrdom of Saint Sebastian;* Gerard David's *Adoration of the Magi;* Quentin Metsys' *Madonna and Child;* Cranach's *Adam and Eve;* Rubens' *Têtes Nègres* (*Étude*); Brueghel the Younger and Brueghel the Elder both. Enough; I've given you an idea. The house in which *Erasmus* lived and worked is a Renaissance treasure, in the Anderlect suburb, and while you are there, look at a gem of the nearby *Gothic church; Brueghel's house* at 132 Rue Haute operates as a museum, but only by appointment: phone 12-45-73. Something else again is the authentically Art Nouveau house of the architect named *Victor Horta* (among his works is the Beaux Arts Concert Halls complex) at 25 Rue Americain. The *Royal Library* is rich with illuminated manuscripts and old prints and engravings. And the *Ixelles Gallery* (71 Rue Jean Van Volsem) is likewise, with French and Belgian Impressionists. There's a choice—very choice —Oriental porcelain collection in the curious *Chinese Pavilion,* 44 Avenue Van Praet. And I have saved a whopper for last: the *Royal Museum of Art and History,* adjoining the Cinquantenaire archway on the Avenue des Nerviens. This is a wide-screen show—collections of the early civilizations of Asia and Africa, as well as Greece, and Rome; and choice European exhibits, particularly so in the case of the decorative arts.

**Other destinations in the environs:** The suburb of Laeken is verdant and pretty. You can't see the inside of the eighteenth-century *Royal Palace* (the principal residence of the royal family), but for a few days each May the *Royal Greenhouses,* with an unusual collection of exotic plants, are open to the public. Earlier kings and queens of the dynasty are buried in Laeken's *Church of Notre Dame.* (But the King's parish church is baroque St. Jacques, on the Place Royale in Brussels.)

Belgium is full of *castles;* it has more than its share, and many are open to the public. In the Brussels area those of note include *Gaasbeek,* which is full of splendid tapestries and furnishings; moated *Beersel,* quite as it must have been in medieval days; and *Grand-Bigard,* another medieval château but full of Renaissance furniture.

TO WATCH

*Son-et-Lumière* (or, if you will, Sound and Light) is a summertime treat on the Grand' Place but usually only on Saturday, Sunday, and holiday evenings. Belgium's now-famous *Ballet du XXième Siècle* (which has had tremendous success abroad, including the United States), directed by Maurice Béjart, performs on home base in the beautiful mid-nineteenth-century *Théatre de la Monnaie,* which is also home to the *Brussels National Opera,* with a wide-ranging repertoire of both contemporary and traditional operas, ranging from Britten's *Rape of Lucretia* to Mozart's *Don Giovanni.* And bless the management: Synopses of the operas are in the printed programs in English as well as French and Flemish. The *Palais des Beaux Arts,* designed by the earlier-mentioned architect, Victor Horta, is the principal hall for symphonic concerts, both local and guest; its diverse program also includes movies, ballet, and art exhibits. The *Conservatoire Royal de Musique de Bruxelles,* on the Rue de la Regence near the Place Royale, is also the site of symphonic concerts. Brussels *Agenda* and the press list theater offerings, in both French and Flemish, as well as movies, which are shown with their original sound tracks, with French and/or Flemish printed titles. *Puppet shows* are an ancient Brussels tradition; *cabaret* is a relatively modern tradition, and not, of course, cheap—you get a little bit of everything including chorus line, jugglers, magician, and a corny comedy act, invariably in a language you don't understand.

## TO STAY

I do not mean to offend the Flemings of Brussels when I say that the good French tradition of hotelkeeping seems to have had its influence in the Belgian capital. (Surely no one will deny that the French are better hoteliers than the Dutch?) At any rate, Brussels is full of good, comfortable, professionally run hotels whose staffs understand what service is all about. The *Brussels Hilton,* while hardly one of the more aesthetically beautiful in the Hilton International group (which I know well and of which I am fond) is beautifully operated. The staff is alert, attentive, quick, smiling, everything works like a charm, the view from the on-high rooms over the town is exceptional, and the location provides the best of both Brussels. By that I mean you are almost across the street from the smart shops of the Avenue Louise, with the museum area of the Place Royale and the Sablon squares close by. And the Grand' Place is a nice fifteen-minute walk. Downtown, I am partial to the *Hotel Metropole,* and have been for years. It is many, many more years old than I, heaven knows, Old School in the best sense, with a Place de Brouckère location right in the heart of things, refurbished guest rooms, and delightfully atmospheric public rooms, including a popular Place de Brouckère gathering-place cafe. Still welcoming as it was some years back when I covered its official opening is the Knott chain's *Westbury,* on the top floors of a skyscraper opposite the Sabena Air Terminal and the Central Railway Station. The guest rooms are immaculately maintained, the wine-dine facilities remain first-class, and the service is deft. The oddly named *Hotel Amigo* (where did that Spanish creep in?) is a modern hotel in Renaissance style, just around the corner from the Grand' Place, with attractive bedrooms, agreeable restaurant and bar, and a loyal returnee-clientele. Goin on from de luxe to first-class: The *Atlanta* is the earlier-mentioned Metropole's next-door neighbor on the Place de Brouckère, elderly but refurbished in modern style; cheerful guest rooms and public spaces. The nearby *President* is smaller but quite as convenient, with small but cheery bedrooms, all with bath. The *Plaza,* in the same general quarter, could be in Paris—luxuriously French Traditional, with good-size rooms, both guest and public. Both the *MacDonald* and the *Brussels Hotel Residence* are very spiffy, particularly the former. They are next-door neighbors, too, but more for regular business visitors who know the city well than for short-time visitors, for they are quite a way from the center. Two convenient downtown hotels that are more reasonable than the foregoing are the *Vendôme* on Boulevard Adolf Max, and the elderly *Grand,* on the Boulevard Anspach.

## TO EAT (AND DRINK)

There are so few Belgian restaurants abroad, and so relatively few Belgians, that if one has not made a study of national cuisines, or visited Belgium, one really has no idea of how extraordinarily well the Belgians cook. It is certainly possible nowadays to eat mediocre or poor restaurant meals in the major restaurant cities of the world. But I would like to go out on a limb and say that this would be difficult in Brussels.

The Belgians themselves are adamant about wanting the world

to know that their cuisine is their own, and not French. Of course. But there is no point in not saying that it is largely French-derived. That, of course, is what makes it one of the great cuisines. There are, to be sure, Dutch and to a lesser extent German and Congolese influences. But the Belgians have wisely seized upon the French fare and built upon it in their own distinctive way. They are more extravagant than the French. They will use richer ingredients and worry less about making every bit of every foodstuff count. They emphasize products that are peculiarly or originally Belgian—like endive, Brussels sprouts, Ardennes smoked hams, venison, rabbit from their woods, and things made using their superlative beer as an ingredient. (The stew called *carbonnade* is the classic example, and there are beer waffles as well.) And by no means are the Flanders specialties to be despised: *tartines* with *siroop*—a black pear syrup; soused herring; *stoemp me spek*—a simple cabbage and potato casserole; *hutsepot,* a beef-lamb stew; and the celebrated capon stew that is *waterzooie*. Brussels, with its central geographical location, boasts markets to which foods are brought daily from regions as diverse as Ardennes and the North Sea coast. The Bruxelloise adore mussels which they purchase at odd hours from street vendors. They would despair if their supply of *frites*—Belgian fried potatoes—were cut off. Their consumption of chocolates—which they make magnificently and which they call *pralines* (*prah-leens*)—is such that you wonder why they are not a nation of roly-polys (they are not). *Gaufres de Bruxelles* (waffles with cream) and *speculoos* (spice biscuits) are specialties. Their butter and cheeses and milk are all very good. They bake breads and pastries superlatively. Their beers—Artois, Gueuze, and Haecht are a few brands—are distinctive, neither Gallic nor Teutonic. And they are also partial to and very knowledgeable about—wine, mostly French, but Luxembourg and German whites are popular too.

Here is a selection of *restaurants* I like. If you are in the market for one major slam-bang meal, my suggestion is a lovely country house a twenty-minute cab ride from the center of town. It is called *Villa Lorraine,* and is among the better restaurants of Europe. The décor is luxurious and the presentation is dramatic. But this is not a gimmicky restaurant. Food is taken very seriously; it is of the Franco-Belgian classic style, with no nonsense. And it is expensive although perhaps a third cheaper than a comparable meal at a de luxe United States restaurant. The wine cellar, I might add, is one of the finest in Belgium. *La Couronne,* in a guild house directly on the Grand' Place, remains as elegant, excellent, and exciting as when I knew it on a first visit to Brussels years ago. Just a couple of short blocks from the Grand' Place, occupying both floors of a charming seventeenth-century house, is the *Restaurant du Bon Vieux Tempe.* The address is 13 Rue du Marché-aux-Herbes, but remember also that you walk from that street down a short alley called Impasse St.-Nicholas to get to the entrance. The furnishings are mostly as old as the house. But the food is good, too, and moderately priced, with grills (the steak au povire is very good) the specialty, and pleasant service. *Restaurant Nicholas,* 8–10 Rue des Dominicaines, also near the Grand' Place, is reasonable, full of locals, and with an excellent and varied set menu. Also inexpensive is the spick-and-span, always-busy *Chez Léon,* 16–22 Rue des Bouchers; the specialty is seafood. Another seafood place—this one very smart, indeed —is *L'Écailler du Palais-Royal,* 18 Rue Bodenbroek, near the Grand Sablon; try the mussel soup and the *waterzooi poisson* —fish substituting for the usual chicken. One of the best seafood buys in town is the *Oyster Bar Dégustation d'Huitres* in the Passage du Nord; order a half lobster and a half-dozen oysters. Food in the hotels of this city is invariably good. My favorite hotel restaurant, for its looks as well as for its good food is the enormous, wonderfully elaborate, high-ceilinged fin-de-siècle *Restaurant Leopold II* at the *Metropole.* Still another recommendation: the department stores. *A l'Innovation,* my favorite of the lot, has a Quick-Bar—excellent for salads, sandwiches, and pastries, and a first-class restaurant (the wine list alone is three pages long) called *Le Finistère,* which is very handsome and very recommendable. Uptown, on the Avenue Louise, the ultramodern *Sarma Department Store* has Le Snack, as well as a third-floor bar—yes, Myrtle, a bar where you can get a real drink—and a smart-looking cafeteria called, appropriately enough, *Le Lift*. The *Pub Louise*—Edwardian indoors but with an outdoor cafe, too—is amusing. Inviting hotel bar-cocktail lounges include the *Amigo;* the *Metropole,* both the bar and the sidewalk cafe; the Polo (off the lobby) and Penthouse (twenty-second floor) of the *Westbury;* and the *MacDonald* Horseshoe, along with its next-door neighbor, the *Brussels Hotel Residence.*

## TO BUY

Not, to be frank, a great deal, in this expensive country where the factory-made is as commonplace as it is in the United States. There are shops selling tawdry souvenirs all about the Grand' Place and the area of the Mannekin-Pis, including what passes for Brussels lace. But the best Brussels souvenir is something to eat. The chocolates, or *pralines*—particularly if you'll soon be flying home—make fine gifts. Among the better chocolate shops are *Neuhaus,* 25 Galerie de la Reine, 27 Avenue de la Toison d'Or, and 1 Rue de l'Amigo; *Godiva,* at 22 Grand' Place and 87 Boulevard Adolf Max, among other locations. Also the department stores (see below). *Val St. Lambert* is the noted Belgian crystal and glass; it is expensive, but not as expensive as in the United States, and a lot of it is very well designed. The factory has its own showroom at 3 Vieux Marche-aux-Grains. *Palais du Crystal,* Rue du Marché-aux-Herbes, is another Val St. Lambert source. *Tissagerie Réunis,* Rue Royale (next to the Astoria Hotel) has fine linens, place mats, tablecloths, handkerchiefs, towels, sheets, does monogramming, and ships expertly. The *department stores* are interesting. *A l'Innovation* ("*A l'Inno*" for short) at Place Rogier and Rue Neuve downtown; *Old England* on the beautiful Place Royale is about as, well, as Old England as you could imagine in Brussels; good quality if hardly avant-garde in style, and of course it has a tearoom. The *Galeries Louise* on the Avenue Louise is full of good shops; *Au-Feu-de-Camp* has modish clothes for both men and women, and *Delhaize* sells food and wines. On Avenue Louise itself, *Libudinic de Rome* is good for books and imported periodicals. *Demanet* has fine jewelry. *Pavilon Louise* deals in Haviland, Limoges, and other china, and silver too. *Rosenthal Studio Haus* is similar to its branches in other cities— china, ceramics, glass, and the like. *Fourrure Actuelle* has high-style women's clothes. *Marthe* is for millinery, *Michel's* for men's clothes.

Don't forget the *bakeries*. I bought two tall *speculoos* figures at a *boulangerie* near the Grand' Place more than a decade ago, and still use them every year as Christmas decorations; they're now hard as rock, but they haven't lost their looks.

## TO NOTE

**Access:** There is excellent air service from the United States. Sabena, the Belgian airline, flies nonstop every day from New York, but it is only one of more than twenty-five international airlines that serve Brussels' international airport, at Zaventem. Kudos to the Belgians for leading the world with the kind of transport that should link every major airport and the town it services: I am talking about the train service between downtown Brussels and Zaventem; it takes fifteen minutes and costs under a dollar. Belgium is a small country, too small for scheduled domestic plane service, but you may rent small aircraft if you like, through Sabena. As for trains, the Belgians' comprise the densest rail network in the world, connecting with those of other countries that link Brussels—and other Belgian points—with all Europe. All of the crack trains—including those of the Trans-Europe Express—call at Brussels. Paris is but a two-hour train ride away; Amsterdam is a good bit closer. Antwerp is less than half an hour away, and the equipment, service, and frequencies are of a high caliber that the United States has not known since before World War II. Motorists will find modern, well-marked highways; both self-drive and chauffeur-driven cars are for hire in Brussels. Bus tours emanate from the capital to throughout the country. Within Brussels there are plenty of taxis, and a modern public transport, as well as local sightseeing tours by bus. **Climate:** It can be damp at any time of year. But it is rarely blistering hot or near-zero cold. Summer (June through August) can at midpoint hit the low seventies, but it is usually in the sixties. Spring and fall (April and May, October and November) average in the fifties, although November can be colder. Winter (December through March) sees temperatures mostly in the mid-thirties, with March usually warmer. **Clothes:** The Belgians dress well, the women frequently very smartly, in Brussels. Visitors are most comfortable dressing as they would in any big city, informally during the day, less so—particularly at better places—in the evening. **Currency:** The Belgian franc. **Tipping:** Hotels, restaurants, night spots, and cafes invariably add 15 percent service charge to bills so that additional tipping is not necessary, although baggage porters and bellhops get about ten francs per bag. Taxi drivers are tipped more in Brussels than in most places; they expect at least 20 percent because of the economics of their profession—and it is what they get from both locals and visitors. Virtually everyone else who performs a service expects a tip, with five francs about the minimum. **Business hours:** Most shops are open from 9:00 or 9:30 A.M. to noon and from 2:00 P.M. to 7:00 P.M.; the big department stores, though open at 9:30 A.M. and go straight through until 6:00 P.M., without lunch breaks. In most cases these are Monday-through-Saturday hours. Additionally, there are evening hours on Friday: The downtown shops stay open until 9:00 P.M., the uptown shops until 8:00 P.M. **Language:** Belgium is officially a trilingual country. The northern half of the country—Flanders—is essentially Flemish (Dutch)-speaking. The southern portion—Wallonia—is French-speaking. There is a very small area near the

German frontier that is German-speaking. Brussels, the capital, though situated within Flanders territory, is officially bilingual (French and Flemish), although most of its citizens regard French as their mother tongue. Street signs, official notices, and much advertising are in both languages. And still a third language is popular in the capital—English. **Local literature:** Brussels *Agenda,* a well-edited, quadrilingual weekly, is distributed through the hotels. The Brussels *Times* and the Brussels *Bulletin* are English-language weeklies. **Further information:** Official Belgian Tourist Bureau, 720 Fifth Avenue, New York; Commisariat Général au Tourisme, 7 Boulevard de l'Impératrice, Brussels, Begium; Brussels Information Center, Place de Brouckère, Brussels, Belgium.

# *Copenhagen*

I am full of prejudices about Copenhagen. I emerged into it from its capacious if unlovely railway station a couple of decades ago, after a long ride from Amsterdam—or was it Hamburg?—and I have been under its spell ever since. When I go back these days, I am as happy as a clam if things go well, irritated almost to the point of feeling that as an aging Copenhagen hand I had been cheated, if standards appear to have been lowered. I expect too much. Intellectually, I realize that Copenhagen has known such phenomenal post-World War II touristic success (it was never, after all, Grand Tour magnet before the war) that it is not always able to cope with the crowds, nor indeed with the temperaments of its own citizens confronting the crowds. But emotionally I expect the city to have quite the same charm it had when the overseas visitor was something of a curiosity. That, of course, is asking a lot of the capital and sole metropolis of so small a country as Denmark, even if Copenhageners—over a million in toto—constitute a full quarter of the national populace.

**National weapons—wit and humor:** What I most like about Copenhagen is the air of today that both it and its people convey, despite the considerable age—eight centuries plus—of their city. There is, coupled with that feeling of grasping the contemporary, an attractive lack of pretentiousness, and more than in any other Scandinavian capital—and a lot of non-Scandinavian capitals, as well—a thoroughly engaging sense of whimsy and humor. When you consider, if you are a Copenhagener, that your ancestors conquered the British before Copenhagen even existed; when you further consider that your home city was the capital, in later centuries, of an empire embracing Norway, most of southern Sweden, some of northern Germany, a bit of the West Indies, and Iceland, and when you ponder the reality that the town in which you live is now the seat of government of a European kingdom only about half the size of South Carolina . . . well, you *require* a sense of humor. (To be fair, one must add that the enormous, hardly green island of Greenland remains Danish, as do the rugged Faeroe Islands, north of Scotland.)

**The Vikings take to the sea:** The pre-Copenhagen Viking period may not have been the Danes' most stylish era, but it was surely the most exciting. By the end of the ninth century, after considerable combat, King Alfred—one of the few early English sovereigns whose names we remember—made peace with the Danish King Gudorm, after which the Danes took over a considerable chunk of England, the while introducing the insular English to the vigorous and skillful Danes, who themselves introduced Christianity to the still unconverted Danes, to the point where—with the aid of some missionary activity—Denmark was essentially Christian by the time it became a united kingdom just a few decades before the year 1000. The first Christian king of Denmark has gone down in history with the quite memorable name of Harold Bluetooth. Harold's ambitious son, Svend, succeeded him and set out, with success, to conquer *all* of England —the England of Ethelred, one of the kings whose names we don't particularly remember, for the good reason, I suppose, that he lost out to Svend and fled to France. Svend ruled as the joint Anglo-Danish monarch (briefly, to be sure), to be succeeded by his bright twenty-year-old son Canute, who was quite possibly the first (but by no means the last) Dane to charm the pants off the Britons. (Denmark, to this day, remains a popular destination with British holidaymakers, its long-ago imperialist background notwithstanding.)

The Union of Denmark and England lasted almost three decades. It was *kaput* in 1042—a good century before a bishop named Absalon fortified the fishing villages that were Copenhagen's antecedents and developed a proper town. The little, not-far-distant town of Roskilde was the seat of the kings, (they are still buried in the Roskilde Cathedral) until the middle of the fifteenth century, when Copenhagen finally took over. By that time the first Queen Margarethe (the second was not to accede until 1972) had achieved an all-Scandinavian union of Denmark, Norway, and Sweden. Although Sweden went off on its own before long, Norway was under Danish aegis for a long, long time— until the early nineteenth century.

**Between the Margarethes—Christians and Fredericks:** There are good reasons for the long span of time between Margarethes: Denmark was ruled by men from the time Christian I took the throne in the mid-fifteenth century until the present Margaret's father—Frederick IX—died in 1972. And with one glaring exception (Hans, who followed Christian I) the kings have alternated in their names for all those hundreds of years. One would be Christian, the next would be Frederick, the next would be Christian, and so on down the line. There have been two Christians you will want to know about. The first was Christian IV. He had all manner of bad luck in matters political and military. But the Danes like him anyway, because he was their great builder-king, not only in Copenhagen (you will be told about him by the locals any number of times as you admire his handiwork) but in the Norwegian capital of Oslo, as well. He not only rebuilt Oslo after a disastrous fire that occurred during his reign, but he renamed it Christiania, after himself, and it wasn't until this century that the Norwegians renamed it Oslo.

But the Danes are even fonder of Christian X. Denmark had remained neutral, in the face of great difficulties, during World War I. In 1939 it signed a ten-year nonaggression pact with

Nazi Germany. The Germans ignored the pact, and their troops marched across the frontier and occupied Denmark in April 1940. King Christian X—already popular as the monarch who as early as 1915 had given the people a modern constitution enfranchising women—remained in his capital, rather than going into exile, as did the monarchs of other occupied kingdoms. He chose self-imposed seclusion rather than yield to the German authorities, remaining throughout the frequently terroristic occupation part of the time as a prisoner at rural Sorgenfri palace, at all times a symbol of the national unity that made possible the remarkable accomplishments of the Danish resistance movement. Christian lived through the early days of post-World War II peace.

His successor in 1947 was Frederick IX. Frederick's reign was a happy reign. Denmark, which had become one of the most progressive of European countries in the time between the wars, quickly rebuilt its economy, diversifying agriculture with manufacturing and industry and other major income-producers like tourism. (The U.S. touristic invasion was accomplished almost singlehandedly, and with a remarkably modest budget, by a bright and witty Dane named Axel Dessau, who had been introduced to tourism when he coordinated the work in Copenhagen of the Danish Allied Committee after the war—welcoming Yankee troops on furlough from Germany to Copenhagen and provincial Denmark. Dessau came to the United States in the early fifties, and with a genius for promoting the lures of his homeland has suceeded in turning us all into Denmark buffs. No country on any continent that I am familiar with—and I have worked with most —has been luckier in the area of tourist development and promotion than has Denmark.) The country's innovative background of a literate populace, achieved with the aid of the unique Danish adult folk-schools, of a strong cooperative movement, of prowess in enterprises as diverse as dairying and the applied arts (Danish butter is no more celebrated than Danish modern furniture), of typical Scandinavian pioneering in social welfare—all these contributed to the modern Danish Renaissance.

**Today's lively Denmark:** The post-World War II era of Frederick IX saw Denmark come into its own, internationally, for the first time since it was a great power. Frederick and his Queen—Ingrid, the intelligent and attractive daughter of Sweden's King Gustav VI Adolph—and their three pretty daughters, became the very models of a democratic monarchy. You would see the Queen in the shops, alone or with a single attendant or a daughter, and absolutely no fanfare or public fuss. The princesses' education was not unlike those of other Danish girls their age. The King loved to drive his own cars, conduct the Danish Radio Symphony, and take his wife and daughters, unannounced, to performances in the Royal Theater of the noted Royal Danish Ballet, of which he was so fond. Frederick and Ingrid traveled to the United States (on their 1960 visit to New York the King read the fairy tales of Hans Christian Andersen to children from the Andersen statue in Manhattan's Central Park) and spread the happy Danish word in many countries. With his family, he created an image of an informal—yet respected—late-twentieth-century monarchy that had never been attempted elsewhere in quite the same way.

In 1953 Denmark had still another constitution, a Woman's Lib one, if you will, that made it possible for royal princesses—not only royal princes—to succeed to the throne. And so when Frederick IX died before his time, after a short and tragic illness in early 1972, his eldest daughter became not only the second reigning Danish queen but the second Queen Margarethe, as well. Married to a French diplomat styled Prince Henrik by the Danes, and the father of Crown Prince Frederick (born in 1968), Queen Margarethe, thirty-one when she succeeded her father, is a tall (5′ 10″), athletic, well-educated, well-traveled, multilingual young lady as fortuitously equipped as any sovereign could be to lead the people of her effervescent kingdom into the twenty-first century.

**Lay of the land:** Copenhagen is a heady mix of the architecture Christian IV adapted from the seventeenth-century Dutch, and the functional Modern of our own century, into which has been sandwiched bits and pieces of intermediate eras, and through all of which weaves more than a million industrious, amusing, and often whimsical Copenhageners, not to mention inordinate quantities of curious visitors, as well as the very occasional neighborhood duck, a bit out of its element, perhaps, but withal crossing at an intersection with its brood and under the protection of the gendarmerie.

Central Copenhagen is capacious, make no mistake about it. But it is—like so much of Denmark—so flat in terrain that it makes excellent walking territory. There is a good likelihood that you will arrive in town at either the *Airlines Terminal* or its across-the-street larger neighbor, the *Central Railway Station.* The street in question is one worth remembering. It is a wide one called *Vesterbrogade*—the distance is just a few blocks, it leads directly into the big *Town Hall Square* (*Radhusplasdsen*), and—this is important—en route it passes by the midtown pleasure gardens called Tivoli. The Town Hall Square is, not surprisingly, dominated by the Town Hall, with its great tower—an important landmark. From it one gains the principal shopping street, which is a continuation—much narrower and differently named—of the earlier-mentioned *Vesterbrogade.* This shopping thoroughfare is distinctive in that it (1) allows no motor vehicles, (2) is known as the Strøget, but (3) actually embraces five streets, one running into the other, namely *Frederiksberggade, Nygade, Vimmelskaftet, Amagertorv,* and lastly, *Østergade.* Don't worry about these names; I repeat, the street is known collectively as Strøget. It is worth remembering, though, that it runs from the Town Hall Square to still another important square called *Kongens Nytorv*

(*King's New Square*). Landmarks for this latter are Magasin du Nord, the major department store, the Royal Theater, the Hotel Angleterre, and the onetime Charlottenborg Palace, which houses the Royal Academy of Art. But to continue. Another major area lies between the two major squares. It is dominated by *Christiansborg,* an immense multipurpose government palace, lying to the right of the Strøget, as you go from the Town Hall Square to Kongens Nytorv. *Nyhavn,* a colorful after-dark-raunchy thoroughfare that is at once the haunt of sailors off their ships and some nocturnal tourists off their rockers, runs perpendicular to Kongens Nytorv, going toward the sea. Not far beyond is *Amalienborg,* the quartet of rococo palaces enclosing their own square, the lot serving as the Copenhagen home of the Royal Family. Amalienborg is but a step or two from the piers where the passenger ships for Oslo tie up. The rest you learn as you amble about, remembering that it's hard to get lost because virtually anyone you might ask for directions speaks good English.

**Choice destinations:** Copenhagen for the visitor is an engaging jumble of destinations. *Tivoli* (open from May through late September) is the heart-of-town park that has no counterpart—anywhere. A Danish genius by the name of Georg Carstensen created it in the mid-nineteenth century between the bastions and battlements that once encircled the city. What had been a moat is now the lake that mirrors the campanilelike Town Hall Tower. The whole of the area is enhanced by flowerbeds that are among the most lovingly tended in Europe. There are gloriously illuminated fountains and fireworks (every evening, these last), an outdoor pantomime theater (in a fanciful Chinese pagoda) that is possibly the very last extant; a concert hall (with its own resident orchestra), whose performances are complemented by nightly outdoor spectacles and still additional (big name this, usually) entertainment in a variety hall. On weekends a longtime tradition in the form of Tivoli Guard—pre-teenage boys in the scarlet blazers and bearskin hats reminiscent of the Royal Guards—march through the grounds, providing oom-pah music for the crowds. There are dance halls and sausage stands and ice-cream parlors and cafes and something like a score of proper restaurants in all categories, a few of them among the very best in the entire kingdom. And off in a corner of its own is an amusement park of the traditional variety. Day or night, Tivoli is the place to meet Denmark—all Denmark—enjoying itself: young, old, affluent, simple, this is the nation's single most popular congregating place. And everybody behaves.

The Copenhagen of the Builder King of the Renaissance, Christian IV, embraces a number of structures. The most unusual building is the long, low-slung *Stock Exchange,* or Børsen, with its memorable spire of four intertwined dragons' tails. *Holmen Church* is where the Royal Family and the Navy brass still worship. It has an historically important chapel, and a baroque reredos and pulpit. The *Round Tower* (*Rundetarn*) connects with *Trinity Church,* and its spiral passage has known any number of distinguished visitors, not least among them being Russia's Peter the Great. *Holy Ghost Church* (*Helligandskirken*), about midpoint on the Strøget, has a sandstone portal dating from Christian IV, but is otherwise from other eras; they blend beautifully. Even more unusual is *Nyboder*—Christian IV's contribution to urban housing that was all too much copied in ensuing centuries. Nyboder is a group of twenty double rows of attached houses— presumably the first such anywhere. He built them to house his Navy, and many—if not all—remain to this day reserved for naval personnel.

Last, there is *Rosenborg Palace,* which had been Christian IV's summer house and is now a museum, dealt with in later pages. The earlier-mentioned *Amalienborg Palace,* home to the Royal Family, is not open to visitors. Still, the square on which the four handsome rococo detached houses of the palace front is one of special beauty, and one could do worse than to arrive there one day at noon to watch the *Changing of the Guard* and— when the Queen is in residence—a parade from the palace into town, to musical accompaniment. Copenhagen is a town of eminently visitable *churches*. Worth peeking into are *Christian's Church* on Strandgade (rococo) and *Frederick's Church* (also known as the *Marble Church* or *Marmorkirken*)—it's the one with the great dome directly behind Amalienborg Palace, about a block away, and is a late-nineteenth-century reconstruction of an earlier church. The *Garrison Church,* on St. Anne Place, is a little early-eighteenth-century gem. The *Franco-German Reformed Church* is worth a look when you're at Rosenborg Palace; it's across the way and is originally late-seventeenth-century, with the parson's house to the rear now doing duty as the *Museum of Musical History. Our Savior's Church (Vor Frelsers Kirke Christianshavn)* has a superb spiral staircase on its elegant spire, with a statue of a figure on a globe at the very pinnacle; only the Town Hall is taller. The baroque sanctuary is lovely. *St. Petri Church,* on St. Pederstraede, though much restored, has a 1304 pedigree, making it the oldest in town. The Danes are nuts about *Grundvig's Church* out on Bispebjerg; it's a 1920s variation of the handsome white churches you see all about the countryside, which are to me infinitely preferable. *Christiansborg Palace,* as mentioned earlier, is a multipurpose structure that is uniquely and sensibly Danish. It is, you should understand at the outset, the third such, the earlier Christiansborgs having gone down by reason of fire, bombardment or what have you. The current palace is rather surprisingly twentieth-century, having been completed 1918–28, but on traditional lines. Within are the Royal Reception Rooms (excessively elaborate and graceless, with an ambience that is heavy-handed, and oddly atypical of the usually excellent Danish national taste in such matters) and the Folketing (the unicameral Parliament), both of which are open to the public, and the Supreme Court and Foreign Affairs Ministry, which are not. In the old wing (which had been the riding school) is the Court Theater, now the Theater Museum, and dealt with in a subsequent paragraph. What have I forgotten before treating museums in a section of their own? *The Little Mermaid?* Heavens, no! Well, you'll take her in on any basic Copenhagen bus tour. She's on a rock of her own at the Langelinie promenade overlooking the harbor. Her sculptor was named Edward Eriksen, and she was, of course, the very same *Little Mermaid* of the Andersen fairy tale.

**Museums in Copenhagen** are special. The three most popular are the National Museum, Rosenborg Palace, and the Ny Carlsberg Glyptotek—and understandably so. But they are only starters. *The National Museum* is mostly housed in a mid-eighteenth-century palace, and runs an exceptionally wide gamut, from Danish prehistory onward, with fine departments on foreign subjects like Africa (outstanding), the Orient, classical Greece, and ancient Egypt. But the don't-miss section is the group of Danish interiors of the seventeenth through the nineteenth centuries, moved to the museum with their original walls, ceilings, and furnishings from all over the country. *Rosenborg,* earlier mentioned as the summer home of Christian IV (in the seventeenth century, its location was considered bucolic, although it is now quite near the center of town), doubles as a museum. The big draws are the exquisite Crown jewels. But the architecture and interiors of the palace are in themselves quite marvelous. And there are, as well, a richly decorated banqueting hall full of rare silver furniture and an ivory coronation chair; and a jumble of other exhibits, ranging from portraits of all the monarchs to every one of the eighteen hundred pieces of one of the first Royal Copenhagen services in the costly Flora Danica pattern, made for the count in 1790. The *Ny Carlsberg Glyptotek* goes back to the late nineteenth century, when it was founded by Carl Jacobsen, the Carlsberg Brewery eminence, to house his collection, considerably enlarged since by the New Carlsberg Foundation, which gets part of the cost of every bottle of Carlsberg you quaff. The museum's lushly planted winter garden is a gem. The Egyptian-Greek-Roman collections are among the best anywhere, and among other treasures the French Impressionists-Post-Impressionists group is particularly special—Manet, Cézanne, Toulouse-Lautrec, Gauguin,

Degas, Bonnard; they're all represented—in spades. Then we move along to the lesser-known museums. The *Royal Museum of Fine Arts* (*Statens Museum for Kunst*) had its origins with our old friend, Christian IV, who had a collection of five hundred paintings. These became the nucleus of a royal collection added to by his successors, one of whom put the lot together into a proper gallery. Their current home is a cavernous 1896 neoclassic pile that was masterfully refurbished in 1969. The chief lure is the old masters collection—Titian, Rubens, Rembrandt, Hals, to name but a very, very few. There is, as well, an absorbing group of Danish works, particularly from the eighteenth century. And there are later and more contemporary samplings from throughout Scandinavia—Norway's Edvard Munch is included—and a French Moderns group, with a number of Matisses among the stars. The *Museum of Decorative Arts* (*Kunstindustrimuseet*) ranks with the similarly titled institution in Paris; it is one of the great such museums in the world; we have nothing to equal it in the United States. Art-loving Carl Jacobsen, who founded the Glyptotek (and also contributed to the Statens Museum for Kunst) helped this museum get started too. Its current home is a treasure of a rococo palace—four wings enclosing a courtyard and originally a hospital—that is happily large enough to house the museum's remarkably extensive collection. The emphasis is international, not only Danish. There are furniture, textiles, ceramics, glass and crystal, metalwork, and other decorative and utilitarian objects from the medieval centuries through to our own. (On a recent visit I was delighted to find on display the same Danish stainless steel flatware designed by Einar Cohr in 1928 that I had purchased decades later in Copenhagen.) *The Theater Museum:* Theater in Denmark has a rich tradition, dating from well before the noted comedies of Ludvig Holberg in the eighteenth century. But it was at that time that the old Court Theater was constructed above the stables of Christiansborg Palace during the reign of Christian VII and his theater-buff wife, Caroline Matilde—a sister of England's George III. The present museum is a maze of memorabilia: the theater auditorium itself, old stage machinery, pictures and prints and playbills, and a section devoted to the ballet, for which Copenhagen is such a noted center. *Ordrupgard* is a World War I-era house in the suburb of that name that is chock-a-block full of French paintings—Impressionists like Degas, Monet, Sisley, and Renoir, but earlier painters too, such as Delacroix, Corot, and Ingrès—all given to the nation by their owner, Wilhelm Hansen, along with his house. The *Resistance Museum* (*Frihedsmuseet*) at Churchillparken, opened in the late 1950s, movingly recounts the work of the astonishingly daring Danish resistance movement during the World War II Nazi occupation years, along with the way the Danish people lived during that dark period. There is a similarly important museum, devoted to the Norwegian resistance, in Oslo. The *Copenhagen City Museum* (*Københavns Bymuseum*), Vesterbrogade 59, occupies a lovely eighteenth-century guildhouse and is a treasure trove of objects having to do with the history of the city. *Jaegerspris Palace,* at nearby Jaegerspris, is a seventeenth-century structure open in summer, with the Memorial Rooms of Frederick VII its highlight. *Louisiana,* among the most enchanting museums of all northern Europe, is worth every minute of the time it takes to reach it and return to town. It is some twenty miles north of Copenhagen. Its nucleus is a century-old house that had belonged to a nobleman who had had three wives, each named Louise. "Hence," as the museum said in one of its publications, "the name: Louisiana, which the Museum had adopted out of respect for such fidelity." The original house serves only as the entrance to a newer structure, which is Danish Modern design at its most sublime, in a sylvan parklike setting. Louisiana's aim is "contemporary art in congenial surroundings." And does it ever succeed—with exhibits a mix of architecture, landscape gardening, painting, sculpture, graphic art, and handicrafts. There are special exhibits, frequently imported, from time to time, concerts and children's programs, and a honey of an outdoor-indoor cafeteria blended in with the museum's library. I don't know of any institution in Denmark that is more successfully able to convey to the visitor, on a single short stay, what contemporary Danish life and art and design are all about.

**Selected excursions:** Because you might not get there otherwise, I have recommended Louisiana in the section on museums above. I want to recommend *Fredensborg,* too. Only twenty-four miles from Copenhagen, its lure is the palace by that name where the Royal Family has traditionally lived in spring and fall. The builder was Frederick IV, before the mid-eighteenth century, but there were extensive alterations in the latter, more rococo period of that century. The result is a gem of a structure at once baroque, rococo, and a bit neoclassical, as well, with a massive, overproportioned and quite marvelous square dome its most distinctive feature. The Dome Room, with an eighty-foot-high ceiling, is among the highlights within, along with the Garden Room, an immense reception salon. The palace's own park, bordering Esrum Lake, is an also-lovely eighteenth-century souvenir. (Fredensborg was particularly popular with the turn-of-century King Christian IX, to whom so many crowned heads were related that he was known as Europe's Father-in-Law. One of his children was Queen Alexandra, the beautiful but hard-of-hearing wife of Britain's Edward VII; they were frequent Fredensborg visitors.) Open only part of the summer; check before you go. *Frederiksborg Castle* (not to be confused with Fre*dens*borg) is another Christian IV masterwork of the early seventeenth century. Mr. Art Patron himself, the Carlsberg Brewery's J. C. Jacobsen, provided the wherewithal to convert it into a museum of national history, in 1878. It interprets Danish history in chronologically arranged galleries, the interiors of which—filled with furniture, paintings, sculpture, and other decorative objects of the subject era—are splendid. The magnificent chapel is where Danish kings were crowned until 1840, since which time there have been no formal coronation ceremonies. *Kronborg* is, of course, the Renaissance castle where Shakespeare set *Hamlet.* It is at Elsinore (Helsingør in Danish, and not to be confused with the Swedish town just across The Sound from it, called Halsinborg). Kronborg is late-sixteenth-century, with its beautifully sited exterior superior to what is to be found within; the best room is the chapel, dating from a century later than the rest of the palace. The *Danish Maritime Museum* is housed in a part of the castle and illustrates the broad-screen story of Danish shipping over the centuries. Of more interest, though, is the *Elsinore City Museum*. It occupies a treasure of a house called Marienlyst, originally sixteenth-century, but virtually rebuilt in neoclassic style in the late eighteenth century; the period rooms are beauties. There are a number of open-to-the-public *stately homes*. One such is *Lenchanborg Castle*—a baroque-rococo manor about sixty miles west of Copenhagen, owned by the Countess of Lenche-Lenchenborg. Another is *Gisselfeldt,* a sixteenth-century Renaissance castle, home to the noble Danneskiold-Samsøe family; it's in southern Zealand.

## TO STAY

The Danes like to create an aura of coziness in their hotels. Frequently, if not always, they succeed. At their best, they are excellent and skilled hoteliers. Recent years, though, have seen a period of such astonishingly full employment that standards have lowered. The most conscientious of hotel managers cannot always be sure if his hotel will have a full staff complement from day to day. (Some hotels, in order to help solve their employment problems, have gotten the government to allow them to bring in English-speaking Filipinos to serve as chambermaids.) Still, one must be prepared for occasional brusqueness at reception desks, occasionally overdelayed room cleanup or room service, and occasionally slow and/or unpleasant service in restaurants, cafes, and bars. The *Hotel d'Angleterre,* on the Kongens Nytorv, is Copenhagen's grand old hotel, a Danish institution that dates to the eighteenth century, which has not allowed itself to coast on the laurels of a venerable reputation. For as long as anyone can remember, newly appointed ambassadors have stayed at the d'Angleterre before presenting their credentials to the reigning monarch. So don't be surprised if you see an envoy in tails and decorations, accompanied by a resplendent royal chamberlain, setting out for an audience with Queen Margarethe at Amalienborg Palace. Every year sees extensive refurbishing and the kind of improvements that are quietly stylish. Bedrooms are impeccably maintained. The suites are a dream. The restaurants include a main dining room that is one of the best places to eat in northern Europe, a newer and more informal and moderate-tabbed bistro-bar called the Krinsen, a honey of a cocktail lounge, and in season an always-crowded sidewalk cafe. The subterranean kitchens and wine cellars—even to a somewhat jaded kitchen inspector like me—are a major marvel of Copenhagen. The *Royal* is the d'Angleterre's major competitor, de luxe in category, but as Danish Modern as the Angleterre is traditional. Owned by SAS and beautifully operated, this sleek 22-story, 292-room sky-scraper is probably the only major hotel extant that was designed *in toto*—building itself, furniture, furnishing, linens, accessories —by a single architect-designer, the late Arne Jacobsen. You may not like every facet of Jacobsen's work, but you cannot but marvel that it was the work of a single, exceptionally gifted man. And there is no doubt that it is, over-all, a building that is hand-some and functional and that wears very well upon repeated visits. There are a variety of wine-dine-dance-drink rooms. The *Sheraton-Copenhagen* is what Copenhagen has needed for a long time: a big (476-room) first-class hotel with full facilities and the virtue of a central location—rarely possible any longer in the built-up downtown sectors of Europe's big cities. Just a couple of blocks from the Central Station, with the Town Hall Square not far distant, the Sheraton-Copenhagen is a 17-floor beauty that was a success with both locals and visitors from the moment it opened its doors in 1971. It could not be more authentically Danish Modern in either its design or its décor. Everything you sit on, sleep in, eat with, and look at is Danish designed and Danish made. Facilities are full-scale, and range from a rooftop *boîte* to and through an enormous coffee shop and cocktail lounges, with posh King's Court one of the very best restaurants in town. The *Palace,* in my earlier Copenhagen days the sole top competitor to the d'Angleterre, remains a first-rate Old School structure with an inspired Town Hall Square location. There has been a good bit of refurbishing, and the ambience is attractive and welcoming. There is a good restaurant-bar (the Viking), the Ambassadeur dine-dance room, and a sidewalk cafe. The *Hafnia* is an elderly charmer, not too big (some 60 rooms, all with bath), and well managed, with the advantage of a central location, a relaxing little bar, and a good restaurant that turns alfresco in summer (or at least on those summer days when it's warm and sunny enough for a Copenhagen restaurant to turn alfresco). The *Kong Frederick,* next door to the Hafnia, has been refurbished in traditional style in recent years and is now a place of considerable style. Bedrooms are small, though—handsome as they are—and because the place has become so fashionable (particularly among the locals), service in the hotel and its restaurant-bar can be curt if you're a nonregular. The *plaza* is the onetime Terminus, restyled with great panache, and like its predecessor, one of the most agreeable hotels in town. The *Alexandra* (named for Edward VII's beautiful Danish Queen) is another of the moderate-size, moderate-level older places—conveniently located, attractively refurbished, welcoming. Its newer, smaller neighbor is the *Ascot,* in a masterfully refurbished elderly structure; bath or shower in all rooms; breakfast only. The *Mercur* is modern, moderately priced, well located, full of Danes (many from the provinces), and thoroughly, unabashedly cozy. The *Hotel 71 Nyhavn* occupies a cleverly restored, three-hundred-year-old warehouse on convenient, historic Nyhavn; there are eighty antique-accented rooms and suites, and a restaurant-bar. The Copenhagen home of my earliest visits, the *Missionhotellet* at 27 Longangstraede, just off the Town Hall Square and a hop and a skip from the Palace, remains a good budget choice. By no means all of the rooms have baths, but some do, and the price is right; this is one of a temperance chain, which means there's no bar. The *Missionhotellet's Annex*—around the corner on Vester-volgade, is smaller but newer—all rooms have shower, and there's a breakfast room, to complement the all-meals restaurant of the bigger Missionhotellet.

TO EAT (AND DRINK)

Danish food is the most Continental-influenced in Scandinavia, and therefore the most varied. When it is good, it is very good indeed. But one must not be under the impression that it is im-possible to order a bad meal. The great Danish gastronomic con-tribution is the *smørrebrød* (literally, bread-butter), the open-face sandwich—shrimp, beef, egg, liver paste, cheese, ingeniously garnished—that all the world tries to emulate, with only partial success. This is the staple at lunch—two or three are quite enough, with a glass of beer, and some of the delicious pastry and excellent coffee to round off the meal. Danish breakfasts can be among the best in Europe. They are quite simple: a basket of assorted breads, rolls, and *Wienerbrød* (literally, Vienna Bread, which is what the Danes call Danish pastry) and a pot of coffee, with a boiled egg if you ask for one. The secret is in the baking; no Scandinavian land bakes more delicious breads, and the Wiener-brød is invariably sublime. So, for that matter, is the coffee. And most hotels use either the Royal Copenhagen or Bing & Grøndahl traditional blue-and-white china service; you can't beat it. Smor-gasbord, as we should all know by now, is Swedish rather than Danish, although the whole non-Scandinavian world has latched onto it. In Denmark, when one sees a buffet it is called a *kolde bord,* or cold board, and is not all that different from those across the Sound; as in Sweden, one eats the cold fish selections first, follows these with the cold meats and salads, moves along to the hot dishes, and concludes with cheese and/or a dessert. Other Danish specialties—pork, ham, duck, goose (not to mention the more prosaic chicken)—are well prepared, and with all of the water surrounding Denmark it should go without saying that fish and seafood (eels, shrimp, and lobster particularly) are favored foods and well prepared. There is a national fondness for sauces, so that one does well to inquire in advance to avert surprises. There is a healthy respect for green salads and vegetables. Desserts are rich and good. So, of course, are the cheeses, butter and rich milk and cream. Danish hot dogs (*pøls*) are oranger than ours, but very good indeed served from street stands, with a tiny hard roll on the side and a blob of mustard for dipping. The aforementioned *smørrebrød* are also available at stands (open night and day on the Town Hall Square and opposite the Central Railway Station) and automatic vending machines. The most popular Danish potable is beer. Though it is now horrendously taxed, it remains among the better of the world's brews; Carlsberg and Tuborg are the undisputed leaders. Before a proper lunch or dinner, *with food imminent* (the stuff is strong), Danes are apt to *skøl* each other with a glass of their superb *Akvavit*—Aalborg is the favored brand, at least with me. It is served very, *very* cold, and invariably followed by a swallow of beer. The Danes are possibly the most *skøl*-prone of Scandinavians. Skølling or being skølled, one always looks one's fellow drinkers *in the eye, at the same time lowering the head a bit* before drinking, looking back at one's companions again—ever so briefly—after drinking. Bars, cafes, and restaurants stock all manner of spirits in this alcoholically liberal country, serving on Sunday as on weekdays, and into the wee hours every morning. *Restaurants:* My first suggestion is that the hotels not be overlooked; some of their restaurants are among the very best in town. The *King's Court* of the *Sheraton-Copenhagen* is one of the handsomest dining rooms in town—Danish Modern décor at its very smartest. And the *haute cuisine* menu, both Danish and international dishes, is equally appealing; a good bet for a festive meal. The *Hotel d'Angleterre Restaurant* is unsurpassed in the traditional category: quietly attractive, with an elaborate menu—classical continental and Danish specialties in profusion, and a wine list reflecting what is probably the finest cellar in the kingdom. The *Hotel Hafnia Restaurant* is particularly appealing when its summer garden is open; but even at other times it is very good indeed. More moderate-priced is *Ekko Danmark,* a handsome modern-décor restaurant operated by the Danish Agricultural Marketing Board and featuring, it should go without saying, Danish specialties made from the very best Danish raw materials. *Wivex* has a range of eateries from posh to the snack type, with year-round entrance from the Vesterbrogade, and summer access from within Tivoli; invariably reliable. The *d'Angleterre's* smart-looking *Krinsen* is a combination bistro and bar with a very Danish and very good menu, and everything very reasonable. The *Royal* has a convenient and inexpensive snack bar. *Krogs Fiske Restaurant* is a happy choice for seafood. The *Spinderokken*—opposite Den Permanente—is agreeable, and typically Copenhagen. *Brønnum's* serves late dinners, for theatergoers. *Det Grønne Trae* is convivial, bubbly Danish in menu and ambience. *Magasin du Nord* and *Illums* have inviting *cafeterias.* And by no means leave Copenhagen without having sampled the earlier-described sausage and sandwich stands. As for *Tivoli,* my recommendation is unreservedly and wholeheartedly for *Belle Terrasse,* with hearty, colorful, old-fashioned ambience, as skilled a staff as one can find these days in Copenhagen, and an ever-reliable Danish-continental menu. There are any number of less-expensive restaurants (*Divan I* and *Divan II* are in the same top category as Belle Terrasse, but I don't think they come up to it), not to mention countless snack bars and the like. Of the hotel bars, the smartest is that of the *d'Angleterre* and the handsomest, that of the Plaza—a capacious, period-style library, and called just that. *Sidewalk cafes* abound in the Town Hall Square and Kongens Nytorv area. You will, of course, be making use of them. But I am not about to recommend any; they tend to be overpriced, and the service is frequently interminable and unsmiling. *Bargain beer:* the cheapest-priced brew (one crown) in Denmark, where beer is heavily taxed, is the Carlsberg in the dispensing machine of the basement canteen at the Carlsberg-affiliated Glyptoteket Museum.

TO WATCH

*The Royal Danish Ballet* is one of a handful of the world's great companies. Its dancers are trained in its own school, from childhood upward, in the tradition of the Russian and Continental ballet academies. Its best-known ballets are romantic, full-length works by the Dane August Bournonville. But the Royal Danes are wonderfully eclectic, performing works ranging from Balanchine's *Symphony in C* to their own young Flemming Flindt's very contemporary *Romeo and Juliet*. This company that knows style, technical proficiency, drama, and—when indicated—humor, has its home base in the lovely mid-nineteenth-century *Royal Theater* on the Kongens Nytorv. (The second stage of the Royal Theater, something from the 1930s, is quite possibly the ugliest structure ever constructed in Denmark; but if the performance is what you want to see, don't let the décor stop you.) The Royal Theater is also home to the *Royal Opera*—commendable, but with nothing like the rank of the ballet company. The first-rate *Danish State Radio Symphony's* concerts are invariably good bets. A good time to visit the city is in May, when the annual *Royal Danish Ballet and Musical Festival* takes place.

Danish *night life* has always been convivial, but of recent years it has become no-holds-barred. Pornography is legal, and although the Danes largely ignore the scene, it attracts the butter-and-egg men who can afford it. The best way to find out what's going on is through the amusement pages of some of the papers, or through one of the incredibly explicit sex manuals. There are any number of shops that sell not only these manuals but all kinds of related materials. One shop, called Porno, is on the

Frederiksberggade section of the Strøget. Another is Shop Bizarre, at Vesterbrogade 60. At either of these—and at many others—one can pick up such manuals as *Tourist Sex Guide* (". . . We welcome you to Copenhagen hoping that this guide will help you to get some funny experiences which are rich in memories.") or the *Sexionary Tourist Guide for the Sex-Life of Copenhagen* (". . . Today a new fairy-tale is being written, one which will make little Denmark even more famous than Hans Andersen was able to. The fairy-tale is about a country whose government have been planning so much ahead that they have given people the right to a free and uninhibited sex-life. . . . Have a good time!"). Aside from this literature—which contains the only ungrammatical English you are likely to come across in Denmark—the big attractions in the porno area are "shows" in "clubs" where the activity usually includes "advanced" strip-tease and porno movies. That at least is the general program for the great majority of clubs for the heterosexual customers; there are gay shows, as well. All of them are expensive (most Danes couldn't afford them if they wanted to); hotel concierges and the porno shops can provide specifics.

## TO BUY

The Danish pre-eminence in contemporary crafts can be attributed to a trio of circumstances. First, the craft tradition is honorable and ancient in Denmark. Living in a cold, damp clime is not, poets and contemporary legislation to the contrary, all love. It is day-to-day coping, and in the case of Denmark it has created a desire over the centuries for what the Danes call *hygge,* and what is best translated into English as coziness and comfort. The Danes are, as a consequence of this yearning, home-furnishings nuts. There are probably more furniture stores, per capita, in Copenhagen than in any other city. But it isn't only chairs and chests. It's a longtime tradition in textiles and silver and porcelain. And although no people are more modern-minded than the Danes, the role of the artisan is diminished less than one might imagine, even with today's mass-produced furniture and glass and china. This is still a land of weavers, potters, jewelers, turners, and joiners. So that the craft tradition is point No. 1 in the Danes' favor. Point No. 2 is the bourgeois, middle-class character that the country has assumed in this century. Almost every family has a home of its own or a comfortable, modern, capacious apartment, and what's more has the wherewithal to furnish it, so that the applied arts industries do not produce only for tourists and an export market. Point No. 3 is the Danish penchant—you might even call it genius—for promotion. No other people has had such phenomenal success in selling not only its country but its bacon, its ballet and, to get to the point of this section of this chapter, its applied arts.

The place not only to survey the scene, but to purchase as well, is the enterprise known as *Den Permanente,* or to translate, the Permanent Exhibition of Danish Arts and Crafts. It was conceived in 1931 by designer Kay Bojesen (you know his teak monkeys and elephants, but do you know his silver?) as an exhibition center for the best of the country's designers. Eventually, it came to sell as well as to exhibit. But it remains nonprofit—whatever profits are made are transferred to a reserve fund for investment in future activities of the organization. And it remains unique in that everything on sale is carefully selected by a committee of five of the designer members elected at the group's annual meeting. The late King Frederick IX, while Crown Prince, was Den Permanente's first patron; after he acceded to the throne his wife, Queen Ingrid—now the Queen Mother—succeeded him, and not only on paper but with considerable conscientiousness, enthusiasm, and expertise. Den Permanente occupies three floors in the Vesterport Building on Vesterbrogade, the wide thoroughfare on which the Central Railway Station also fronts; they are almost opposite each other. The beauty part of this place is that you find the old, classic greats of Danish design here, and you can be sure that each year's bright young hopefuls will be represented too. In furniture, for example, there will be specimens of the work of Hans Wegner, one of the great chair designers of our time; Arne Jacobsen (the earlier-mentioned designer-in-toto of the Royal Hotel); Finn Juhl; and Borge Mogensen. In silver, although one does not find the earlier work of the late Georg Jensen himself, there are contemporary Jensen designs, both in stainless and silver; there are the now-classic paper lampshades of Kaare Klint (himself a pioneer furniture designer). There are pottery, posters, inexpensive machine-made ceramics, and one-of-a-kind originals by Bjørn Wiinblad; textiles and jewelry, even paintings and sculpture. The gift department's wares range from kitchenware to offbeat games. And there is an inspired souvenir department, one of the first (and still, sadly, one of the very few) whose stock contains not a single solitary Cheapie Ugly; no matter how inexpensive, every bit of merchandise in the department is of the same high design standard as the expensive stuff. Additional note: Den Permanente ships reliably and expertly. Bigger, jazzier, splashier, and with considerable non-Danish wares among its huge stocks is the multi-floor Strøget store known as *Illums Bolighus* (not to be confused with the older Illums Department Store). Built about a rather overpowering atrium, with balconies ringing it, and—being profit-making commercial—without the standards of Den Permanente, the fact remains that it does stock a lot of first-rate merchandise, from kitchenware through furniture. *Georg Jensen* is a treasure trove of sumptuous silver. The flatware designs alone, created by Jensen himself (including the best-selling Acorn pattern, designed in 1915), by the late Count Sigvard Bernadotte of the Swedish Royal Family, and by such contemporary Danish luminaries as Henning Koppel and Søren Georg Jensen, make this store visit-worthy. (Prices are about half those in the United States.) But there are, as well, copious selections of hollow ware, silver jewelry, goldwork, and inexpensive stainless steel; a new addition is the smart Jensen Boutique, with clothes and accessories. *Royal Copenhagen* and *Bing & Grøndahl* have for long run neck-and-neck as Denmark's top two in china and porcelain. They are neck-and-neck as neighbors, as well, next door to each other on the Strøget. *Royal Copenhagen's* dinner-service classics are the Blue Fluted service—within financial reach of the reasonably affluent traveler; and the Flora Danica (an early set of which is, as earlier mentioned, on display at Rosenborg Palace, which only zillionaires can afford, but which everyone can look at). (Don't miss the little museum displaying the firm's special treasures—off the landing on your way upstairs.) There are cheaper services, in faience— a ceramiclike texture that is not as costly as porcelain. And if you go to the top floor you'll find yourself in a mob scene among the seconds—which are much cheaper. Not to be mentioned in the same breath is Royal Copenhagen's attempt at contemporary ceramics and stoneware; there's a separate department for it, and it is about the ugliest stuff purchasable in Scandinavia, has been for years, and probably will be for some time to come. And as for the porcelain figurines: *Chacun à son gout.* But no question: The ladies love 'em. The difference between Royal Copenhagen and *Bing & Grøndahl?* Not a great deal. Look at the latter as well as the former, and compare. B & G has done some interesting things in kitchenware—casseroles and the like. And while you're there, don't forget to pick up B & G's gratis map of Copenhagen, recommended in this chapter as the best available. The major department stores are super. *Magasin du Nord,* which dates from the time (along with the Hotel d'Angleterre) when the Danes liked to name things in French, occupies a pair of disparate structures. The original is a late-nineteenth-century Beaux Arts beauty fronting on the Kongens Nytorv, and the newer addition is a Danish Modern functional pile on the Strøget. An hour or two, going from floor to floor (home furnishings, furniture, housewares and a convenient cafeteria are all in the upper reaches) is time well spent. One might do likewise at *Illums,* more conservative perhaps than *Magasin,* but no less interesting, and with a Strøget main entrance, and an Elizabeth Arden beauty salon among its lures. The earlier-mentioned *Bjørn Wiinblad, enfant terrible* of post-World War II

Danish design, has opened a shop of his own at Ny Østergade 11, in which are to be found his charming posters; his droll, one-of-a-kind ceramics (they are very costly, even on home base); and a range of the other things he has turned his hand to in recent years. Happily, only the Danish stuff is present; the fussy, gilt-decorated china and doodads he took to designing for the German firm of Rosenthal (superb when they contain a minimum of vivid color, in the application of which he is not always discerning) in recent years, and for which he should be ashamed of himself, is happily absent. Danish glass and crystal, although never having achieved the worldwide reputation of that of Sweden, is hardly to be despised. Holmegaard, one of the top producers, sells its stuff at the *Kastrup Holmegaard* shop, 12 Nyhavn. The silver and the woodenware of *Kay Bojesen,* the pioneer silver designer I mentioned earlier in connection with the founding of Den Permanente, are on sale in the Bojesen shop at 47 Bredgarde. *Johannes Hansen* (Østergade 24-B) has what is probably the most complete selection of chains designed by Hans J. Wegner—No. 1 in his field. *Ekko Danmark,* an earlier-recommended restaurant operated by the Danish Agricultural Marketing Board, has a delicatessen in connection, which sells a variety of artfully packaged parcels of Danish food—cheese, ham, sausage, bacon, shrimp, pâté—and even the delicious dark Danish rye bread. They'll ship for you, guaranteeing freshness upon arrival. To get an idea of what Danish baking and pastry-making is all about, pop into the *Trianon Bakery* on the Strøget. They bake for the Royal Count; one sampling indicates why. *Pottemagerstuen,* at Graabrodretorv 1, is a pottery shop—expensive and with all kinds of stuff, some of it junk; you just might find a bargain or two. Which brings me to the importance of a square—the very same Graabrodretorv on which that shop is located. It is just off the Strøget (to the left as you go from the Town Hall Square to Kongens Nytorv, and about midway down the shopping street); it is, like the Strøget, a for-pedestrians-only thoroughfare, and it leads to another pedestrians-only thoroughfare, this one called Fiolstraede, one of the major *antiques shops* streets. The other antiques area comprises streets on the other side of the Strøget: Laederstraede, Kompagnistraede, and Hyskenstraede. Good shops in this area include *Countess Irene Laurvig,* Laederstraede 5-A (full of the unexpected, from old Flora Danica china to turn-of-century souvenirs ; *Erik Vejerslev,* Hyskenstraede 7 (particularly strong on eighteenth- and nineteenth-century crystal, glassware, and china; and *H. Danielsen,* Laederstraede 11 (gold, silver, and a good deal else). And to close: the *partially duty-free shopping area at Kastrup Airport,* in case you forgot Danish products—anything from cheese and ceramics to Aalborg Akvavit and Cherry Heering liqueur, not to mention the usual Scotches and gins, and tobacco—if you *still* haven't stopped smoking.

TO NOTE

**Access:** Copenhagen is the principal terminus for daily SAS flights from New York and other North American gateways; that airline is, of course, the national airline of Denmark and its fellow Scandinavian kingdoms, Norway and Sweden. There are Pan Am flights direct from the United States as well, and any number of other international airlines fly to handsome Kastrup Airport, finally equipped with moving sidewalks to complement two-wheel scooters, which are fun *if* you don't have too much hand baggage —and don't lose your balance! Kastrup is the destination of intra-European and intra-Scandinavian as well as transatlantic flights; SAS flies throughout the north country (its hop to Malmo, Sweden, just across The Sound from Copenhagen, is one of the shortest international flights on the planet) and the Continent, and almost any major European airline you can name has Copenhagen in its network. There are cheap airport buses from Kastrup to the central Air Terminal adjoining the Royal Hotel; taxis, though, are not overly expensive, since the distance is not all that great. Getting to Copenhagen by train is great fun. The nearest major continental points you might be coming from are Amsterdam or Hamburg, from which there are express trains that go north into the Jutland (or mainland) portion of Denmark and, with the aid of modern train- and car-carrying ferries, traverse the Danish islands of Funen and Zealand to Copenhagen, which lies at the eastern edge of Zealand (with Malmo, Sweden just across The Sound). Coming from Britain—another enjoyable route—one would go by train to the British North Sea port of Harwich, thence transfer to a Danish luxury liner for the overnight journey to the Danish port of Esbjerg, thence completing the journey eastward by Danish State Railways (and ferry) to the capital. There are also good rail-ship routings from both Stockholm and Oslo. Motorists would follow routes not dissimilar from those of the trains, utilizing the same ship transfers. *Within Copenhagen* there is modern public transport (no subway, but a good rapid-transit surface railway to the suburbs), as well as taxis (many of whose drivers are English-speaking) and self-drive cars (with or without drivers). If you are able to stay in a central Copenhagen hotel you'll be able to walk, most of the time. There are bus and boat tours of the city and environs, with a variable standard as regards the dispositions of conductors and starters; some can be unpleasant and patronizing. The Town Hall Square—in front of the Palace Hotel—is the starting point for the lot of them. **Climate:** Late spring through autumn are the nicest months. Spring is coolish and can be damp, but when the sun shines, no city is lovelier. Summer (June, July, and August) is mostly a high-sixties period, although there is the occasional heat wave when Copenhageners swelter in the seventies. May and October are fiftyish. November through March is cold weather (mostly in the thirties), although in January and February the mercury can drop to the crispy twenties. Copenhagen is quite the most southerly of the Scandinavian capitals, but even so the late spring through early autumn evenings are extra light, particularly in July and August. **Clothes:** Younger people dress quite as casually in Copenhagen as do their counterparts in New York, London, and Amsterdam. But Denmark is essentially a middle-class country where the tie and the jacket—after dark—are welcomed in better places. A raincoat is as requisite an article of clothing as it is in London, Dublin, Edinburgh, and Amsterdam. So is a collapsible umbrella. **Currency:** The krone, or crown (plural: kroner), divided into one hundred øre. **Tipping:** Restaurants and cafes add a tax and a 15 percent service charge, so that additional tipping is not necessary; the concierge in your hotel should be tipped upon departure if he has been of special help, and bellhops expect about a kroner and a half per bag, as do luggage porters in the terminals. Tip taxi drivers about 15 percent—no more. **Business hours:** Shops are usually open without lunch-hour closing, from 9:00 A.M. to 5:30 P.M., Monday through Thursday; on Friday many stay open until 7:00 or 8:00 P.M., but on Saturday they close at 1:00 or 2:00 P.M. **Language:** Danish is a Scandinavian tongue, closer to Norwegian than Swedish, with its own distinctive pronunciation. (Danish can sound to its detractors like gargling; I happen to like the sound of the language.) The Danes are quite as remarkable as the Dutch and Norwegians when it comes to speaking English. Virtually every Dane, from the age of, say, five upward, is astonishingly bilingual in English. **Local literature:** The hotels all carry the giveaway called *This Week in Copenhagen.* The best map I have been able to find is a little gem published as a giveaway by *Bing & Grøndahl* (the porcelain firm at 4 Amagertorv, Copenhagen). There are picture albums and books in English about the capital, in the shops. **Further information:** Danish National Tourist Office, Scandinavia House, 505 Fifth Avenue, New York; Scandinavian National Tourist Offices, 612 South Flower Street, Los Angeles; Danish Tourist Board, Banegardspladsen 7, Copenhagen V, Denmark.

# Dublin

In no European capital is one more immediately and wholly enveloped in the life style of the people—and the complex, bitter-sweet heritage that is theirs—than in Dublin. It is a transformation that occurs almost as you alight from the plane. Before you have your directional bearings you have already had several conversations with locals. Mundane or profound subjects, or whatever. That is all it has taken to immerse you.

It is not the same in London, or in Edinburgh, or in Brussels or Madrid, for that matter. I wonder each time I return why it is like it is. The American connection has a lot to do with it. Both Americans and Irish are former colonials of the English, and many Americans are of Irish origin. It is the accent; we Americans are suckers for it. It is the humor; the Irish personality has had such a strong influence on the American that the senses of humor of no two countries are more similar. And it is the drama—melodrama, if you will—of all that Ireland has endured for so many centuries. You have only to pass the post office on O'Connell Street—the site of the fateful 1916 Easter uprising that led to sovereignty—to realize that Dublin's story is Ireland's story.

**Melodrama of the centuries:** There is little that has happened in Ireland that the capital has been spared. It may not have been smack in the heart of things when the populace was composed of those oddly named Picts, but then came the Gaelic-speaking, red-haired Celts and the provinces whose names are still used, like Leinster and Munster and Connacht—all under the overlord who lived at Tara, which was very close to the present Dublin. St. Patrick introduced Christianity in the fifth century, and Ireland's Golden Age followed. For three hundred years—from the sixth through the ninth centuries—Irish monks, operating from a network of universitylike monasteries, roamed England and the continent, not so much as preachers but as teachers of the Latin and Gaelic cultures. It is only because the period following the Golden Age was so violent and destructive that many of the still-standing monasteries are roofless. Even so, there remain illuminated manuscripts (the Book of Kells in Trinity College's Library is the most celebrated) and religious objects in finely worked gold (one has only to look through the National Museum) and stone crosses and ruined churches that bear witness to this period of greatness that was especially remarkable, given the geographical isolation of this island.

**Golden Age to Troubles:** The end of the Golden Age was virtually the beginning of the Troubles. These started with the invading Normans in the eighth century. Those that had not been assimilated were driven out by the tenth century. In the twelfth, the Pope awarded Ireland, as a papal fief, to the King of England, and although there was Irish authority in this region or in that, the English gradually tightened their control, in time for no less a monarch than Henry VIII to bring the whole island under his rule, the while anglicizing the chieftains. Henry's wives had no more reason to be unhappy with him than the Irish. From his time onward, over a period of some four centuries, England exploited Ireland shamelessly and mercilessly. Subject peoples in the most remote corners of the British Empire could not have known a harsher, more exacting master than did the people of the green island just across the Irish Sea from England. The Irish were not slow to react. They rebelled on three occasions during the reign of Elizabeth I. Elizabeth followed with an action that has had repercussions to this day: Her government planted a community of Scottish Protestants in the Irish Province of Ulster.

But it was not only British sovereigns who took out their frustrations on the Irish; Cromwell did likewise, massacring the unruly, and continuing his predecessors' policy of the confiscation of land and the institution of the vicious absentee-landlord system that reached a peak of ugliness in the mid-nineteenth century, when impoverished tenants were evicted from their farms if they could not pay rent. When the potato blight struck at that time, Ireland had a population of 8½ million. Within half a decade, a million Irishmen had died of starvation, and within the next half decade, more than 1½ million emigrated, mostly to the United States. (Economic conditions, until recently, have been such that the emigration movement has never stopped; the population of the republic in 1971 was only 2.9 million.) The famine was followed by militant political action. There were rebellions in 1848 and 1867. In 1870, the brilliant Parnell was successful in popularizing the Home Rule movement, to end the Act of Union under which, since 1800, the kingdoms of England and Ireland had been united, to the great detriment of Ireland.

**Home Rule, independence and unimpaired wit:** The years leading up to the turn of the century saw enactment of Land Acts that led at long last to ownership of their land by the tenants. Home Rule was enacted at the same time World War I erupted, but its operation was suspended. Two years later, in 1916, saw the Easter Week rising that resulted in the proclamation of the Irish Republic. But before the republic actually came into being there was a period of armed resistance to continued British rule, and a civil war within Ireland over the terms of the Anglo-Irish Independence Treaty. In 1937 Ireland adopted a new constitution. It remained neutral during World War II, although many Irish volunteered to fight with British forces. Finally, in 1949, the Republic of Ireland, as we know it today, came into being, unaffiliated with the British Commonwealth, but 'ere long a valued member of the United Nations and on an equal footing with Britain for the first time in the centu-

ries-long period of their association. Withal, the country retained
its distinctive culture (is it any wonder that the government makes
an effort to sustain the Irish language?), the while producing great
writers out of all proportion to its size (Swift, Goldsmith, Sheridan,
Wilde, Shaw, Yeats, O'Casey, Joyce, Behan—to name some).
Ireland was practical-minded enough to realize, upon achieving
sovereignty, that political freedom was not enough, and it mobilized
sufficient drive and proficiency to confound the world in the post-
World War II years, with its conversion from an essentially agricultural economy to an essentially industrial one, with tourism
—skillfully promoted—emerging as a major industry. Through it
all the Irish wit, and sheer genius at conversation, have come
through unimpaired. It is as though every Irishman instinctively
realizes that without these, what with all that has gone before,
there would be no Ireland today.

### TO SEE

**Lay of the land:** Dublin is not a big city, but there is more
here than meets the eye. The name to begin with, or rather the
two names. Dublin comes from the Irish *Dubhlinn,* meaning black
pool, a not particularly attractive bit of imagery. But what your
friends will see on the postmark of the cards you mail home will
be the currently official Irish designation, *Baile Atha Cliath*—
a name older than Dublin, and translating as "town of the Hurdle
Ford," descriptive, perhaps, of the ancient settlement that was but a
ford on the Liffey River. Since that time there has been considerable action in this now peaceful, albeit lively metropolis of half a
million. Vikings held the town in the tenth century; the English
routed them in the twelfth, when King Henry II himself crossed
the Irish Sea to hold court in Dublin, which for a period was the
center of the English government. In the following century, the
Black Monday massacres of English residents was a highlight.
Cromwell personally commanded the landing of his Republican

troops during 1649, and four decades later the dethroned Catholic, James II, came to Dublin to hold his final Parliament. His Protestant successor, the Dutch-born William III—ruling with his English wife, Mary—took Ireland, including Dublin, as a result of the apparently everlastingly consequential Battle of the Boyne the following year. William and Mary continued the policies James I and Cromwell had followed, of "plantation"—whereby Irish land was confiscated and awarded to absentee English landlords. At the same time their legislation effectively deprived Catholics of civil rights and discriminated against them economically.

The eighteenth century, anti-Irish policies notwithstanding, saw Dublin become the No. 2 city of the British Isles, under the aegis of a splendid Viceregal Court in Dublin Castle, and with an affluent English and Anglo-Irish gentry creating a Georgian-design city of extraordinary beauty. The nineteenth century and, indeed, several decades of the present century, were times of struggle in the Irish capital, and frequently of violence—the insurrection of Robert Emmet in 1803, the Fenian uprising in 1867, the Post Office uprising of Easter 1916 that led to the guerrilla war against the English Black and Tans. The destruction of those years has long since been repaired. More recently, though, the city has been confronted with a threat common to many cities in many countries. The bulldozers of public-be-damned builders have had some success in razing irreplaceable monuments of the city's architectural greatness. The Desmond Guinness-led Irish Georgian Society is fighting them, but no one can yet predict the ultimate winner. It behooves the interested and concerned visitor not only to see Dublin while the seeing is to be had, but to support the Irish Georgian Society (address: Merrion Square, Dublin, Ireland).

**Orienting yourself:** Central Dublin is easy to get about. *O'Connell Street,* much-photographed at the point where it approaches the *Liffey River* and the *O'Connell Bridge,* is as good a starting point as any. O'Connell Street extends all the way to *Parnell Street,* with Parnell Square's eighteenth-century Rotunda Hospital

and the Municipal Gallery of Modern Art just beyond. Return
now to the O'Connell Bridge and cross the Liffey. The part of
town you enter is the area of the better shops, most, but not all
of the better hotels, the government, most museums, and some of
the finest Georgian houses. Once over the bridge, you have left
O'Connell Street; it becomes *Westmoreland Street.* Take it to the
first major intersection—to one of the architecturally great in-
tersections of all Europe, for that matter. You will see the entrance
to Trinity College on your right, and the old Irish Parliament—
now the Bank of Ireland—to your left, along with a thoroughfare
named *Dame Street.* Dame Street is worth remembering because
it leads to Dublin Castle, with the two Church of Ireland cathedrals, Christ Church and St. Patrick's, not far distant. Return
now, though, to Westmoreland Street, continue walking it, and
you will find that it has taken its third (and last) name: *Grafton
Street.* Streets like *Nassau, Duke,* and *Anne* lead left from shop-
lined Grafton into the interesting *Government-Museums-Georgian
houses-boutiques area.* Continue down Grafton, though, and you
bump right into *St. Stephen's Green.* There are few lovelier small
parks on the planet. University College lies down the hill from
the far side of the green. It is a modern, Catholic-oriented university, whereas the famous and venerable Trinity College is
essentially Protestant.

**Choice destinations:** Lest you get bogged down in the inspection of the interiors of public buildings, I suggest that you amble
about first for a look at the façade of residential *Georgian
Dublin.* Ulick O'Connor, in his short but delightful history, *The
Gresham Hotel 1865–1965,* describes the Georgian house: "The
façade would have been austere. The effect is achieved by elegant
proportion of window and door and the great height of the
houses: yet not so high as to dominate the thoroughfare below,
but built in delicious congruity with it. The Georgian architects
knew the value of light and air. They built wide streets and bent
stone until it accommodated the clouds." Georgian houses, great
and small, are scattered all about the extensive older parts of the

city. One sees them in the little streets off Grafton and Nassau and in the St. Stephen's Green area. *Merrion Square,* though now without the fine British Embassy that was tragically burned in early 1972 as a protest against the British killings of thirteen Northern Irish Catholics, still has some exemplary brick houses whose interior stuccowork is typical of Dublin Georgian; it was designed in 1762. *Mount Lovejoy Square,* though newer (it dates to 1818), has been allowed to deteriorate over the years, but is the focal point of the Irish Georgian Society's preservation fight. The house at No. 47 has been restored and is open to visitors, and No. 50 is the society's Dublin headquarters. *Henrietta Street* (leading to the King's Inns) is lined with big Georgian houses. Though generally not open to the public, there are some fine nonresidential Georgian buildings of interest, including the law courts building called the *King's Inns* (a word or two with the porter might result in an informal tour); the riverside *Custom House*—an enormous and everywhere-viewable Dublin landmark from without and eminently inspectable within; the *Four Courts,* also on the Liffey, designed by the same James Gandon who was architect of the Custom House, and with a central dome from which the quartet of High Courts radiate; the *Bank of Ireland,* the onetime Irish Parliament that is a globally celebrated masterwork dating to 1729, with the original House of Lords (now the Board Room) the room to beg admittance to; and two hospitals—the eighteenth-century *King's Hospital* (known also as the *Blue Coat School*) and the pre-Georgian, seventeenth-century *Royal Hospital,* whose main hall and chapel are exceptional, and whose neighbor is the historic, recently restored *Kilmainham Jail.* A bit of a drive from the center is a little treasure of a mid-eighteenth-century structure that was designed as a pleasure pavilion for one Lord Charlemont. It has the not easily forgettable name *Casino Marino,* resembles nothing so much as a little Greco-Roman temple (Romans were imported to construct it), and is full of architectural surprises. To get in, you must go first to the religious institution known as the O'Brien Institute and ask for the priest with the key to the casino, which is on the Institute grounds. Let yourself in with the key (it appears to be the original), remembering, of course, to return it to the priest. *Marsh's Library* has such relatively limited open-hours that I mention it at this point. It is so much more than the oldest library in Ireland. It is a wonderful oddball of a place, what with stalls—still seen if not still used—in which the librarian locked you up while you read the books you had borrowed. The books are all quite as old as the beautiful structure itself, and it goes back to 1707; the volumes are on subjects ranging from Hebrew and Greek to medicine and theology. To get in when the gate and front door are locked, hop over to nearby St. Patrick's Cathedral and look up one of the clergy on duty, or the verger, asking if you might borrow the key. As at Casino Marino, don't forget to return it; it's an antique. *Mansion House,* not open to the visitor, is a somewhat showy but nonetheless elegant Queen Anne house—white, with black trim—that is the official residence of Dublin's lord mayors.

**Dublin basics:** *Dublin Castle* is originally thirteenth-century, but as seen today is a hodgepodge of periods and styles surrounding a central court. There is a Heraldic Museum, and there is a neo-Gothic onetime Protestant chapel in which the resident lords lieutenant of Ireland worshiped; it is now a Catholic church. But what you want to see are the late-eighteenth-/early-nineteenth-century *State Apartments,* recently restored and refurbished, and used by the Irish government for official receptions. One glance and you have an idea of how opulently the Crown's representatives lived. The Throne Room—all white and gold and high-ceilinged—is out of a fairy tale. There is the delicate oval Wedgwood Room, the oblong Victorian Drawing Room, and the smasher of the lot, St. Patrick's Hall—royal-blue carpeted, with gilded Corinthian columns supporting a brilliant frescoed ceiling. Dublin's *City Hall,* a fine eighteenth-century domed structure, (originally the Royal Exchange) is the castle's next-door neighbor.

It contains, besides municipal offices, a collection of a hundred-odd royal charters and the traditional regalia of the city—a sword and mace. *Trinity College Dublin* was established by no less august a sovereign than Queen Elizabeth I. What one sees today, though, is mostly eighteenth-century, with some nineteenth- and twentieth- added for spice. It is the older buildings, surrounding a series of fine quadrangles, that are the best. These include a chapel, theater, dining hall, museum, and the justifiably famed old (1712) library, with its collection of several thousand illuminated manuscripts, including the medieval Irish *Book of Kells.* The old library is entered through a somewhat incongruous but nonetheless handsome new library, whose entrance is some distance through the quadrangles from the main college entrance. The two chambers of Parliament (*Dáil,* the lower, and *Seanad,* the upper) meet in *Leinster House,* a mid-eighteenth-century mansion that had been the home of the Dukes of Leinster; open to visitors when not in session.

**Churches:** Until 1869, when Prime Minister Gladstone was successful in having legislation enacted in London that "disestablished" the Church of Ireland (which is the Anglican, or Protestant Episcopal Church), it was supported by tithes of the Irish people. That explains in part how a city with a small minority of Anglicans like Dublin could afford two Anglican cathedrals. The elder of the two, *Christ Church Cathedral,* dates to 1172, and is the Church of Ireland cathedral for the Diocese of Dublin and Glendalough. *St. Patrick's* is the Church of Ireland's national cathedral. Its oldest portions are twelfth-century, but there are thirteenth- and fourteenth-century additions. In the early eighteenth century, satirist Jonathan Swift was the cathedral's dean; he is buried there. Unlike the Anglicans, the majority of Catholics were unable to build anything like a cathedral until the early nineteenth century, when the *Pro-Cathedral of St. Mary* went up. It is a modest, neoclassic structure, lacking the good looks that buildings of this style often achieve. Seventeenth-century *St. Mary's Church*—O'Casey was baptized here—is far handsomer. *St. Audeon's Church* (Church of Ireland) is the city's only medieval parish church; there's a twelfth-century door, and bells that are more than six hundred years old, while the arch next to the church is all that remains of the original town walls.

Of the **museums,** the *National Gallery* is the leader. When appointed in 1964, Director James White took a near-moribund institution dating from 1864 and brightened and refurbished it masterfully, adding additional gallery space in several extensions and rehanging the collection with imagination and verve. There is now a refreshing sense of style, and many superior paintings among the collection of six thousand—Fra Angelico, Michelangelo, Rubens, Rembrandt. Actually all the major European schools are represented, from the fourteenth century onward, and there is an excellent Irish section. The *National Museum* is another treat, particularly its Antiquities section. There is a display of medieval Irish goldwork that is an absolute dazzler. The *Chester Beatty Library* is a recent addition to the Dublin exhibition scene. It contains the priceless books and manuscripts —the Oriental ones are the most special—of a rich American who left his collections and the library to the Irish nation; the lot constitutes a major Dublin surprise package. The *Municipal Gallery of Modern Art* occupies eighteenth-century *Charlemont House,* on Parnell Square. There are worthy Irish and continental works. The *Civic Museum* is another Georgian building, this with an octagonal main hall that had been the city council chamber. The subject matter is Dubliniana.

If you make but one excursion out of Dublin, the destination should be *Castletown House,* County Kildare—the finest Georgian country house in Ireland. It was built in 1722 to designs by Alessandro Galilei, an Italian whose work you have seen if you know the façade of St. John Lateran Church in Rome. Galilei designed this house for William Connolly, who was the speaker of the Irish House of Commons, in Palladian—the style inspired by the classic buildings of Rome and Greece. Over the years, Castletown, like a number of fine country houses in Ireland, had sadly deteriorated. Some years ago, the Irish Georgian Society began to restore it. (The society's headquarters are in the house.) It was a slow, room-by-room process, undertaken only as funds were available. It has been completed—grounds and all—and it is a place of especial beauty.

TO WATCH

*The Abbey Theatre,* the National Theatre of Ireland, has a well-deserved global reputation. Its gifted repertory company mostly—but not entirely—presents works of noted Irish playwrights like O'Casey, Synge, and Behan. There are times when the law specifies that they must be presented in the Irish language, but most of the time they are acted in English. The only sad note in the Abbey scene is the theater itself—an appallingly nondescript contemporary structure that has all of the importance of a neighborhood cinema. The *Dublin Focus Theatre,* on Pembroke Place off Pembroke Street, is a remarkable institution in still-conservative Ireland. (The Catholic hierarchy-influenced government still censors books, plays, and the like, and bans imports of titles it doesn't like; you can't, for example, buy any of the novels of a fine contemporary Irish writer like Edna O'Brien.) At any rate, the Focus is avant-garde and experimental; more power to it! *The Gate* is the home of the usually first-rate Michael MacLiammoir productions of noted plays—Wilde, Shakespeare, and the like. The *Olympia* is another legit house. The *Gaiety* packs 'em in with variety, or what we used to call vaudeville in the United States. Dubliners adore *movies;* downtown has a number of big houses.

## TO STAY

There's no capital in Europe with finer service in its hotels
than Dublin. They're darlins, that's what they are. All Irish, for
one thing. Dublin is unlike other capitals with full employment,
where foreign labor has to be imported for hotel and restaurant
jobs. The economics of Irish life are such that the Irish themselves want the available jobs. And they are, traditionally, very
nice to people. They seem pleased to see you. They smile.
They say "Please" and "Thank you," and they make pleasantries
about the weather, and would you know their relatives in Utica?
Moreover, managements of the better Dublin hotels are professional and competent. Things usually work. (This is not always
the case in the provinces, where the people are quite as kind, if
not as efficient.) What I like about the *Royal Hibernian
Hotel* is its location, on Dawson Street, in the heart of the most
attractive and convenient part of town. I like its great age as
well. (How many hotels, even in England, can say that George
IV was among their guests?) The modern top-floor addition
almost but not completely spoils the Georgian façade. Maintenance is not in every instance quite all that it might be. But
within, enjoy the public rooms (afternoon tea or a drink in
the Royal Hibernian lounge is always a treat), bedrooms are
comfortable, and the atmosphere is relaxing. There are a number
of restaurants and bars, including one of the former that is among
the very best in northern Europe. The *Gresham Hotel* is way
at the foot of O'Connell Street, near Parnell Square, in a part
of town that is no longer the center of things. But it is, in every
other respect, exceptional. It was founded in 1817 and is now
in its third home; its second—on the same site—was destroyed
during the Anglo-Irish war in 1922. The present building is a
near-copy of that Georgian structure. The period-style rooms are
quite the most tasteful in town; the suites even more so. The

restaurants and bars are among the best, and the management is first-rate. The elderly *Shelbourne,* on St. Stephen's Green, is the very same that novelist Elizabeth Bowen wrote an entire book about. Its public rooms have been drastically remodeled since that time, in a not entirely felicitous contemporary style. But Trust Houses-Forte now runs the place, and runs it very well indeed; they have updated many of the bedrooms, adding quantities of private baths. The old-fashioned Horseshoe Bar is about the nicest drinking parlor in town, and the restaurants are very good. *Buswell's Hotel,* on Molesworth Street near the Parliament, is a century-old period piece, modernized but still with the ambience of Old Dublin. Bedrooms are spotless and comfortable (many have bath), there are a pair of spacious, attractive lounges, and there's a good restaurant; a charmer. The smallish *Russell Hotel* is a longtime occupant of St. Stephen's Green. It is under the management of the same competent Kingsley-Windsor group that runs the Royal Hibernian. The restaurant is renowned. The little drinks-lounge is pleasant, but the look of the place is so Plain-Jane-understated as to be almost drab. Well-located *Jury's Hotel,* where I stayed on my first Dublin visit a couple of decades ago, was at that time no more than a not-very-well-run second-class house that had seen better days. But in the last decade it has been thoroughly refurbished, smartly redecorated, and reborn as an absolutely first-class hotel, with good management, agreeable rooms (many with bath), and a full range of quality restaurants and bars. The *Moira Hotel* on Trinity Street is a hop and a skip from Jury's, and under the same management, although smaller and a mite less luxe. But, like its sister hotel, it has been cleverly updated. Rooms (many with bath), public rooms, restaurant—all are attractive. The big (314-room) modern *Dublin Inter•Continental* is such a friendly, well-managed place that I wish it were central, so that I could have put it up at the head of this section with the down-town leaders. It is in the Ballsbridge section (near the also modern, circular-shape American Embassy). The bright, spacious rooms all have baths, the locals enjoy the restaurants and bars (a sure sign that they're good), and the service is of the high caliber I've enjoyed in Inter•Continental hotels around the world.

## TO EAT (AND DRINK)

There is good food to be had in Dublin, particularly in the leading hotels. Fare in better places is French-style—which is nothing new in Dublin; there has long been a tradition of Gallic cookery in this capital. Irish food is similar to the English, with Irish variations. Irish soda bread, for example, is distinguished, Irish, and delicious; so is the whole wheat bread. The local shrimp—big ones called Dublin Bay prawns—are excellent, as are the oysters. The smoked salmon is on a level with that of Scotland—very high indeed; trout and sole are likewise. The Irish are big meat eaters; their beef is good, and so is their mutton and lamb (they do not care much for veal, and as a result have little of it). All the pork products are special, bacon and Limerick ham in particular. Game birds like grouse and pheasant are well prepared. And don't forget Irish stew! Although Irishmen have been making Irish whisky for half a millennium, it has never caught on as well as it might in the United States, despite occasional promotional spurts from the Irish distillers. It is an excellent drink, one that deserves to be given a chance on home territory by even the most avid Scotch drinkers; there are four major brands, all good: Powers, Jameson, Paddy, Bushmills. Guinness stout is an Irish beverage, which you may or may not like, but you owe it to yourself to try it. Beers—Harp and other brands—are similar to those of England. And the liqueur made with an Irish whisky base—Irish Mist—is an after-dinner delight. *Licensing hours:* On weekdays they are 10:30 A.M. to 11:00 P.M. in the winter; 10:30 A.M. to 11:30 P.M. on weekdays in the summer. For some odd reason the wicked cities of Dublin and Cork—but not the rest of the country—must observe a dry hour—from 2:30 to 3:30 P.M. each day. Sunday hours are from 12:30 P.M. to 2:00 P.M. and from 4:00 P.M. to 10:00 P.M.

If I am asked by a short-term visitor to recommend a restaurant for the one evening he has available, it is the *Lafayette Restaurant* of the *Royal Hibernian Hotel*. Occupying a trio of formally styled rooms, this is among the best to be found in northern Europe. The menu is classic French. You will not find a finer trolley of *hors d'oeuvres* in Paris. And so it goes with every category—fish, meats, vegetables (especially), and sweets. There is a good wine list, and the service is skilled and professional. The other Royal Hibernian restaurants are good too. The *Rotisserie* specializes in grills, both meat and fish, and features several spit-roasted specialties. The *Bianconi* is an attractive coffee shop. And there's a congenial basement cocktail lounge, as well as main lobby-lounge for drinks or delicious afternoon teas. The Russell Restaurant has long been the most universally respected in Dublin. It is, to be sure, authentically French, but I don't think, if my most recent dinner is any example, that it is as good as it used to be. The service was far from exceptional, but what is more important, neither was the food. And without these, there seems little point to undertake an expensive meal in such an unattractive dining room. The *Shelbourne's* animated *Saddle Room* is a super spot for grills—both meat and fish—and roast beef any way you like it. That same hotel's main restaurant, while not as good-looking, offers well-prepared Continental-Irish dishes from an extensive menu; good cellar, too. There is also a convenient grill/coffee shop with both counter and table service, and the earlier-recommended Horseshoe Bar. The *Gresham's* most recent restaurant is the smartly got-up *Hunting Lodge Grill* in the basement—spit-roasted specialties, good steaks, and a select group of popular "hot-pots" —including an Irish stew that I suspect is unsurpassed in Ireland. The traditional-décor, traditional-menu main restaurant is excellent, and there is also a honey of a sleek-lined coffee shop called *Tain* but pronounced *than*. The Inter•Continental's *Martello Roof* is popular with local couples who like to dance with their dinner; the *Dubliner Bar-Lounge* in that same hotel is another good place to meet Dubliners. *Jury's Copper Grill* in the basement is one of the best-looking eating places in town; fondue Bourguignonne and roast duck are among the specialties; the menu is an Irish-continental mix. That same hotel's *Antique Bar* is precisely that—and wondrous to behold. There are some amusing pubs that are ideal for lunch. *Neary's Chatham House Pub,* on Chatham Street, is one of the best; there are upstairs and downstairs dining rooms, a long, busy bar, and youngish, sophisticated customers, as well as the wonderful old-timers that make an Irish pub an Irish pub; try shrimp salad or cold salmon. The *Restaurant of the National Gallery,* a relatively recent addition, is a wise luncheon choice. *Bewley's* is a venerable, ever-popular place but still good; drop in for coffee or tea, with a piece of their own cake or pastry. *Brown, Thomas Department Store's* second-floor *Tea Room* overlooks Grafton Street and is pleasant. *Switzer's Department Store* has a good restaurant on the first (up one flight, for us) floor, and a quick-service cafe as well. *The Long Hall,* Great George's Street, is a late-nineteenth-century pub that is the most sumptuously embellished in town—mahogany, cut glass, gilding, the works—and a gang of chatterboxy locals all enjoying drinks and TV. *Mulligan's,* on Poolbet Street, is another good pub choice, drawing a heavily journalistic crowd convinced that its trio of barmen—each of them a partner-owner—serve up the "best pint of stout in Ireland."

## TO BUY

Dublin is a very agreeable place to shop, or even to browse. The stores—big ones and boutiques—are inviting, and the salespeople are nice to talk to and are so *polite*. To look for are Irish hand-woven tweeds—by the yard or made up into men's and women's clothing; those thick, off-white, handwoven Aran-style sweaters, again for both men and women; that exquisitely handblown, hand-cut Waterford crystal—glassware, decanters, bowls, even chandeliers; Arklow and Belleek china and pottery, and other ceramics, too; and the good Irish whisky (this last from the duty-free shop at Shannon Airport). And an especially good buy in Dublin are antiques. What I suggest first, though, is a look around in both of the leading department stores, *Brown, Thomas* (the smarter of the two), and *Switzer's*. Neither of them is as large as the London, Paris, or Copenhagen department stores, so that getting about doesn't take long. Both are good on Irish clothes and tweeds (both men's and women's); Irish linens (from tablecloths to handkerchiefs, china, and crystal, as well as the usual other departments); and both pack, ship, and accept credit cards. *Noirin Kennedy's The Weavers Shed,* at 9 Duke Lane, is a tiny place with beautiful things—all of them woven. *Cleo,* at 3 Molesworth Street, has one of the most stylish selections of knitwear in town—Aran-type sweaters, stoles, skirts, and the like. *Creation Boutique,* on Duke Street just off Grafton Street, is where I bought an Aran-type sweater years ago; it has worn beautifully; both men's and women's, each in a number of styles. *Market Ireland,* 75 Grafton Street, has well-designed ceramics, handmade jewelry, contemporary crystal, and textiles, too. *Fergus O'Farrell,* 24 Duke Street, has some interesting Irish crafts. *The China Showrooms,* 81 Grafton Street, has what surely must be the biggest selection of Waterford Crystal anywhere, with the possible exception of the factory in Waterford. They carry—according to my count—at least fifty-two shapes of glasses alone; packing, shipping. *Irish haute couture* designers have retail shops. If I were you, I would go to *Sybil Connolly,* 71 Merrion Square, if only to see her splendid Georgian house, not to mention the clothes. See also *Vera Hennessy,* 17a South Anne Street, and *Irene Gilbert,* 117 St. Stephen's Green. *Richard Alan,* 59 Grafton Street, is a shop selling Irish (including Donald Davies) and imported women's clothes. *Louis Wine, Ltd.,* 31–32

Grafton Street, has been an antiques shop since 1840. New York-born Mrs. Wine, the current owner, takes time with clients, even notifying them by mail if things that might interest them come into stock. Wine's has what is one of the largest collections of antique silver in Europe or America, and one of the best concentrations extant of sterling, from early seventeenth- to early nineteenth-century. The silver is mostly Irish, but there is English and French as well; although, of course, Irish is rarer, and of excellent workmanship. Irish furniture is much scarcer than Irish silver—a pity, because Irish versions of English styles often tend to be vigorous and striking. Other good antiques dealers include *Gerald Kenyon,* 37/37 South William Street; *Georgian Shop,* South Anne Street; *Dandelion Green*—a series of dealers' showrooms all under one roof, across from St. Stephen's Green; and *Orken Brothers,* away from the center of town, at 28A Upper Ormond Quay, a huge, messy warehouse, with occasional treasures to be found among masses of junk; for the knowledgeable shopper interested in digging up silver, porcelain, paintings, furniture, glassware, or metalwork—and who is competent at bargaining.

### TO NOTE

**Access:** There are nonstop transatlantic flights via Irish International-Aer Lingus, TWA, and Pan Am, usually via Shannon International Airport, west of Dublin, with Dublin's own airport the second stop. The idea behind all this is to get you to explore the Ireland beyond Dublin before reaching the capital. Coming from Britain, you have your choice of air (Aer Lingus, BEA) from London, Edinburgh, Manchester, and other points; or ship, from Holyhead on the Welsh coast to Dun Laoghaire, the port of Dublin. Continental connections are best made by air; Aer Lingus flies to many points and a number of continental airlines reciprocate, with services to Dublin. Getting about, in town, is either by modern buses (they're painted green, of course), metered taxis, or on one's feet, this last the most enjoyable. There are good local sightseeing tours, and others, excellently and most reasonably conducted by CIE, the national transport firm, take one by bus and/or train to points throughout the republic. **Climate:** It's rarely too cold, and seldom heat-wavey. Winter (November through March) averages in the low forties. Spring is fiftyish and can be delightful. Summer comprises June, July, August, and some of September—months that average in the high fifties, going into the sixties; seventy is a scorcher. And autumn is nippy. Keep your collapsible umbrella and raincoat with you, as you would in Edinburgh and London, and you'll be prepared for whatever moisture develops. Not that there are not a fair share of glorious sunny days. **Currency:** the Irish pound, at par with Britain's, is divided into 100 pence, written "p". There ½p, 1p, 2p, 5p, 10p, and 50p coins; there are £1, £5, and £10 notes, as in the past. And you are still likely to come across coins of the old currency. A shilling is the equal of 5p, and the coins are the same size; a florin—the two-shilling coin—equals 10p, and the 50p coin is equal to the old ten-shilling note. If you are a newcomer to Ireland, the recent decimal system will seem a lark; if you've been going to Ireland for some time, though, it takes getting used to, as the locals will assure you. **Tipping:** Hotels add a service charge to the bill; still, bellhops expect about 10p a bag; and hall porters expect a gratuity—but only if they have performed a special service for you. Give chambermaids 10p a day, if it's a nice job they've done for you. If service is not added to restaurant bills, tip 15 percent, and bring it up to that if the service charge is less. Tip taxi drivers 15 percent. **Business hours:** Stores are usually open from 9:00 or 9:30 A.M. to about 5:30 P.M., with no lunch-hour closings, no late evenings, and the inconvenience of midday (usually 1 P.M.) shutdowns on Saturday. **Language:** There are two official languages, Irish being No. 1. Irish is Ireland's own variation of the Gaelic of the Scots, the Welsh of Wales, and the

Breton of Brittany. Lots more Irish spoke it than now, until the
middle of the last century, when it began to fade except in more
remote areas. Learned societies such as the Gaelic League and
nationalist groups began reviving it at the turn of the century.
It has been taught in the schools—compulsorily—since the early
twenties, and civil servants are required by law to know it. The
government and all those Irishmen who have been working hard
over the years to preserve this beautiful and ancient tongue deserve our thanks (Irish even has its own handsome alphabet;
you'll see it on the bilingual street signs). But we are, heaven
knows, indebted to them also for retaining English as the No. 2
official language; else how would we communicate with our
Irish friends, and—this is not to be underestimated—vice versa?
**Local literature:** The *Irish Times* is the leading paper, but there
are, of course, a number of others; there are many magazines,
and the shops are full of books about the country and its
capital. **Further information:** Irish Tourist Board (*Bord Failte*
—if you would like it in Irish), 590 Fifth Avenue, New York;
135 South LaSalle Street, Chicago; 681 Market Street, San Francisco; 7 King Street East, Toronto, with headquarters in Dublin;
Dublin Tourist Information Bureau, 14 Upper O'Connell Street,
Dublin, Ireland.

# *Edinburgh*

It does not seem probable, let alone possible at this point in time, with the twenty-first century approaching. But here is a European capital that is in part a medieval town beneath a castle on a crag—and an exquisite Georgian town lies right alongside it. Edinburgh has never been ordinary, neither architecturally, nor geographically, nor historically.

Glasgow overpowers it today, in size and economic importance, and in no way can it compete with the global pre-eminence of London, in that portion of the realm lying south of the Tweed. Still, Edinburgh is a proud city: proud of its past—bloody and turbulent though much of it has been; proud of beauty so striking that not even rain or mist diminish it; proud of the stubbornness with which it holds onto the gray stone monuments of its history, in an era when plastic dominates.

I first realized how strong is the sense of history of these people when, some years back, I found myself in a town on the South Island of distant New Zealand. Its first inhabitants, colonists come out from Scotland, named it Dunedin—"fortress on a ridge." This was the name Edinburgh's first inhabitants gave their settlement, only to have the ancient Angles take the "edin" from Dunedin—resembling the "Edwin" of the king at the moment—and add the suffix "burgh." It stuck.

**History-book sovereigns:** Edinburgh, with its great age and its

great castle, figures in Scottish history from the very beginning.
For a small country whose monarchs have come from the south
for a couple of centuries now, it is even more remarkable than
it might otherwise be, for the gallery of memorable sovereigns
it has produced.

Take Duncan, whom Shakespeare was to write about, and
who was among the earlier of the kings, reigning almost a thousand years ago. His trusted general, Macbeth, murdered him,
took over the kingdom, and himself reigned for seventeen years—
ably, according to accounts. But Macbeth paid for his crime
when Duncan's son Malcolm killed him and became King Malcolm III. Malcolm's career deserves notice. First, he married a
lady named Margaret, sister to the pretender to the throne of
England. Second, though he embroiled Scotland in war after war
during a reign of nearly four decades, he was able to keep his
kingdom independent at a crucial time. Third, wars or no, his
devout English-speaking wife reorganized the church in Scotland,
de-emphasizing the major role of the Gaelic-speaking clergy in
favor of English-imported priests from the south who played a not
insignificant role in encouraging Scotland's linguistic drift from
Gaelic to English. Fourth, Malcolm had the distinction of being
husband to a lady who was sainted by the Catholic Church (not
for her work in the area of language, but rather for her piety
and devotion to the poor), being father to four sons who became kings of Scotland and, as if that were not enough, to two
daughters who became queens of England. Considering the relationship they were to have in ensuing centuries—both warlike
and peaceful—it is as well that St. Margaret helped bring the
English language to Scotland; the two peoples have been able to
communicate with each other ever since, if not always amicably.

**France, the Stuarts—and Mary Queen of Scots:** Disputes of economic, religious, or political natures for a long while impelled the
Scots to take the French as their allies against the English. France's
role in the affairs of the two countries was never more important
than toward the end of the sixteenth century. James V, a Stuart,

was married to the French Mary of Guise, who succeeded him as Queen Regent upon his death, and who obtained permission of the Scottish Parliament to have their daughter Mary raised in Catholic France at a time when the Protestant Reformers were gaining strength in Scotland. While still a young woman, Mary had married and become the widow of young King Francis II of France. Upon the death of her mother in Edinburgh Castle, Mary returned to the land of her birth to reign as its queen. She married the Earl of Darnley, an English cousin; saw her Italian secretary, Rizzio, murdered in Holyrood Palace by courtiers presumably working with Darnley; became implicated in the later death of Darnley; and married again (her third and last husband was the ill-fated Earl of Bothwell), against the advice of her nobles. She then found herself embroiled in a test of wills with her cousin, Elizabeth I of England, only to spend the last two decades of her life a prisoner of Elizabeth in a succession of drafty English castles, before losing her head at Fotheringay. (Antonia Fraser's recent excellent biography, *Mary Queen of Scots,* is recommended pre-Edinburgh reading.)

There was, however, more than melodrama in Mary's story. There was much irony as well. For it developed that Mary's only child—her son by Darnley—succeeded her as James VI of Scotland but, in addition, came to rule as James I of England—the first joint sovereign of the two long-antagonistic kingdoms. It is this same son of the beautiful but unlucky Mary Stuart whose name was given to the Protestant Bible in general use today and also to Jamestown, the first English settlement—founded in 1607 —in America.

**Act of Union:** Almost a century elapsed—a century full of animosity—before, in 1707, the Act of Union properly dotted the i's and crossed the t's and gave Scotland the representation that was rightfully hers in the British Parliament (to whose House of Commons it sends seventy-one members). And while not absolutely everyone on both sides of the border has lived happily ever after (Scottish nationalists made away with the Scots' ancient

Stone of Scone from London's Westminster Abbey, where it was part of the coronation chair, on the eve of Elizabeth II's coronation), the two countries have shared the same monarchs ever since, as well as a number of common government services. A member of the Cabinet in London, the Secretary of State for Scotland, represents the Scots who have, over the years, rightly insisted upon certain institutions of their own. (The Church of Scotland, for example, is Presbyterian, not Anglican, and the laws of Scotland, as a result of Scotland's earlier ties with France, are closer to those of France than of England.)

Ever since Victoria's time, sovereigns have spent part of every summer at Balmoral Castle in the Highlands, while the official Edinburgh residence of the Royal Family is the same Palace of Holyrood House—largely rebuilt by Charles II, to be sure—where Mary Stuart saw her secretary murdered.

TO SEE

**Lay of the land:** You can't miss in Edinburgh. Edinburgh Castle is always there to guide you as a landmark. Even the traveler with no sense of direction whatsoever finds his way about this capital with little effort. The medieval Old Town extends from Edinburgh Castle down a succession of four streets, one following the other—Castlehill, Lawnmarket, High Street, and Canongate—and collectively known as the *Royal Mile,* to the Palace of Holyrood House. There is no more romantic a walk in all Europe. The wide and splendid thoroughfare called *Princes Street*—with the parklike Princes St. Gardens on the side facing the castle—separates the Old Town from the New Town. This last mentioned was new in the eighteenth century, when Robert Adam played a major hand in its design. Its core is laid out gridiron-style. The gridiron's boundaries, lengthwise, are the aforementioned Princes Street and *Queen Street,* with *George Street* —a thoroughfare of fine shops and other quality establishments—

sandwiched between these two. There is a gem of a square at either terminus of the square: *Charlotte,* at the end nearer the Castle; *St. Andrew,* opposite. One gains George Street from Princes Street by any one of five streets running perpendicular to these two: *Charlotte Street, Castle Street, Frederick Street, Hannover Street,* and *St. David Street.* Aside from the castle, there's one other elevated sector of the town visible from all about. With the structures atop it, you might think it a kind of Acropolis. Actually, it is called Carlton Hill.

**Choice destinations:** Edinburgh's requisites are *Edinburgh Castle* and the *Palace of Holyrood House.* Let's take the castle first, for a number of reasons, one being that it is open on Sunday. Not much is open on Sunday—in Edinburgh or anywhere in Scotland, and anything that *is* deserves a salute; the castle has ours. It perches atop an eminence 270 feet above Princes Street. It has been around a long time. That very same King Edwin—earlier mentioned as the king for whom Edinburgh is named—was among the early tenants; others of note were the same Malcolm III and his sainted wife Margaret, whose contributions to Scottish history are discussed in earlier pages. Indeed, the oldest structure within the castle complex is the lovely little Margaret Chapel, named for the saint-queen, and in Romanesque style, (which in Britain is called Norman). Of more interest, though, is the room where Mary Queen of Scots gave birth to James VI of Scotland and I of England. To be inspected, too, is the big hall that has served variously as banquet room and parliament and is now a museum of old weapons. The Scottish Regalia is in a room that invariably has a long queue at its door, but the bejeweled crown is spectacular and worth a wait. The *Palace of Holyrood House* is open only when neither the Royal Family nor the head of the Church of Scotland (during the Church's annual General Assembly) is occupying it. It was first used as a royal residence by Mary Stuart's grandfather, James IV, but after the Restoration (Edinburgh had been rather a busy place during the Charles I–Cromwell period),

Charles II largely, but not completely, rebuilt it. You may see
Mary Stuart's supper room, and there is a plaque where the body
of David Rizzio, her Italian secretary, was found, after his murder
in that little chamber, by courtiers with whom Mary's second
husband, Lord Darnley, was collaborating. Bonnie Prince Charlie,
the Stuart prince who cut such a dashing figure when he tried in
vain to gain the throne with the aid of Highland followers in 1745
(and who later sadly roamed the Continent a drunk), entertained
at Holyrood, and King George IV (better known for building the
Royal Pavilion at Brighton while his father, George III, reigned)
gave a ball on the occasion of his Edinburgh visit in 1882; he delighted his Scottish subjects by wearing full Highland dress. The
*High Kirk of St. Giles* (purists resent it being called a cathedral)
is an unusual squarish Gothic structure, quite distinct from the
Gothic one sees in England, and whose single tower is topped by
an equally unusual crown-shaped dome; this is believed to be the
oldest part of the building—early twelfth-century. The loveliest
part of the interior is the Thistle Chapel. The four-century-old
*Parliament House* is interesting, in part because it is no longer a
Parliament House; hasn't been since the Act of Union in 1707,
and its functions were taken over by Westminster—not always to
the satisfaction of the Scots. It is interesting also because it is now
a courthouse; Scotland's highest tribunals meet here. *Edinburgh
University,* founded by James VI, is best known abroad for its
medical school, but architecture buffs will want to admire its Old
College—an early-nineteenth-century masterwork built from designs by Robert Adam. Even the most ardent admirers of Mary
Queen of Scots will find *John Knox's house* worthwhile. For one
thing, it is not certain that that fanatically anti-Catholic and un-
relenting adversary of the Queen actually owned the house, although he is believed to have lived in it for some time. It is, in
all events, late-fifteenth-century and typically Edinburgh of the
period. The *Canongate* section of the Royal Mile contains a number of fine houses, many restored; *Moray House*—now a school,
but try to have a look—is among the most exemplary. So are

the structures—the White Horse Inn among them—of *White Horse Close,* a onetime coach terminus. Pop into historic *Canongate Kirk,* the seventeenth-century church whose minister is traditionally the Edinburgh chaplain to the sovereign. The *New Town's* general plan, earlier described, is mostly late-eighteenth- and early-nineteenth-century, with considerable work by Robert Adam, that era's great architect-designer. With the help of his brother James, Adam drew on the designs of ancient Rome and Greece, eliminating heaviness and pompousness from them, much like the Palladian villas of northwestern Italy. Adam's houses, furniture, decorative objects, and entire areas of towns (as in Bath, for example) are to be found throughout the British Isles. Although the principal architect for the New Town was a twenty-three-year-old Scot named James Craig, it was Adam who designed Charlotte Square as an integrated unit. Its north façade is considered one of his best pieces of work. All of *George Street*—the main thoroughfare of the New Town—is a visual delight. Particularly worth viewing within are the *Church of St. Andrew and St. George,* a Georgian gem with superb plasterwork in its oval ceiling; and the *Assembly Rooms,* splendidly proportioned and hung with great crystal chandeliers that serve, during the annual Edinburgh festival, as headquarters for the Festival Club, which visitors join on a membership basis. *St. Andrew Square* is at the opposite end of George Street from Charlotte Square; most of its handsome houses are now bank-occupied. And there is still another major Robert Adam building: *Register House,* opposite the main post office, on Princes Street. The monument you cannot help but see in the Princes Street gardens that looks like the detached campanile of a Gothic church—without the church—is the *Scott Memorial.*

**Museums** are an Edinburgh treat. Picture gallery, restored house, or what have you: They are the presentations of pros. The one to start off with—at least for any visitor who is curious about Edinburgh's rich historical background—is the *Scottish National Por-*

*trait Gallery* on Queen Street. The idea is not unlike that of the
National Portrait Gallery in London—to give you an idea of what
the country's past was all about by letting you look at pictures of
the people who made it, painted by their contemporaries. The
starting date is the mid-sixteenth century, and the pictures of the
early Stuarts—all six Jameses, Mary, Mary's beautiful French
mother, Mary of Guise; and later Stuarts, too—Bonnie Prince
Charlie as a lad and as a debauched man in his fifties; his com-
mon-law wife, Charlotte, Duchess of Albany and . . . but look
yourself; you'll recognize many portraits you've seen reproduced
in books. The *National Museum of Antiquities* occupies the ground
floor of the building housing the *National Portrait Gallery,* and is
full of surprises—weapons and shields and more mundane objects, too. The *National Gallery of Scotland* occupies a striking
neoclassic pavilion on Princes Street. There is a section devoted
exclusively to Scottish painting of the seventeenth, eighteenth,
and nineteenth centuries that is illuminating for many of us un-
familiar with this national group. The ones to look for are Sir
Henry Raeburn (perhaps the best known), Allan Ramsay, and
David Wilkie. The larger part of the gallery is devoted to English
and European painting. Every major school is represented, from
French Impressionists like Gauguin, to Spaniards like Zurbaran,
Italians like Tiepolo, and Dutchmen like Hals. The *Scottish
National Portrait Gallery of Modern Art* concentrates on work
of this century from the British Isles and the Continent; it's out
at the *Royal Botanic Garden,* and the setting is as high-caliber as
the pictures. The *Royal Scottish Museum* is an old-fashioned
hodgepodge from the middle of the last century—with lots of
things for the school kids in science and technology sections, but
with some priceless art objects (everything except paintings) from
throughout Europe and Asia (Moslem enamels, Meissen porcelain,
to give you an idea). There remain the less conventional museums
in antique buildings. *Canongate Tollbooth* is a municipal repository for Highland costumes. Neighboring *Huntly House* is full of
oddities relating to the city's history. *Lady Stair's House* centrally

locates exhibits by and about the Scottish Big Three Writers
group—Stevenson, Burns, and Scott. *Dean Village* is an absolute
charmer of a reconstructed hamlet just a few minutes from the
heart of town.

**Suburban excursions:** A pair of worth-visiting stately houses are
*Lauriston Castle,* at Davidson's Main, some five miles from town,
and dating originally to the sixteenth century, with early nineteenth-century refurbishing, and valuable furnishings; and *Hope-
toun House,* twelve miles distant near Furth Road Bridge at
South Queensferry, which is the Robert Adam-designed home
of the Marquess of Linlithgow, and a place of great beauty, in a
splendid setting. I wouldn't bother bringing the *Zoo* to your
attention—the world is, after all, full of zoos—were it not for
the penguins. They constitute the biggest captive colony of their
species—anywhere. And every day they leave their enclosure for
a walk among their fans; the Edinburghers call it the Penguin
Parade. Everyone has a good time, the hammy penguins most
definitely included. *Cramond* is a village on the Firth of Forth,
the North Sea estuary that is Edinburgh's outlet to the sea. It is of
Roman origin—minor treasures excavated are in the earlier-
mentioned Huntly House museum on the Royal Mile—but
the major lures, aside from a harbor for sailboats, are the restored
eighteenth-century houses and a tower going back to medieval
times. *Rosslyn* is a little village some eight miles from town that is
the site of Rosslyn Chapel, a fifteenth-century beauty. *Swanston*
is still another village, this noted for its thatched, whitewashed
houses surrounding a traditional green, with a house nearby that
was a retreat of Stevenson's. *South Queensferry* is the village
from which you can get a fine view of the two bridges spanning
the Firth of Forth; the newer of the two, by far, was opened by
Queen Elizabeth II in 1964 and has a central span of thirty-
three hundred feet; the older—the rail bridge—has been going
strong since 1890. *Plewlands House,* a seventeenth-century National Trust of Scotland property, is in the neighborhood. I doubt

if you are going to want to go swimming—the water this far north
is chilly. But the locals are brave, and used to it, and given a bit
of sun they flock to the long beach or the enormous pool at
*Portobello;* there are a promenade, fun fair, and other amenities
in connection. Last but hardly least is Edinburgh's historic port,
*Leith.* It has been in business for some eight centuries. Mary
Queen of Scots landed there in 1561, and George IV about two
and one half centuries later. St. Mary's Church is about the only
building dating to Mary's era.

## TO WATCH

*Massed bagpipers* constitute the bulk of the *Beating the Retreat* spectacles on the Edinburgh Castle Esplanade, usually presented in the spring—a couple of times each week in May and
early June. In summer, from June until September, *Princes Street
Gardens* are the scene of all manner of alfresco entertainment,
especially fun when it's typically Scottish. *The Scottish National
Orchestra* is the Edinburgh-based symphony whose home is *Usher
Hall,* where it performs regularly. The roaming *Scottish Opera*
gives occasional Edinburgh performances. *Plays* are performed
in a number of theaters—the *Lyceum, Kings,* and the *Church Hill*
are among these. And this being Britain, *movies* are popular;
there are a number of first-run cinemas downtown. The town's
big annual show—as it has been since 1947—is the *Edinburgh
Festival,* which usually runs from mid- to late August through the
first half of September, with specific dates varying each year.
This is one of the oldest and without question one of the very
best of the European festivals. Companies from the world over
present a rich program of music, drama, opera, ballet—and the
*Scottish Military Tattoo.* There is a film festival in conjunction.
Bookings for both festival *and* for a roof over one's head at festival time must be made *way, way* ahead.

## TO STAY

Edinburgh has the same hotel problem as the Scandinavian capitals: how to fill hotel rooms in off-season winter. The answer: Have few enough of them so that you can get through the cold-weather months. There is, as a consequence of this understandable policy, a tight situation in the late spring, summer, and early autumn. And there is another situation, not common to Scandinavia, but still typical of the British Isles: private baths in hotels are regarded as desired only by royalty and rich Martians. The Scots, like the English, are only just beginning to realize that ordinary middle-class folk—and not only American by nationality—are accustomed to private baths with their hotel rooms, and have been for some time (unless, of course, they are British —and that includes Scottish). We must still, therefore, carefully specify private baths when booking. The choice is not wide, but it is good, in Edinburgh. My preferred hotel is the *George,* one of the fine old houses of George Street, that for some years now has been masterfully transformed into a full-facility hotel. The public rooms have a smart period ambience, neither overbusy nor overquiet. (There is no more pleasant place in Edinburgh for afternoon tea.) The guest rooms are either recently refurbished or contained in a new wing carved out of an adjacent building; most have bath. The landlord is Grand Metropolitan, the British group that does a good job with good hotels on two continents. The *Roxburghe* is the genuine article—an original Charlotte Square mansion that has been converted into a luxury hotel of considerable beauty. Some fifty of the seventy-odd rooms have private bath, and there is a very good restaurant and a bar. The *Caledonian* is a cavernous British Rail institution on Princes street. A team of very clever decorators has taken full advantage of the elaborate plasterwork, high ceilings, and capacious public spaces for a bold, imaginative, and generally successful refurbishing job, which has included quantities of desperately wanted private baths. The staff—some of it spirited across the border from England— at times patronizes the unpretentious Edinburghers, let alone unpretentious guests from across the Atlantic. The *North British,* at the other end of Princes Street, has the same owner—British Rail —and is of the same vintage as the Caledonian; it is a mite smaller, perhaps, similarly well equipped, and with similar renovation of both public spaces and guest rooms. Trust Houses-Forte's Edinburgh property is the *Carlton,* just over the North Bridge from Princes Street, and quite as well located as the earlier-mentioned hotels. The Carlton has a forbidding exterior, but good old Trust Houses has fixed up things inside to the point where you *know* you're going to get a private bath: *Every* room has one. And all the rooms—though not overly large—have been brightened up. The *Scotia* is moderate-priced and embraces a group of joined Georgian houses on Great King Street; there are a charming restaurant and bar.

### TO EAT (AND DRINK)

One is not bowled over by the food in Scotland, but it is considerably superior to what many visitors to these isles dare dream. It is no longer true, in Britain, that once you leave London you're a goner, gastronomically. The world—most particularly Europe —has gotten smaller. Britons, including Scots, flit back and forth to the Continent once or twice or thrice a year. It is making a big difference, particularly in Edinburgh, which probably has more foreign visitors than the combined total for every other British city outside of London. (When, for example, was the last time you were in Manchester?) The good things are not dissimilar from the good things in England: copious breakfasts, with oat scones perhaps, toast (ice-cold and on silver racks to cool it quicker, unless you specify "hot buttered"), eggs, bacon/ham/sausage, the inevitable half a broiled tomato, and coffee, with the

especially Scottish addition of a bowl of oatmeal. Afternoon tea is
a treat. The Scots, like the English, bake very well—their own hot
buttered scones are a globally known specialty. But biscuits and
cakes and pastries are good, too. And so are the tea sandwiches.
Roast beef, as in England, is invariably tasty, thick, and rare.
Soups, especially Scotch broth (made with barley and mutton)
and cock-a-leekie (chicken-based and with leeks) are excellent
when well prepared.

The Scots like fish. All those trout fishermen you've read about
in novels do indeed exist, and their catches, simply grilled, are
very good. So are grilled kippers (a breakfast favorite of mine).
The smoked salmon are among the best such on the planet.

As for beverages, aside from tea and coffee, you will have
heard of Scotch whisky. It is spelled *whisky* in Scotland, as in
Britain, and in both places its nationality is implied; one simply
says "whiskey." Good as the whiskey is, it can't be drunk at just
any old time. Weekday *licensing hours* for hotels, pubs, and
licensed restaurants are 11:00 A.M. to 2:30 P.M. and 5:00 P.M.
to 10:00 P.M. All pubs (and, sad to relate, most restaurants) are
closed Sunday. Hotels, though, may serve drinks from 12:30 P.M.
to 2:30 P.M. and from 6:30 P.M. to 10:00 P.M. on Sundays, although not all of them choose to. Licensed restaurants may serve
liquor with meals on Sundays from 12:30 P.M. to 2:30 P.M. and
from 6:30 P.M. to 10:00 P.M.

Quite the most outstanding restaurant in Edinburgh is not really
in Edinburgh. It's about a fifteen- to twenty-minute taxi ride from
downtown. It's called *Prestonfield House* and it is an architecturally exceptional seventeenth-century house whose guests have
included none other than our own Benjamin Franklin, who
scooted up while he was ambassador to France. I don't know that
I would go quite that distance, but it's surely worth the ride from
Princes Street. The architect was the very same who redesigned
Holyrood House for Charles II; possibly for that reason there's a
Charles II portrait on the premises. The whole ground floor is
given over to eating and/or drinking, in a pair of bars and a pair

of dining rooms, no two alike, and each sumptuously furnished in exquisite pieces of the period. The fare is at once Scottish and continental, and of high quality; and there are a few bathless bedrooms upstairs. *Cosmo* is an Italian-owned and -staffed restaurant on Castle Street, just off George, that sets a superb table: Pastas, veal dishes, salads with the genuine article—oil-vinegar-touch-of-garlic dressing, and a rich and delicious *zuppa Inglese.* Italian wines, too. Moderate. The *Scots Kitchen* is the basement grill of the North British Hotel, and as good a place as any to sample national specialties, even including haggis if you insist; I prefer piggly wigglies. Continuing with the Scottish theme, you may order just about any and every species of Scotch whisky extant—more than half a hundred. Also with authentic Scottish fare is the *Epicure,* on Princes Street. *Restaurant des Ambassadeurs* is the George Hotel's principal dining room—Corinthian columns supporting a high, elaborately plastered ceiling, unusually good wine list, French menu, dancing to an orchestra. The same hotel's *Perigord Room* serves a popular-price buffet at lunch and dinner. The Caledonian Hotel's *Pompadour Restaurant*—one of the nicest in town—is a stylish Louis XV room with a classic French-style menu; the same hotel's main dining room is less expensive, and the kind of hotel dining room that can give hotel dining rooms a bad name. The Carlton Hotel's *Carvery* is quite possibly Edinburgh's best restaurant buy. It features lunch or dinner including a first course of soup or appetizer, an entrée of Scotch beef, roast leg of lamb or roast leg of pork, which you (or the chef) carve at the counter (as much as you like, of course), and a choice of desserts. Everything is delicious. The *Consort Restaurant* is in the Roxburghe Hotel's basement, and unlike the rest of this charming period-piece of a hotel, it is tartan-plaid-modern, with a good, moderate-priced, British-Scottish-continental menu. *Pubs,* offering some atmosphere and cheap but good lunches, include the *Abbotsford* (3 Rose Street) and *Scott's,* at 202 Rose Street. *The Doric* (15 Market Street) is a congenial pub, with both drinks and snacks, but has a popular restaurant in connection. *The Cramond* is worth the journey from town to the Firth at Forth; it's a lovely seventeenth-century inn, serving exceptional meals, as well as drinks. Both *Jenner's* and *Forsyth's* department stores are good for tea and cocktails, as well, while the *Woolworth* store near Waverly Station is known for its cottage and meat pies.

TO BUY

Woolens and knit goods, which the Scots make so skillfully, are no cheaper in Scotland than in England, and not much cheaper in either country than in the United States, so that they are no bargain—which is not to say that you might not like to look over the tempting selections for men, women, and children at *Jenner's,* the *Scotch House,* and *R. W. Forsyth,* all fine old Princes Street stores, and *Anderson's,* another quality shop of long standing, on George Street. *Highland Home Industries* is a commendable nonprofit organization whose purpose is to promote continued traditional craft production—and market the results. Scottish-born Queen Mother Elizabeth is the patron, and on sale are a tremendous variety of handwoven tweed, tartans, rugs; pottery and other ceramics; knit goods, and a variety of smallish souvenirs (including tile plaques with the coats of arms of Scottish clans, for friends at home, bearing their names). Another George Street source of interesting handmade articles is the *Royal Repository for the Sale of Gentlewomen's Work,* at No. 137. On the Royal Mile's Canongate, the *Scottish Craft Centre* makes its headquarters in venerable Acheson House; it is a national organization of craftsmen whose work it sells; one finds pottery, woodwork, jewelry, batik, tapestries, and silver embroidery—to name a few. Standards are high. *Taste,* at 46-A George Street, is as modish a men's and women's clothing accessory shop as you'll come across. *Harry Chernack,* on Rose Street, sells antique silver, while other Rose Street emporia include such boutiques as

*Buzz* and *Focus. Mowbray House,* 51 High Street, specializes in Georgian furniture. *West Bow* is the name of the Edinburgh street that is loaded with antiques shops.

TO NOTE

**Access:** Scotland's international airport is at Prestwick, whose origins go back to World War II, when it was an air base. It is closer to Glasgow than Edinburgh, but there is bus service to both cities. There is transatlantic service via BOAC, Pan Am, and SAS. Edinburgh's own little airport, Turnhouse, is but six miles from town. BUA-Caledonian and BEA fly into it frequently from a number of British Isles points, including London and Dublin. There is excellent British Rail service between Edinburgh and London, with both daytime and overnight luxury trains making the run. There are modern buses and good highways. Remember that Britons—and that includes Scots—drive on the *left.* Within Edinburgh, there is good bus service. The comfortable traditional-style taxis are a pleasure to ride in; they're metered, and there's an extra charge for whatever luggage is carried up front with the driver. Self-drive and chauffeur-driven cars are available from a number of sources, and there are well-organized bus sightseeing tours. **Climate:** You must count on a wee bit o' rain. Keep your raincoat and/or collapsible umbrella with you as you would, say, your wallet or handbag. Edinburgh is one of the few capitals that looks beautiful even when wet. But there are visitors who are known to have seen it in the sunshine; I am one of them, and there is nothing lovelier. Temperatures do not go to extremes. Winter (November through March) averages in the mid- to bottom forties, with lows mostly in the mid-thirties. Summer (June, July, and August) is mostly sixtyish, although there are low-seventies days in July and August. Spring and autumn (April/May, September/October) are usually fifties months. **Clothes:** Edinburgh, it is well to remember, is only a fraction of the size of London, and is in many respects more conservative. Not that the younger crowd aren't quite as mod in their dress. As casual as you like during the day, less so in the evening. **Currency:** The pound is divided into 100 pence, written "p". There are ½p, 1p, 2p, 5p, 10p, and 50p coins; there are £1, £5, and £10 notes, as in the past, but note that the Scots have their own banknotes, as distinct from those of the Bank of England; there is usually no difficulty, though, in using the English notes in Scotland. You are still likely to come across coins of the old currency. A shilling is the equal of 5p, and the coins are the same size; a florin—the two-shilling coin—equals 10p, and the 50p coin is equal to the old ten-shilling note. **Tipping:** Hotels usually add service charges to bills, so that additional tipping is not necessary, except in the case of bellhops, who should get 10p per bag, and others who perform really special services, the hall porter included. Tip taxi drivers 10 to 15 percent. **Business hours:** Most stores are open from 9:00 A.M. to 6:00 P.M. Monday through Friday, but on Saturday many are open only until 1:00 P.M. And to complicate matters, certain stores close Tuesday or Wednesday afternoons, instead of Saturday. Thursday evening is late night—8:00 P.M. **Language:** Scottish-accented English is a joy to hear, and rarely, if indeed ever, difficult to understand. **Local literature:** *The Scotsman,* and the other Edinburgh papers, of course. Shops abound in guide and picture books on the city. **Further information:** British Tourist Authority, 680 Fifth Avenue, New York; John Hancock Center, Chicago; 612 South Flower Street, Los Angeles; 1712 Commerce Street, Dallas; 151 Bloor Street West, Toronto; 602 West Hastings Street, Vancouver. Scottish Tourist Board, Rutland Place, Edinburgh, Scotland; City of Edinburgh Tourist Information and Accommodation Service, 1 Cockburn Street, Edinburgh, Scotland.

# *Helsinki*

Helsinki is a low-profile capital. By low-profile I don't mean that it is without tall buildings, but rather that it is not out to knock you dead. You must take it on its own terms—an agreeable conglomerate of early-nineteenth-century neoclassic coupled with the bold, severe, and frequently exciting structures of the Finnish Modern Renaissance—the decades beginning after World War I, when Finland gained complete independence from the Russians, and continuing right up to today, and the Finlandia Hall of Alvar Aalto.

Even though the Russians, during the time that Finland was a Grand Duchy of the Romanovs' empire, allowed the Finns a good deal of leeway in the area of self-government, it is difficult to appreciate that Finland, as a sovereign republic, was born as recently as 1917. Visit Helsinki today and the Finns—gracious, attractive, living comfortably and contemporarily—belie the hard times they have known even in their own time, let alone earlier eras. Finland is on the razor's edge between East and West. It has not been allowed to forget it for a long, long time.

**West from the Urals:** The Finns, like their fellow Finno-Ugric language group confreres, the Estonians and the Hungarians, came west into Europe from the Urals as long ago, possibly, as the beginning of the Christian era. By the eighth century they had taken possession of what is now their country, displacing the original inhabitants—the Lapps—who fled to the Arctic north and have remained there ever since, retaining their own language and a considerable amount of their culture. The Finns then had a four-century breather on their own, toward the end of which their raids on the Swedish coast became irritable to the Swedes' King Eric IX. That was when he led his forces across the Baltic and not only conquered but Christianized the Finns (they remain mostly Lutheran—like their fellow Scandinavians). In the sixteenth century, Finland was created a Grand Duchy of Sweden, and Swedish became the official language. As time went by, Finland found itself caught in the uncomfortable middle between antagonistic Russia and Sweden, and suffered severely. In 1721 Czar Peter I took the Finnish province of Viborg, and less than a century later, all of Finland found itself Czarist territory.

**The Swedish centuries:** But Finland, for a good century, was to fare better under the Russians than under the Swedes. The Czars gave the Finnish Grand Duchy its own constitution, and it enjoyed semi-independence with its own Parliament and a democratic regime completely separate from that of Russia proper. Still, the enlightened Russian rule did not stop the development of Finnish nationalism, a continuing facet of which was the Finnish-Swedish language conflict. Toward the turn of this century, the Russians commenced a Russianization policy in Finland. The Finns were not buying. There was a general strike in 1905, and Russia's fortunes during World War I made it possible for the Finns to declare themselves an independent republic in 1917. Even that was easier said than done, for a Finnish civil war resulted, with the pro-Russian Reds on the one hand versus the pro-republic Whites, under the man who remains the national hero, Field Marshal Mannerheim. The Mannerheim forces, with German help, won, and within a few years there was even Soviet recognition.

The Finns who, like all northern peoples, are plagued by an excessive fondness at times for alcohol (those long winters, you know), tried Prohibition in their infant years as a republic. It was as disastrous as in the United States, but repeal came a little sooner and more mercifully in Finland (1931) than in America.

**The republic's growing pains:** The thirties were the years in which Finland became known for being the only European country to pay its World War I debt to the United States, and even now, in the seventies, there are vast numbers of us in the United States who know nothing else about Finland. It is as well that those debts were taken care of by the time of the eve of World War II, or chances are they never would have been; for in 1939 the Soviet Union invaded Finland, and the following year the Finns found themselves ceding the Karelian isthmus—and a lot more—to their giant neighbor.

In 1941, understandably smarting and wanting to regain the territory they had lost, the Finns joined the Germans in their attack on the USSR. Britain, but not the United States, declared war on Finland at this time. The Soviets' retaliation was massive and lasted until, in 1944, Finland capitulated and gave back what the Russians had earlier taken, plus a good deal more. To add to their woes, the Soviets insisted that the Finns flush out the German troops who by that time had occupied northern Finland; in order to do so, battles ensued that resulted in near-total destruction of the towns of the north. As a result of the Peace of Paris (1947), the Finns agreed to pay the Soviets three hundred million dollars. Within a short while they paid up all but seventy-five million dollars of their reparations, which the Soviets canceled.

**On the razor's edge:** Later, post-World War II years saw them deal effectively with their own Communist Party (it had participated in coalition governments in a minor way, but lost out completely in the 1971 elections), rebuild the devastated north, and develop the rest of the country in the areas of industry, housing, transportation, communications, and international trade (pulp and paper are major sources of revenue from abroad), to the point where their standard of living is one of the highest in Europe. Although Finland has refrained from any military alignment with the West (it remains punctiliously neutral, the Soviets still being a major neighbor), it has joined Denmark, Iceland, Norway, and Sweden in the Nordic Council, served a two-year term as a small-power member of the UN Security Council, and joined the European Free Trade Association as an associate member. It *is* Scandinavia. But it *isn't* Scandinavia. It is Eastern-influenced. But it is as Western as the day is long. It is, when you get down to it, hard to define. Only of one thing is one sure: the marvel of the strength of Finnish culture and the miracle of Finnish independence. Ask a Finn how it has happened this way and he replies with a one-word answer: *sisu*. That is a Finnish term translatable in English only as "guts."

TO SEE

**Lay of the land:** Although Helsinki has almost a 4¼-century history at the time this is written—it was founded by command of Swedish King Gustav Vasa in 1550 to compete with the Estonian port of Talinn for some of the area's trade with Russia—it did not become a town of consequence until the early nineteenth century, and then for two reasons. The first was that in the course of being taken from the Swedes by the Russians it burned down. The second was that Czar Alexander I, who had promised Finland autonomy under his crown, decided to remove the Finnish capital from the ancient city of Turku—in the west, closer to Sweden—to Helsinki. And the new Helsinki, Alexander concluded, had to have the look of a capital rather than just another port. It was decided that this look would be neoclassic. Hired to execute it was a German-born architect who had never quite gotten over the brilliant neoclassicism of Italian-designed St. Petersburg. Though without the marble that had always been considered requisite for neoclassic construction, Engel made do with bricks and wood. He followed the plan suggested: The old market square was to be enlarged to become a forum fringed by administrative buildings and dominated by the principal church and a broad esplanade, which would divide the old part of the city from the new.

Engel's Helsinki remains the core of today's Helsinki. Starting with the *harbor,* one takes one's bearings from Engel's original buildings in and around it: the President's Palace facing the water, always with the traditional guards in and about their pillboxes at the gates; the nearby smaller palaces, which are respectively the Town Hall and—having the place of honor among foreign diplomatic missions—the Swedish Embassy. On the broad pavements of the square is the daily produce market, which draws all of Helsinki to its mostly female-operated stalls. And in the water, tied up at piers, and anchored farther out, are ships of all sizes and nationalities, some Finnish, most foreign, with flocks of pristine white gulls adding to the animation.

But Engel hath wrought more. Backdrop for all of this is *Senate Square,* a hop and a skip to the rear. The great domed structure that is the Lutheran Cathedral—atop a high flight of steps on a little mountain of its own—dominates, while all about are public edifices of great dignity. One is the original University of Helsinki building, housing a magnificent library and a splendidly decorated Great Hall. And another is the old Senate.

The earlier-mentioned esplanade of the original plans is just that: a broad, boulevardlike thoroughfare lined with cafes that are a summertime Helsinki delight. The *Esplanade* (*Esplanaadik-atu* in Finnish) extends from the harbor to a junction where it terminates, and at which points another principal Helsinki thoroughfare begins. It is *Mannerheimintie,* which leads past the monumental Railway Station to—among other things—the Parliament, or Eduskunta, and the National Museum. There is still another major street to be reckoned with. It is *Aleksanterinkatu.* It runs parallel with Esplanaadikatu—from Senate Square into Mannerheimintie—but rather than being a green boulevard, it is Helsinki's principal shopping street.

The foregoing are by no means all of Engel's works; old parts of the city are dotted with them, ranging from the Guards' Barracks on Kasarmintori to the elegant onetime Governor General's Residence (during the Russian period) on Esplanaadikatu, now used by the Council of State for dinners and receptions and which, somehow or other, one does well to see.

**Choice destinations:** Helsinki is possibly the most offbeat, architecture-rich capital of Europe. There is nothing ancient. The oldest monument is the mid-eighteenth-century *Suomenlinna Fortress,* on an island of its own in the harbor—and it is a destination of value. The early nineteenth century is best represented by the neoclassic brilliance of the earlier-mentioned Engel-designed *Senate Square and harbor area.* Here the requisites, to recapitulate, would include the *President's Palace* (if you can wangle your way in, aim for the Hall of State and the Hall of Mirrors), the *Town Hall* (go in and see as much as you can), and these highlights of the Senate Square: the entry and conference halls of the *Senate,* the great domed *Cathedral* (yes, it *is* worth climbing all those steps to have a look inside), the splendid interior—a rotunda and a trio of vaulted halls—of the *University Library,* and the main *University building.* Noteworthy architectural works of this century are numerous; let me suggest my favorites. The foremost, surely without doubt, is Eliel Sarrinen's *Railway Station.* Built between 1906 and 1914, this is surely the great rail terminal of the planet, embodying all the elements of a model public building—the strength of the immense, exaggerated arch of its main entrance, the drama of the tower that gives it a landmark significance, the detail of the stone façade, the capaciousness of the high-ceilinged interiors. Equally outstanding in its own right is the *Olympic Stadium,* designed by Yrjo Lindegren and Toivo Jantti in 1934, for the 1940 Olympics—which never took place—and added to for the 1952 Olympics—which, happily, *did.* In my work I find myself looking at stadiums all over the world. I have seen bigger stadiums, newer stadiums, more famous stadiums; nowhere, though, is there a more beautiful stadium. Aside from

the earlier Eliel Saarinen (whose son, incidentally, was the noted
American architect Eero Saarinen), no Finnish architect is more
internationally noted than Alvar Aalto. Helsinki is a particularly
rich repository of Aalto projects. The newest is *Finlandia House,*
which opened in late 1971 and overnight became the world's most
talked-about—and admired—concert/congress hall. It consists of a
1750-seat main auditorium, a smaller chamber music hall seating
350, a restaurant, a cafeteria, and a number of smaller meeting
rooms. The main decorative material is white marble but, instead
of the traditional red-and-gold accents, the color scheme is a blend
of white, varying shades of gray, and black. The hall—whose
auditorium has the irregular, unsymmetrical boldness typical of
Aalto—is part of a coordinated civic and cultural center that the
aging Aalto—seventy-four when *Finlandia House* opened—
planned for the city's Toolo Bay area. *Other Aalto works* include
the 1958 Concert Hall of the House of Culture in the Sornainen
area; the library and public hall of the National Pensions Institute (1956); the bank building at Fabianinkatu 29 (1965); the
interior of the Savoy Restaurant on Esplanaadikatu (1937); and—
all in the Munkkiniemi area—a 1954 apartment house at Riihitie
12–14, the 1956 structure at Tiilimaki 20 which is Aalto's studio,
and the private house called Villa Aalto at Riihitie 20, which was
Aalto's first Helsinki building (1937). Scandinavia is justifiably
celebrated for the contemporary satellite towns that ring its older
cities. *Tapiola,* outside of Helsinki, is one of the most outstanding.
Dating mostly from the mid-fifties and planned to have a population of about twenty-five thousand, with construction still continuing, it comprises a trio of residential areas all of which share a
central commercial, cultural, and administrative center. Tapiola
is by no means the work of a single architect, but rather of many,
with the result a mingling of styles, designs, sizes, shapes, and
concepts. Aarne Ervi's central complex—wherein are a shopping
center, large department store, and other public and commercial
buildings—is noteworthy, as is Aarno Russuvuori's 1965 church
on Tapionraitti.

If architecture is one special Helsinki treat, *museums* constitute a second. The *Ateneum,* in a neo-Renaissance building that went up in the late nineteenth century, is divided into two major sections. One is devoted to Finnish Modern painting and sculpture, about which foreigners know relatively little. It is strong and vigorous—not unlike the Finns themselves—and very likable indeed. The other part of the museum has foreign art, ranging from African and Henry Moore sculptures to paintings by Picasso and Miro. The *Amos Anderson Art Gallery* specializes in the offbeat—lots of shows from abroad, and very popular with young Helsinki. The *Arabia Museum* is in the Arabia porcelain factory, in itself a major Finnish cultural/industrial asset. Arabia for more than a century has produced not only china but individual, one-of-a-kind works of art by its own gifted ceramists, internationally known names like Rut Bryk, Kaj Franck, Toini Muona, Friedl Kjellberg, Michael Schilkin, Birger Kaipiainen, and my old friend, Kyllikki Salmenhaara. Arabia retains a group of these leading artists to work in private studios in a seperate section of the plant. They are much like artists in residence at universities, creating what they wish, as they wish, at their own speed. If you aren't able to get to the museum, you can see a bit of contemporary work at *Arabia's gallery on Esplanaadikatu.* The earlier mentioned *Suomenlinna Fortress,* on an island in the harbor, contains two worthwhile museums—the *Ehrensvaard* (residential interiors in the Commandant's House) and the *Armfelt* (early-nineteenth-century art, furnishings, and objects from a country manor house). The *Finnish National Museum* in an early-twentieth-century Saarinen building, which you might mistake for a courthouse, on Mannerheimintie, is at its best in the Ethnological Department, with the exhibits of Finnish folk art. The towered home where artist *Akseli Gallen-Kallela* worked, and which he built before World War I, is a museum of his graphics and paintings. The *Helsinki City Museum* occupies a gem of a mid-nineteenth-century house that's quite as much of a treat as the exhibits. The house in which *Marshal Mannerheim* lived, with his own furnishings,

memorabilia, etc., is another surprise. So is the rare late-eighteenth-century house called *Tuomarinkyla Manor,* with its exhibits
of Helsinki-made furniture and furnishings of the period.
*Suerasaari* is an open-air museum of the kind one sees frequently in Scandinavia—a maze of interestingly furnished farm
and town houses and shops brought from throughout the country.
Sports fans will like the *Finnish Sports Museum* in the earlier-
praised Olympic Stadium; exhibits range from what may well
be some of the most venerable skis extant to a pair of Finnish
runner Paavo Nurmi's track shoes dipped in gold.

**The sauna:** When I took my first sauna in Finland, a decade
and a half back, at a little club on a mini-island in Helsinki
Harbor, I treasured the certificate I was awarded at bath's end.
There was no question but that I was the first on my block to
sit in a wood-walled cabin with the temperature close to 200°.
But if the Finns have succeeded in exporting any facet of their
culture in recent years, it is the sauna. The whole world takes
saunas now, and I suspect that visitors to Finland are now apt
to forget that the sauna is a Finnish gift to the well-being of the
universe. In rural Finland, farm families take a sauna together
every Saturday night, usually in the separate sauna building that
is located near one of the countless thousands of lakes that are a
commonplace of the Finnish landscape. From hot bath they plop
into the water (it makes no difference if it's summer or winter)
and then go back for some more heat; the hot-cold operation is
usually repeated several times, after which bathers relax in an
adjacent room over a beer before dressing. There is nary a
modern apartment house in Finland without its sauna; tenants
are signed up for regular times of their own in the bath. Additionally, there are public saunas and saunas in leading hotels—open
to guests, of course. The leading ones in Helsinki include the
Palace, Marski, Inter•Continental and Hesperia. Shower baths, of
course, substitute for lakes in urban saunas, but some of the
country's resort hotels are able to provide traditional alfresco cold-
water and even the old-fashioned log sauna houses, for the "smoke"

rather than the more modern "steam" type of heat. Rare is the
Finn—young, old, male, female—who does not take to the sauna
at least once a week. In Finland, families that sauna together
stay together. Businessmen close deals in the sauna, politicians
plan, scheme, and deliberate in the sauna. Finns consider the
sauna a major source of whatever physical stamina they possess,
of their emotional well-being, of *sisu*—the tenacious strength of
the nation and its people—that has made it possible for Finland
to thrive in the face of odds that would have been the despair of
similarly handicapped countries through the centuries.

### TO STAY

My favorite Helsinki hotels are neither its newest nor its
handsomest. One, for example, is the *Palace*. It was aesthetically
exciting when it went up after World War II, but its smallish,
quiet rooms are pedestrian today. Still, its situation, alongside the
waters of Helsinki Harbor, and with sumptuous views from its
public spaces and its front rooms, makes it No. 1 with me. So
does the excellent fare—among the very finest in the city—in its
Grill, and the convenience of the location. No. 2 is the *Marski*,
newer by a decade than the Palace, though hardly more attractive.
Bedrooms are more spacious and less cell-like, however, and
the location is about as central and in the heart of things as one
could want. There is a lively disco in the basement, a congenial
lobby-floor bar-lounge, a next-door cafeteria, and a second-floor
main dining room that is surely the most depressing public room
in Finland. Although I am told that the service has greatly improved from the time when I stayed there, I have never cared
for the *Vaakuna*. It is of an odd, Finnish Modern era that never
quite made it aesthetically. I mention it here only because it is
one of the bigger hotels in the top category, and its location—
opposite the railroad station—could not be more convenient. And
I mention also the first-class *Helsinki Hotel*—comfortable if un-

exceptional, and also well located. Two newer top-category hotels, well away from the core of downtown near the Finlandia House congress/concert hall, on Toolo Bay, are the good-looking 294-room *Inter•Continental* (of which Finnair is a major shareholder), with rooftop dine-dance room, lobby-level coffee shop and bar, and saunas; and the *Hesperia,* with a disproportionately large number of singles (much needed in Helsinki) among its 285 rooms, and a full range of luxury facilities.

TO EAT (AND DRINK)

Finland's great culinary treat is the July–August crayfish binge. In every good restaurant you see groups wearing great red-and-white bibs gorging on seven or eight of the minilobsters, to a vodka/beer accompaniment. But the rest of the year one eats well, too. The cuisine is far closer to that of Finland's western neighbors, the Swedes, than its eastern neighbors, the Russians. Indeed, one would have to look hard to find any Eastern influence whatsoever. With all those thousands upon thousands of lakes, plus an extensive seacoast, fish plays a major menu role—fresh-water and ocean species, both. The Finns are very big on potatoes, too; on soups, which they prepare very well, and on salads, which are invariably garnished with dill (as are other dishes), as in Sweden. Smoked reindeer meat is a specialty from the north country. Dessert pancakes with cloudberries and cream or ice cream are delicious. So, invariably, is smorgasbord, in Finland called *voileipapoyta,* and as in Sweden eaten in sections: start with appetizerlike dishes, go on to the cold meat and cold fish platters (there is invariably a selection of herring prepared in different ways), then help yourself to the hot courses, and follow with cheese and dessert. Finnish breads, particularly the dark rye varieties, are very good and so is this country's variation on the Scandinavian flatbread theme. In Finland flatbread is known as Finncrisp and constitutes, in my view, the tastiest in all Scandinavia. Grilled steaks are always available in restaurants and are usually served with well-prepared French fries. Vegetables are fresh and usually not overcooked. If solids are Western-derived, the most popular liquid obviously has Eastern origins. I refer to vodka, which has the role in Finland that is reserved for aquavit in the other Scandinavian countries. It is excellent, is served chilled, and is often followed by a beer chaser. Taken in an old-fashioned glass on the rocks, it is an admirable substitute for the pre-dinner dry martini many Americans enjoy, and is much cheaper than would be a cocktail composed of imported gin and vermouth. A good Finnish liqueur is Mesimarja, made from the Arctic-region berry of that name. Food is good in certain of the leading hotels—the *Palace* (second-floor Grill, rooftop restaurant, bar with harbor view) in particular, and the newer *Inter•-Continental* (both its rooftop Ambassador with dancing and cheaper Brasserie), and *Hesperia,* and outside of town, the *Kalastajatorppa—Fisherman's Cottage* if you want a translation —in its own woodsy seaside compound, and with dancing and entertainment. Also out of town—in eighteenth-century Suomenlinna Fortress on its own island in the harbor, and open only in summer, is the atmospheric *Walhalla. Motti* (Toolontorinkatu 2) is noted for both Finnish and international dishes. *Adlon* (Fabianinkatu 14) is posh, expensive, and offers dinner, dancing, gambling, and entertainment. *Konig* (Mikonkatu 4) is good for after the opera or concert—supper and drinks. The *Royal,* adjoining the Swedish Theater, is traditionally reliable; nice in the summer with its terraces (the lower one is crayfish headquarters in July and August). For lunches and snacks, there are *Fazer's* (Keskuskatu 6)—a Schrafft's-type place, and one of many run by the country's largest candy manufacturers; *Esplanaadikappeli,* a cafe in the center of the Esplanade, near the Market Square end; the restaurant of *Stockmann's Department Store* (the *voileipapoyta,* or smorgasbord, is a favorite here), and the cheap, quick chain of *Columbia Cafes* all around town, where, be warned, not much English is understood. And, to have a look as well at the building itself—the restaurant and cafeteria at the Alvar Aalto-designed *Finlandia House.*

## TO WATCH

Language barriers notwithstanding, there is considerable evening diversion. *Finlandia House*—its acoustics are as excellent as its design is striking—is for symphony concerts and other musical events; I would go to hear the telephone directory read aloud if for no other reason than to see the place. The *House of Culture auditorium,* designed by Aalto, as was Finlandia House, is also the scene of symphony concerts, as is the perfectly magnificent neoclassic *Great Hall of Helsinki University.* The *Helsinki Opera House* is a rather intimate, rather charming late-nineteenth-century structure that houses the Finnish National Opera—a good company—and its ballet, which I have seen on a number of occasions and which deserves to be better known abroad. The *Helsinki City Theater*—or if you want it in Finnish, *Helsingin Kaupungin Theatteri*—is among the most splendid of contemporary-design playhouses anywhere in the world, and frequently is the scene of Finnish-language productions of well-known American musicals. If you've seen the musical at home, or at least know the score, you can easily get away with seeing the show spoken and sung in Finnish; the productions are first-rate professional. Consider also the *Swedish Theater,* which often does Swedish-language versions of musicals or plays you might be familiar enough with to want to see. And remember the movies; features go on at six-forty-five and eight-forty-five, and the foreign films have printed titles, with the original sound track, rather than dubbing. The *Helsinki Festival* usually takes place in May; lots of music, ballet, theater, and opera.

## TO BUY

Finnish handicrafts and Finnish industrial design are the most distinctive in Scandinavia. It is a marvel of Finland that with all of the trials it has faced during this century—and earlier—that its artists and artisans have been able to create and produce to the point where they have won for Finland an enviable international reputation in these fields. Outstanding are the furniture (architect Alvar Aalto is also a designer of classics of Finnish Modern furniture, and but one of many in this area); ceramics, pottery, porcelain (I have suggested seeing the museum of the Arabia factory earlier in this chapter): textiles—handwoven wools and hand-blocked cottons for draperies and for clothes; the famous handwoven high-pile *rya* rugs, plastic tableware (the best-looking, most reasonably priced I have seen in any country), and jewelry. Your first stop should be the *Finnish Design Center,* Kasarmikatu 19, for a look at the current design scene; nothing is sold, but retail sources are given for all articles.

Look next at the street-floor gallery of the *Arabia* factory's top ceramics designers downtown at Esplanaadikatu 14; then have a look at Arabia's vast range of china, casseroles, kitchenware, and the like at their upstairs exhibition on the fifth floor at Esplanaadikatu 25. (Nothing is sold, but retail sources are given). Follow this with a look at the exhibits of the glass and crystal of the *Iittala* glass factory (Tapio Wirkkala and Timo Sarpaneva are among its leading designers) at Esplanaadikatu 14 (second floor). As at Arabia, no sales are made, but retail outlets are given. Then hie yourself over to the great Finnish institution that is *Stockmann's Department Store*—with either money, credit cards (Diners Club or American Express), or travelers checks. And prepare to lose your head, at least if contemporary design is at all your scene. You may have all the help you like in spending your money here. Ask at the first-floor in-

formation desk for a personal shopper to take you all around
the store, if you would like one. (It's not necessary, as many
salespeople speak English.) The desk will also give you a floor-by-
floor directory and a good gratis map of Helsinki. And they
will explain how, after making all your purchases, you may pay
for the lot in travelers checks or with your credit card, get an
export discount if one is current, and have things well packed
for shipping, if desired, at the store's export department. Stockmann's is an excellent source for Arabia china, crockery, and
one-of-a-kind ceramics; Iittala glassware (much of its comes in
boxed sets, easy to carry with you), plastic dinnerware, and
serving pieces (ask for Fiskamin brand, in striking colors—white,
red, green, yellow, orange, even violet), cotton textiles by the
meter, whimsical toys and toddlers' picture books, furniture, *rya*
rugs (both hand- and machine-made, or the do-it-yourself kits
for same), men's, women's, and children's clothing (some of it
very smart), tasteful souvenirs, while-you-wait shoe repair, capacious paper shopping bags of which you may have need, the
biggest bookstore (it's called *Akademia*) in town, with a big
English-language section; and the earlier-recommended restaurant.
*Elanto* is a department store run by the countrywide cooperative
union by that name; less smart than Stockmann's but not without
its share of interesting wares. Check the basement for housewares, the second floor for cotton fabric by the meter, the top
floor for furniture. *Sokos,* Mannerheimintie 9, is still another
major department store; china and such are on the second floor.
*St. Henrik's Market,* in the shop-filled tunnel under the Railway
Station, is a big place, with imports as well as Finnish things.
There is a good deal of junk. But there are also some worthwhile
things, *and* it is open on Sundays from noon to ten in the
evening. *Marimekko* is the most noted name in Finnish textiles
and in women's sportswear. It is not cheap but it is high-style,
both as regards the clothes and the hand-blocked fabrics. There
are several Marimekko shops—at Keskustkatu 3 (clothing), Kale-
vankatu 4 (furnishing fabrics by the meter), and Fabianinkatu 31

(drapery fabrics). *Friends of Finnish Handicraft,* Lonnrotinkatu 4, is very big on handwoven drapery fabrics, placemats, table-cloths, needlepoint, and embroidery, and *rya* rugs and the like, which are sold from a round-the-corner shop, *Suomen Kasityon Ystavat,* at Yrjonkatu 13, seventh floor. *Asko,* Mannerheimintie 8, specializes in Finnish furniture and is expert at shipping. The *Artek* shop at Keskustkatu 3 is one of the few selling Alvar Aalto's furniture, and light fixtures. *Kalevala Koru,* Keskust-katu 4, is a charmspot full of traditional-styled jewelry that is not necessarily expensive, and an unusual selection of handmade craft gifts that is tasteful. And for closers—or, for that matter, openers—there is the earlier-described *Market Square* at the harbor. The lady vendors are themselves attractions, but so are their wares—flowers, produce, fresh fish, even handmade rag rugs that you are tempted to take home with you. Note also the oblong pavilion near the Palace Hotel, at the water's edge. Inside are butcher, fish, and cheese stalls, and one selling absolutely delicious dough-nuts called *possu;* only the strong-willed can resist buying a bagful.

## TO NOTE

**Access:** The logical means of approach is via the Finns' own airline, crackerjack Finnair, which flies Helsinki–New York via Copenhagen and Amsterdam; it also connects Helsinki with any number of European cities, both East and West, not to mention Scandinavian destinations, including Finland's own midnight sun territory in Lapland. There is also service via SAS and Pan Am from New York, and BEA flies from London. Helsinki's airport, new and one of Europe's handsomest, is about twelve miles from town; airport buses to the city are cheap; and taxis are fairly inexpensive. To reach Helsinki by train, the most direct route would be from Copenhagen or Oslo to Stockholm, trans-ferring to a ship linking the Swedish capital directly with the port of Helsinki. A much longer route, obviating sea travel, would take one from Copenhagen or Oslo north by rail to Swedish Lapland, thence east into Finnish Lapland, and south to Helsinki; motorists could follow a roughly similar route in their cars. Finnish highways are generally good, and there is a sophisticated bus network, particularly popular in Lapland. With its extensive coast and many inland waterways, there are a variety of boat services; the earlier-mentioned ones linking Helsinki with Stockholm are most comfortable; there is also service on modern ships to Germany and to both Leningrad and Talinn (Estonia) in the Soviet Union. Central Helsinki is relatively compact and exceedingly walkable but there is modern public transport and good taxi service, not to mention a number of car-hire services. **Climate:** Something like a third of Finland is north of the Arctic Circle, to give you an idea of how northerly it is. It should not be surprising, then, that summer is relatively short: June, July, August, and early September, with average temperatures in the high fifties and (in July) low sixties. You might call May spring and October autumn; each of these months has weather in the forties. Winter temperatures are often in the twenties, with crisp, snowy weather. **Clothes:** As informal as you like during the day, but after dark Helsinki is generally jacket-and-tie territory. Men tend to dress more conservatively than in, say, Stockholm or Copenhagen. But Helsinki ladies, particularly the good-looking younger crowd, have quite a couture of their own, and dress modishly. **Currency:** The Finnmark, or markka, is divided into one hundred pennia. The Finnmark is written "Fmk". **Tipping:** Service charges (15 percent in hotels, 11 percent in restaurants) are added to the bill, and that takes care of tipping. Period. Give a porter or bellhop a mark per bag, and hatcheck girls the same for your coat; that's happily *it;* cabbies, hairdressers, and barbers are not tipped. **Business hours:** Most shops are open from 8:30 A.M. to 5:00 P.M., Monday through Friday, with no lunch-hour closings; on Saturdays they close at 3:00 P.M. **Language:** The national language is Finnish; it is the mother tongue of 93 percent of the population. However, there is an affluent, influential minority whose first language is Swedish, and to keep these people happy— they are Finnish citizens too—Swedish is officially designated as the second official language after Finnish. The Swedish-speaking Finns are less snobbish about their attitude toward the Finnish language than they used to be—particularly younger people—but it is still possible to encounter Swedish-speaking Finns who would have you believe that their group constitutes the saviors of the republic. Finnish, the majority language, is nothing like the Swedish-Danish-Norwegian group. It is a part of the Finno-Ugric group of languages, and its only cousins are Estonian (which Finns can partially understand) and Hungarian (which they cannot). Finnish does not use the letters b, c, f, w, x, and z, there is no gender, and the same word stands for "he" and "she"; there are few prepositions, but instead there are fifteen cases of the noun. Finland (a Swedish word) is *Suomi* in Finnish; the Finns, *Suomalaiset.* "Thank you" is *"Kittos."* "How are you?" is *"Mita kuuluu?"* When pronouncing Finnish, *always* accentuate the first syllable (Helsinki is pronounced *Hel*-sinki, not Hel-*sink*-i). Thus endeth my Finnish lesson. These days, I am glad to be able to report, a lot of Finns—particularly in Helsinki—have taken the trouble to learn English, so that one has considerably less difficulty in communicating than in the past. This, however, is a development of only the past half decade, for which we must all be very grateful. **Local literature:** *Helsinki This Week* is a hotel giveaway, but not nearly as good as its counterparts elsewhere. *Helsinki in a Shopping Bag* is a nifty little booklet by the Association of English-Speaking Wives. *The Helsinki Architectural Guide* is an illustrated quadrilingual paperback compiled by a group of architects for architecture buffs. *Facts About Finland* (Otava Publishing Company) is a frequently revised compendium in paperback. Bookshops stock a variety of books and picture albums on the capital and the country. **Further information:** *Finnish National Tourist Office,* Scandinavia House, 505 Fifth

Avenue, New York; Scandinavian National Tourist Offices, 612
South Flower Street, Los Angeles; Finnish Tourist Board, Mikan-
katu, Helsinki, Finland; Helsinki City Tourist Office, Pojh. Es-
planaadik 17, Helsinki, Finland.

# *Istanbul*

Like West Berlin, itself the subject of a chapter in this book of capitals, Istanbul is today capital of absolutely nothing. But it was until half a century ago, and it had been, for the preceding seventeen of the Christian era's twenty centuries. Istanbul—as Constantinople and Byzantium—had controlled a succession of three empires that profoundly affected the course of European affairs, from London to Vienna.

It is, to be sure, a city that straddles two continents; the Bosphorus separates its Asian from its European sectors. Its people are overwhelmingly Moslem by faith. For four and a half centuries—the mid-fifteenth until the early twentieth—Constantinople was an essentially Eastern City. But its Western Christian roots—those implanted by the ancient Greeks of early Byzantium and the succeeding Romans—cannot easily be dismissed. The great mosques that give Istanbul its distinctive skyline are essentially Byzantine in design, different from the domed Byzantine churches that preceded them only because of appended minarets and appropriately changed interiors.

That same Christian background is apparent when one observes that Istanbul today is the seat of the Ecumenical Patriarch who heads the Orthodox Church in Turkey; of the Patriarch of the Armenian Church (Gregorian); of the Patriarch of Cilecia, who heads the Armenian Apostolic Church in Turkey; of the Bishop

of the Chaldean, or Nestorian Uniat Church; of the Titular
Bishop of Gratianopolis, who heads the Greek Byzantine Rite in
Turkey; of the Apostolic Delegate, who represents the Pope in
Rome; and, additionally, of the Grand Rabbi, of the mostly
Sephardic Jewish community. (Turkey is the only Moslem country
in the world exchanging diplomatic missions with Israel. It is one
of the few countries in the world—Mexico is another—where
the wearing of clerical garb is prohibited by law, except in places
of worship.)

**The fabulous Ottomans:** I think, though, that the biggest surprise
in this land of surprises is that the Turks are not Terrible. We
have heard so much about them through history books and from
Hollywood as cruel warriors and oppressive captors and merciless
victors that it is almost something of a letdown, when we meet
these descendants of the Ottoman sultans and their grand viziers
and intriguing courtiers, to find that they are among the most
hospitable and gentle of hosts.

There is no denying that we might have found their forebears
more glamorous. I have a series of postcards, purchased in Istanbul,
illustrating court costumes of the Ottoman Empire with the titles
of the wearers indicated for each—Custodian of the Arms of the
Sovereign, Head of the Black Eunuchs, Chief Lackey Who Keeps
and Carries the Dresses of the Sovereign, Head of the Court
Concierges, Head of the Suite of the Prime Minister in His
Unofficial Visits, Master of Ceremonies of the Ministers, Head
of the Money Minting House, and even Official Charged with
the Underclothing of the Ministers.

It was pure Arabian Nights, that empire of the Ottomans.
But then, neither the domains of the Romans or the Byzantines
that preceded it were backwaters. The early Byzantium goes back
to the sixth century before Christ, and was named, so it is
thought, after an early Greek king named Bizas. Its location on
the Bosphorus helped it do well from its earliest period; so well,
in fact, that in the second century A.D. the Romans, under Emperor Severus, captured it. And in 330 A.D. Emperor Constantine

moved the seat of his government eastward from Rome to Byzantium, becoming known first as Seconda Roma, eventually as Nova Roma, and only later as Constantinople. Rome brought more than government with it; language (the Latin then spoken by the Romans) and culture followed, too. (The town's inhabitants soon became called *Romani;* that became shortened to *Rum,* which to this day is a Turkish word meaning people of the West.) In 395, the Roman Empire had become unwieldy, and was chopped in two, with Constantinople heading the eastern sector.

**Justinian's Constantinople:** The sixth century saw Constantinople enjoy its first Golden Age, under Emperor Justinian. He won back Africa from the Vandals and took parts of Italy from the Ostrogoths. He was a great builder—St. Sofia was one of his projects; but possibly most important, he codified Roman law, an accomplishment that profoundly influenced subsequent legal history. Later, Greek influence became so popular—after a lapse of centuries—that Greek replaced Latin as the official language. Subsequent Byzantine centuries were not unlike those of other empires; one power after another—Persians, Bulgarians, Russians, Hungarians—all besieged, or tried to besiege, Constantinople, creating just enough weakness for it to become acceptable to the advances of Arabs and, more important, of Turks come from Asia to the plains of Anatolia.

What had happened is that Constantinople had become a cultural melting pot—a fine thing in itself, but it was not working as well as it might, what with the various groups—Turks, Russians, Jews, Germans—antagonistic toward one another. In the ninth century the Syrian-led Iconoclasts destroyed priceless works of religious art in their anti-Christian violence. Later, Italians from Venice and Genoa came to settle in, amassing so much wealth that they aroused the native Byzantines who, in 1182, rose up against them. The Italians did not forget; that uprising was to be Byzantium's undoing, for this was the time of the Crusades. The Italians were successful in influencing the Crusaders to attack Constantinople. It fell to them in 1403, virtually destroyed, and was never again strong. Succeeding centuries saw the neighboring Turks organize themselves and develop culturally, politically, and militarily. Under a bright twenty-one-year-old sultan, Mehmet the Conqueror (you will see a miniature of him smelling a rose in Topkapi Palace), they took Constantinople in 1453. It was the end of the Byzantine Empire.

The Ottoman sultans were never—even into this century—to understand representative government, or the needs and concerns of the great mass of their mostly impoverished subjects. Still, their socially and politically reactionary dynasty fostered a culturally magnificent empire not without refinements in many areas, and with levels of sophistication—in matters aesthetic—that the West was only able to marvel at. From the beginning there was an appreciation of the Byzantine inheritance. Already existing structures like Justinian's St. Sofia were left standing and were converted to use as mosques rather than razed.

**The Brilliance of Suleiman the Magnificent:** Under Suleiman the Magnificent the empire reached its zenith. His armies made conquests in the Balkans and the Mediterranean basin; he occupied Hungary. His armies were victors over the Persians, his navy was one of the most powerful extant. All the while he effected reforms—military, educational, and particularly legal— these last earning him the name Suleiman the Law-giver. At the same time he was a lavish patron of poetry and painting and the applied arts, most definitely including architecture. It was under Suleiman that the greatest of the Turkish architects, Sinan, built the Suleimanye mosque. Still, this remarkable man was hardly without faults. Even though he gave his unusually competent grand vizier, Ibrahim, more power than grand viziers customarily held, he had him strangled, without apparent provocation. He was later held responsible for the murder of one of his sons, Mustafa, only because his No. 1 wife, Roxelana, wanted one of her two sons to succeed to the throne. Later, Suleiman saw to it that the unfavorite of those two sons was eliminated. It was only one of a number of instances over the centuries where the ladies of the harem were to exert fatal influences on imperial actions.

From the early Ottoman period through the early nineteenth century, the Sultans lived in Topkapi Palace, which by the time they vacated, had become a city within a city. The early nineteenth century saw the beginnings of European influence in the court. Turbans were forbidden and were replaced by fezzes. Courtiers' long gowns were replaced by obligatory trousers. The first newspaper was printed. A Western-style mail service was begun. The university was founded. In 1856, a sultan attended a foreign ambassador's ball, and not long after, there were the first sultanic visits to Europe. All the while, though, palace life became more lavish and expensive—the court had moved from Topkapi to neo-baroque Dolmabahce—and representative government was making no headway. After two sultans were ousted in the 1870s, Turkey got a constitution of sorts and a window-dressing parliament. But things were not going well.

**The Young Turks—and Ataturk:** The subject states of the enormous empire were becoming restless. There were military reverses. The original Young Turks—whose name has since been taken by similarly dissident, reformist groups in other countries—forced the abdication of Sultan Abdul Hamid in 1909. In 1914, with the outbreak of World War I, Turkey and Germany signed a secret agreement, with the latter advising the army of the former. Later that year, the Allies declared war on Turkey, and at war's end the Ottoman Empire was vanquished and dismembered.

The last of the sultans, Mohammed VI, capitulated to the Allies, who occupied his capital and sought to administer what was left of his empire through him. Meanwhile, the young genius whom history remembers as Kemal Ataturk gained political power in Anatolia, the vast plain that is Asian Turkey and that constitutes the great bulk of the country. The last sultan was deposed in 1922 (he died four years later in San Remo, Italy); moreover, the institution of the sultanate was abolished, and law forbids entry into Turkey of any member of the Imperial Family.

The Republic of Turkey was founded. Ataturk, its first President, had no hesitation in using dictatorial methods to transform the ancient and archaic remnant of an empire into a twentieth-century republic. He disestablished the powerful Moslem hierarchy, the while allowing freedom of religion. He forbade the wearing of the Moslem fez. He attempted to liberate women, although legislating the removal of the veil was not as easy (not out in the villages where tradition dies hard) as with the fez. He Romanized the Arabic alphabet. He turned Turkey toward the West in additional matters—technical, industrial, educational. He introduced wide-scale public education so that Turkey now has more than half of its populace literate, in contrast to about a tenth when the republic was born. And—in an attempt to make a clean, fresh, republican state—he moved the capital from ancient Istanbul to the then-obscure town of Ankara, smack in the center of the Anatolian plateau. He died in 1938, only fifty-eight, of cirrhosis of the liver, in Dolmabahce, the ex-imperial palace that he had turned into a public building. It is a measure of the continuing respect of his people for him that the clocks in the palace were stopped at precisely the moment he died—five past nine—and have not been wound since.

**Modernity—and unsolved problems:** Post-Ataturk Turkey has only begun to solve its problems. The rural poor remain grindingly poor and backward (in great contrast to the urban populace). The military considers it necessary to step in and take over when government instability manifests itself (although Turkey has a multiparty system and a critical press). The youth of the country is impatient with poverty, only-partial democracy, and a foreign policy that includes NATO affiliation and NATO/U.S. bases on Turkish soil—in a country that not only shares a land border with the Soviet Union but controls the waterways (Bosphorus, Sea of Marmara, Dardanelles) through which Soviet ships must pass from the Black Sea to the Mediterranean. Still, the traveler familiar with the Moslem world and the still-slow, tradition-dictated pace of other Moslem countries, cannot but marvel at the modern miracle that is modern Turkey. The same traveler is grateful that the city that was the symbol of the old Turkey is confident enough of its future to retain the monuments of a past at once spectacular and indelible.

TO SEE

**Lay of the land:** Rio de Janeiro, Hong Kong, Sydney, perhaps. All told, there are few cities whose setting is such an exquisite blend of land and water and architecture. Credit must go first to the early Greeks who settled the place, and the Byzantines and Romans who followed, building a proper city. But it was Sultan Mehmet the Conqueror who knew a splendid setting when he saw one. He built Topkapi Palace, and to this day the view from its terrace is the most enviable in town.

Let me repeat the basic Turkish geography lesson you may not remember from the sixth grade. Locate the Black Sea on a map. Then look at the Aegean-Mediterranean Seas. The body of water separated by a finger of land from the Aegean is the Sea of Marmara, and the channel cutting through—joining the Marmara and Aegean-Mediterranean—is the Dardanelles. Continue eastward into the Sea of Marmara, look north, and there is another body of water linking Marmara with the Black Sea. That is the Bosphorus. Its eastern shore is the continent of Asia and a portion of the city of Istanbul. Its western shore is the continent of Europe and another—the more important—portion of Istanbul. Now we subdivide the European sector of Istanbul. It is bisected by a glamorously named body of water—an arm of the Bosphorus —called the Golden Horn. There are no bridges, only boats, between European and Asian Istanbul. But two bridges span the Golden Horn to join the two parts of European Istanbul. One of these—Galata Bridge (appearing on some maps, to confuse you, as Koprusu Bridge) is the heart of town, a veritable crossroads of the universe. I remember that on my very first visit to Istanbul I walked across Galata Bridge the day I arrived, late in the afternoon. There were sleek white passenger liners—a Soviet ship out of Odessa, a domestic Turkish maritime vessel next to it—tied up at the north end of the bridge, in the newer sector of the city. I was a part of a motley crossing-crowd—pedestrians wearing not only the Western garb of the city but also the pantaloons and aprons and coveralls worn over the centuries in the villages; passenger cars that had seen better days; taxis that were making an effort at modernity; the passenger-packed *dolmas;* farmers leading their clattery horsecarts with dusty sacks of grain as their cargoes; laughing, animated student-cyclists. And dead ahead, in the old part of the city, were needle-thin minarets—a principal glory of Turkish design—framing the domes of the mosques of an unsurpassable skyline.

Istanbul has been known to put off newcomers because it is without the scrubbed-up quality of many cities in the West. There is no doubt about it: It conceals neither its age nor the poverty of many of its residents. It is, in this respect, more Middle Eastern—at times shabby, at others falling apart at the seams—than European, and for those to whom it is an introduction to the Levant, the ambience can at first appear jarring and grating. A period of adjustment is required in which one comes to understand that the old cities at Asia's edge are far better organized than seems apparent. Istanbul demands of its inspectors a sense of proportion—for its sweeping natural situation; a sense of design—for its art and artisanship; and a sense of history, to evaluate all of these in terms of its egalitarian present and autocratic past.

Before setting off, it is as well that the visitor be apprised of the situation of the hotels vis-à-vis the most interesting destinations of the city. The hotels are clustered in the *new European part* of the city, *north* of the Galata Bridge, in the general neighborhood of Taksim Square. With some important exceptions, the places the visitor wants to see are concentrated in the *old European part* of the city, *south* of the Galata Bridge. The distance between the two is considerable. It can easily take a half hour by car through dusty, snarly, difficult traffic—particularly in summer. That is why I recommend hiring a chauffeur-driven car for that portion of one's Istanbul visit—say a couple of days, anyway—that will include requisite sightseeing. I should not have to add that it will pay to make every effort to secure a knowledgeable driver.

**Choice destinations:** *Topkapi Palace* comes close to being the be-all, end-all Istanbul destination. It is bits and pieces of everything Ottoman Turkish—the cloak-and-dagger sultans, their art and architecture, their clothes and their cooking, their manners and morals. Sultan Mehmet the Conqueror began building Topkapi in the mid-fifteenth century, and his successors kept adding to it all the way through the middle of the nineteenth century, by which time the imperial entourage had moved to the more Western-design Dolmabahce Palace in the newer part of the city. The *Golden Horn*-Bosphorus-view situation at the edge of the old city's peninsula on the site of the earlier Byzantine acropolis is inspired, and so is the walled city-within-a-city concept of the palace. Topkapi today is a dual destination. One goes to see the centuries-long residence of the Ottoman emperors and their harems. And one goes to see the contents of the Turkish Republic's premier museum.

The *palace* embraces a trio of sections: *outer,* with the kitchens (now a part of the museum), stables, storerooms, staff quarters; *inner,* the *sanctum sanctorum* cluster of buildings where sultans and their personal staffs lived; and the *harem,* about which more later. Among the important rooms are the Sultans' Audience Chamber, the beautifully decorated wooden Pavilion of the Sofa, the masterfully tiled Baghdad Pavilion; the high-ceilinged and surprisingly elaborate Circumcision Chamber, wherein imperial princes were circumcised. The *harem* was reopened in late 1971 after meticulous and expensive restoration lasting more than three decades. Well over a hundred of its more than four hundred apartments, halls, corridors, baths, paved courtyards, and gardens are open to visitors. The opulent harem—with its glazed tiles, gilt archways, silk brocades, and rich velvets—was perhaps one of the few institutions of Ottoman life that the movies did not exaggerate. Torture chambers with vats of boiling oil may or may not have been the fantasy of Hollywood script writers. But the harem was not fiction; the only men who ever entered it were the sultans themselves and the male members of their family, along with their castrated, mostly black eunuchs. (The concept of the eunuch, to be fair to the Ottomans, originated with their Constantinople predecessors, the Byzantine emperors, and spread to various parts of the Middle East; the eunuchs were brought as slaves from Africa, usually from among groups of boys singled out for the eunuch trade; castration operations are reported not always to have been completely effective, and eunuchs are known to have risen to high position, at least one attaining the status of a Byzantine general.) The harem's inhabitants were at once slave girls and princesses, these latter fathered by the sultans and often married off to rich merchants or princes upon reaching maturity. Otherwise, the harem's inhabitants stayed within its walls. In the Hall of the Sultans their mentors arranged elaborate entertainments for them, sometimes even importing foreign musicians and opera companies. (Lady Wortley Montague, in her eighteenth-century Constantinople letters, reported that many harem ladies were literate and lived quite cultivated lives.) Quite as opulent as that chamber are the rooms inhabited by Roxelana, the favorite wife of Sultan Suleiman the Magnificent, whose intrigues are recounted in the earlier pages of this chapter.

The Topkapi museums are substantial enough to be the subject of a separate visit or two, to the palace compound. The *Treasury* is the most dazzling subdivision, with the magnificent jeweled dagger that was the basis of the plot of the film, *Topkapi,* but one of a number of breathtakingly beautiful exhibits. In the *Portrait Gallery* one sees a collection of the miniatures at which the Turks excelled. Two stand out: Mehmet the Conqueror, in white turban and blue robe, smelling a red rose; and Suleiman the Magnificent, in a pale blue robe, attended by two courtiers. There is a section of normal-size portraits of the sultans as well, with the striking likenesses of Mustafa III and Abdulhamid I, the ones to single out. Still another gallery shows off the elaborately embroidered *caftans,* and other garments of the sultans—some two-score cases of them, with jeweled swords often accompanying them. Other rooms are devoted to the fine art of Turkish embroidery, Turkish tiles and pottery, Turkish china and glass, and, in the architecturally outstanding ex-palace kitchens, cooking utensils that convey the idea of the importance the sultans attached to cuisine. There are, as well, extraordinarily good collections of both Chinese and European porcelain.

*The great mosques* follow Topkapi in importance. *St. Sofia,* built as a Byzantine church, later served as a mosque, and its architecture became the prototype of the mosques that were built after it. (The principal change was the addition of minarets, a maximum of four except the Blue Mosque, with its six.) That is why I classify it as I have. It is a work of such genius that it is difficult to believe that Emperor Justinian dedicated it more than fourteen hundred years ago. The interior's tremendous height—the equivalent of a twelve- or fourteen-story building of today—gives it a nobility difficult to describe. The mammoth mosaics of the Emperor Justinian and Constantine, of the Virgin Mary and of Christ with the Virgin Mary and St. John the Baptist flanking him, are major works of art. And the stone-carving, the detail of the arches, windows, and galleries, are exceptional, too. St. Sofia, a museum since the advent of the republic, is a major Istanbul experience. The *Blue Mosque,* known also as Sultan Ahmet Mosque, is an early-seventeenth-century work of massive proportions (thus six minarets rather than the usual four), great elegance, and the exquisite interior—blue-green tiles in intricate designs cover the surfaces of the domed ceilings—that has given the place its name. *Suleimanye* bears the name of its builder, Suleiman the Magnificent; it is the masterwork of the architect,

Sinan, whom Suleiman commissioned to build the countless
mosques and palaces that earned him a reputation of Turkey's all-
time No. 1 architect. The courtyard is especially inviting; the
interior is dominated by a dome that admits light through its 138
windows. And a bonus is the tomb of Suleiman and his infamous
wife Roxelana. Istanbul has other beautiful mosques. If you
have time for some, consider *Rustem Pasa*—adjoining the venerable *Egyptian* (*Spice*) *Bazaar* (itself worth a visit), designed by
Sinan and with exceptional tilework within; *Beyazit,* early-sixteenth-century and with unique stalls especially built for vendors
of perfume and rosaries; and *Sehzade,* still another Sinan work,
built by his patron, Suleiman the Magnificent, as a memorial to
the two sons whose appalling fate is recounted in earlier pages of
this chapter.

**Museums:** Topkapi is only a starter. Perhaps the biggest surprise in this area is the *Archaeological Museum,* particularly to
the visitor who has not given much thought to the geography of
Turkey—and the classical Greek and Roman settlements within
its frontiers. The Aegean and Mediterranean coasts of Turkey
contain classical ruins—Ephesus is the most outstanding example—that rival those of today's Greece. This museum, founded
more than a century ago as the Imperial Museum, is full of fine
specimens, in two floors of galleries. The requisite exhibits are
the elaborately decorated sarcophagus of Alexander the Great,
dating to the fourth century B.C.; a fine head of Alexander,
from the third century B.C.; and a full-length draped statue of
Alexander, from the second century B.C. The *Tile Museum* is
housed in the building opposite the entrance to the Archaeological
Museum (whose original home it was). Little ballyhooed, this is a
smallish but choice repository of the art of the Turkish tile; a
don't-miss. The *Museum of Ancient Oriental Art* is another neighbor of the Archaeological Museum, and in the galleries of its
single-floor building exhibits dazzling Babylonian antiquities and
also of the classical Greek, Assyrian, Arabic, and Hittite eras;
the last-mentioned was the dominant ancient civilization of the

Anatolian plateau which constitutes the bulk of modern Turkey. The *Museum of Turkish and Islamic Arts* is a repository of treasures not come upon in the other museums, most particularly carpets, which have been a traditional Turkish applied-arts form for many centuries. There are a couple of galleries full of antique rugs, both Turkish and foreign; other displays range from illuminated Korans and manuscripts to antique jewelry. The setting is a onetime soup kitchen built by the architect Sinan. The *Istanbul City Museum* is housed in a charming white marble fantasy that had, some centuries ago, served as a little school, which had been built in the seventeenth century by an intellectually and charitably minded white eunuch who rose from the ranks to high harem office. The contents rank with those of the best city museums in Europe—memorabilia through the centuries—clothes and coffee pots, etchings and inkwells, pens and porcelains. *Kariye* (known also as *Chora,* the original Greek name), though the last-listed museum in this section, is hardly of little consequence. It is a onetime Byzantine church with ancient antecedents. Over the centuries it became a showcase of some of the finest mosaics of Byzantine Constantinople. They were covered up in later centuries during the period when Kariye was converted into a mosque (there is still a single minaret beside it, from that time). But with the advent of the republic, the chalk surface was removed from the mosaics, which constitute some of the finest extant. There are fine frescoes, as well. They are to be seen in the sanctuary.

**Other destinations:** *Dolmabahce Palace* is where the sultans moved their court when they got bored with Topkapi, and wanted something a little more Western. This was during the early-nineteenth-century reign of Abdulmecit, the first of the dynasty to be really curious about Europe—and to do something about it. The palace fronts the Bosphorus in the newer side of European Istanbul, almost directly below the Istanbul Hilton. Its style is what might be called Arabian Nights-Baroque-Victorian, if you can imagine such a mix. It is so absurdly gaudy and so pre-

posterously ornate that you can't get angry with it. You enjoy
it. And I don't mind telling you that I *have* enjoyed it.
The Society of American Travel Writers convened in Istanbul
in 1967, and the Turkish Government hosted the writers at a
supper-dance in the palace's Great Hall. A waltz beneath the
great central 750-bulb chandelier—a gift of Queen Victoria—
in that ornate room is a waltz not easily forgotten. Nor, for that
matter, is a tour of Dolmabahce's harem. The simply furnished
room in which Ataturk died in 1938 is preserved as it was, as
a memorial to the founder and first president of the republic.
*Beylerbeyi* is a somewhat newer, smaller Bosphorus-shore imperial palace, erected in 1865; like Dolmabahce, it is a rather
bizarre Turko-European mélange, with a number of sumptuous
reception rooms, a harem, and its chief claim to fame the 1869
visit of Napoleon's Empress Eugenie. *Rumeli Hisari* is a fortress
on the Bosphorus which, with its medieval crenelated towers, was
constructed by Sultan Mehmet the Conqueror more than five
centuries ago. The *Underground Cisterns*—still water-filled, as
they have been since the time of Byzantine Emperor Justinian,
who built them—comprise a full dozen tanks delineated by a
series of stylized Corinthian columns. There are *ferry boats*
to the Asian side of Istanbul—surely you will want to personally
experience the unique intercontinental aspect of the city. There
are boats as well to the *Princes Islands,* pleasure gardens for
the locals during the warm-weather months, with restaurants,
cafes, and facilities for swimming. And it is pleasant to drive
along the European Bosphorus shore toward the Black Sea, at
least as far as *Tarabya,* an area that is agreeable in summer, with
a fine hotel, swimming facilities, cafes, and a number of good
seafood restaurants.

## TO WATCH

During the warm-weather months there are frequent presentations of classical Turkish plays by the National Theater (with earphones for simultaneous translation), of performances by the Janissary Mehter Band, and of music and ballet at *Topkapi Palace;* some of these are part of the annual Istanbul Festival. Additional summer-months performances—drama and concerts—take place at *Rumeli Hisari Fortress,* on the Bosphorus. Check for *Son et Lumière* (Sound and Light) at such splendid summer settings as *St. Sofia* and the *Blue Mosque.* In winter, the opera and ballet companies of the Turkish State Opera come from their home base in Ankara to perform periodically at the *Opera House;* there are plays—presented, of course, in Turkish—at the *City* and other theaters; and there are periodical *concerts* at locations that hotel concierges are familiar with. Some, but not all, cinemas show imported *movies* with the original sound track and Turkish printed titles; at these, you're in luck if you know the language of the country of origin; hotel concierges can advise. Belly dancers or no, Turkish *night clubs* are easily skippable, and no cheaper than their counterparts anywhere. That of the Istanbul Hilton and the restored old Galata Tower are as reliable as any.

## TO STAY

If the Turks tend to be less loquacious than the neighboring Greeks, they are not a whit less charming as hosts. Tourism is newer as an industry to them, but the last decade has seen them make astonishing strides in the expansion of every facet of their tourist plant—from highways to hotels. The *Istanbul Hilton* is some two decades old, and is to Turkish tourism what the Caribe Hilton was to the beginning of tourism in Puerto Rico and throughout the Caribbean. Pre-Hilton Istanbul had no idea of what the casual foreign tourist was all about. A government development corporation commissioned Hilton International to supervise the design and construction of the new hotel and to operate it. I first stayed there shortly after the opening, and it has never, over the years, allowed its standards to lower, even though it is only just beginning to face major competition; few hotels in uncompetitive situations are so high-minded. Bedrooms are generous-sized, baths de luxe. The lobby, both capacious and comfortable, leads to a covered terrace-cafe overlooking formal gardens, with the shoreline of the Bosphorus—a mosque highlighting it—beyond. The ships plying between the Black Sea and the Sea of Marmara are a constant passing parade, and Asian Istanbul is across the water. The restaurants (about which more later) are Hilton high-standard; so are the bar-cafes, and—big bonus—there's a honey of a pool for lunchtime or predinner dips in summer. The modern *Divan,* smaller, cheaper, and less luxurious than the Hilton, but modern, comfortable, professionally staffed, and with full facilities, is nearby. It has the even newer, also pleasant *Hotel Unver* as a same-category neighbor offering solid competition. The *Park Hotel,* closest of the lot to busy Taksim Square, is also the oldest, by some decades. Its Bosphorus-view location almost rivals the Hilton's—there's a nice cafe for drinks or coffee and an atmospheric restaurant—but the plant has been allowed to age not quite as gracefully as it might; a pity, because the place has character. I doubt if you'll want to put up there if the city itself is the reason for your visit, but you should know about the modern, handsome *Tarabya Hotel,* at Tarabya, on the Bosphorus shore en route to the Black Sea, if for no other reason than that you may want to go for a meal or a drink. The guest rooms are attractive, and there's a pool. Also quite a way from town, but also worth knowing is the *Cinar Hotel,* at Yeskiloy, near the airport: contemporary, sleek-lined, with full facilities, including a *boîte,* pool, and beach of its own—these last-mentioned all popular with the locals in summer. Two other good bets for day's swimming excursions are the beach club of the *Carlton Hotel* and the *Lido Swimming Club;* your own hotel can arrange your admittance. But mind: 30 million dollars' worth of additional hotels are going up—a quartet of them: the 29-story, 400-room Bosphorus-view *Sheraton Istanbul* near Taksim Square; the 27-story, 432-room *Istanbul Inter*·-*Continental,* also in the Taksim Square area; and two moderate-category hotels, the *Macka* and the *Tepebasi.*

TO EAT (AND DRINK)

The extraordinary finesse, sophistication, and diversity of the Turkish cuisine should not come as a surprise to anyone who has inspected the onetime capital of the Ottoman Empire, visualized its opulence, and been made aware of the enormity of the empire when it was at its peak. (The kitchens at Topkapi Palace, still open to the public, are said to have had staffs ranging in the thousands.) It is difficult to say just how much the Turks improved their cuisine by exposure to the foods of their subject peoples, or whether it was the Turks, with an innate culinary sense, who magnanimously brought their dishes to the lands they occupied, thereby raising local cooking standards. Surely Ottoman imperialism has played its role, one way or the other, or both ways. What is so sad is that the republican Turks, while maintaining the high standards of the cuisine they inherited at home, have done little about spreading the good word about it abroad. One rarely comes across a Turkish restaurant of any consequence or importance abroad. The visitor to Istanbul, therefore, is in for some surprises. His first area of concentration should be the appetizers (*meze* in Turkish) preceding lunch or dinner. One may order three or four, or six or eight. They run a wide gamut— from a dish of black olives, green peppers, tomatoes, and cu-

cumbers, to more elaborate things like artichokes with fresh fennel, gray mullet caviar, stuffed mussels, smoked eels, fried eggplant, or carrots with yogurt, and *dolma,* the same stuffed vine leaves that the Greeks serve. Soups can be imaginative, too— yogurt soup with fresh mint or red lentil, for example. Fish and seafood can be sublimely good—grilled skewered swordfish with bay leaves; the local variation of sole, and the Bosphorus fish-delicacy (always caught at night by lantern-equipped fishermen) known as *lufer.* The local lobsters and shrimps are excellent. Grilled meats—*shish kebab, doner kebab*—the Turkish counter-part of the Greek *souvlaki* (or vice versa?) vertically grilled on a spit, yogurt kebab, (broiled lamb served on typical flatbread with yogurt), and roast baby lamb. The crumbly white goats' milk cheese that the Greeks call *feta* is *adirne* to the Turks, and equally as good. The Turks are adept at salads; they can be simple greens dressed in oil and vinegar, or composed salads on a buffet table. The pastries include the honey-sweet *baklava* and the delicate little cakes comprising layers of the pencil-thin *philo* dough that the Hungarians might well have pre-empted for the strudel they invented, when the Turks occupied Hungary half a millennium ago.

Turkish wines are as much an unknown quantity abroad as the food. There are both white and red domestic varieties, and both can be good. Kavaklidere is a favorite dry white; Kulup Sarabi or Kulup Kalite, good dry reds. Ah, the Turkish coffee! It's made in the little individual copper or brass pots, using beans that have been ground to a powdery substance. It is always black and thick, but is sugared (or not) as you prefer when being made so that you should order it as you like it: *sekerli* (extra sweet), *orta* (sweet), or *sade* (without sugar). The Turks' favorite apéritif is *raki* (Yeni is a good brand). It is the anisette-flavored drink that turns cloudy when water or ice cubes are added to it (that is the best way to drink it), and it is similar to the French anisette and the Greek *ouzo.* The Turks also make their own version of cognac (spelled *kanyak*), and a good quality of vodka. Efes is the brand-name of a leading beer, but there's a lot of Danish Tuborg about, not to mention a wide range of imported spirits. Despite its un-Turkish name, the *Roof Rotisserie* of the *Istanbul Hilton* is the town's best Turkish restaurant. Hilton International, wherever it operates, makes a point of hiring the best local chefs available to cook the local cuisine at its most typical and delicious. Istanbul is a perfect example of this policy at work. The room is handsome—with that fabled Bosphorus view. The service is Turkish professional at its very best, and most important, there is an extensive menu of authentic specialties, all of them well prepared and beautifully served, from *meze* (some thirty of these appetizers are on a typical menu) to Turkish pastries.

The Bosphorus has a number of restaurants lining its shore, on the European side; they are generally unpretentious, but they can be very good indeed. *Facyo,* not far from the Tarabya Hotel, is one of the very best. The *meze* are among the tastiest in town, and the swordfish kebab exceptional; grilled meats are good, too. Two other oldies that remain first-rate are the neighboring *Feliz* and *Fidan;* it is easy to confuse them, but it makes no difference: They are both fine, especially for grilled fish. *Liman Kokantasi* serves lunch only and is located upstairs—overlooking the Bosphorus and the Golden Horn, near the Galata Bridge—in a building owned by Turkish Maritime Lines, which operates the restaurant; the view is fascinating, the food authentic. *Galata Tower Restaurant* is in a restored sixth-century tower, not far from the bridge; convenient for lunch if you're in the area. *Abdullah* used to be Istanbul's leading restaurant and worth every lira of the taxi fare to get out to it and back to town; it has deteriorated. If a country drive does interest you, I would instead recommend *Beyti,* out near the airport; agreeable ambience and good kabobs—doner, shish, and mixed. The *Hotel Divan's outdoor cafe* has excellent pastry. The *Terrace Cafe* at *Topkapi Palace* has an inspired view of the Golden Horn and both Bosphorus shores; fine for coffee, Coke, and a snack after sightseeing the palace.

### TO BUY

There are wonderful things to buy in Istanbul, but shopping
can be a tricky proposition, done alone or without some knowledgeable Turk along. There are many touristy-souvenir shops
near the hotels in the Taksim Square area, and in the main
shopping streets off the square. You don't need any help to
inspect these places, but they have little to recommend them.
For the lot, you're on your own, without any specific suggestions
from me, except to bargain in the case of more expensive articles.
The place to shop—and surely this will come as no surprise to you
—is the *Grand (or Covered) Bazaar,* first constructed in the
fifteenth century by Mehmet the Conqueror, enlarged a number of
times (Suleiman the Magnificent was among the enlargers), rebuilt
at others, as a result of earthquakes or fires—most recently in
1954. There are several *thousand* individual shops, and the visitor
who enters the labyrinthine maze without someone who knows
his way is making a mistake. (Here, one bargains for everything.)
Shops are grouped together according to category, as they have
been since the founding: Rugs are in one area, antiques in
another, jewelry in another, housewares in another. For the visitor
from abroad it seems to me that the most interesting sections are
those vending jewelry (new, elderly, or antique), carpets (new,
elderly, or antique), and antiques—this latter covering a multitude of sins. The jewelry tradition is ancient and honorable;
the work is in gold—a lot of it is 14-karat, with pearls, garnets,
turquoises, opals, sapphires, and diamonds used in the designs.
The most popular article of jewelry sold (you will see them on
every female tourist who has been in town longer than, say,
six hours) is the harem ring. It is, actually, a cluster of several
gold rings joined together, and embellished with various precious
or semi-precious stones. There are, as well, brooches, bracelets,
necklaces, and rings for men as well. The jewelry section of

the Grand Bazaar has more than its share of dealers; browse and select, as you like, preferably with the advice of a knowledgeable Turk. The antiques shops are repositories of icons, old jewelry, carpets, and all manner of objects, large and small. Many have great appeal. Once again, it pays to be with someone who knows about these things, if you yourself do not. As for icons, my counsel is the same as in the chapter on Athens: Beware; there are lots of good copies. Of the many *antiques dealers,* several whose wares I found interesting were *Arnak Bey* and *E. Civanyan; Jakob Y. Salhosfili and Edip Cansever;* and *Abdullah L. Chalabi.* In the carpet section, a shop operated by *Cemal Aksoy* sells handsome handwoven goats' hair blankets that may be used as rugs (or rugs that may be used as blankets, as you will) in shades of black, brown, or natural; they ship, and reliably—as I made a test in their case. *Aleksan Kuyumcuoglu* sells good-looking old Anatolian and Persian rugs, in both silk and wool. Time was when Turkish-made *suede* jackets and coats, for both men and women, were excellent buys and of at least fair quality. Design has, however, deteriorated, the quality is no better, and prices are considerably higher. That leaves the *Spice Bazaar,* also known as the Egyptian Bazaar and, so far as I am concerned, a requisite Istanbul destination, shopper or no. They are all there, much as they have been for centuries: the spices and condiments, and so many of the foodstuffs that go to make the Turkish cuisine. Displays are intriguing and tempting, and the crowds great fun to mix with. Find the shop called *Ipek* and buy a bagful of typical and traditional candy—either halva (which you may know from the United States), or my favorite, Turkish Delight, this country's answer to the gumdrop of the West.

TO NOTE

**Access:** Unless you have time on your hands, fly. Pan Am has direct service from the United States. Turkish Airlines, the well-run government-owned national carrier, connects Istanbul and Ankara with major Western European cities, and many Western European airlines connect their capitals with Turkey. There are cheap airport buses from Istanbul's international airport at Yesilkoy into the city, which is about fifteen miles distant, but taxi fares are nice and low. Arrival by train can evoke memories of all those old *Orient Express* movies, because Istanbul is still the eastern terminus of the still-running *Orient Express,* which connects it with London and Paris via Sophia, Belgrade, and Milan. There are other express trains to other parts of Europe, including Athens. There are bus services from Western Europe, utilizing the same routes as motorists, who enter Turkey from either Bulgaria or Greece. Within Istanbul, taxis are your best bet, along with the Istanbul version of the jitney-type taxis seen in other cities of the world. Here they're called *dolmus.* This means stuffed, and when you ride them you'll understand the reason for the name. They cruise defined routes along main thoroughfares leading from one part of town to another, and they stop with some regularity en route, to discharge or pick up passengers, who pay a bit more than they would in public transport, but less than in a taxi. (The word for "stop"—when you want out—is *"dour."*) Istanbul is big and spread out. It is not a walking town, and if one has limited time and wants to take in a fairish amount, I recommend hiring a chauffeur-driven car; driving oneself through this complex city could be time-consuming and self-defeating, at least on a short touristic visit. There are basic bus-sightseeing tours. **Climate:** Istanbul is a temperate-zone, four-season city, with mild winters, hot summers, and moderate in-between seasons. Winter (December through March) averages in the forties, occasionally dipping to the thirties in January and February, when snow is not uncommon. Summer (June through part of September) averages around seventy going into the eighties in July and August. Spring (April and May) and autumn (October and November) average between the mid-fifties and mid-sixties. **Clothes:** Urban Turks wear Western-style clothes, but only a very small upper class is able to concern itself with the nuances of style and fashion. Casual dress is the rule during the day, in warm weather, and in the evening, too, at the outdoor restaurants and cafes that are popular; jacket and tie are needed only in the relatively few dressy places. **Currency:** The unit of exchange is the Turkish Lira (TL). It is divided into one hundred kurus. **Tipping:** Tips are important to Turks in the service industries. Tip restaurant and cafe waiters about 10 percent, even if a service charge is included in the bill. In hotels, bellhops expect about 2½ liras per bag, as do baggage porters in terminals. Leave chambermaids a few liras a day if the room has been taken care of nicely. Taxi drivers expect about 10 percent. **Business hours:** Shops are usually open from 8:30 or 9:00 A.M. until noon, and from 1:30 P.M. until about 6:30 P.M., Monday through Saturday. **Language:** Turkish, with the alphabet—for nearly half a century now—the very same Roman one we ourselves use; Western words have crept into Turkish, in which they are written phonetically, as they sound. You'll be surprised how much you'll be able to understand, reading menus, signs, and the like. In Istanbul, English is spoken in hotels, leading restaurants, transport terminals, and some shops. Where it isn't, try French—the other popular Western language. **Local literature:** An English-language paper, the *Daily News,* is published in Ankara but circulates also in Istanbul; it is intended primarily for the country's long-term English-speaking residents, but it is of some value to tourists, too. A weekly, published in English, called *Outlook,* is a pro-government publication, good for background. Locally published English-language guidebooks are all about; the English is not always intelligible, but the pictures are pretty.

**Further information:** Turkish Tourism and Information Office, 500 Fifth Avenue, New York; Ministry of Tourism and Information, Istanbul Branch, Istanbul Hilton, Istanbul, Turkey. The best map of Istanbul was published by the ministry in 1968—and is so dated. It was superseded by an inferior map in 1970, subsequently reprinted; but you're in luck if you find the 1968 edition.

# *Lisbon*

If you start out feeling sorry for Lisbon, you are not going to
like it. What you have to recognize is that Lisboners like their
town the way it is: Europe's most unabashedly old-fashioned
capital. This is, after all, the seat of government of Europe's
Mississippi, and it is as well to bear it in mind to spare oneself
frustration. Portugal is about No. 0 on the Continent when it
comes to things like literacy, per-capita income, and the prevalence,
at least in rural areas, of amenities like indoor plumbing, running
water, and electricity. Even in the area of representative government, Portugal has moved only at an elderly snail's pace since
the demise of the low-profile, albeit repressive, four-decade Salazar dictatorship. And although Britain, France, Belgium, and
Spain have long since relinquished their African colonies, Portugal
continues to spend a disproportionately excessive proportion of
its limited means to battle those Africans fighting for their independence in Angola, Mozambique, and Guinea-Bissau.

**Personal versus plastic:** You simply have to be in tune to
the plus factors of this believe-it-or-not anachronism. And they
are not to be despised, in the mother country, if hardly in the
colonies: personal versus plastic service; the handcrafted versus
that of the machine; the tried and traditional versus the faddish
(mind, I did not say *fado*—about which more later); the relatively
intimate versus the monolithic massive; and, surely not the least

important, a culture that still has not come to worship the bulldozer.

I do not mean to infer by these introductory remarks that Lisbon is without a high-rise or, for that matter, the telly. (The entire republic has a solitary television station, which is probably more than enough; we might all be the better for having such minimal TV.) But when one thinks what might have been to-day, for this once-great world power, the mind boggles. Surely no other European land that had reached such a pinnacle has had quite such a fall.

**Romans and Lusitanians:** Early-early Portugal appears to have been free-for-all territory for everybody in the general vicinity. There were the Romans (whose great legacy was the Romance basis of the Portuguese language), and the Lusitanians, from whom the Portuguese (who sometimes also call themselves Lusos) consider themselves primarily descended. Then, though, in the eighth century, came the Moors. They really settled in, staying until the mid-thirteenth century, when they were expelled. Their influence on the country was quite possibly the most far-reaching it was to have in Europe. They altered the language (aside from Romanian, Portuguese is the most non-Romance-*sounding* of the Romance group), and they made profound contributions to the Portuguese culture in areas ranging from architecture to cuisine.

Portugal's Golden Age more or less coincided with Columbus's discovery of America. Indeed, Columbus, who had a Portuguese wife, went to Spain's Ferdinand and Isabella with his westerly route to India proposal only after he had been turned down in Lisbon. Still, the Portuguese had hardly been stay-at-homes during this era. A decade before Columbus set sail in 1492, Diego Cão had sailed up to the mouth of the Congo River, thus beginning Portugal's long relationship with black Africa; Cão sailed still farther south half a decade later and came across the cape that had been called Tempest, renaming it Good Hope. These ventures were the result of considerably earlier sorties undertaken by the remarkable son of King João I, whom we know as Prince Henry the Navigator.

**Prince Henry, Da Gama, and Magellan:** Henry set up a think-tank for the intelligentsia of the marine world at the promontory of Sagres at the southwestern tip of the country (it is a visitor magnet to this day). His captains discovered Madeira in 1420 and the Azores in 1427. The success at Good Hope was nothing more than a theory of his that came to pass. By the end of the fifteenth century, the Treaty of Tordesillas had awarded Portugal the eastern half of South America (Brazil today is where the great bulk of the world's Portuguese is spoken), with Spain getting the rest. In 1498 Vasco da Gama sailed around the coast of Africa, stopping at still-Portuguese-controlled Mozambique en route, and reaching India several months later. The following year a chap named Gaspar Corte Real came upon Newfoundland, of all places. And, not long after, a ship of the fleet of the Portuguese captain Magellan was the first to circumnavigate the globe.

What should have been ensuing centuries of smooth sailing —to say the least—for a country that had been so instrumental in opening up such vast and consequential areas of the planet, were anything but. The period between the end of the sixteenth century and the beginning of the twentieth saw Portugal at times under Spain, at times under Napoleon, for a brief period in the odd situation of being ruled from one of its colonies—King João VI and his family fled to Rio de Janeiro in 1807; later there followed the loss of Brazil (which itself, for a period, became a monarchy).

**Monarchy to dictatorship:** Of monarchs, during the periods of independence, there were the usual quota of weak ones. (Kings Alfonso VI and Sebastian, and Queen Maria I were insane.) Much of the nineteenth century saw intrigue and confusion in and about the throne. In 1908, King Charles and his son were assassinated, and his successor—Manuel II—lasted only two years. In 1910, revolution changed this ancient kingdom into an infant republic, which proved to be anything but a panacea. Antonio de Oliveira Salazar, who had been finance minister, took over the government in 1928—there had been little more than confusion since the revolution—and Portugal has been a fascistic "corporative state" ever since.

Portugal was neutral during World War II, friendly with Franco and the Axis powers early in the war, later veering toward the Allies, to the point where it provided them naval and air bases. As for Lisbon, it had not been such a center of attention since Prince Henry's time. It was the Continent's great communications and spy center. Although Portugal was at first turned down for United Nations membership after the war, it was eventually taken in. Indeed, until Greece's elected government was overthrown in 1967, it was the only authoritarian power that was a member of the North Atlantic Treaty Organization. Salazar's successor, Marcello Caetano, a former minister of colonies, took over from the ailing Salazar in 1968 (Salazar died in 1970), and there have been welcome surface changes—criticism allowed here and there, a bit of satire in the theater, the appearance in Lisbon of a Soviet circus, modernization of aspects of the economy, pro-European Common Market policies. Still, the forces that control Portugal—the military, the financiers, the conservative Catholic Church hierarchy—continue to exert the influence that is likely to keep Portugal not appreciably different from what it has been.

TO SEE

**Lay of the land:** This most stubbornly archaic of the European capitals is beautifully sited—on a series of hills that slope down to the Tagus River Estuary, itself now spanned by what is surely the city's—if not the whole country's—finest piece of contemporary architecture: the Salazar Bridge, a long-needed modern connection with the south.

The Portuguese have always been good at town planning. One

has only to see the handiwork of their builders and architects and engineers wherever they have been—Rio and Bahia, in Brazil, for example; Angola's Luanda, Mozambique's Lourenço Marques; the enclave on the China coast that is Macao—to appreciate that they knew what they were about when they laid out a city. There are always elements of logic and symmetry, with the square —*praça*—serving both as congregating center and as directional marker. Lisbon begins with the *praça* known officially as the *Praça do Comercio,* but popularly as the *Terreiro do Paco.* It fronts on the water, with its other three sides lined by arcaded, eighteenth-century neoclassic buildings, now mostly occupied by government ministries. In the center is a sculpture of a figure atop a horse, cast in bronze—King João I. (The square, because of the darkish hue of the color of the bronze, is sometimes also called *Black Horse Square,* to further confuse the visitor.) At any rate, one gets into town from this square through a graceful arch leading into the commercial thoroughfare known as *Rua Augusta.* This shop-lined street leads directly to still another principal square, officially *Praça Dom Pedro VI,* but popularly the *Rossio.* Still another commercial street, *Rua Aurea,* parallels Rua Augusta, leading also from the Terreiro do Paco to the Rossio. Unlike the serene Terreiro do Paco, the Rossio is lined on three sides with busy shops and buzzing cafes (alfresco in warm weather) and on the fourth by the early-nineteenth-century National Theater. Now then, to continue the game of dual names. The street known as *Rua do Carmo* leads into the *Rua Garrett* —these are as busy as any streets in town—which in turn gives onto a smallish square known as the *Largo do Chiado.* Because of the name of this square, both of the streets connecting it to the Rossio square are collectively known as the *Chiado.* Continuing inland from this area, the next important square after the Rossio—and very close to it—is the *Praça dos Restauradores.* It is the close-to-downtown terminus of the wide, boulevard-like thoroughfare called *Avenida Liberdade.* Restauradores more or less marks the end of old Lisbon. Avenida Liberdade leads directly to the circular *Praça Marques de Pombal* (named for the mid-eighteenth-century minister who rebuilt the city after a severely destructive earthquake), the big *Parque Eduardo VII* adjoining it, and a number of newer hotels. I have left out one major area of old Lisbon; it is the venerable quarter known as the *Alfama,* and it lies beneath the *Castelo São Jorge,* the whole area roughly paralleling—to the right as one goes inland—the earlier-described region lying between the waterfront Terreiro do Paco and the Rossio.

**Selected destinations:** All of the area delineated in the preceding Lay of the Land section—from the shore of the Tagus to the Praça dos Restauradores—is well worth exploring on foot. I would like to suggest some stopping-off places within this area, and without it as well.

The single most beautiful destination in the whole city is the cloister of the *Jeronimos Monastery* in the ancient waterfront quarter of the city known as Belem (Portuguese for Bethlehem). No other structure in the capital better typifies the peculiarly elaborate Portuguese version of Gothic architecture known as Manueline. Situated near the site of the harbor from which da Gama's ships sailed, and erected in 1502 shortly after their return, the monastery embraces the *Church of Santa Maria,* with an exquisite interior that leads to the cloister, with its double-story gallery, and that also contains, in a newer wing, a *Museum of Archaeology.* The landmark that is *Belem Tower* is nearby. It is a five-story fortification, worthy of interior inspection. *Castelo São Jorge* and the Alfama constitute the city at its oldest. The castelo —or what is left of it—goes back, in part at least, to the fifth century. There are still a number of towers and ramparts remaining, and a garden built among them that is a favorite promenade area for Lisboners. The view of town and the Tagus is extraordinary. Downhill toward the water is the *Alfama,* a marvelous maze of steep and narrow streets and streetlets (go slowly to savor the houses and churches and shops and mini-squares) that lead precipitously down to the Largo do Chafariz de Dentro, where the locals gather for after-dusk gossip. There are some *churches* of special interest. The twin-tower *Cathedral* is a rather plain twelfth-century structure partially rebuilt after the eighteenth-century earthquake, with a lovely cloister. *Igreja de Madre de Deus* (Mother of God) is part Manueline, part baroque, part Renaissance (the cloister), part neoclassic, with some Renaissance (and earlier) paintings in the chapel. *São Vicente de Fora* is Renaissance-era, with some particularly good tiles.

As for *museums,* you would think there was nothing but the one devoted to old royal coaches, the way the tour guides would have it. There are, however, a few dandies. The *Museu Nacional de Arte Antiga* is a gem among the national art galleries of Europe, which is saying a great deal. It contains the perfectly splendid Capela de Santo Alberto, a sixteenth-century Carmelite monks' chapel moved to it, in toto. Its most treasured work is a fifteenth-century polyptych attributed to Nuño Gonçalves, the Adoration of St. Vincent, but there are any number of additional Portuguese paintings of the fifteenth and sixteenth centuries, portraits mainly, distinguished by their strong, vibrant color, with the subjects coming through as substantial individuals. The eighteenth century is well represented too, and there are some old foreign masters as well. Of equal Portuguese interest is the *Museum of Decorative Art* (you may have to ask for it as the *Fundacão Ricardo Espirito Santo Silva*. It occupies a seventeenth-century palace that had belonged to a long line of counts who knew what luxury living was all about, as you will see from the sumptuously furnished salons. Then there is the *Museu Calouste Gulbenkian*. Not particularly Portuguese, to be sure, but oh, wow! The gift of an immensely wealthy Armenian, it occupies a parklike campus of its own. The principal building is a low-slung, futuristic travertine-faced pavilion. The collections, displayed with great style, are of great beauty, value, and, often, rarity: exquisite artifacts from ancient Egypt, Greco-Roman sculpture, tiles and carpets of Islam, lacquerware, porcelains and other

Oriental treasures. Europe is no less magnificently represented —a French medieval illuminated manuscript here, a Tyl Riemenschneider carved-wood Virgin there, paintings by Van der Weyden, Rembrandt, Ruysdael, Carpaccio, Fragonard, Dégas, Renoir, and Gainsborough, to name some. And, in addition: sculpture, carpets, bronzes, crystal, furniture, jewelry, and tapestries.

*The Royal Palaces* are outside of town. The older of the two, at *Sintra,* is mostly fourteenth- and sixteenth-century, with an odd pair of conical kitchen chimneys the most distinguishing architectural details. The interiors are beautiful, with particularly fine tilework on the floors, of course, but lining entire wall surfaces as well, some doorways in the Manueline style, Renaissance and baroque furniture. Noteworthy are the Stag Room, with its domed ceiling; the charming Hall of Swans; and the king's bedroom. The palace at *Queluz* is eighteenth-century, a kind of Franco-Portuguese rococo of great charm, with its pink-white-green façade, and interiors of considerable elegance: the very formal Ambassadors' Hall; the Sala das Mangas, with its exquisite blue-and-yellow tile walls; the chandeliers and paneling of the ballroom and the royal bedrooms; the gun room frescoes; exceptional furniture throughout; and sculpture-accented gardens.

### TO STAY

The Portuguese have not the innate knack at innkeeping that seems to come naturally to the neighboring Spaniards. By and large, though, one does well enough. In Lisbon, the trend in recent years has been to build hotels, like the modern Ritz and the much newer Sheraton, away from the city center in and around the Parque Eduardo VII sector—fancy and well manicured, to be sure, but too far out to be able to walk conveniently into the absorbing older quarters that are, after all, what Lisbon is all about. Trend or not, my preferences are central. The *Avenida Palace,* elderly and architecturally handsome, with graceful public rooms and capacious bedrooms, and a fine location, had been allowed to deteriorate pitifully, but has been tastefully refurbished at considerable effort and expense, and is now just the sort of hotel I enjoy—luxurious, with the heart of town walkably convenient. The *Mundial,* a hop and a skip from the Rossio Square gives the impression of being busy, busy, busy, but is well run and has a fine rooftop restaurant. The *Imperio* is another downtowner (Rua Rodrigues Sampaio 17), as are the simpler *Borges* on the popular shopping street, Rua Garrett, and the also unpretentious *Infante Santo,* down near the waterfront, with nice Tagus views from some rooms. Outside of town, in the seaside resort of *Estoril* (which will never, at least for me, have the appeal of the French or Italian Rivieras), the *Palacio Estoril* looms large as a de luxe hostelry of the old school, good-looking, impeccably maintained, beautifully operated, right in the heart of things, with its own pool, a restaurant of consequence, bar-lounge, *boîte,* and the ugly modern casino its nearest neighbor. The public beaches are a two-minute walk; Lisbon is a half hour or so distant on the earlier-mentioned commuter railroad.

## TO WATCH

The beautiful old *Teatro Nacional de San Carlos,* on the Rossio, is home to the National Symphony, and whatever ballet and opera Lisbon is able to offer. A number of theaters present Portuguese-language plays. The *Restaurante Folclore* is presumably the town's leading locale for folk dances of this country, and it is—to be charitable—best avoided; the program is amateur, and the accompanying dinner is no better. That leaves the movies and *fado.* The movies you can see at home; *fado,* you can't. For it, one frequents dimly lit cafes where singers pour out their souls —and concurrently the composite soul of Portugal—with very sad songs. *Fado* is Portugal's emotional safety valve, its counterpart to Spain's *flamenco.* Many of the *fado* cafes are in the atmospheric old Alfama quarter, appropriately enough. You may go for dinner (book for about 9:00 P.M.) and the show, or later for drinks and the show. *Lisboa a Noite, Frigata Real,* and *A Severa* are good choices.

TO EAT (AND DRINK)

The Portuguese cuisine is not among the more distinguished of Europe. It has none of the excitement and inventiveness of Spanish food at its best, if one wants to make a comparison with the neighbors to the east. There is, of course, heavy emphasis on seafood. Pork with clams is the best and most inventive dish I have ever had in Portugal. Grilled sardines—the sardines Portuguese themselves eat are monsters in contrast to what they can—are also very good. One is liable also to run into lobsters and crabs that are very good when prepared simply. *Caldeirada,* a fish stew, is excellent when well prepared. Cod, or *bacalhau,* is to the Portuguese what an *entrecôte* is to the Frenchman; they prepare it in multitudinous ways, which are all very interesting—if you like codfish. Desserts have a Moorish overtone—too sweety-sweet for many tastes. The bread can be good; the coffee varies. The national drink is, of course, wine. Now, *that* can be excellent. Portugal's most famous wine, port, comes from around the northern, No. 2 city of Oporto, and is, of course, a sweetish after-dinner wine, at least when red. (Most red port is exported to Britain, where it remains popular.) White ports are nice as apéritifs, as are some of the Madeiras—Sercial is a recommendable dry one—from the Portuguese island of that name. Except for the much-exported rosés, Portuguese table wines are not much known abroad, but can be very good. Ribatejo and Colares are two reliable types.

Now then, for Portuguese food at its most sublime, a lunch or dinner at the *Avis Restaurant* is indicated. Though not on the premises of that late lamented No. 1 hotel, the restaurant is largely staffed by alumni of the hotel. It is in a lovely old house at Rua Serpa Pinto 12-B, downtown, embraces a bar and a trio of antique-furnished dining rooms, with superlative service. The *Tavares* (Rua da Misericordia 24) is an old-timer that has retained its elegance and its very good traditional fare. *The roof of the Mundial Hotel* is a super place for dinner. There is a fine view of town, the ambience is animated, the service that of real pros, and the food some of the best in the capital. The *Grill of the Ritz Hotel*—a structurally modern edifice with décor and ambience attempting to emulate the style of the grand palacelike hostelries—is a posh eatery in the town's poshest hotel, with fine fare. The *Escorial,* near the Rossio, is chromy-modern in décor, with tasty, typical cuisine, and smiling service. The *Veranda do Chanceler* is Charmsville (Rua da Vigario) in the Alfama. The *Gondola* is indicated in warm weather for lunch or dinner on the terrace. *A Quinta* has two plusses: Portuguese food at once first-rate and authentic, and a splendid site affording panoramic views. *Café Suiça* affords a good view of Rossio Square action; pause for coffee, tea, a sandwich, or a Coke, for that matter. *Bernard* is a similarly relaxing snack-stop on the Rua Garrett.

## TO BUY

What the Portuguese excel at is pottery. The Spaniards' ceramics are very nice indeed. But they can't compare with what's done in Portugal for sophistication, design, and color. Their tiles —*azulejos*—are superlative as well. I have looked in many Lisbon shops, and elsewhere in the country, and seen quality and design nowhere that could touch that at the shop called *Sant' Anna,* downtown at Rua do Alecrim 9. You'll find bowls, platters, ashtrays, planters, dinner services (cups and saucers, plates, and other pieces may be bought separately), and other objects. *Solar do Velho Port,* Rua San Pedro de Alcantara 45, is the port wine industry's exhibit-sample center; taste any of scores upon scores of ports, and buy what you like at any wine or grocery shop. *Antiques* remain available, at any number of shops. Portuguese eighteenth-century blown glass is a particularly good buy—and there is a good bit available. *Antonio Trinidade,* Rua do Alecrion 81, is an interesting antiques shop. Portugal is a good place to buy *linens*—hand-embroidered from Madeira—usually on ecru or white organdy; or of simpler designs on actual cotton or linen, from the northern provinces. There are, as well, placemats, bridge sets, luncheon sets, tablecloths, napkins, guest towels, aprons, and heaven knows what all else of similar ilk. Some of it is beautifully done, a lot is souveniry, tourist-tacky. *Rua Augusta* and *Rua Garrett (Chiado)*, and adjacent streets are loaded with shops selling the *black-and-red roosters* that are a Portuguese trademark, as well as *cork* products (it is a shame that this handsome natural Portuguese product is invariably fashioned into gimmicky souvenirs), the inevitable regionally costumed dolls, and other bits and pieces. I have purchased in several of them, but will not recommend one over the other; they all appear rather drearily similar.

TO NOTE

**Access:** Lisbon is about as close as you can get to North America and still be in continental Europe. There are nonstop flights from New York via our own TWA, TAP (the Portuguese national carrier), and Swissair. TAP has very limited domestic service—to Oporto in the north or the Algarve in the south—but it flies also to Madeira, the Azores, and Portugal's African colonies. There is frequent service between Lisbon and its Iberian neighbor, Madrid, and with the rest of Europe. Portuguese long-distance trains are, to say the least, adventurous. The suburban line from Lisbon's downtown Cais do Sodré station to Estoril and Cascais is, however, cheap, clean, and reliable, if hardly streamlined. The major highways are good, and there are car-hire services in Lisbon, with or without chauffeur. If you hire a chauffeur-driven car for anything beyond half a day, do your best to get a knowledgeable driver; not all of them are. Getting about Lisbon is best accomplished on foot, if you are wise enough to stay in or near downtown. Taxis are plentiful and cheap, however; they're metered. There is a public transport system, of course, which includes a subway, the Metropolitana. Basic sightseeing tours by bus, within and without the city, are, of course, available. **Climate:** Lisbon's weather is one of its strong points. Even the winter months are mild, with averages in the low fifties from November through March. Spring (April and May) is sixtyish, while the summer (June through August) is in the seventies. September and October are sixtyish. **Clothes:** The Portuguese dress conservatively, and except for the small upper-middle and upper classes, quite squarely. The traveler expecting Lisbon to approximate Madrid in the areas of style or chic is in for a surprise. Jackets and ties are expected in the evenings in the better places. **Currency:** The unit of exchange is the escudo (which very often comes out as *skootch,* when pronounced by the locals). **Tipping:** This is a poor Latin country and wages are low, so that small tips above the inclusive service charges at restaurants and cafes are not out of order. Bellhops and baggage porters expect about three escudos per bag. About the same per night for the chambermaid is appreciated. A taxi driver will thank you for 10 percent, but 12 or 15 would be more like it. As for the others: They all expect something, not much, but something. But the Portuguese are invariably polite, and if you don't have the change you won't get a dirty look. **Business hours:** Generally, stores are open from 9:00 A.M. until 1:00 P.M. There's a two-hour lunch break, with afternoon hours from 3:00 P.M. until 7:00 P.M., Monday through Saturday. **Language:** Portuguese is probably the most difficult to pronounce and to understand of the Latin languages, except, perhaps, for Romanian. The Portuguese are understandably proud of their language and, also understandably, they don't relish being addressed in Spanish, even though many of them understand that language. Still, if you know Spanish and are getting nowhere in your attempts at communicating with someone in any other language, try your Spanish; your listener may admit to understanding you. Recent years have seen a phenomenal increase in English-language fluency, particularly in Lisbon, where there is considerably less difficulty in communicating than was the case, say, a decade ago. French-speakers will frequently find that that language will stand them in good stead. **Further information:** Casa de Portugal, 570 Fifth Avenue, New York; Ministry of Information and Tourism, Directorate General of Tourism, Foz Palace, Praça dos Restauradores, Lisbon, Portugal.

# *London*

It may well be that London has always tried harder because it is an island city, physically detached from the larger Continent, and anxious to prove that the English Channel and the North and Irish Seas were quite the reverse of barriers to its development. Your Londoner today is neither aggressive nor restless nor impatient. But surely his forebears must have been. Else how would such a great and beautiful and, for long, powerful city have evolved on a dampish, northern island?

**The name's the thing:** Not that London was without certain advantages. A head start for one. And a name that stuck, for another. The Celts—poets then, as now—were calling the place Lyndin—a name with a nice ring to it that meant waterside fortress—as long ago as the first century of the Christian era, when the Roman legions happened up from France to settle in. Always better at adapting than originating, they simply Latinized Lyndin to Londinium. There was a brief period, not long after their arrival, when it was touch and go whether they would stay. The Celts' own queen, Boadicea by name, tried to oust the rascals from the fort they had built. But to no avail. Roman walls went up, Roman laws were introduced, the Roman culture, and the Latin language; all had been implanted by the time of the Roman exodus four hundred years later.

There followed that confusing, albeit alliterative run of the "E" kings—Egbert and Ethelwulf and Ethelbald and Ethelbert and Ethelred and Edmund and Edred and Edwy and Edgar. Until Alfred the Great—no one has explained his refreshingly distinctive name—none of this "E" crowd was especially London-oriented. Alfred changed all this. He chose London as his capital, which was an achievement in itself. But he was, as well, a pursuer of peace in an age when war was the norm. Additionally, he set his people's sights on education and literacy, first setting up a school for his largely illiterate nobles, and second, ordering translated the handful of important books of the time from Latin—still the literary tongue of his realm—to English. After settling in, he gave London its first proper government.

**1066 and all that:** London then was the easterly sector of what all these subsequent centuries has been called The City, and that continues to jealously guard its independence of the rest of London. Its government was such that with the invasion of England by William the Conqueror in 1066, the City of London was treated with separately, allowing its citizens to democratically elect their officials, as they had since Alfred's time. The Tower of London —or at least the White Tower, its nucleus—went up during William's time. But just before then, William's predecessor and boyhood chum, the sainted Edward the Confessor, had begun to personally supervise the building of Westminster Abbey to replace an earlier church that had been on the site. It was Edward, with his attention to the Abbey at Westminster, who succeeded in transferring the Court and government from the Tower area of the City to Westminster—where it has remained for almost a millennium, with hardly a break. All the while, under later kings like Richard I (who gave The City the Lord Mayor and corporation form of government it has never abandoned) and Henry III (who built still another Westminster Abbey—the one we know today), London continued to expand, economically as well as architecturally and politically. The medieval centuries saw the craft and trade guilds become important. Lawyers formed their still-extant Inns of Court.

**Henry VIII: six wives, three children:** At midpoint in the mid-fifteenth century, England had spent a hundred fruitless years fighting to retain her French territory, to no avail. The ugly civil strife with the beautiful name—War of the Roses—between Yorks and Lancasters, followed, with Henry VII's victory at Bosworth Field, and then the eventful reign of his son, Henry VIII. Political turmoil, war, disease—nothing stopped London's growth. Although Holbein and other painters had to be imported from the Continent, there was no dearth of domestic architects or artisans. Henry VIII's reign saw Hampton Court erected, as but one of many Tudor-style forerunners of later Renaissance building. It was Henry VIII, of course, whose complex marital situation led to the break with the Roman Catholic Church and the establishment of the Church of England. The religious schism resulting was to trouble England for many successive reigns. Three of Henry's half-dozen wives bore him children, and each reigned: the bright but sickly youngster, Edward IV, for half a decade; the bitterly unhappy Bloody Mary for still another half-decade, which was marked by her disastrous marriage to Spain's Philip II and a wholesale massacre of Protestant subjects thereafter; and then Elizabeth I—the spinster Elizabeth, during whose forty-five years on the throne England became a world power to be reckoned with. Elizabeth resumed the Protestantism of her father over the fanatic Catholicism of her half-sister. Elizabeth's fleet defeated the great Spanish Armada of her ex-brother-in-law and spurned suitor, Philip II. Elizabeth's knights—Raleigh was, of course, but one—secured the colonial empire of the New World.

**The first Elizabeth's England:** It was Elizabeth's reign that produced Shakespeare, Marlowe, Spenser, Bacon, Drake. The Renaissance architecture of these years took its name from the Queen; these were the decades of the great Elizabethan country houses like Knole and Kent and Moreton Hall; of sprouting new colleges at both Oxford and Cambridge; of elaborate formal gardens setting off the manors and palaces; and of design that formed the basis of the succeeding reign. Jacobean—named for

James I—is best typified by Hatfield House, the manor that went up on the grounds of an earlier, smaller house where Elizabeth succeeded to the throne; followed by the pure Renaissance style of Inigo Jones.

The ill-fated son of Mary Queen of Scots (whom Elizabeth imprisoned and beheaded), already James VI of Scotland, succeeded Elizabeth as James I of England. We know him best for his still-used version of the Bible. He ushered in a troubled era. Charles I, his successor, was so disliked by Parliament that it tried him for high treason and then chopped his head off. (You may see a statue of him in Whitehall, not far from where he was beheaded.) The bleak, stern Commonwealth of the Cromwells, father Oliver and son Richard, followed—but only for a decade. Charles II (in the company of orange-vending Nell Gwynn) effected the spirited Restoration—not as lavish, perhaps, as the contemporary France of Louis XIV, but one that put London in high spirits, completely unprepared for the tragedy of the plague that killed off a third of its citizens, only to be cruelly followed by the Great Fire that razed almost the whole of the City. A young inventor and astronomer—not trained as an architect—named Sir Christopher Wren, designed a new St. Paul's Cathedral as a memorial to the old one claimed by the Great Fire. He designed more than half a hundred additional churches, inspiring an entire school of followers, who created much of the London of ensuing decades.

**The furniture monarchs—Anne, William, and Mary:** The Catholic-Protestant confusion engendered by Henry VIII continued, even now, to influence the choice of occupants for the throne, to the point where Catholic James II was booted out and Protestant Dutchman Prince William of Orange was called across the North Sea to reign with his English wife Mary, one of the two Protestant daughters of the deposed James II. The second daughter, Anne, followed William and Mary to the throne, and had more success giving her name to the handsome Renaissance school of furniture and design that sprouted over England than to giving birth to an heir—or even heiress. Poor Anne, who reigned only a dozen years, was pregnant seventeen times by her rather simple Danish husband, but only one child lived, to die a young eleven. Anne, like her predecessors William and Mary, lived away from the center of town, mainly in the palace at Kensington, part of which is now the home of Princess Margaret and the Earl of Snowdon, and the rest of which is open to the public. (Anne moved about though, to ancient Windsor and Tudor Hampton Court in summer, and to St. James's Palace in town as well as Kensington in winter. She never visited Scotland as Queen, although the important Act of Union came about during her reign.) Anne was so proud of the Duke of Marlborough's victories that she built Blenheim Palace for him as a gift from the nation. (The duke's wife, Duchess Sarah, was Anne's great friend while he was away fighting England's battles, but the two—Sarah and Anne—parted enemies.) Blenheim Palace, now a major excursion destination out of London, was, several centuries later, the birthplace of Winston Churchill.

**The Teutonic-origin four Georges:** German relatives—the easy-to-remember four Georges—succeeded heirless Anne on the throne. Of these, only the last two were interesting: The long-reigning George III, because of his repressive policies, lost England its non-Canadian colonies in North America; and George IV, because, while Prince Regent during his father's latterly insane years, he commissioned a genius named John Nash to build what we now term Regency London. What Wren did for Renaissance London, Nash did for the capital of the early nineteenth century, with Regent's Park, Regent Street, Waterloo Place, and Carlton House Terrace. (Alas, "Prinnie's" Carlton House—his town palace—is no more. But his Royal Pavilion at Brighton is as enchanting as ever it was.)

**Eighteenth-century brilliance:** The city had not, to be sure, stagnated during the eighteenth century, which saw the construction of Grosvenor, Hanover, Bedford, and Soho Squares and which was, after all, the great era of Georgian architecture and applied

arts ranging from silver to furniture. Inigo Jones (whose Whitehall Banqueting House is a requisite London destination) introduced the neoclassic Palladian into London from Italy, and
the great Robert Adam later became its chief practitioner in
Edinburgh (see the chapter on that city) as well as London, not
to mention Bath. Cabinetmakers like Chippendale, Sheraton, and
Hepplewhite furnished the elegant Georgian houses. Slender-
spired colonnaded churches—St. Martin's-in-the-Fields in London's
Trafalgar Square is a prime example—went up in profusion. And
the style found great favor in the American colonies, where we
still often refer to Georgian houses and churches—as well as
latter-day adaptations like banks and schools—as "colonial."
English painters came into their own—late, if contrasted with the
Continent—but great: William Hogarth, Sir Joshua Reynolds,
Sir Thomas Lawrence; and those other painters of beautiful English ladies and beautiful English landscapes: Gainsborough, Romney, Raeburn, Lawrence.

**Victoria's sixty-four year reign:** Victoria ascended the throne in
1837 and stayed there—much of the time in mourning at Windsor
for her German-born husband—until 1901. Her reign of sixty-
four years was the longest in English history, and saw England
evolve into a democratic nation during a long, mostly peaceful era.
Victorian London is to be seen at every turn—The City of course
is full of the heavily proportioned construction of the era, and
the neo-Gothic houses and mansions—and all of these styles
crossed the Atlantic to America. But so much else bears the name
of that long-reigning lady: furniture, interiors, fiction, and hardly
the least, morals. This was the age when Britain consolidated
her far-flung empire, and even the late-twentieth-century traveler
is not allowed to forget it. My *National Geographic Atlas* lists
nearly three-score Victorias around the world, ranging from the
capitals of British Columbia, the Seychelles, and Hong Kong, to
the falls of the Zambezi River dividing Zambia from Rhodesia, the
territory on the map designated Victoria Land, Antarctica; a
state in Australia; a creek in Alaska; a beach in Manitoba, a

fjord in Greenland; a harbor in Ontario; a river (the Victoria Nile) in Uganda; a point with capital P in Burma; just plain towns in Illinois, Kansas, Texas, and Virginia (only one of which states, incidentally, is a onetime British colony). Victoria reigned for so long that her portly heir, Edward VII, was sixty when he acceded. His reign was short—just under a decade—but still it constituted an era, though not as giddy as we have been led to believe. Edward VII never gets quite the credit he deserves for his diplomatic talents. He was an intelligent man, and his tact and brains had a lot to do with the development of cordial Anglo-French relations, which were to prove so valuable in World War I. Britain emerged a victor from that conflict, and the decades before World War II saw—among a lot else—the first Labor government under Ramsay MacDonald, and the abdication that the world has never stopped talking about: that of the popular, brand-new-to-the-throne Edward VIII, who became the Duke of Windsor and the husband of a twice-divorced American, Mrs. Wallis Warfield Simpson.

**Churchill and the current Elizabethan era:** World War II was Britain's darkest yet bravest hour. Following Nazi Germany's invasion of Poland in 1939, Britain entered the war. The coalition government of Winston Churchill led it to victory, although after the invasion and occupation of France in 1940 it fought alone, until joined by the United States at the end of 1941. London suffered from repeated World War II bombings. Great portions of it were blitzed, and many of its people were killed or wounded. No people were braver than Londoners during World War II, and at no era in history were the British and American peoples closer than during World War II and the immediate post-World War II years. Chances are that the Underground platform at which you wait for a train was slept upon by countless Londoners in the course of almost nightly air raids. (The extraordinary depth of the Underground stations—many twice as far down as are those of, say, New York—were a major factor in saving many lives.)

The popular wartime king, George VI, was a postwar casualty.
He died in 1952, and his elder daughter, Princess Elizabeth,
became Queen Elizabeth II while animal-viewing in the bush
lodge called Treetops during an official visit to Kenya. (You read
a bronze plaque to that effect on the Treetops terrace, while you
sip your afternoon tea in the company of a gregarious family of
baboons, who come each afternoon to be fed hot scones.) Elizabeth and her husband, Prince Philip, the Duke of Edinburgh—a
former Greek prince and nephew of Lord Mountbatten, the last
British viceroy of India—have four children, the Princes Edward
and Andrew, Princess Anne, and the eldest and heir apparent,
Charles, Prince of Wales. In a sense Britain has come full circle
in this second Elizabethan era. It was during the reign of the
first Elizabeth that the empire became great. It has been during
the second that it has been largely dismantled, former colonies
around the world now mostly sovereign republics voluntarily as-
sociated with the Commonwealth of Nations—proof, if ever it
was needed, of the eternal magnet that is—in the economic sense,
at least—Britain. But if the empire is lost, Europe is gained. The
Common Market approved Britain's bid for admission in 1971.
Of course, there will always be an England—and a London as its
capital.

TO SEE

**Lay of the Land:** The beauty of London comes through from
the window of one's sedate black taxi, from the moment of
arrival: The campanile of Big Ben and the tower of Parliament
over the Thames, Victorian grandeur and Georgian elegance, Regency crescents and Renaissance palaces, the polished brass of
Mayfair and its glossy little shops, Wren churches, department
stores, pageantry that is positively medieval in its splendor, and bus
conductors that are earthily Cockney.

London's geography—that is a slower matter. It takes longer to master. It requires memorization, and then lots of footwork, despite the enormity of the area involved. Forget about the complexity of the manifold boroughs of the entity known as Greater London. What interests most visitors is the West End and the City, contiguous areas on the north side of the Thames. Look at your map and let me try to orient you very broadly. Start in *Piccadilly Circus,* the best-known if hardly the best-looking of London's squares. This is the core of the visitor's West End. Almost due north is *Regent Street,* with its great stores. Almost east is *Shaftesbury Avenue,* worth remembering because it leads to the maze of legitimate theaters which are a prime London lure, and to the foreign restaurants of *Soho.* Walk south on an extension of Regent Street or on *Haymarket,* running parallel to it, and you are in the ancient *St. James's* area. The first major cross-street is smart *Pall Mall,* and one walks east on it to enormous *Trafalgar Square,* with its fountains, Nelson Column, and such landmarks as the National Gallery, National Portrait Gallery, and the Wren-style Church of St. Martin's-in-the-Fields. Walk through the square, continuing east to the *Strand.* In just a few blocks it changes its name to *Fleet Street,* at once newspaper center of the country and the beginning of the original, still separately governed, *City* area, the economic and financial center of the Commonwealth. The Strand is as good a place as any to cross one of the many bridges leading over the Thames to South London. *Waterloo Bridge* leads one to the modern Royal Festival Hall, and just beyond, Waterloo Station. If one went farther east, the crossing could be made on *London Bridge,* with Gothic Southwark Cathedral just over the water. Return now to where we started, Piccadilly Circus. Walk directly west on the broad thoroughfare known as *Piccadilly.* Within a few blocks, just beyond the Royal Academy of Arts, you will come to a street running perpendicular to Piccadilly, in a northerly direction. It is fashionable *Bond Street.* You may walk it due north until you come to the major intersecting artery called *Oxford Street*—a major shopping thoroughfare with middle-category stores and a major department store, Selfridge's. Return, now, to Piccadilly, and continue walking west. The park on your left is *Green Park.* Contiguous with it are *Buckingham Palace Gardens,* with Buckingham Palace overlooking them; and *St. James's Park.* The most impressive approach to the palace is via *The Mall,* a handsome artery cutting through St. James's and Green parks. Return once again to Piccadilly. Continue walking along it until it terminates at *Park Lane.* Turn right onto Park Lane, and walk along it to the north. The park it is named for is *Hyde Park,* which it fronts. It is the locale of a number of fine hotels, and it is the western frontier of *Mayfair,* whose maze of charming streets provide the stuff of limitless exploration. Still another major park—*Regent's,* with its remarkable zoo—is way to the north of Mayfair. *Kensington*—where many visitors live and which all want to at least partially explore —lies to the south of Hyde Park, and *Chelsea* borders it, along its southern flank, stretching to *Cheyne Walk* and the *Chelsea Embankment* on the Thames. For the rest, discover as you go. London's chief surprises for the pedestrian are its *squares—Belgrave* and *Cadogan, Grosvenor* and *Berkeley, Portman* and *Manchester, Hanover, Cavendish,* and *Chester*—this last heavily inhabited by affluent American expatriates.

**Choice destinations:** To begin, the *Essential London*—I often wish that my first destination on my first trip to London had been the *National Portrait Gallery* (St. Martin's Lane, at Trafalgar Square). The idea is to give you an idea of what Britain has been all about, these many centuries, by means of portraits of its leading personalities—not only kings, queens, and royal mistresses, as important as they were, but politicians, writers, poets, and musicians; the work of such painters as Reynolds, Romney, and Lawrence, and many foreign painters, too. On my last visit, the museum was passing out a folder "intended for the visitor with only a limited period of time at his disposal." It suggested viewing these "Six Famous Portraits in Fifteen Minutes": Sir Walter Raleigh by Nicholas Hilliard; Queen Elizabeth I by Gheeraedts the Younger; Henry VIII by—of course, you know—Holbein; Shakespeare by an unknown artist; Samuel Pepys by Joun Jahls; and the Brontë girls—Charlotte, Emily, and Anne —by their brother, Branwell. I would go on then to the major remaining souvenir of medieval London, the *Tower of London.* Its thousand-year-old nucleus is the wall-encircled White Tower, wherein were imprisoned quantities of illustrious personages. The Tower complex includes the Armoury Museums (housed in the White Tower and a Renaissance annex); two chapels—St. John's and St. Peter-ad-Vinculai; and, of course, the Crown Jewels. *Westminster Abbey* is London's great Gothic treasure, and it is where, since Edward the Confessor built it a millennium ago, every sovereign—save two—has been crowned, from William the Conqueror to Elizabeth II. Henry VII's Chapel—named for the monarch who built it—with its exquisite fan-vaulting, a magnificent choir, the venerable oaken Coronation Chair, the Poets' Corner (with memorials to immortals like Chaucer, Milton, and Shakespeare), and the tombs of kings and queens, including both Elizabeth I and Mary Queen of Scots. The *Houses of Parliament* —frequently referred to simply as "Westminster"—are splendid mid-nineteenth-century neo-Gothic. Both the House of Commons and the House of Lords are in the principal main building, officially called the New Palace of Westminster. The Lords, smaller and more elaborate of the two chambers, includes a throne for the monarch—who by tradition does not visit the Commons. (The annual Opening of Parliament by the sovereign takes place in the Lords.) The much more capacious Commons is post-World War II, its predecessor having been a casualty of the war. *Westminster Hall* is virtually all that remains of the medieval Westminster Palace. It was originally built in the eleventh century, but was largely rebuilt in 1399. This is where Charles I was tried, and it served for centuries as a law court. Visitors are admitted to both houses and to Westminster Hall, for purely sightseeing purposes, at certain specified times. Additionally, it is possible to watch the Commons and Lords in session—I highly recommend this—from their Strangers' Galleries. British Tourist Authority, hall porters in hotels, the American Embassy (for Americans), and the Canadian High Commission (for Canadians) can be helpful in this respect. The *British Museum,* of all the London museums, is the one to zero in on, as a first choice. It is the most marvelous of the catch-all museums, full of treasures from every corner of what had been the world's greatest empire—and then some. The building, erected well over a century ago, is not the easiest in which to find one's way about. It is, indeed, so complicated that the museum includes a big map in the pocket of the guidebook it sells. Even more helpful than the map are the guards—old-timers most of them, and of inestimable value in getting you to what you want to see. Exhibit highlights include the Rosetta Stone; the Shakespeare First Folio; one of the original drafts of the *Magna Carta;* some of the great Egyptian, Roman, and Greek antiquities, including the statue from the Erectheum of Athens' Acropolis (which the Greeks still want returned); and the best specimens in the world of the sublime sculpture of the Ife and Benin cultures of Nigeria. *Hampton Court,* though away from central London, is a requisite excursion destination. Begun in the early sixteenth century by Cardinal Wolsey, it became a royal residence when the cardinal—in a vain attempt to remain in Henry VIII's good graces—made a gift of it to the King, whose successors lived in it through the reign of the second George, in the mid-eighteenth century. The medieval portions, built by Wolsey and Henry VIII, form the bulk of this complex of quadrangles. But there are, as well, newer and equally splendid late-seventeenth-century additions, which William and Mary had Sir Christopher Wren design. *Windsor Castle* is as essential an excursion destination as Hampton Court, for it is the largest and oldest royal residence, dating back a millennium, to William the Conqueror. Its St. George's Chapel is a fifteenth-century masterwork; St. George's Hall, the State Apartments, the medieval Round Tower, and the 4800-acre Great Park are its other especial treats. You may or may not like *St. Paul's Cathedral,* but if nothing else a visit to it will get you into the heart of the City, with its multitude of lures. St. Paul's is considered Wren's greatest work; he designed it to replace the old Gothic St. Paul's after the Great Fire of 1561. The building is full of Wren's genius, but its general Gothic layout—which the authorities at the time insisted upon—seems to be inappropriate for its Wren-Renaissance design; the ambience is cold and formidable, unlike so much else of Wren's work, particularly his smaller churches. Of interest is the Jesus Chapel, a memorial to Americans who died in Britain during World War II. *Kensington Palace* is still another London landmark with Wren associations—and with William and Mary connections as well. King William III had Wren make additions and alterations to the place when he took it over in 1689, as a respite from the damper neighborhood of Whitehall, which he considered not at all healthy for a chronic asthmatic like himself. His sister-in-law, Queen Anne, made additional enlargements during her reign, as did Anne's successor, George I, who had William Kent decorate the interiors with sumptuous painted walls and ceilings. The park-like gardens without are lovely (they include Queen Anne's Orangery), and there are surprises within, like Queen Victoria's bedroom and nursery. She was born at Kensington, as was Queen Mary, wife of George V, and grandmother of Queen Elizabeth II. Kensington is the only inhabited royal palace in town whose state apartments are visitable. Living elsewhere on the premises are the Queen's sister, Princess Margaret; her husband, the Earl of Snowdon; and their children, Viscount Linley and Lady Sarah Armstrong-Jones. And in still another part of the palace—you may tour it in conjunction with the State Apartments—is the *London Museum,* founded during the reign of George V and Mary, with exhibits relating to the history of the city from Roman times—ranging from Renaissance jewelry to a Victorian fire engine, and including a slew of royal wedding dresses and coronation robes, Elizabeth II's among them. You don't need a dinner invitation to pop in and have a look at the *Banqueting House,* Whitehall. Like Hampton Court, it was originally Cardinal Wolsey's. His sovereign, Henry VIII, took it over after Wolsey's comeuppance, and turned it into the Whitehall Palace that was used until—as I mentioned earlier—asthmatic William III wanted the country air of Kensington. A fire destroyed the works, but in the early seventeenth century the gifted Inigo Jones built what you see—a great rectangle of a neoclassic pavilion. The ceiling was commissioned by the ill-fated Charles I; its painter: Peter Paul Rubens. Oh, wow! *Changing of the Guard at Buckingham Palace* and *Changing of the Horse Guards at Whitehall* are as essential as the Eiffel Tower in Paris or the UN in New York. Buckingham Palace is the Royal Family's London home. It is named for the Duke of Buckingham and Chandos, who built it in the eighteenth century, selling it to George III in 1761. George IV had Nash remodel it in the early nineteenth century, and Queen Victoria—who eventually took it over as her town house—made changes, as did George V, as recently as 1913. The only parts of it open to the public are the Queen's Gallery and the Royal Mews (see Museums, later on). Should you ever get invited inside, the rooms to see are the State Ballroom, where the Queen conducts investitures and other ceremonies; and the Throne Room, with its marble frieze of the Wars of the Roses. The Changing of the Guard takes place at 11:30 A.M. daily; get there a little early, so you can see. And take in, as well, the Changing of the Mounted Household Cavalry daily at 11:00 A.M. (10:00 A.M. on Sundays) at the Admiralty, Whitehall. (A less spectacular ceremony takes place there at 4:00 P.M. daily.)

**Other London treats:** *Chiswick House* (Burlington Lane) is probably the greatest pure Palladian villa outside of the prototypes in the Veneto region of northern Italy. Chiswick was built in 1725 by Lord Burlington after his return home from a Grand Tour, where he saw the originals in Italy. The interiors are by the same William Kent who did the ceilings of Kensington Palace. Edward VII lived there for a period. There is a resemblance to Jefferson's Monticello. *Guildhall* is the Town Hall for the City of London. Originally eleventh-century, it was largely restored after World War II damage, but still is impressive. It is where Freedom of the City ceremonies and the yearly Lord Mayor's Banquets take place. *Grosvenor Square* is originally eighteenth-century, although much of it now is neo-Georgian twentieth-century. Among the neo-Georgian buildings is the former American Embassy, now the Canadian High Commission. The Americans are now housed in a decidedly contemporary Eero Saarinen building—handsome and appropriate for the site—whose oversized eagle was the subject of controversy when the building opened in 1960. To be noted, too, is Sir William Reid Dick's *statue of Franklin D. Roosevelt,* who was President during World War II when the United States and Britain collaborated closely. (It is something of an irony, surely, that Americans have to travel across the Atlantic to see a memorial to one of their great Presidents. All New York has to honor FDR is a street in his name, which the natives still refer to as the East River Drive. Washington has been squabbling for years over the form an FDR Memorial will take, but none as yet exists.) *Lincoln's Inn* is a sanctuary of tranquillity in the midst of The City; half an hour's stroll through it is indeed a London treat. It is one of the so-called Inns of Court, which traditionally control the practice of law in England, and which include resident quarters for lawyers, as well as other facilities. Lincoln's Inn (not named for our Abraham) goes back to the fifteenth century. There is a little bookshop near the entrance that sells a charming guidebook. What you want to see are the Old Hall, built the year Columbus discovered our shores; the New Hall, late-nineteenth-century; and the big library. *Marlborough House* is where the late Queen Mary lived until she died in 1953. It is now used for Commonwealth conferences, and the like, and is open to the public. Wren built it for the same Marlborough to whom Queen Anne awarded Blenheim Palace in the country, in recognition of his battlefield victories. The chief lures are a staircase mural of one of the great duke's battles, and a chapel. *Regent's Park* was designed by Nash for George IV, while he was still Prince Regent. It's a beauty, bordered by superb houses, and including Queen Mary's Garden, an aviary designed by Lord

Snowdon, and one of the biggest and best and most delightful zoos
on the planet, with the attendant Londoners—young and old—
of not much less interest to the visitor than the animals themselves.
The *Chelsea Royal Hospital* is one of the anachronisms that
makes London interesting. Charles II founded it as a veterans'
hospital in the seventeenth century—much like the Louis XIV-
established Les Invalides in Paris. It is still another Wren work,
with additions by Robert Adam, among others. The chapel is
open to the public, as are other parts of the complex. The old
chappies you see all about in traditional red coats are the inmates
—Chelsea pensioners, they're called. *Somerset House,* on the
Strand, went up in the late eighteenth century as an office building
—London's first. It is an immense quadrangle of a structure with
a massive inner courtyard and some especially interesting decorative details. Step in to have a look when you're passing by.

**Museums, greater and lesser:** Taking time out for London's museums—beyond the British Museum—is, I know, easier said than
done, given the diverse lures of this city. But it is time well spent;
some of the great ones of the world are in London. The *National
Gallery* is so conveniently located on Trafalgar Square that I
marvel that more of my countrymen don't visit it. It houses one
of the superlative collections of old masters, but it is strong as
well on the French Impressionists. The Italian medieval work—
Masolino's *Saints John the Baptist and Jerome,* for example—is a
joy. One sees, as well, Bronzini and Titian, Bellini and Botticelli
among the Italians; Vermeer and Rembrandt (represented by
nineteen paintings) among the Dutch; Goya and Velasquez among
the Spaniards; and the Golden English eighteenth century of
Reynolds, Gainsborough, and their contemporaries is not neglected. The *Tate Gallery* is outstanding for its specialties, British
painting from the Renaissance onward, and modern work from
the Impressionists through to, say, last week. In the English sections there are fine Hogarths, Gainsboroughs, and Reynoldses.
But the star of the Tate is J. M. W. Turner, the early-nineteenth-

century English painter who was a good half century ahead of his time, and who is better represented at this museum than at any other. There are strong Constable and Blake sections, too, and some fine French Impressionists and Post-Impressionists. The *Courtauld Institute of Galleries* is a unit of the University of London. The specialty is Impressionists and Post-Impressionists— the finest such assemblage in Britain. They are all on hand: Bonnard, Degas, Pissarro, Seurat, Renoir, Roualt. Manet's *A Bar at the Folies Bergère* is alone worth a visit to the Courtauld; so are the Van Goghs and Gauguins. The *Victoria and Albert Museum*—the "V and A" to Londoners—is a unit of the group of museums devised by Queen Victoria's German consort, Prince Albert, after his successful Great Exhibition of 1851. Victoria herself laid the foundation stone in 1899, not long before she died; her son, Edward VII, opened the building in 1909—not long before he died. The V and A is nothing less than a great repository of the decorative arts. Not only British. And not only decorative. The fine arts are well represented, too. The emphasis is on European work from the Middle Ages onward. Not unexpectedly, English furniture and furnishings are particularly strong. But you will find all manner of treasures from paintings by Raphael to Renaissance ship models of solid gold. The special shows are invariably imaginative. *The Queen's Gallery,* with its own separate entrance, is, along with the Royal Mews, the only part of Buckingham Palace open to the public. It displays objects—old paintings, for the most part—from the exceptionally rich and high-caliber Royal Collections. The *Royal Mews,* also a part of Buckingham Palace, just has to be the greatest old-coach museum of them all. The sumptuous rococo eighteenth-century Gold State Coach has been used at every coronation since George IV's. Newer than the coronation coach, but hardly less elaborate, is Queen Victoria's railways coach— all royal blue and gilt, and quite the equal of anything Lucius Beebe devised along these lines in the United States; it is but one of a number of royal conveyances in the *Museum of British*

*Transport.* The *British Theatre Museum* is all that its title indicates—Sarah Siddons' Sheraton dressing table, letters, manuscripts, photos, costumes (including one of Nijinsky's), and all manner of memorabilia relating to the theater in this most theater-loving of countries. The *Wellington Museum* occupies Apsley House, the magnificent mansion on Hyde Park Corner that was the home of the first Duke of Wellington, and was donated to the nation as a museum by his current descendant. The most spectacular exhibit is in the dining room—a service of silver plate from the Regent of Portugal that took well over a hundred silversmiths several years to create. But the handsome house—an attraction in itself—is full of Wellingtoniana. *Sir John Sloane's Museum* occupies its donor's early-nineteenth-century house. Like similar museums in Boston and Stockholm, its contents are not allowed to be altered, by terms of the donors' wills. Fortunately, Sir John, an architect, had good taste in paintings, furniture, and other objects; it's a lovely place. The *Wallace Collection* occupies an exceptional town house on mellow Manchester Square. It was a gift to the British people from the widow of Sir Richard Wallace who, with his ancestors, had collected it mostly in France. The Renaissance paintings are the chief lure—the great Dutch and Flemish artists are all present. But the French are big—eighteenth-century, mainly. And so are the Spaniards and English. Painting is only part of the collection; there is armor and some very good French eighteenth-century furniture—among a great deal else. I am dignifying *Madame Tussaud's* by including it in this section of selected museums, only because you will have heard of it, and you may want to go. I say, do so. Unless you see them, you can't believe how awful the wax statues are, at least of the personalities whose faces we are familiar with from newspapers, films, and television. A bit out of town now for these last two: The *Greenwich* complex is one of the least appreciated in London, at least by foreign visitors. There's a lot to take in. The Royal Naval College started out as a palace for Charles II. Wren later turned it into a hospital; his Painted Hall is the finest room within, along with the chapel. *Queen's House* was still another royal residence, this for Charles II's wife, Henrietta Maria. Inigo Jones designed it in neoclassic style; it shelters the *National Maritime Museum,* with exhibits on naval subjects through the centuries. To be seen, too, is *Cutty Sark,* not the whisky but the doughty sailing ship for which it was named. *Kenwood,* out in Hampstead, is at once an extraordinarily beautiful Robert Adam-designed house (the library is its finest room) and a first-rank gallery of the paintings that had belonged to the late Lord Iveagh. Rembrandt, Vermeer, and Hals are represented, along with Englishmen like Turner, Gainsborough, Romney, Raeburn, Reynolds, and Lawrence.

**Some interesting churches:** *Southwark Cathedral* does not attempt to compete with Westminster Abbey. But it should. Across the river, in South London, it is, after Westminster, the greatest Gothic church in London. It dates to the thirteenth century, although it has had restoration, mostly of good quality. Very big, very beautiful. *Westminster Cathedral:* There are some six million Roman Catholics in Britain, and enough of them live in and around London for it to constitute an archdiocese headed by an archbishop of cardinal's rank, whose seat is the turn-of-century Westminster Cathedral. The style, a nice, refreshing change in London, is Byzantine. A slim campanile is the exterior landmark. Within, there are fine arched nave, and mosaic-decorated chapels. *The Temple Church* (near Lincoln's Inn) goes back some eight hundred years, combining Gothic and Romanesque features very impressively. The *Chapel Royal* is the only part of St. James's Palace open to the public—and then only for Sunday services. It dates back to the Renaissance, and was the scene of Queen Victoria's wedding. The *Queen's Chapel* in Marlborough House was designed by Inigo Jones and is open regularly for services. *The Guards' Chapel,* in Wellington Barracks, originally from fairly early in the last century, was almost completely destroyed in World War II, and has been interestingly rebuilt, with

military motifs incorporated into the décor. It is open daily and
for Sunday services. *Grosvenor Chapel,* on South Audley Street
in Mayfair, is handsome eighteenth-century and was much used
by. It is early-eighteenth-century, designed by James Gibb, a
Place, was designed by Nash for George IV, which should be
recommendation enough for you to see it. There are two churches
dedicated to *St. Botolph* in London; the one in Aldersgate is the
more interesting in that it is at once medieval and eighteenth-
century. *St. Bride,* a Fleet Street landmark, is also originally
medieval, was rebuilt by Wren, bombed in World War II, and
was once again reconstructed, with the aid of Wren's plans. Pepys
was baptized in the church font. *St. Martin's-in-the-Fields* is a
Trafalgar Square landmark; see it from within, when you pass
by. It is early eighteenth-century, designed by James Gibb, a
follower of Wren, and it was a prototype for many churches in
the United States; *St. Mary-le-Strand,* in the City, is still another
fine Gibb work.

**Some writers' houses:** *Carlyle's House* is handsome early-eighteenth-century, on smart Cheyne Walk along the Thames, in
Chelsea. *Dickens' House,* on Doughty Street, is where he finished
*Pickwick Papers,* and houses the Dickens Fellowship and that
organization's Dickens Museum. *Keats' House* is in Keats Grove,
Hampstead. It is where he wrote "Ode to a Nightingale," among
other things; full of Keatsiana.

TO WATCH

*Theater:* London is the greatest of theater cities, with more
than twice as many legitimate theaters as New York. The fare is
varied—classics, musicals, new comedies and dramas, even imports from across the Atlantic that you may have had trouble
getting tickets for in New York. Prices are not as cheap as in
former years, but theater still is a major London bargain. Buy
tickets at booking offices of theaters, if you have time. But do

not hesitate to use ticket brokers; major hotels have branches of them, and they are all around town. Their fees are lower than their American counterparts', and for the visitor with limited time they provide a valuable service. All brokers have printed schedules of what's-playing-where, for the asking. Daily newspapers carry them, too. And so does *What's On,* one of the weekly counterparts of New York's *Cue* magazine, though with a format that makes it difficult to read. Evening performance times vary; some at seven-thirty, some at eight. There are usually *two* matinees on Saturday, late afternoon and evening, but there is no consistency here, either. Note that what we call the orchestra —or main level—of a theater, the British call stalls. Most of the legitimate theaters are in and around Shaftesbury Avenue near Piccadilly Circus. They are all equipped with bars that sell soft drinks, beer, and liquor at intermission; additionally, usherettes serve intermission cookies and coffee on trays, at one's seat, if ordered when seated. They also vend boxes of chocolates, a favorite theater food in London.

Of equal import with the theater is the mid-nineteenth-century *Royal Opera House, Covent Garden;* it is the home of the first-rank Royal Ballet and of the Royal Opera. Performances for popular Covent Garden attractions can be the most difficult to get seats for. Watch for ballet also at the *Sadler's Wells Theatre* and occasionally at other locations, and note that the Sadler's Wells Opera Company performs at the *London Coliseum,* and that, as a matter of policy, all of the operas it presents are sung in English. The architecturally interesting oval-arena-shape *Royal Albert Hall* went up in 1870 as a memorial to Queen Victoria's consort. It is a major locale for musical events—concerts by the Royal Philharmonic and recitals—along with the post-World War II *Royal Festival Hall* in South London, across the Thames, and its newer neighbor, *Queen Elizabeth Hall. Wigmore Hall* is used for chamber music and smaller concerts. The big first-run *cinemas* are mainly in and about Leicester Square; you can see the same movies at home, but if you like you may buy tickets for these big movie houses in advance at their booking offices or through the theater ticket brokers. *Son et Lumière* (Sound and Light), though normally presented outdoors, sensibly moves indoors in London. The locale—in summer only—has been St. Paul's Cathedral in recent seasons. *Gambling* is legal in Britain, and London has a number of casinos. *Crockfords* at 16 Carlton House Terrace and the *Twenty-One Club* (8 Chesterfield Gardens) are probably the best-known of the lot: members only, which means take your passport along. The *discothèque,* French though its name may be, was born in London, and still thrives. *The Scotch,* in a basement off the alley called Mason's Yard, is among the more fashionable. Your hotel hall porter can up-date you on the contemporarily popular discos. *Night clubs* are expensive and predictable. I make no recommendations. Of the *dinner-dance-floorshow restaurants,* those of *Quaglino's,* in the Meurice Hotel, and the *Savoy Hotel* are top rank. And there is pleasant *dinner-dancing* at such hotels as the *London Hilton, Grosvenor House,* and *Dorchester.* Last, but hardly least, is the classic London Sunday afternoon diversion: listening to the soapbox oration at *Marble Arch corner of Hyde Park.* The subject matter is limitless, the speakers and the crowds just possibly the London you've been looking for all along.

## TO STAY

When a London hotel is running beautifully, there is none better. Service is gracious and flawless. Everything will look well, taste well, work well. What must be borne in mind is that the better, older London hotels have considerable experience in catering to Britain's upper classes and peerage, and that there is no more knowing or demanding a clientele—anywhere. At the same time, it is well to note that one is no longer completely guaranteed an English experience in an English hotel, as used to be the case. With the exception of chefs in the better hotels' kitchens, staffs

were always local, very often the sons and daughters or grandsons
and granddaughters of old-timers in the same places. The ambience was English. And the language was English. Recent years
have seen changes. English is not always understood. The English
way of doing things is sometimes more foreign to staff members
with whom you come in contact, than with *you*—the short-
term visitor. And standards can vary. Still, managers of better
hotels are doing their best to cope with the vicissitudes of the
employment situation. By and large, they are coping very well
indeed. A final word: New-hotel construction proceeds at a rapid
pace in London, but in this, of all European capitals, one still
is warned to book hotel space in advance, arriving with written
confirmation in hand, regardless of the season of the year.

Here are some hotels that I like, with a *de luxe* group for starters.
The *Dorchester,* on Park Lane overlooking Hyde Park, is—or
at least has been for me—an extraordinary hotel experience.
The luxury is the kind that English interior designers—Oliver
Messel in this case—create so well, combining traditional furnishings with contemporary fabrics and colors, with the results
bright and warm and welcoming. The services—reception, hall
porters, waiters, barmen, chambermaids, doormen—are about as
consistently good as I know at any hotel on any of the six continents. More on this later, but this is an exceptional place to eat,
too; grill, restaurant, tea lounge, or even via room service, where
a multicourse lunch or dinner is served a course at a time by
the floor waiter. The ordinary bedrooms are particularly spacious.
But the suites—the many regular ones and the extra-luxe
Roof Garden series—are especially sumptuous. The *Hyde Park*
is an Edwardian dandy whose backyard is Hyde Park. (No
other hotel may make that statement.) It has been masterfully
refurbished to the tune of several millions over recent years
—David Hicks is among the decorators—and gifted Trust Houses-
Forte management has brought an ambience to the place that is one
of the most winning in town—alert, animated, attractively peopled.
The bedrooms and suites and the brand-new baths therein are

special treats. So is lunch in the park-view restaurant, or drinks in the lively lounge. The *Savoy,* in the hurly-burly dominantly Victorian-era Strand, is a good bit away from more sedate Mayfair. But the location is more convenient than one might at first imagine, and there is more than meets the eye behind the rather formidable façade. Service is what has made the Savoy. It is click-click, knowing, professional. The hall porters are masters of their art. The reception people could pass for diplomats. Hitchcock could use the barmen and waiters—or, for that matter, the chamber-maids—in a movie. Get away from the prosaic-looking—albeit perky—lobby, and the old-fashioned-size bedrooms and suites are an absolute delight. To lunch or dine or drink or dance in the Savoy is genuine London pleasure. The *Ritz,* on Piccadilly, is the kind of pure, unadulterated, eighteenth-century French luxury transported across *La Manche* to London that we dream about. Exquisite is the only way to describe the look of the place. The glass-roofed pavilion called the Winter Garden is—all crystal chandeliers and paneled walls and Louis XV chairs—nothing less than London's most inspired afternoon-tea locale. All of the public spaces—lobbies, bars, and most especially the Louis XVI Restaurant—are quite super, and so are the bedrooms and suites. Service is very knowing and very nice. The *Connaught,* on Carlos Place in Mayfair, is quite as though some English friends were putting you up in their town house. Nothing French here—dark-beamed, turn-of-century, very smart English-English. Accommodations are quietly luxe. The paneled bar is in and of itself a worthy destination. And the restaurant warrants additional comment on a later page. *Claridge's,* not far away on Brook Street, another Mayfair address, has made a specialty of royalty over the years (since 1838, to be precise). And done very well at it. The original Claridges were a butler and his wife, a housekeeper, who had worked for the gentry. But a solitary royal signed the register in 1860, to be visited by Queen Victoria. And the crowned heads have not stopped since. Commoners, though, are welcome. There is nothing distinguished about the eighteenth-century décor, except that it is elaborate, and that ceilings are high. Part of the staff still is liveried, as in days of yore, and one drinks—tea or stronger stuff—in the lobby rather than in a detached bar-lounge, the better to watch the clientele pass in review. Accommodations are elaborate and the proportion of suites, as you might imagine, is exceptionally high. The skyscraping *London Hilton* on Park Lane raised eyebrows among the locals when it opened in the early sixties—the first luxurious contemporary-design hotel in town. Muttering, muttering about those upstart colonials coming over here to run a hotel. Well, the Hilton International people pioneered in London as they have in San Juan, Addis Ababa, and other parts. Their beautifully run tower—its guest rooms are as handsome as the striking views they afford—has often been emulated, but seldom with the success of the London Hilton. (Success has been such that a second Hilton—the Kensington Hilton—is going up.) The ambience of the place blends Britain with just enough of the sassy transatlantic colonials to make things interesting. There are a variety of wine-dine spots, and the location is excellent. *Grosvenor House,* another Park Lane landmark, went up in the late twenties. Its architect, Sir Edward Lutyens, was the very same whom the Crown had earlier commissioned to design a new capital for India, when it was determined that it was time to move on from Calcutta to New Delhi, long before Indian independence was taken seriously in Whitehall. Well, if Lutyens' New Delhi is now Indian, his Grosvenor House is now Trust Houses-Forte, who have put some seven million dollars into a kind of refurbishing whereby you enjoy the up-to-date quality of it all, but you still recognize the Grosvenor House you've known. The lobby is big and humming-busy. The two residential wings—they are connected by the lobby and public rooms—boast zingy accommodations. There are fine new restaurants and drinking parlors, but tea in the lounge remains a happy London pastime. And the whole is masterfully managed. The *Churchill,* on Portman Square just beyond Selfridge's on Oxford Street, was Loew's Hotels' first European operation. Operators of

de luxe New York leaders like the Regency and the Drake, they
knew what they were about in the big-city hotel business. They
planned carefully. The Churchill is a good-looker from the outside façade inward. Ellen Lehmann McCluskey, the New York
designer who created the interiors of the Regency, crossed the
Atlantic for the Churchill. Her stamp—appropriately Regency—
is again evident. The rooms and suites are lovely, and so are
the public spaces, including what has to be the most beautiful
coffee shop in London. The reborn *Berkeley* on Wilton Place in
Knightsbridge, retains the spirit—traditional, elegant, a stickler
for personal service—of its predecessors not to mention its antique
furnishings, marble mantels, and wood paneling; and there's a
rooftop, roofed-in swimming pool, as well as a restaurant and bar.
The *Stafford* (16 St. James's Place) is understated, old-school,
smallish, and very smart, with the kind of personal service rarely
encountered today.

Of the *first-class* hotels—as distinct from those of the luxury
group—I like these: The *Cavendish,* on Jermyn Street, just opposite Fortnum & Mason, is a modern version of a well-known
oldie that had occupied the same space. The location is one of
the most convenient in London, with West End theaters and
Mayfair equally walkable. The rooms are functional-comfortable-
modern. The public area—including a round-the-clock restaurant
and a cozy bar—are inviting, and the service, particularly hall
porter and reception, is Trust Houses-Forte at its very best.
The *Meurice,* just around the corner from Jermyn Street,
on a little thoroughfare called Bury Street, is a winsome old-timer
that has been agreeably updated. You may know it as the hotel
housing the even more celebrated Quaglino's Restaurant-Cabaret,
but the period-style accommodation and the smiling service are
hardly to be despised. The *Basil Street Hotel,* on the street from
which it takes its name, in Knightsbridge, is a hop and a skip
from Harrod's, but assuming that shopping in that estimable store
is not your only reason for a London visit, let me capsulize the
Basil Street's other attributes. The first is ambience. There is a

delightful English country air about the place, thanks in large part to eighteenth- and early-nineteenth-century décor. The second is convenience: There's a fine restaurant and a newer, amusing cafe. And the third is value: Almost every room has bath, and rates are among the most reasonable in town. The *Charing Cross,* attached to the Charing Cross Station at Trafalgar Square, is a prime example of how well British Transport Hotels have spruced up their old properties. The Charing Cross is a turn-of-century souvenir of an era when things were built very grandly, with high ceilings, elaborate plasterwork, palatial reception areas, and huge bedrooms. British Transport has redecorated and modernized so that one enjoys all of the style of the old with contemporary amenities like private baths (most rooms have them), super wine-dine facilities, and expert service. The *Strand Palace* is value-packed. The location is the Strand, the exterior elderly, the interior so up to date that every room has bath; there are varied eat-drink locales, and the lobby has a nice buzz to it. The *Waldorf* is another City landmark; Aldwych is its address. The façade is splendid neo-Renaissance, and the public rooms—including a trio of restaurants and five bars—are handsome, particularly the Templars Grill, with its murals depicting the history of London. A modernization program has resulted in every room having its own bath. Management is good Trust Houses-Forte. The *Russell,* on Russell Square not far from the British Museum, is still another example of how well Trust Houses-Forte can take a *grande dame,* of Edwardian vintage, and modernize it, the while retaining its aura of old. All rooms have bath, and there's a nifty restaurant and bar. The *Cumberland,* at Marble Arch on Oxford Street, is British hotelkeeping at its no-nonsense best. The idea is comfort rather than luxury, and at sensible tabs. Rooms are cheery, and all have private baths. The lobby is big and bustling and there are several restaurants and bars, one of them exceptional. The *Mt. Royal* is a nearby Marble Arch neighbor, not as attractive but in the same general worth-knowing-about category. *Fleming's Hotel* and the *Green Park Hotel* are a pair of Half

Moon Street opposites, with enviable Mayfair locations. Both are agreeably elderly, moderate in size, with restaurants and bars, refurbished to the point where most rooms have private baths and under the management of Grand Metropolitan Hotels—the crackerjack group that has properties all over London, the Continent, and even New York, some of them distinctly top rank. The *Clifton-Ford* and the *Londoner* are another pair of Grand Metropolitan neighbors. These two are both on Welbeck Street, a bit north of Oxford Street, near Manchester Square and the Wallace Collection. All of the bedrooms in both these inns have private baths, and both hotels have restaurants and bars. The *Grosvenor Court* is a Grand Metropolitan, too; I mention it because it is well situated on Davis Street, at Oxford, with Bond Street and Grosvenor Square close by. Most rooms have bath, and there's a restaurant-bar. *The Royal Court* is an always-reliable oldie, on pleasant Sloane Square, that has been modernized to the point where almost all rooms now have private bath; restaurant and bar.

## TO EAT (AND DRINK)

I have known English food since a few years after World War II, while I was studying in England. You still needed ration coupons—even to eat in a university dining hall. There were relatively few eggs, the famed English beef was a sometime thing, and the continental gastronomic influence—bless it many times over—had not yet made inroads. Times have changed over the years, most especially in London. The influx of people from all over the Continent and the Commonwelath during and after World War II, for one reason or another, brought the cuisines of the Continent, and Asia, to London in force. Coupled with that was the increase, year by year, of Britons vacationing on the Continent —even low-income Britons who before the war invariably stayed at home, holidaying at Brighton, Bournemouth, Torquay, or on the Cornish coast. All of this interchange has been gastronomically beneficial. It has created an interest in, and often a knowledge of good cooking among people of the lower classes and made it possible for upper-class and aristocratic Britons—who have always eaten and drunk well—to indulge their culinary fancies more than in the past. You have probably been told many times, for want of too much else to say, that Britain is blessed with good raw materials—the meat, the fruits, vegetables, the fresh fish and seafood. All of that is true, but no more so than in most countries of Europe or North America. England cooks some things very well. Roast beef, roast mutton and lamb, and the mutton and lamb chops; roast pork, grilled bacon, mixed grill, steak and kidney pie, Dover sole, oysters, shrimps. Baked goods—cakes, pies, cookies, crackers, shortbreads, whole-wheat and brown breads, muffins, scones, the dessert called trifle (a kind of English *zuppa Inglese*), jams, and jellies. Cheeses, like Cheddar and Stilton, milk and cream, particularly the sublime clotted cream from Devon and Cornwall. Chocolates and candies. Tea. Cooked vegetables are often disastrous. Potatoes, considering how many of them are eaten, are frequently misunderstood. Gravies and sauces are best ordered on the side, except in good places. Simple things like hamburgers and hot dogs, which the British think they prepare as well as we do, can be just *terrible*. And so can attempts at continental dishes—particularly if they are at all complex—when undertaken in the more modest places. The best rule is to order the simplest things. Undeniably good is the traditional big breakfast: porridge, bacon and eggs or sausage (*always* served with a silly little grilled half-tomato), chilled toast (served on racks designed to expedite the chilling, better suited for letters and often used for same), and tea and coffee. Equally good—though not as easily come across these days—is afternoon tea; bread and butter, little triangles of sandwiches, perhaps hot scones and/or muffins, cake and cookies, and a pot of tea. (Afternoon tea is not to be confused with "high tea," which is simply a synonym for supper.) The attractive way in which the

English serve meals is never to be taken for granted. The way a table *looks* has traditionally been more important than the actual food consumed. One has only to consider the beauty of English silver, china, and dining furniture over the centuries to appreciate what I mean.

As for drinks, tea is of course favored at teatime, and as the principal in-between pick-me-up. When I first knew England, the English swore to heaven they would *never, ever* use our insipid tea bags. Well, they have succumbed, more's the pity. If their tea—thanks to the bags—is no longer as consistently good, their coffee has improved, thank the good Lord, with appreciation as well to the Italians, who have taught them *espresso*. The English drink quantities of room-temperature beer—the kind closest to ours is called lager, although hotel bars carry Danish, Dutch, and German imports. Scotch whisky is just plain whisky in Britain, the nationality being implicit. The upper classes have always been quite serious wine drinkers, and they are very knowledgeable about wine, too. Britain has for long imported more sherry than any other land. (The British very sensibly give sherry parties rather than cocktail parties, when they want to keep costs down.) They gave the name sherry, to the Spanish *jerez*. They drink considerably more sweet port, after dinner, than the Portuguese, who make the stuff. They are very big on table wines, mostly French. (In this connection, note that they call red Bordeaux "claret.") Commonwealth wines are imported, too; the best are the Australian reds, with which one does well to get acquainted. English gin is as good as Scottish Scotch, and the water is everywhere drinkable, although it is a little-appreciated fact that the English appear to drink even less water than the French, or other continental Europeans—at least in public places. English restaurateurs don't want to be bothered with serving a non-revenue-producing beverage like water, and water-addicted Americans and Canadians must often beg, and beg again, before getting their glassful.

Here are some restaurants that I like. I don't think you can do better than the *Cafe Royal* (Regent Street, near Piccadilly Circus) if you want splendor as regards both food and setting. The latter is turn-of-century Edwardian opulence. The former is a menu that blends the classic style of France—a duck *pâté,* for example, or *truite meunière aux pistaches*—with English specialties like bread pudding or roast lamb. There is a choice of rooms, with the Grill the smartest. Service throughout is Old School Super. The *Connaught Hotel Restaurant* offers a menu mix not unlike the Cafe Royal, except that it is perhaps even more English, and the décor is far less ebullient. Tempters include *Assiette de Saucisses Assorties*—a sampling of sausages, Dover sole, and what has to be England's premier dessert trolley. Precede your meal with drinks in the bar, from where you may order. The *Savoy Grill* (that hotel has a restaurant as well) has the most engaging eatery-ambience in London. It's big and busy and buzzing with the talk of a good-looking clientele, both domestic and imported. Seafoods, grills, French-accented dishes—the whole menu is well-nigh faultless, and the service is rendered mostly by old pros. The *Terrazza* (19 Romilly Street) is a kind of Savoy Grill as regards ambience, at least, with the added attraction of an Italian accent. The crowd is as intriguing here as the pasta. But one does well to order a veal dish, or one of the chicken or shrimp specialties, as well; as good an Italian meal as you'll get in London—which is saying a lot in this trattoria-filled town. *Leith's* (92 Kensington Park Road) has a following of royals as well as untitled eaters. The lures are few but good: game casseroles, for example, seafood bisques, roast duck. Very smart. *La Napoule* (8 North Audley Street) is very French (except for the waiters, who are skilled Spaniards) and very good. Order the *terrine du chef* and the grilled red mullet. And don't pass up the pastries. The *Dorchester Grill* is one of the handsomest of London restaurants and serves excellent food, from an extensive, predominantly French-style menu. The seafoods and fish dishes are noted, but the steaks and roasts are equally exemplary. Note the wine list; it is one of the best in the U.K. *Scott's* on Mount Street is a fine traditional restaurant where the emphasis has long been capital E for English—and for Excellent. Steak and kidney pies, roast beef, steaks; friendly, too. The *Ritz Hotel's Louis XVI Restaurant* is the most eye-filling restaurant in town: pure and beautiful eighteenth-century French, with the classic French dishes of the menu the most interesting. And service is as classic as the *carte*. The *Gay Hussar* (2 Greek Street) typifies the foreign flavor of Soho, in this case Hungarian—and authentically. Chicken paprika, *gulyas, strudel,* of course, good Hungarian wines, engaging Hungarian service. *Lacey's* (26 Whitfield Street) is smallish, offbeat, and under the aegis of a cookbook author, who practices what she preaches, with English-continental dishes. *Manzi's* (Leicester Street, just off Leicester Square) is an oldtime seafood place that I have long enjoyed. The *moules marinière* are very good, and so are all the fish, Dover sole naturally included. *Il Girasole* (Fulham Road, S.W. 3) occupies a white stucco cottagelike interior that spells Sicily; good Italian food. The *Causerie* in Claridge's Hotel serves a dull buffet lunch, with ungracious waiters seating you and bringing coffee—only if you want a cheap meal in a famous hotel. *M. J. Embertson* (5b Shepherd Street in Mayfair, near the Dorchester) is a minuscule oyster place—the bivalves themselves, or a bisque, and wine. Not cheap but very good. *Martinez* (Swallow Street, just off Regent Street, just off Piccadilly Circus is a Spanish restaurant—paella, gazpacho, guitarist—that has been going strong for at least as long as I know London. Lunch in the *Hyde Park Hotel Restaurant* is as enjoyable as one could ask at midday. The picture-window view is of the park, from the only hotel that has the park as a backyard. The room is handsome, high-ceilinged, traditional, and the menu runs a wide gamut of French-style specialties. Precede the repast with a drink in the hotel's cocktail lounge. With its big Indian population, London is the best city outside of India for the distinctive food of that country. *The Shah* (Drummond Street, Mayfair) is about as good a source of Indian curries and the like as you'll find. One of the most sensible developments in English eatery in recent years has been the inexpensive help-yourself-to-roast-beef restaurant, at which a waiter serves you everything but your main course, which you help yourself to, at a counter, with a chef to assist. Selections usually include a joint of beef, roast lamb, or roast pork. These places usually are called *The Carvery.* There's a good one in the *Cumberland Hotel,* Marble Arch, and another at the *Strand Palace Hotel,* Strand. The old-fashioned high-ceilinged *Charing Cross Hotel Restaurant* (Trafalgar Square) has been beautifully restored to bring out the fine decorative detail. But the food—hors d'oeuvres, pastries, cheeses, not to mention entrées—is tasty, too. Worth remembering is the *Ribblesdale Restaurant* of the Cavendish Hotel. It's sleek-modern in ambience, serves fine fare, and— this is important—is open round the clock, every day of the year. The *Piazza* at *Grosvenor House* is another late-late cafe. And finally, half a dozen good *pubs for lunch.* The *Audley,* in Mayfair's South Audley Street, gives you a choice: the Gilded Cage in the cellar, the main floor pub proper, and Annie's Attic upstairs. All three are amusing, congenial, and with good, solid fare. The *Rose & Crown* is on Old Park Lane (off Piccadilly)—good-looking crowd, good lunches. The *Grenadier* (18 Wilton Row) goes back at least to the early nineteenth century, when it was called *The Guardsman* and George IV was a customer. The clientele today is very smart Belgravia, the lunches excellent, and the service smiling. You may go for dinner as well. (Note, please, that you enter through Grosvenor Crescent, just off Hyde Park Corner, passing by foot through Old Barrack Yard; easier than it sounds.) The *Chelsea Potter* is a gregarious King's Road lunch spot. The *Bunch of Grapes,* on Brompton Road, is Victorian, and with good vittles. Of this quintet, *The Archer* is the oldest; it's a neighbor of the Tower of London, and is good to know about in connection with a Tower visit. Still another lunch spot in connection with still another visit: Hampton Court Palace. The name of the restaurant is the *Mitre Inn*—it's very near by. *Afternoon tea* is a treat when taken in the *Winter Garden* of the Ritz Hotel, Piccadilly—sandwiches and cakes, with white-glove service to match; the setting is sumptuous Louis XV. The *Dorchester Hotel Lounge,* Park Lane, is still another *luxe* locale, and you get a little more to eat. At *Claridge's Hotel,* a liveried waiter will serve you in the lobby so that you can watch the passing parade. The *Waldorf Hotel* lobby—elaborately Edwardian—is another pleasing tea spot. Outside of the hotels, there is no question but that *Fortnum & Mason* is the place to go. Choose the handsome restaurant on the fourth floor over the always-crowded (but also good) Fountain—which has tables as well as counter—on the Jermyn Street side. More reasonable—as it has been for a long time—is the *Ceylon Tea Centre* (22 Lower Regent Street), with the tea genuine Ceylonese, of course (you may buy tins of it) and satisfying sandwiches and cakes. The *Danish National Centre* (2–3 Conduit Street) serves fifty types of Smørrebrød, the Danish national open-faced sandwiches. The department stores—*Harrod's* and *Selfridge's* most particularly—serve afternoon tea, often in more than one location. And there are the myriad *Lyons* teashops, where one can get sandwiches, snacks, desserts, tea, and coffee, and the much larger and more elaborate *Lyons Corner Houses* scattered about the major commercial districts; each of these has more restaurants and tea shops than you know what to do with. The nicest of these is on Oxford Street, near Marble Arch; aside from the counter tea places, it has a remarkably good and inexpensive steak house that I can recommend. *Museum-eating* is a convenience of consequence in the course of gallery-hopping. Agreeable museum restaurants include those of the Victoria and Albert, Tate, British, National Gallery, National Maritime (Greenwich) and Kenwood (Hampstead).

And lastly, *pubs for drinking,* in contrast to the lunch ones listed above. *Dirty Dick's* (202 Bishop's Gate in East London) boasts proudly that it hasn't been cleaned up in a couple of hundred years. Its spider webs are its trademark. The *Lamb and Flag* (33 Rose Street) is a theater-district landmark worth remembering for after the play. The *Salisbury* (St. Martin's Lane) is another after-theater magnet. The *Waterman's Arms* (1 Glenaffric Avenue, way out east) is a cab ride away from the center, but there's a very loud music hall band for a bonus, along with considerable local convivality. The *Prospect of Whitby,* down around the docks and known to cabbies, replaces the band with a quieter guitar and a respectably historic ambience that extends to the early sixteenth century. *The Mayflower* (117 Rotherhithe Street) is another atmospheric oldie named for the Pilgrims' ship, near the church (St. Mary's) where its captain is buried, and with a Thames view. The *Anchor Tavern,* on the Southwark side of the Thames, dates to Elizabethan times, and is a jumble of intriguing bars and eateries, with the also-venerable *George Inn* a near-neighbor (and with tasty English specialties in its restaurant). Though hardly pubs, the *cocktail lounges* of the leading hotels are pleasantly atmospheric for drinks; these include the *Savoy* (whose house specialty, the Prince of Wales, deliciously blends champagne, lemon juice, Cherry Heering, and strawberries, but whose martinis are also excellent, *Ritz, Connaught, Dorchester,* and *Hyde Park.*

## TO BUY

The beauty part of shopping in London is that it's all done in English. Sometimes this is not a beauty part at all: It's too easy, which can result in its becoming too costly. But shopping in the English language would not be all that worthwhile if there were not worthy wares. Believe me, there are. Not, mind you, that there are any bedrock bargains. Everything that is exported to the United States is, of course, somewhat cheaper on home ground, but not all that much. No, it is the design and quality and variety— and the smart way in which things are displayed and merchandised—that keep us in stores for disproportionately greater periods of our time in London than should be the case—if we want to see other aspects of the city than the insides of its emporia.

First, though, where to shop? I would break London down this way: (1) *Piccadilly*—between Piccadilly Circus and Green Park (moderate to expensive); (2) *Regent Street*—from Pall Mall to Oxford Street (moderately high to expensive); (3) *Oxford Street* —from Marble Arch to Charing Cross Road (moderate); (4) *Knightsbridge,* including Brompton Road and Sloane Street and Fulham Road (moderate to expensive); (5) *King's Road, Chelsea*—from Sloane Square to Beaufort Street (moderate to expensive); (6) *Mayfair*—roughly the area bounded by Park Lane, Regent Street, Piccadilly, and Oxford Street, and including Old and New Bond Streets, Curzon Street, and Savile Row (expensive); (7) *Soho,* including Shaftesbury Avenue—moderate; (8) *Strand*—from Trafalgar Square until the name changes to Fleet Street (moderate).

Purchases of substance may be made tax-free, with the savings considerable. Better stores can provide you with details.

The **street markets** are an intrinsic part of the London shopping scene. They include *Camden Passage* (Saturday only), with antiques among its wares; *Caledonian Market* (Friday only), antiques; *Portobello Road Market* (Friday and Saturday), antiques; *Billingsgate* (of course, you have heard of this one), fish, Monday through Saturday, from 5:30 A.M.; and *Petticoat Lane,* (another famous one), with clothes and what-have-you, Sunday from 9:00 A.M. to 2:00 P.M.

The **department stores** rank with those of the major North American cities and a very few other cities (Tokyo, Copenhagen, Stockholm, Paris) as among the very best. Concentrate on the Big Two. Start with *Harrod's,* in Knightsbridge, the undisputed top dog of the lot. Prices range from moderately high to expensive. Stop first at the information counter on the main floor and ask for a leaflet listing department locations. Then case the place from stem to stern, from antiques to apples, and not excluding clothing, accessories, gifts, and housewares, and a variety of places to snack or lunch. No. 2 is *Selfridge's,* on Oxford Street, near Marble Arch. The price level is lower, but the range is impressive, and there are good buys frequently to be made. Though not a department store, *Fortnum & Mason* comes close in its unique way. It goes back to the eighteenth century, when it started out as a fancy grocery, which it still is. But after you've looked at the foodstuffs and delicacies and wines of the main floor, take in the clothing and accessories of the upper floors, not forgetting the earlier-recommended restaurant and fountain. **Leather** is of exceptional quality in England; the findings on bags, wallets, luggage, and briefcases are usually superior to those on the Continent. Bond Street has many good shops. *Harrod's* and *Fortnum & Mason* both have good departments. *Silver*—reproductions and contemporary designs—can be seen at many fine shops, including *Mappin & Webb,* 170 Regent Street, and *S. J. Phillips,* 139 New Bond Street. **English china and pottery** is justly celebrated, and among the very best of London values. Aside from department stores like *Harrod's* (which has an excellent china department) there are such shops as *Gered* (174 Piccadilly), specializing in Spode and Wedgwood; *Chinacraft* (Burlington Arcade and other locations), with a variety of makes, and *T. Goode* (20 South Audley Street. **Clothing fabrics by the yard** is another good buy, assuming you have someone at home to make it up for you, whose labor is not so high that it will make the total cost exorbitant. Good scources include *Liberty's* (210 Regent Street), a fine old store whose exported fabrics, neckties and the like, are famous —particularly their hand-blocked prints, and *The Scotch House* (2 Brompton Road and 84 Regent Street), the Edinburgh firm with the largest selection of tartans extant, and a great deal else of beauty and quality. *Bookshops* are everywhere, and the department stores have big departments. The books can be good buys, and the quality works are beautifully designed and printed. Two interesting sources are *Foyle's* (119 Charing Cross Road), where the danger is that you may spend the entire day browsing, and *Her Majesty's Stationery Office* (49 High Holborn and 423 Oxford Street), at which are on sale the low-priced but frequently fascinating publications published by the government on a wide range of subjects. **Stationery** is nowhere more elegant than in

England—plain, printed, or engraved with name and address or monogram. Bond street is full of tempting sources. One especially super one is *Frank Smythson, Ltd.,* on New Bond Street; they'll ship your order to you, if it's not ready when you leave town, and they'll keep the dye—or plate—so that you can reorder. **Kitchen equipment** may not seem like a British specialty, given the erratic quality of British food, but the noted cookery writer, *Elizabeth David*—whose books have surely been the major stimulus behind England's post-World War II interest in Mediterranean-area foods —has opened a shop so that her readers may without difficulty buy the kind of cooking equipment she considers essential for a good kitchen. The location is 46 Bourne Street, and if Mrs. David is on hand when you stop in, she'll be glad to inscribe *A Book of Mediterranean Food, French Country Cooking,* or whichever other of her volumes (most are Penguin paperbacks) you would like to buy. **Food shops:** The earlier-mentioned *Fortnum & Mason*—for tinned teas, cookies, honeys, condiments, and heaven knows how many other edibles that you may want to buy for self or gifts; and the also-earlier-mentioned *Harrod's*—whose food department (the marble-counter meat area, the live-fish tanks, the berries in leafy boxes) is a major European gastronomic attraction. *Richoux,* South Audley Street near Adam's Row, vends its own luscious chocolates, and doubles as a very fancy coffee shop. **Linens:** *Robinson & Clever,* on Regent Street, have a big selection of the linen dish towels (tea towels to the British) that are one of the best cheap souvenirs of England, at once utilitarian and typical, thanks to the local design-motifs. **Umbrellas,** as well as walking sticks, are best when British. *Swaine, Adeney Briggs & Sons* (185 Piccadilly) is a noted source. **Handicrafts** are not the sort of thing one expects in Britain, but there are exceptional selections at the *Crafts Council Galley* (12 Waterloo Place) and the *Commonwealth Crafts Centre* (35 Victoria Street), where they come from Commonwealth countries around the world. **Perfumes, soaps, and colognes**—the last two for men as well as women— make welcome gifts from Britain if they are the English ones made by *Floris* (89 Jermyn Street), who have purveyed their men's and women's scents to the Crown since George IV's time; or *George F. Trumper* (9 Curzon Street), the greatest old-fashioned barber shop of them all, which for long has put up its own lime cologne in an old-fashioned bottle whose stopper is a leaden crown. **Men's barbers** don't have the business they used to, with so much long hair. But here are two. A conservative favorite I have known for years is the above-mentioned Trumper's. More contemporary is the unisex shop called *The Crimpers* (80a Baker Street; telephone 466-4522 and ask for my barber—Saul). Among the many excellent **women's hairdressers** are Leonard's, 6 Upper Grosvenor Street; top models like its high-style trademark.

**Knitwear and sweaters,** are somewhat cheaper than when exported to the United States. Aside from department stores like *Harrod's* and *Selfridge's,* one finds good things for both men and women at *Jaeger* (204 Regent Street) and *The Scotch House* (2 Brompton Road). **Children's clothes and toys** are delightful at *Small Wonder* (296 King's Road)—up to the age of six; *Pollocks Toy Theaters* (44 Monmouth Street); and—for clothes, not toys—*Marks and Spencer* (458 Oxford Street and branches)—one of a chain of cheap-clothes stores nationwide. *Gloves* are not cheap but of fine quality. *The Glove Shop* (138 New Bond Street) is a good men's source, while *Harrod's* and *Dickens & Jones* (another of the department stores) have excellent women's glove departments. **Men's shoes and boots** are available ready-made at every turn. The big English specialty, though, is hand-made footwear, and it's not cheap. *Henry Maxwell* (9 Dover Street) and *Codner, Coombs & Dobbie* (21 Jermyn Street) are two celebrated specialists. *Lotus* (43 New Bond Street) is for casual, heavy-duty walking, wet-weather, and hard-work shoes and boots for men and women. *Women's shoes* are not of as much interest to visitors in England as men's, but the *Chelsea Cobbler* (165 Draycott Avenue) makes them up to order; and *Lillery & Skinner* is noted for its huge ready-to-wear stock. **Women's clothes** could be the basis of a whole chapter. There are the couturiers like *Norman*

*Hartnell* (26 Bruton Street) and *Hardy Amies* (14 Savile Row). There are the department stores and big specialty shops: *Harrod's, Harvey Nichol's, Simpson's, Jaeger,* and so many others. And there are countless *boutiques.* Here are a few: *Bazaar* (138a King's Road)—Mary Quant originals; *Fenwick* (63 New Bond Street)—current but not faddy; *Foale & Tuffin* (1 Marlborough Court, off Carnaby Street)—currently "in," trendy stuff; Malabar (311 Brompton Road)—unusual Indian silks; *Piero de Monzo & Dean Rogers* (Fulham Road)—highly original designs, including some for gents. **Men's clothes** is a where-do-you-begin proposition. The major clothing stores—good ones—include *Acquascutum* (100 Regent Street), whose raincoats are a specialty: *Austin Reed* (103 Regent Street)—including their trendy Cue Shop; *Jaeger* (204 Regent Street); *Simpson's* (203 Piccadilly), which is big on Daks trousers, has an upstairs avant-garde section, a restaurant, and even a theater-ticket broker; *Burberry's,* good for rainwear as well as other clothing; and the *Way In Shop,* upstairs at *Harrod's*—a dark, cavelit maze with music, coffee, snacks, and way-out clothes. *Custom*—or "bespoke," as the British so quaintly call them—*tailors* are many, along Savile Row and other Mayfair streets. Two good ones are Charles Stevens at 53 Brick Lane, in the City, with lower prices than Savile Row; and *Blades* (8 Burlington Gardens), which is more contemporary than many of the bespoke places, and, thanks to its New York branch, has an idea of what Americans are wearing. If you would like a bowler (derby) or a trilby or just an everyday felt *hat,* splurge with a purchase from *Lock's,* an ancient St. James's landmark. *Handmade shirts* are a very personal London souvenir. *Hawes and Curtis* (2 Burlington Gardens) are specialists. The gang back home always likes *ties* from London, even if they are hardly the bargains of long ago. *Liberty's* (210 Regent Street) has its own silk prints. *Washington Tremlett* (Conduit Street) has classic and contemporary styles. *Turnbull & Asser* (71 Jermyn Street) is an aged institution that went mod a few years back, losing some of its *politesse* in the process, but emerging with some handsome, albeit expensive, four-in-hand and extra-wide bow ties. Men's *boutiques* and small shops abound. *John Stephen* (52 Carnaby Street and other locations) pioneered the Carnaby Street brouhaha; moderate prices. *John Michael* (18 Saville Row and on the King's Road, as well) is smarter and more expensive. And then there are the amusing *unisex boutiques; Apple* (94 Baker Street) and *Hung on You* (430 King's Road) are two of many. **Antiques:** There are still considerable quantities of English seventeenth-, eighteenth-, and nineteenth-century furniture, ceramics, porcelain, books, maps, paintings, clocks, tapestries, and other objects available in London, not to mention antiques of other areas— France, Italy, the Middle East, the Orient—which cost more. One can buy at the big noted dealers and auction houses, but also to be considered are smaller places—often with good prices— on Knightsbridge's Brompton Road, Chelsea's King's Road, Kensington's Fulhmam Road, and the Portobello Road. To be noted also is the big annual *Antiques Fair* held for a fortnight in mid-June at Grosvenor House Hotel. Here are some well-known sources: *Mallett* (with a branch at Bergdorf Goodman in New York) is in the ex-home of the Duke of Westminster at 2 Davies Street, and is also at 40 New Bond Street; the fanciest antiquery in the kingdom, with both domestic and French wares. *Frank Partridge* (40 New Bond Street) is also very good, very expensive, and with French as well as English stock. Other top dealers include *Stair & Co.* (Mount Street, near the Connaught Hotel); *Bond Street Silver Galleries* (111 New Bond Street); *Aubrey Brocklehurst* (124 Cromwell Rd.)—English clocks, watches, barometers; *Bernard Quaritch* (5 Lower John Street)—old, rare books; and *Dark & Rendlesham* (498 King's Road)—English furniture from Elizabethan to the seventeenth century. There are several *antiques "supermarkets."* One of the bigger ones is *Hypermarket* (26–40 Kensington High Street)—a hundred dealers have stalls, and all guarantee refunds if fakes—perish the thought—are unintentionally sold to customers. The two famous **auction houses** are *Sotheby's* (affiliated with Parke, Bernet in New York),

34 New Bond Street, and Christie Manson & Wods (8 King Street).

TO NOTE

**Access:** More airlines fly from the United States to London than to any other European capital. These include Britain's BOAC, America's TWA and Pan Am, Australia's Qantas, Air-India, and Japan Air Lines. British airlines—mostly British European Airways—link London and the capitals of Europe, whose countries' own carriers provide additional extensive air service. There is, as well, considerable domestic air service within the British Isles. London Airport, at Heathrow, is fourteen miles from town, making taxis a fairly expensive proposition; the airport buses, to the several London air terminals, run frequently, and are cheap and efficient; taxis are readily available at the air terminals in town, to take passengers to hotels. There is excellent train service between London and the continental capitals and Ireland, thanks to trains coordinating with ship sailings across the North and Irish Seas and the English Channel. British Transport's domestic rail services are good; there are crack luxury expresses to Edinburgh. Car-carrying passenger boats transport automobiles between the Continent and Britain, which has a modern highway system, but where driving remains on the left-hand side of the road—not always easy for visitors, including pedestrians, to accustom themselves to. Within London, there is excellent public transport. The subway, or Underground, is one of the best such in the world; maps of the Underground system are easily available. The bus system is good, too, and foreign visitors enjoy riding upstairs on the double-decker buses; fares are taken by conductors who come to one's seat, charging *according to destination.* London taxis are especially designed as taxis, with plenty of leg room in front of one, and plenty of head room so that it's easy to step in and out; they are the most civilized such conveyances of any country on the planet. They are metered, but nominal extra charges are made for luggage. Self-drive and chauffeur-driven cars are easily hired from any number of London firms. The latter—particularly *Take-a-Guide* (11 Old Bond Street), which is staffed by well-educated young people driving their own cars—are an excellent idea if one is interested in getting about a lot, both in town and the surrounding countryside, in a relatively short time. It is much quicker when a knowledgeable local person, who knows the area and its attractions, is at the wheel and making suggestions on itinerary and the like at the same time. **Climate:** Milder than you may think, and frequently drier than you might think. Every season is good for London. Summer (June through August) averages in the sixties, with seventies as highs in July and August, and the occasional scorcher of a heat wave—say, maybe eighty—which throws the town into a tizzy. (There is normally no need for air conditioning, so that when it does get this hot, one feels it; men do especially, as there is normally no occasion for them to have the summer-weight suits that Americans wear during the hot-weather months.) Spring (late April and May) and autumn (late September and October) are generally fiftyish. Winter (November through March) averages in the low forties, although thirties weather is not uncommon in January and February. Moisture of some sort or other can appear at almost any time, not necessarily with notice; that is why Londoners carry umbrellas as habitually as the rest of us do Kleenex. Raincoats—even in summer, which can be cool—are a convenience, too. This is not to say, though, that "bright periods," as the British weathermen call them, are all that infrequent. **Clothes:** It started in London, the mod clothes-long hair phenomenon, and it continues. London is the most tolerant of world capitals—along with New York—as regards attire. Which is not to say that it is not well dressed. On the contrary, its designers, for both men and women, are among the most talented extant. And Londoners are clothes-conscious. Better places, particularly after dark, still prefer gents in jackets and ties rather than turtlenecks, and like to see women correspondingly well got

up. **Currency:** The pound is divided into 100 pence, written
"p". There are ½p, 1p, 2p, 5p, 10p, and 50p coins; there are
£1, £5, and £10 notes, as in the past. You are still likely to
come across coins of the old currency. A shilling is the equal of
5p, and the coins are the same size; a florin—the two-shilling coin
—equals 10p, and the 50p coin is equal to the old ten-shilling
note. **Tipping:** Generally, restaurants and cafes do not add a service charge, so tip 15 percent. Tip bellhops and baggage porters
10p per bag. Tip doormen 5p for getting you a cab. Tip hall porters—that's English for concierge—an average of 10p–20p per
day, but only if they've performed special services for you during
your stay. Tip taxi drivers 15 percent, but not less than 7p or 8p.
**Language:** There is a tremendous fuss sometimes made by both
Britons and Americans as regards the differences between the
English spoken in the two countries. In the two decades-plus that
I have been visiting Britain, I have never encountered a bit of
difficulty, nor do I know anyone else who has. I am not, therefore,
about to give you a "vocabulary" of Britishisms; any American
with an even average IQ figures these out as they come his way.
And vice versa with our British cousins. **Local literature:** Where
do you begin with this category, in London of all cities? There are,
to start, guide books and picture albums on London of varying
quality. The earlier-mentioned *What's On in London* is for sale
at newsstands, and is full of information, albeit typographically
difficult to plow through. Of the newspapers, I regularly read
the *Guardian* (formerly the Manchester *Guardian,* but for some
time published both in London and Manchester); the *Times* of
London (the Personals are no longer much fun, but the letters
to the editor can be amusing, and the daily Court Circular keeps
you abreast of what the Royal Family is up to, day in and day
out), and the *Daily Telegraph;* these are all national dailies,
with the *Guardian* the most politically liberal, the *Telegraph* the
least; and the *Times* the best of the lot to acquaint oneself with
the ramifications of British eccentricity, as witness this, my all-
time favorite *Times* Personal: "IDENTICAL TWINS required to

travel as social secretary/P.A. to English lady with large family, large house and big headache. Requirements: one of the girls must be able to type, have organized mind and speak French; the other to receive guests, supervise staff and generally organise house. High salary, interesting life with much travel for the twins that fill these qualifications. Please write first with photo to . . ." Most of the remaining national dailies are sensational-type, that you can read through in about six minutes, always feeling, upon completion, that you haven't gotten your money's worth. The political weeklies are excellent, particularly the *New Statesman and Nation* and the *Economist.* The glossy magazines are beautiful to look upon (the British are typographers, typographic designers and printers of the first order). I have long been a sucker for the *Illustrated London News.* You have to be British to laugh at many of *Punch's* cartoons. But there are so many; they don't seem to go out of business the way their counterparts do in America. Check any newsstand; you'll find plenty to tempt. **Further information:** British Tourist Authority, 680 Fifth Avenue, New York; John Hancock Center, Chicago; 612 South Flower Street, Los Angeles; 1712 Commerce Street, Dallas; 151 Bloor Street, Toronto; 602 West Hastings Street, Vancouver; 64 St. James's Street, London, S.W. 1, England; London Tourist Board, 4 Grosvenor Gardens, London S.W. 1, England (with branches in Victoria Station, BOAC Air Terminal, and the Underground Concourse in Piccadilly Circus).

# *Luxembourg*

It has taken me a number of visits, stretched over a pair of decades, to appreciate Luxembourg for what it is—a town that evolved from a medieval fortress into a place of solid, middle-class charm that has miraculously preserved so much of its astonishing past that you marvel at its being the capital of a rich little country that makes most of its money from an anything but quaint steel industry.

**Medieval fortress to Common Market Co-capital:** You would never say that Luxembourg is unsophisticated. Our planet's only sovereign Grand Duchy, doubling in spades as co-capital of the ten-nation European Community/Common Market, can simply not be written off as Simple Simonsville. The word is unpretentious. It is satisfaction enough to Luxembourg that it had counts who doubled as Holy Roman Emperors and ruled realms as far afield as Hungary and the Bohemia that we now know as a region of Czechoslovakia. And so, barely beyond earshot of such neighboring fleshpots as Paris, Amsterdam, and Brussels, little Luxembourg City goes about its business, with a minimum of effervescence, perhaps, but knowing precisely what it is doing, in a setting where everyone knows everyone else and is never too busy to say "hello" and "How's the family?"

For something like nine of its more than ten centuries, Luxembourg has been a fortress of one formidable sort or other. Not many towns have so distinctive a background. The town began as a castle built at the site of the eminence known today as the Bock Rock, jutting out over the Alzette River atop the deep and dramatic cliffs that are still a hallmark of the town. The builder was Count Sigefroy, first of a dynasty of sovereigns bearing the title "Count," who were in later centuries to lead not only the Holy Roman Empire but a diverse assortment of kingdoms and duchies and counties in the most unlikely sectors of Europe. The medieval centuries saw Luxembourg as a community of some five thousand souls—peasants and tradesmen and merchants—all living within the fortifications, and gradually expanding, with newer walls built. The third wall's builder was one of the most famous of Luxembourg counts—John the Blind, who was later to become Holy Roman Emperor and King of Bohemia, and who is buried in the Luxembourg Cathedral.

**Four centuries of invaders:** By the middle of the fifteenth century the sovereigns had changed their titles. They were dukes instead of counts. But a rose by any name. . . . The dynasty expired and the neighbors were eager to move in. The King of Burgundy did just that in 1443. For four succeeding centuries, Luxembourg was considered fair game by one power or another. There were Spanish Hapsburgs interrupted for a spell by France's Louis XIV. And then there were Austrian Hapsburgs, French republicans, and the French under Napoleon. If they all had one thing in common, it was their efforts to make Luxembourg the superfortress of Europe. Over the centuries came appurtenances like bastions and redoubts and batteries and the fantastic network of underground passages known as the *Casemates,* which are still a Luxembourg landmark.

During those long Fortress Luxembourg centuries, civil needs gave way to military. The populace lived along crowded, narrow, fireprone, not particularly hygienic streets that were considered little more than afterthoughts. The various occupiers looked upon Luxembourg as a military prize, and its inhabitants as caretakers. But the Vienna Congress, in 1815, changed things in

Luxembourg as it did in so much of Europe. Luxembourg City became, once again, the capital of a country at least nominally independent, albeit under the aegis of the newborn Kingdom of the Netherlands. (To this day the Luxembourg flag is identical with that of the Netherlands: three horizontal stripes: red, white, and blue.) It found itself, as well, a member of the Germanic Confederation, which meant that it remained a fortress with a sizable complement of Prussian troops. Less than two decades later, neighboring Belgium, having won *its* independence from the Dutch kingdom, proceeded to annex to its realm a substantial chunk of the Grand Duchy of Luxembourg that remains known as the Belgian Province of Luxembourg; it had constituted the major portion of the Grand Duchy's territory, and was a complete loss; the land remaining is but thrice the size of the five boroughs of New York City. But foreign powers continued to make decisions for Luxembourg. In 1867 the French and the Prussians got together on neutral territory—in London —to resolve their differences, with a result being the Declaration of Luxembourg as a "perpetually neutral" grand duchy. This meant the dismemberment of Fortress Luxembourg. Off went the troops and down came the battlements.

**A grand duke to the throne:** A modern city began to be constructed, and not long thereafter, in 1890, with the accession of Wilhelmina to the Dutch throne, Luxembourg gained a Grand Duke-in-residence of its very own. World War I saw the neutral little country occupied by German forces for four long years. The Germans returned again in 1940, to invade and occupy the Grand Duchy. Grand Duchess Charlotte, her family, and the cabinet fled to London to set up a government in exile for the duration. Luxembourg was liberated by the Allies in 1944. A few years later, in 1949, the country abandoned its traditional neutrality to join the North Atlantic Treaty Organization. Additionally, it teamed up with Belgium and Holland to form the Benelux Economic Union, from which evolved the European Common Market. During the years of the Truman Administration, Luxembourg achieved a fame of sorts in the United States when President Truman appointed party-giver Perle Mesta as our ambassador to Luxembourg (the appointment served as inspiration for the Broadway musical *Call Me Madam,* with Ethel Merman starring as the ambassador). Some years later, in the Johnson period, Patricia Harris became our envoy—the first black American woman to become an ambassador.

In 1964—in the manner of Dutch Queen Wilhelmina, during whose reign Luxembourg gained its first Grand Duke—Grand Duchess Charlotte voluntarily abdicated after forty-five years on the throne. She was succeeded by her son, Jean, born in 1921, and married to the former Princess Josephine-Charlotte of Belgium. Grand Duke Jean and Grand Duchess Josephine-Charlotte have five children, the eldest of whom, Prince Henri, born in 1955, is heir-apparent.

Their Royal Highnesses are the constitutional monarchs of Luxembourg's some 350,000 subjects. The government is headed by a prime minister, who governs in conjunction with a bicameral Parliament. The upper house, the twenty-one-member Council of State, is appointed. Real power rests with the elected fifty-six-member Chamber of Deputies, with the Christian Socialists and Socialists the leading parties, and the Socialist-dominated trade unions of the steel workers a power to be reckoned with. But there is, apparently, another power to be reckoned with: women's lib, with a U.S. twist. Luxembourg City, which has known two lady ambassadors from the United States, got its first female mayor in 1970—a young woman named Colette Flesch, who is a graduate of America's Wellesley College.

### TO SEE

**Lay of the land:** Luxembourg can seem geographically complicated, if you let it. Start walking about, though, and you soon see how easy it is to find your way. Assuming that you are staying in the neighborhood of the Railway Station—the *Place de la Gare*—bear in mind that there are two principal thoroughfares for you to consider for walks to the heart of town. One is the *Avenue de la Gare*, which leads into the *Boulevard Franklin D. Roosevelt*, in the central area. And the other is the broad and handsome *Avenue de la Liberté*, which leads onto the *Pont Adolphe*, a bridge that leads over the *Perusse Valley*, becoming the *Boulevard Royal*, off which is the core of town. An even newer bridge—the sleek-lined *Pont Grande Duchesse Charlotte* —is appropriately contemporary and leads to the new Kirchberg Plateau sector, which is dominated by the European Community headquarters. What I've dealt with so far has all been elevated, upper-town territory. Below, lying along the river, in the valley, are sectors of the city that are actually suburbs, and lead to the rural areas of the grand duchy.

Specifics for singling out? The over-all view of town and valley and battlements and ancient monuments is Luxembourg at its most memorable. I would take it in by means of a walk on the *Corniche Promenade*. The venerable suburbs of *Clausen* (where Common Market founder Robert Schumann was born), Grund, and Pffaffenthal are below, and at walk's end is the Bock Rock, which has played such a key role in Luxembourg's history. From late spring through autumn—the high season months—the *Casemates* are open to visitors. These are the passages hewn out of rock, extending some fourteen miles in all. They once connected some three-score minor forts with the citadel proper. Within town I would have a look inside the Gothic-Renaissance *Cathedral of Notre Dame,* with the tomb of the most celebrated of the counts of Luxembourg, John the Blind. The capacious structure next door is the *National Library* (take a peek if you like). It was originally a Jesuit college, with the cathedral originally a Jesuit church. The mainly Renaissance *Grand Ducal Palace* (not open to the public) was, like the Royal Palace in Amsterdam, built as a town hall, and goes back to the late sixteenth century. A nearby onetime palace now serves as the *Chamber of Deputies* (the upper house of Parliament has its own building). And the *ministries* of the government are to be found in still other fine old mansions, the Ministry of Foreign Affairs and the Ministry of State most particularly. The *State Museum* (Musée de l'État) is not big, but it has some choice exhibits, and I would certainly have a look around, concentrating on the Roman sculpture—which is exceptional—and the paintings of Luxembourg artists, most especially Joseph Kutter, a Post-Impressionist who was known for his strong, vibrant-hued paintings of both people and places, and who died in 1941. There are a number of small *churches* and chapels that are eminently visitable, some of them deftly tucked into the walls and crevices of the old fortress-city. But even though they are all Roman Catholic (Luxembourg is an overwhelming Roman Catholic country), they are not always open, particularly some of the smaller ones. Try, though, to see *St. Michael's,* which, even though it dates mainly from a rebuilding in 1509, was, after all, consecrated in 987. The street with the principal shops—the nicest ones—is appropriately named the *Grand Rue,* and is just above the Cathedral area and not far from the busy *Place d'Armes,* which is the site of the *City Tourist Office* (also known as the *Syndicat d'Initiative*). More distant, though—across the earlier-mentioned Grand Duchesse Charlotte Bridge—is spanking new *Kirchberg.* The good-looking skyscraper that dominates it is the Luxembourg headquarters of the *European Common Market.* (The other offices of the Common Market are in Brussels.) It is in this building that the European Economic Community's Council of Ministers meets for some three months of each year; for some unfathomable reason visitors are not allowed on tours. Not far away is the futuristic façade of the strikingly designed *National Theater;* try to take in a performance, if only to see the interesting interior. For the rest: Walk. Walk all about the central city. Peek in and out of shops, cafes, churches, courtyards, what have you, remembering that the narrower and hillier the street, the more rewarding the prospects.

**Farther afield:** Luxembourg beyond the capital is so nice and compact—about sixty miles long and less than forty miles at its widest—that it's a joy to explore. This is a region embracing verdant, neat-as-a-pin farmland; vineyard-covered hillsides flanking the Moselle River, which delineates the German frontier; venerable villages that are delightfully inviting for refreshment/ sightseeing pauses; and almost everywhere, castles atop dramatic eminences. It may not be quite Graustarkia, but it comes as close as you can find in today's Europe. In as little as a day, one can undertake a surprisingly leisurely and diverse survey, and with a couple of days an overnight pause is a prospect hardly to be despised. An itinerary that I followed with considerable pleasure—starting and ending in the capital—was roughly circular in a clockwise direction. Highlights included the old churches of *Mersch; Colmar-Berg,* site of the viewable (but unvisitable) summer palace of Grand Duke Jean; *Ettelbruck,* with its monument to World War II's General Patton, and the surrounding *Ardennes Hills* (Patton and some five thousand American troops who fell in Luxembourg are buried at the *U.S. Military Cemetery at Hamm,* outside the capital); *Diekirch,* with a ninth-century church, bits of Roman mosaic, and extensive facilities; *Vianden,* with a fairytale castle in ruins on one craggy hill above it, and a not-to-be-missed funicular leading to still another; *Beaufort,* on a plateau in the relatively rugged Moellerdall Mountains area; *Echternach,* bustling (at least in Luxembourg terms) with visitors attracted to its *Benedictine Abbey,* aged houses, vast *St. Willibrod's Basilica* (largest in the Grand Duchy), and fifteenth-century town hall; *Remich,* heart of the Moselle vineyard country, with wine-tasting at the *Café Beau-Sejour;* and last—preferably for an overnight stay—*Mondorf-les-Bains,* Luxembourg's answer to Vichy, Baden-Baden, and Carlsbad, with its appropriately named

*Hôtel du Grand Chef,* one of Europe's relatively few Old School hotels in the grand—very grand—manner.

## TO STAY

Luxembourg hotels tend to be small in proportion to their environment. Which is quite as it should be. They have the nice, homey, bourgeois feeling that one comes across in the Benelux area, and in provincial French and German towns as well. More often then not, service is efficient, smiling, and personal. And nowhere, anywhere, is cleanliness closer to Godliness! Floors gleam, crystal sparkles, silver glistens, windows are immaculate, and so are linens and closets and dresser drawers. Indeed, it is in its relatively intimate hotels that one realizes one is in the small capital of a small country. I have stayed in Luxembourg City's top two hotels and like them both very much. The *Kons,* on the Place de la Gare, opposite the Railway Station, is elderly and charming, with capacious public rooms full of nice old furnishings and paintings, a first-rate restaurant, an also-excellent basement grill, a cozy bar, and attractively refurbished guest rooms with modern baths. If you feel that the noise of the Place de la Gare would be too much for you, ask for an inside room; the courtyard is agreeable. But the outside rooms, which I prefer, everywhere afford a panorama of the life of the square— Luxembourg, being Luxembourg, is not all that noisy. One more plus: The lady in charge of reception is a darling; she's been on the scene for years, and there is little likelihood of her not being there for many more to come. Perhaps a bit flossier than the Kons, but no more luxurious, is the *Cravat,* with an elaborate lobby off of which is an even more elaborate—you might even say fussy—bar-lounge; a popular-price cafe, much frequented by the locals; a more expensive up-one-flight main dining room; and very comfortable, nicely furnished rooms, with efficient baths.

These, then are the top two. But their space is limited, so that if you must make another selection, consider the *Central Molitor* —Luxembourg-spotless, thoroughly refurbished in antiseptic hospital-style décor (all rooms have baths, not to mention direct-dial phones, wall safes, and Rube Goldberg-type bedside push-buttons for all manner of things, including opening of the bedroom door!); it also has a reasonably priced restaurant-cafe. Bear in mind, also, the *Rix Hotel,* which is perhaps better known for its restaurant (see below) than for its rooms, these last being comfortable, clean, and with modern baths. The *Eldorado,* diagonally across the Place de la Gare from the Kons, is smallish, with a somewhat jarring modern façade that can put one off. Still, within, the welcome is warm, the rooms adequate, and the second-floor restaurant convenient, and noted particularly for the super-jumbo, multicourse breakfast that is included in the room rates. As for the *Holiday Inn* in the shadow of the European Community Headquarters at *Kirchberg:* the less said the better. If the Luxembourgers felt that they had to have an American-connected hotel in this prestigious area, one would have thought their approach would have been to a firm like Hilton International, Inter·Continental, or Sheraton. Instead, Holiday Inn is on the scene—lots of plastic, lots of neon in the ugly sign out in front, and so completely blind a copy of a graceless stateside prototype in almost every respect that the brochure—prepared for the Luxembourg inn—boasts in large type, locally printed, "Your Host from Coast to Coast," even though little Luxembourg is not the United States and is coastless. Luxembourg's oldtime leader, the *Alfa,* on the Place de la Gare, is a far cry from what it was when I first knew it; it has seen better days. Countryside? My recommendation is the earlier-mentioned *Hôtel du Grand Chef,* at the little thermal resort of Mondorf-les-Bains. The baths adjoin it, the Luxembourg-French frontier is in the backyard, the ambience is as delightfully rural-Old School as you could want, there's an inviting lounge for drinks, and the restaurant is surely one of the most superlative in this corner of Europe.

## TO EAT

One eats supremely well in Luxembourg. The cuisine is basically Franco-Belgian in derivation, with Germanic overtones. Happily, neighboring Holland—never particularly noted for its gastronomy —has not had as many culinary as political connections with the Luxembourgers. To look for: paper-thin smoked Ardennes ham; smoked pork and broad beans; local fresh-water fish, including pike, trout, and crawfish; game in season; delicious pastries; good bread. As for beverages, Luxembourg is one of those special countries where both the local beer and the local wine are good. This tiny country has no less than eight breweries, and they turn out good brews to an ever-thirsty populace at mighty attractive tabs. But Luxembourg's dry white Moselle wines are excellent, too—and reasonably priced, with government control through the device of the "Marque National" label on approved bottles. Also good are the local plum brandies—Quetsch and Mirabelle. It is no longer safe to say in any country, including France, that it is impossible to get a bad meal. But the chances of disappointment in Luxembourg are relatively few. The inner man is considered vital by the Luxembourgers. The restaurants of the recommended hotels, particularly the *Kons* and *Cravat,* are excellent, as are their lesser-priced cafes. The *Eldorado Hotel's* dining room is good, too. But of the independent restaurants, my vote goes to *Au Gourmet.* In the general neighborhood of the Cravat Hotel, in a seventeenth-century house, this restaurant is quietly handsome, impeccably operated, and with a classic French-style menu that is particularly strong on the local fresh-water fish (trout, especially) but numbers steak-au-poivre and coq au Riesling among its specialties too, not to mention game—hare, pheasant, partridge, quail, and wild duck—when in season. Very good, too, is the *Pavillon Royal,* in the Rix Hotel. As I mentioned earlier, the restaurant is perhaps more celebrated than the hotel. The food is basically French-classic, with innovative Luxembourg accents. Two further recommendations: One is for the ancient establishment known as *Namur,* on Grand Rue. The lures are chocolates—pralines, as they are called in French—that are the finest in the land, and pastries, to be taken with a cup of morning coffee or afternoon tea. The other is the *Cafe des Artistes*—where locals gather often for uninhibited sing-alongs, at the piano. And there is always the celebrated disco called *Blow-up.*

## TO BUY

Scrumptious, outrageously rich chocolates by the box at the aforementioned *Namur,* or at *Steichen,* its chief competitor, is a Luxembourg requisite. Of note, too, is the little-known, locally made Villeroy & Boch china and porcelain. The quality is excellent (the firm has been making the stuff since 1770); a number of the traditional design patterns—particularly the blue-on-white "Vieux Luxembourg"—are very good-looking, and prices are reasonable, with five-piece place settings going for as little as three dollars. A good retail outlet is *Maison Lassner,* 46 Place Guillaume. The *Duty-Free Airport Shop* makes a specialty of Luxembourg's Bernard Massard Champagne, its noted white Moselle wines, and its Morabelle and Kirsch *eau-de-vie.* Wines are strictly controlled for quality, by the government, by means of necklabels reading "Marque National." Don't buy any without this legend.

## TO NOTE

**Access:** History has shown that Luxembourg has at times, over the centuries, been almost too conveniently located for its own good. Too small to support a transatlantic service of its own national airline, Luxembourg is fortunate in that Loftleider Icelandic Airlines has for some years utilized its international airport as its principal continental European terminus, connecting the Grand Duchy with New York's Kennedy Airport by means of bargain-rate jet flights with intermediate, layover-allowed stops in Iceland. The also cheap-fare jets of International Air Bahama fly the Atlantic between Nassau and Luxembourg. The national carrier. Luxair, is possibly the least-known of any in Western Europe; I have found it to be first-rate—efficient and reliable, with agreeable service aloft, and tasty meals as well. Luxair has a fairly extensive European route, with particularly convenient service to London, Paris, and Frankfurt. Several other European airlines serve Luxembourg, too. Rail service is excellent—trains go in and out of Luxembourg from all directions, and include the Trans-Europe Express. Motorists will find well-maintained roads. Self-drive cars from the leading international firms, and local ones, too, are available in Luxembourg City, from which emanate bus tours of both town and countryside. The central portions of Luxembourg City are pleasantly walkable, but there is public transport, of course, and a taxi fleet. **Climate:** The weather is the same kind of expect-anything situation that prevails elsewhere in the Benelux region, or to the north, for that matter. Summers are supposed to average in the sixties, but I am here to tell you that there can be hot spells, and that there is virtually no air conditioning. By the same token, winters are generally mild— in the thirties—but they can be colder, and very raw indeed. There does not appear to be as much rain as in Belgium and Holland, which front the North Sea, but don't expect anything like the Nevada desert. **Clothes:** The youngsters dress about as modishly as kids do everywhere, but their elders are on the conservative side—not that they any longer shock easily, what with two constant streams of Common Market and touristic visitors. **Currency:** Thanks to its economic union with Belgium, the Luxembourg franc is at par with the Belgian franc. Remember that while you may use Belgian francs in Luxembourg, you may *not* use Luxembourg francs in Belgium, although you may, of course, exchange Luxembourg for Belgian francs at a Belgian bank. **Tipping:** Luxembourgers are among the least tip-happy of Western Europeans. Restaurants and cafes add the service charge to the bill (between 10 and 15 percent), and there's absolutely no need to tip additionally. Tip taxi drivers 10 to 15 percent, and tip airport porters and bellhops about 10 francs per bag. **Shopping hours:** Generally, they are 8:30 A.M. to noon, and 2:00 P.M. to 5:00 P.M., except on Monday, when the shops do not open until 2:00 P.M. **Language:** Well, it's like this: The *official* language is French, but virtually everyone also speaks German, and a great deal of English, as well. However, a Luxembourger tells another Luxembourger by his Luxembourgeois, or, as it is more often called, Letzeburgesch—the spoken language which, as much as any other manifestation of the national culture, serves as a binding, uniting force. **Local literature:** Ask at your hotel for a giveaway called, variously, *La Semaine à Luxembourg, Diese Woche in Luxembourg,* and *Luxembourg Weekly.* **Further information:** Tourism Section, Consulate General of Luxembourg, 200 East 42nd Street, New York, New York 10017; Office National du Tourisme, P. O. Box 1001, Luxembourg City, Luxembourg; Luxembourg City Tourist Information Office, Place d'Armes, Luxembourg City, Luxembourg.

# Madrid

Madrid, though it may not like to think of itself in this way, is quite the upstart among the Latin capitals of Europe. Rome conquered the ancient world. Lisbon traded with the Phoenicians but became Portugal's proper capital in the early twelfth century. Paris had a patron saint of its own as early as the fifth century, but had been a town since after Caesar's conquest. Madrid—smack in the barren interior, without so much as a proper river running alongside it—was little more than a fortress until the fourteenth century.

**A relatively late start:** At that time, in 1329, the *cortes,* or parliament, of Castile honored it by meeting there. And a century later, Ferdinand and Isabella took up occasional residence; Emperor Charles V did likewise. But it was not until the middle of the sixteenth century—in 1561—that Charles V's son, cool and cruel Philip II, made Madrid the capital, although it was not until Philip's son became king that it began to be built up as such. There are, today, bits and pieces remaining of medieval Madrid. Philip II's gloomy Escorial is exurban, but the Plaza Mayor—constructed during Philip III's Golden Age reign—is surely the major Renaissance monument. Still, one must go elsewhere in Spain—Cordoba, Granada, Seville, Toledo, Burgos, Leon—to view its great architecture. So indeed must one look elsewhere for the beginnings of the nation that became great only after it united to fight a brilliant Afro-Arab enemy—the Moors.

The earliest Spaniards didn't have Spain to themselves for long. The Romans took them over two centuries before Christ, and Christianized them in the succeeding centuries. The Germanic Visigoths followed, remaining as overlords for some time. But in the eighth century the Spaniards were to know a new conqueror. The Moors came from across the Mediterranean in North Africa. They might well have taken all of Europe had not the Franks contained them in 732. Still, they held onto their Spanish territory despite internal squabbling—enough to weaken them to the point where northern Spaniards could realistically consider ousting them.

**The Moorish and Jewish contributions:** It took time—several centuries, during which the Moors implanted their rich Moslem culture, as did the highly skilled and gifted Jews—both of which groups lived amicably alongside the Christians. Eventually, the two major Spanish kingdoms, those of Castile and Aragon, were united in the fifteenth century, when Ferdinand II and Isabella married. Then came 1492. Isabella sent the Genoan, Christopher Columbus, off to find a new route to India, and Spain had the good luck to be the discovering power of a new world. At the same time, Ferdinand and Isabella's troops captured Granada, the last remaining Moor stronghold. In their zeal to create a unified pan-Spanish kingdom, Ferdinand and Isabella expelled the Jewish community—which took its skills and capital to the Netherlands and other countries, to the detriment of Spain, where it had been of substantial cultural and commercial importance. Later, the Moors—who had been forced to convert to Christianity—were also expelled and constituted another loss of significant importance. Still, Spain had its new world—almost all of South America (Brazil went to Portugal), Central America, the southern part of North America (including Mexico), and the Philippines as well, became Spanish territory in the sixteenth century. Spain was the New World's first power. Charles V concentrated on unification of the country. His son, Philip II, went a step farther. Although he did not begin the Inquisition, he was fanatic enough to have made it an ugly force, not only in Spain but in the Spanish Netherlands, where his policies were so oppressive that the northern area—now Holland—successfully revolted. Dutch losses were as nothing compared with what followed. After his wife—England's stubborn and unhappy Catholic "Bloody Mary" —died four years after they were married in England, he proposed to Elizabeth I, and was promptly, albeit politely, turned down. In 1588 he sailed his "invincible" armada to defeat the fleet of the queen who had spurned his hand—and was defeated. The loss of the armada signaled the start of a bad-luck period for the great Spanish Empire.

**Cervantes, El Greco, and De Vega:** Madrid, rather paradoxically blossomed culturally under Philip III: Cervantes created his immortal *Don Quixote,* Lope de Vega wrote his plays, El Greco and Zurburan painted; and the distinctive Spanish Renaissance design-style evolved in architecture and decoration, crossing the Atlantic to the colonies of the Americas, to have lasting effect. The succeeding reign saw Philip IV serve as patron of such luminaries as the painters Rubens and Velasquez. (Indeed, because of the attendance of Velasquez in his court, few rulers in history are more painted than Philip IV.) The Bourbons were the first to live in Madrid's mammoth French-style Royal Palace; they ushered in a French-influenced era—of decadence, bigotry, and corruption in high places, and an impoverished peasantry; attempts at reform were futile. In 1808 Napoleon humiliated Spain by occupying it and installing his brother, Joseph Bonaparte, on the throne. With the help of Wellington's British forces, the French were ousted a decade later, but another decade saw virtually all of the South American colonies independent. The Spanish-American War at the end of the last century ended with the loss of the Philippines, Cuba, and Puerto Rico.

**An empire lost, a new republic, civil war:** The twentieth century brought few improvements—strikes and demonstrations forcefully repressed, Primo de Rivera's military dictatorship, and finally, in 1931, the departure of the last reigning king—Alfonso XIII —and the advent of a republic whose first president, Alcala Zamora, resigned in protest against the extreme anticlerical legislation enacted by the Cortes. In 1936, the Popular Front— composed of liberal republicans working with Socialists and Communists—won the national elections, so overwhelmingly that reactionary forces led by General Francisco Franco precipitated a rebellion that plunged the country into a bloody three-year civil war that took more than a million lives and set the stage for World War II.

Franco's Insurgents received substantial help from Nazi Germany (whose bombing of the defenseless village of Guernica is immortalized in the monumental Picasso painting at New York's Museum of Modern Art) and Fascist Italy, whereas the Loyalist republicans—led by Catalonian nationalists in Barcelona and by the Basques—had little outside help except that of an International Brigade (in which some six hundred Americans served) and token support from the Soviet Union. The Loyalists made a remarkable stand. They managed to hold Madrid until the end of the war—a feat, considering their inferior numbers and their internal differences.

Its own war over, Spain remained neutral in World War II, although its partiality toward the Axis powers resulted in the United Nations initially turning it down for membership in 1948, finally admitting it almost a decade later.

**The Franco dictatorship:** The post-World War II years have seen the government—dictatorial though it remains—make commendable efforts to bind up the wounds of a bitterly divided land, at the same time very gradually lessening oppressive controls, to the point where the press is a bit less restricted; and conversational criticism of the government is tolerated, even if public opposition is not. The country remains a monarchy. Generalissimo Franco and his Cortes made a point of bypassing the Pretender to the throne—Don Juan, son of Alfonso XIII—

even though he wanted the job, in favor of his son Prince Don Juan Carlos (whose wife is the former Princess Sophie, sister of exiled King Constantine of Greece). Prince Don Juan Carlos is slated to be Franco's successor as head of state and reigning King of Spain, as well. His reign will, hopefully, see Spain happier, more prosperous, and more socially and politically progressive. But this evolution, if it is to be peaceful, will no doubt continue slowly. The Roman Catholic Church remains the state church and most of its hierarchy—if not all of its clergy—remains conservative; a new liberal wing is the exception. Even in the area of religion, though, there has been change; the major cities, five centuries after the Inquisition—at last have legally operating Protestant churches and Jewish synagogues (Madrid has ten of the former, two of the latter). The United States Government, so often partial to dictators the world over, courts Spain's leaders by means of presidential and vice presidential visits, and regular renewals of the generous U.S.-Spanish defense agreements. Spain's young people are its hope; they continue to make known their desire for a voice in government policies. But it is all of Spain's people—gentle, hospitable, attractive, proud—who impel even the most antifascist of visitors to return again and again.

TO SEE

**Lay of the land:** Madrid's beauty lies in its style. It is expert at elegance. What it lacks in individual monuments of architectural greatness, it compensates for with the sweep of its boulevards, the dramatic fountains and heroic sculpture of its circles, the splendid proportions of its plazas, the emerald lawns and rainbow hues of flowers in the parks and gardens, the smartness of the shops and cafes and, surely, the most important, the modish Madrileños who populate them. Say what one will about Spain's kings, there is no gainsaying the care and skill and attention they lavished on their capital. Post-Civil War Madrid—the city was severely damaged during the Insurgents' siege—manifests the same good Spanish architectural sense of earlier eras. There is a solid, important, built-to-last quality about contemporary office towers and apartment houses that is in refreshing contrast to their counterparts in virtually every city of the world, from Philadelphia to Paris.

Think of Madrid's two superimportant thoroughfares as forming a cross. The vertical artery is the multinamed *Paseo.* Working northward, it begins as the *Paseo del Prado,* later becomes the *Paseo de Calvo Sotelo,* and concludes as the *Paseo de la Castellana.* The horizontal artery—crossing it west to east—begins as the *Calle Mayor,* but for the great bulk of its length it is the *Calle de Alcalá.*

The point where the Paseo and the Alcalá intersect is the *Plaza de las Cibeles,* a circle identified by a statue of the goddess Cibeles in a chariot powered by a lion, the lot fountain-surrounded. Cibeles is an important crossroads because Madrid's principal shopping street leads from it: This is *Avenida Jose Antonio,* but it has another equally popular name—*Gran Via.* Note that its terminus is the skyscraper-filled *Plaza de España.* Return, though, to the Alcalá, take it east a bit to another circular plaza, *Independencía,* and turn north. The street you enter—*Calle Serrano* —is also important, for its shops are the smartest in town. Return to Cibeles and walk south on the Paseo del Prado; in a few blocks you reach *Plaza de Canovas del Castillo,* around which are not only the Palace and Ritz hotels—landmarks both, these—but, more important, the Prado Museum. The Botanical Gardens are due south, and the *Parque del Retiro*—one of the most beautiful in Europe and worthy of as leisurely an inspection as you can give it—is to the east. Return again to Cibeles, and go west on the Alcalá. The first major square you reach is the ebullient *Puerto del Sol.* This is where Spain quite literally begins, for all principal highways going into northern, southern, eastern, and western Spain emerge from the "Kilometer O" point in the center of the square. Continue west on the Alcalá—it now becomes the

*Calle Mayor*—and take your time, for you are approaching Philip III's early-seventeenth-century Plaza Mayor, entered through a series of archways and, within, a coordinated grouping of superb Renaissance structures, the most noted being the *Casa de la Panadería*. Continue west on the Calle Mayor—the extension of the Alcalá—and you reach the southern extremity of the massive Royal Palace, known also as the Palacio de Oriente, after the *Plaza de Oriente,* fronting it.

**Choice destinations:** The *Prado Museum* is at once the choicest destination in Madrid and one of the handful of the planet's great art galleries. Repeat visitors to Madrid, myself among them, head for it automatically, first thing, as soon as they are checked into their hotel. It is a dignified neoclassic building named for the street it faces (officially it is the Museo Nacional de Pintura), and it goes back to the late-eighteenth-century reign of Charles IV, when the idea of it—as a natural science museum—was first hatched. Ferdinand VII changed the contents from science to art, and it opened in 1819, as the Museo Real, with a nucleus of three hundred paintings from the royal collection. That number has been increased more than tenfold. But it is quality as well as quantity that makes the Prado great. Still, the numbers of Spanish masters are hardly to be discounted. There are half a dozen galleries of Velazquez (whose work Spaniards are fonder of than those of any other painter), three galleries of El Greco, and no less than nine rooms full of Goyas. It is, of course, the Spanish school that is best represented. Besides the Big Three—Velazquez, El Greco, and Goya—there are Murillo, Zurbaran, Morales, Gallego, Juan de Juanes, Coello and Cano. The Italians appear in profusion too—Titian and Tintoretto most especially, but Veronese, Botticelli, Fra Angelico, Lotto, Tiepolo, Giorgione, and Raphael as well. Dating from the time when the Spanish Hapsburgs ruled the Netherlands are such Flemish and Dutch masters as Rembrandt, Van Dyck, Rubens, Jordans, and Teiniers, not to mention Germans—including Durer and Memling. You will see your favorites—Moro's painting of Bloody Mary, Philip II's second wife; Velazquez' Philip IV of the waxed mustachios; the wide-skirted *infantas* of the same Velazquez; El Greco's solitary Savior and his somber Saints Andrew and Francis; Murillo's beautiful Holy Family, Goya's *majas,* clothed and otherwise, as well as his beautiful royals and nobles, and the contrast of the ferocious satire of his later years—a period some experts now believe was caused by an illness induced by a form of lead poisoning that could have resulted from the excessive quantities of white paint he used.

The *Royal Palace* is a quantity-over-quality proposition. It is as though the eighteenth-century Bourbon kings wanted to say to their French cousins, and to anyone else who would listen, that Madrid could play the palace game, too. And did it ever. It is surely questionable whether even the palace's long-term inhabitants ever saw all of it. Charles III was the first regal tenant, in 1764, and Alfonso XIII—who fled in 1931—the last. (Generalissimo Franco still uses the palace to receive diplomats.) The heavy, graceless exterior is matched within by one overdecorated chamber after another. There are individual touches—brocades, chandeliers, pieces of furniture, carpets, tapestries, paintings (some Goyas among them), paneling—throughout that are of fine quality. But, put together, the effect, more often than not, is jarring. It should be apparent that this *casa* is not *su casa,* at least unescorted. Guided tours leave every quarter hour or so, and take at least an hour (there are full-length and abbreviated tours; the latter are quite sufficient). The most spectacular rooms include the Gasparini Salon and its anteroom; the chapel; Queen Maria Christina's and Queen Marie Louise's digs; the state dining room; and the throne room. There are museums of *royal coaches* and *royal armor* in connection.

*Remnants of old Madrid*—medieval and baroque, that is— are relatively rare, and for that reason worth searching out. No Catholic capital, save Dublin, appears to have fewer distinguished churches than Madrid. But there are some. *San Nicolás de los Servitas,* near the Plaza de la Villa, is reputedly the oldest, a medieval structure with Moorish—or *Mudejar,* as the Spaniards say—influences. *San Pedro el Real* is about as venerable, and near the *Moreria,* the old Moorish quarter in the vicinity of the Plaza de Marques de Comillas. There are several baroque churches—*San Placido* and *San Martín,* both by the same architect, and *Las Trinitárias,* somewhat newer. *San Francisco el Grande* (1761) is *grande* only because of the enormity of its dome and rotunda—it is quite ugly. *Ermita de San Antonio de la Florida,* in and of itself, is not a great deal more attractive than San Francisco el Grande. The lure is a series of frescoes by Goya, which he painted on the ceiling of the dome in 1798, on King Charles IV's order. The subjects are typical *Madrileños*—laughing workmen, lovely ladies, frisky youngsters, ordinary workmen. The *Capillo del Obispo,* or bishop's chapel, in the Plaza de Marques de Comillas is a Renaissance gem with a reredos that is one of the best-kept secrets in town. The *Ministry of Foreign Affairs* is a handsome old palace on the Plaza de Santa Cruz that you might try to peep into, even lacking diplomatic credentials. The *Teatro Real,* Plaza de Oriente, has the finest interior of any theater in the city. It opened in the middle of the last century and long served the capital as its opera house. There is no longer, alas, a national opera or ballet company, but there are concerts in the theater in the winter.

Leaving aside the Prado, Madrid's *museums* are strangely empty of visitors, even in the height of the season. They are Madrid's secret touristic weapon. They are super—worth prolonging one's stay two or three extra days, to take in. I cannot, to begin, imagine any American—North, South, or Central—not being fascinated with the *Museo de America.* It occupies a big building of its own in the style it contributed to Spanish Colonial America at Ciudad Universitaria, the sprawling modern campus of the University of Madrid. The collections embrace all of the indigenous cultures of Spanish America as they related to the culture of Spain, with which they were combined with the arrival of the conquistadors and the missionaries. One sees maps, paintings, tiles, tapestries, religious objects—all manner of Spanish Americana—the lot giving us an idea on home ground of the tremendous cultural debt we in America owe to this former mother country. The *Museo Romantico,* along perhaps with the earlier-mentioned Teatro Real, embodies the Madrid of the romantic nineteenth century. It is at once the most imaginatively conceived and the most charmingly executed of the capital's museums. (By charming I mean a grinning museum guard who operates an 1850 children's music box for you, upon your approaching it.) The setting is the Madrid town house of the late Marques de la Vega-Inclan, and its contents. The rooms of the house are museum enough: a chandelier-lit, instrument-filled ballroom; a dining room with a decorated ceiling and Spain's equivalent of English Regency dining chairs, to give you an idea. There are, as well, paintings of aristocratic Madrileños and their families and the kind of memorabilia of the era that is not easily come by. The lot is sheer delight. The *Museo Cerralbo* is still another nobleman's house, that of the seventeenth Marques de Cerralbo. It is late-nineteenth-century, and far grander, to be sure, than the smaller and older house that is now the Museo Romantico. The rooms themselves are more palatial than residential: a grand foyer and staircase, a Beaux Arts ballroom that will knock your eye out and, if you please, the marques' personal *armory.* The collections run to furniture, porcelain, antique clocks, and jewelry. Then come the paintings: Spaniards like Ribera, Pacheco, Zurbaran, and El Greco, and such foreigners as Titian, David, Veronese, Van Dyck, and Poussin. The *Museo Lazaro Galdiano* houses the remarkably comprehensive collection—embracing the arts (and not only painting) of all Europe—of a wealthy and discerning private collector. There are treasures of medieval Spain such as cannot be seen elsewhere in Madrid, as well as paintings by Velazquez, Murillo, El Greco, and Goya, among others. There are Byzantine enamels, da Vinci portraits, a Virgin by David, and a Granada cloth-of-gold mantle. No small museum in Europe is of higher caliber. The *Monasterio de las Descalzas Reales* is a convent that was founded by a daughter of Emperor Charles V, Princess Juana of Austria, after her husband died. The building had earlier served as a royal residence—indeed, Princess Juana had been born in it. But even after it became a religious house, it sheltered royal ladies other than its founder, thus the name of the order: *Descalzas Reales,* or Royal Unshods. The décor is appropriately regal. Paintings include works by such masters as Brueghel and Titian, not to mention numerous Spaniards. The grand foyer and staircase are positively Renaissance Palatial, with a memorably decorated ceiling. The chapel is a beauty. There are collections of religious vestments and religious relics. The *Monasterio de la Encarnación* is still another ancient convent that is partially open to the public; it, too, had a royal founder—Margaret of Austria, wife of Philip III. Though with nothing like the splendor of the Descalzas Reales, there are paintings, vestments, a fine choir in the chapel, and an exceptional reliquary. In the *Museo Nacional de Artes Decorativas* the genius of Spanish applied art—particularly in the Renaissance and baroque periods—comes to life in a series of period rooms. Every facet of the decorative arts is represented, particularly those at which Spain excelled—including leather, wrought iron, and ceramics, which it inherited from the Moors, as well as more European specialties like tapestries and glass. A bonus is the collection of mostly baroque Christmas creches. The *Museo Español de Arte Contemporaneo* sets out to show viewers that modern Spanish painting has not all been done by expatriates like Picasso, Dali, and Miro (the first two of whom are represented in the museum). There are works by a number of other contemporary Spanish painters, most of whose names we don't know, but much of whose work is worthy.

*El Escorial,* Philip II's monastery-palace outside of Madrid, is perhaps more essential to see than the city's own, not particularly Spanish, Royal Palace, for an understanding of Spain, its history, its culture, and the mysticism that is frequently bound up in its piety. Philip II built only partially beautiful El Escorial as a monument of thanksgiving to God for a victory over the French.

It is a masterwork of symmetry. You enter through the central
Court of the Kings, with the monastery's church dead ahead, the
palace to the left, and the monastery to the right. You may find
yourself not always able to enjoy Philip's somber aesthetics. The
greatest single attribute of El Escorial is its enormous façade, seen
from far enough away to afford perspective. Within, one can
pick and choose. There is, for example, a superb portrait of
Philip by Titian (in the basic-black with white ruff that was, in
effect, his uniform), a moving *Christ* by Cellini, a brilliantly decorated library, the unusual *St. Maurice* by El Greco in the Chapter House, and the well-furnished interiors of the living quarters of
the palace.

## TO WATCH

To watch, in Madrid, as in all Spain, means two things: flamenco
and bullfights. *Flamenco* is Spain's emotional safety valve—the
bittersweet dances, song, and guitar music that at their best are a
major art form. Flamenco—of Andalusian, not gypsy, origin—
is for an intimate cafe, not a big theater's stage. The performance
is rarely good if close rapport has not been established between
the performers and the audience. A typical company—each of
whose members is traditionally garbed—the wasp-waisted men in
black, the women in flounced, polka-dotted gowns—includes the
ever-so-important guitarist, one or two male dancer-singers, several female dancer-singers, and an older woman who not only
sings and dances but is as well the good-natured den mother of
the group. In larger companies, there are separate *bailladores*
(dancers) *cantadores* (singers), and *jaleadores* (clappers of the
rhythm) as well. There are smart and unsmart places that are
good for flamenco in Madrid, and there are unconscionable tourist
traps, with the food as tacky as the dancers are shabby. Here are
three places that I like very much. The poshest of the lot is *Cafe
de Chinitas* (Torija 7), which is at once a first-rate restaurant in

stylized baroque setting, and a forum for flamenco, with a company of considerable talent. Go for dinner at 10:00 or 10:30 P.M. and stay for the show. *La Zambra* (Ruiz de Alarcon 7), less elaborate, is recommended for late evening—after eleven—for the show only. It has a loyal following of Madrileños. *Los Canasteros* (Barbieri 10) is another late-evening, show-only place that retains a high level of flamenco. Note that at the late-show flamenco places you pay only for what you drink—but don't worry, the tabs are high enough, for the cover is included in the price of the first drink. *Bullfights* are generally a Sunday afternoon (and sometimes Thursday) diversion from late spring through early fall, at the *Plaza Monumental de las Ventas,* the major ring, or the smaller *Vista Alegre.* The *corrida* is a Spanish national pastime that every red-blooded Hemingway-read American is familiar with. The fights are preceded by a musically accompanied parade of the resplendently attired *matadores* (bullfighters, who do the actual killing), usually three in number, and a like number of *picadores*—the mounted-on-horseback bullfighters with spears, with which they stab or "pick" the bulls, to weaken them for the *matadores,* who first attack them with darts and then —with the aid of the scarlet cape, or *muleta*—make the kill. The earlier-mentioned *Teatro Real* (Plaza de Oriente) is the one-time Madrid opera house dating to the mid-nineteenth century. It is quite the most glittering theater in town, and if you have a chance, during the fall through early spring season, take in a performance of the *Orchestra Nacional.* There is no longer any national opera or ballet company, but the *Teatro de la Zarzuela* frequently presents performances of troupes from Barcelona and other cities. There is legitimate theater; performances are, of course, in Spanish. Ask your hotel concierge for current attractions.

TO STAY

Spain's tremendous influx of tourists in recent years—they come from all over Europe, and all of Latin America, as well as the United States—has resulted in an extensive plant, constantly expanding, as well as training facilities to insure a professional standard of service. To this must be added the Spanish penchant for hospitality; Spaniards, though with nothing like the effusiveness of their fellow Latins in Italy, are instinctively adept at welcoming strangers and putting them at their ease. And they are good housekeepers, too. Madrid is one of the neatest and cleanest of capitals. In the *lujo,* top-luxury category, the flawlessly operated *Palace* is a standout. The staff are real pros, many of them old-timers. The traditional-style public rooms—lobby, lounges, restaurant, bar, and the grill in particular—are agreeably animated. The nearby and very grand *Ritz,* under the same expert management, is smaller, more elegant, more sedate, quieter. The bar and restaurant are exceptional, as is the garden restaurant in summer. The lounge is an agreeable setting for afternoon tea. The bedrooms and suites are probably the most beautiful in Spain. The *Fenix,* a part of the Spanish Husa chain, has a becoming understated smartness, a good Paseo de la Castellana location, spacious guest rooms, and all facilities, including a bar and a restaurant that goes alfresco in warm weather. The *Meliá Madrid* (Princesa 27) is zippy Spanish Modern, a sleek skyscraper with skilled Meliá chain service and handsome public rooms—including a variety of wine-dine areas. The *Luz Palacio* is towering and contemporary but with traditional-style décor in its tasteful public rooms and bedrooms. It's well managed, too—part of the Interhotel group, which has good properties throughout Spain. The *Castellana Hilton*—Hilton International's first hotel in Europe—is smartly located, capacious, comfortable, and as popular with locals as visitors. In the first-class category, the *Gran Via*—on the Gran Via (Avenida Jose Antonio) has a perky lobby and convenient cafeteria as well as restaurant and bar, and pleasant rooms. The *Menfis,* also on the Gran Via, has been a leader for some years; the bar is congenial, and the restaurant is good. Its next-door neighbor, the *Washington,* is under the same management, and of the same first-class category, with a similarly attractive ambience. The *Caltrava* is an inviting newcomer at Calle Tutor 1.

## TO EAT (AND DRINK)

Spaniards, when it comes to the matter of Americans identifying their food with that of Mexico, have the patience of saints. Mexicans, because of their country's historic association with Spain, eat some Spanish dishes. But Mexican food is essentially derivative of the cuisine of the Mexican Indians. Spain has no Indians. Spanish food is Spanish.

At its best, it is at once subtle and uncomplicated. Spanish cooks, for whom mechanical refrigeration is a mostly urban, relatively recent convenience, rely on fresh ingredients. They do not season heavily. Sauces, not common, are simple. Broiled or grilled meat—lamb, mutton, veal, kid, and some beef—are popular. Cod—*bacalao*—is perhaps the major fish, but there are others, and seafood—clams, squid, crab, mussels, lobster—play important roles in the Spanish cuisine. Vegetables are often more interesting in the form of salads than as cooked dishes, although artichokes and eggplants are well prepared. Poultry is common. Wild game—partridge in particular, but quail and rabbit, too—is more eaten in Spain than in any other country I know. The soups of the provinces can be excellent; *gazpacho,* an uncooked blend of tomatoes, oil, peppers, onions, and seasonings, served chilled, is a summer treat. *Tapas,* the appetizers served with drinks or as the first course at lunch or dinner, constitute Spanish food at its most imaginative and delicious. There are always

Spain's own delicious olives and almonds, of course, but there are tidbits like fried mussels or clams; the tiny fritters known as *bunuelitos; empanadas*—turnovers with various fillings which, when small, are called *empanadillas*. The classic Spanish dessert is the simple caramel custard known as *flan* and not unlike France's *crème caramel*. Fresh fruit—figs very often, nuts, and cheese are a common dessert, along with small black cups of coffee. Spain's most celebrated dish is named for the two-handled metal pan it is cooked in: *paella,* with its saffron-flavored and -colored rice base covered with a mix of chicken, red peppers, shellfish, and sometimes other fish too, as well as green peas for color, and seasonings including garlic and onion. I can always do without the green peas and the fish, but these ingredients are usually the bases of a Paella Valenciana, or what has come to pass for that. No two chefs make a paella the same way; you will sample it in various places and come to your own conclusions about the combination that most pleases you. Spaniards are not big butter eaters, and they cook more with their own excellent olive oil than with anything else. Their bread and rolls often look like those of France and Italy but are not as good.

Spain is wine country; it is the third-largest wine-producing land in the world and there are vineyards in virtually every area. *Rioja* is the best-known wine region; there are both reds (*vino tinto*) and whites (*vino blanco*) from that area, and both can be very good. The wines of Catalonia—the region of which Barcelona is the chief city—are also commendable. Restaurants often serve house or regional wine by the carafe; it is generally adequate, but bottled wine is so inexpensive that it pays to live a little dangerously. And remember—at least for luncheon on hot summer days—the chilled wine punch that is called *sangría*. Spanish *brandy* is the best in the world, after the cognacs of France. Lepanto, made by the firm of Gonzales Byass, and Carlos I ("Carlos Primero"), made by the firm of Pedro Domecq, are probably the finest brands, both superior enough to be taken home as gifts. I have left sherry—*Jerez* in Spanish, *Xérès* in

French—until last. It comes from the area around Jerez de la Frontera, in the southwestern part of the country. As with Portugal's port wine, it is much more popular with the British (who frequently give sherry parties as a substitute for more expensive hard-liquor cocktail parties) than with us. Sherry is the apéritif par excellence. Spaniards, when they want to order a dry one, simply ask for a *fino; amontillado* (the very same Poe wrote about) is not quite as dry, but is also very satisfying as a premeal drink.

Meals are late in Spain. There is no question but that the pattern takes getting used to—but not more than a day or two. Lunch at two is normal, with dinner seldom earlier than ten, but as late as eleven. Fasting is not expected between these two meals; a snack—*merienda*—is usually taken at six or seven, unless one is going to have drinks with accompanying *tapas;* eight or eight-thirty is the time when the cocktail hour commences.

Service in restaurants tends to be very good; Spain is one of the remaining European countries that does not import foreigners to work in its restaurants and cafes. (It *exports* a lot of its people to do just this, as one finds, for example, in London.) Spaniards staff Spanish restaurants, and more often than not they know what courtesy, promptness, and efficiency are all about.

For a top-rank lunch or dinner, my honors go to *La Peurta de Moros* (Don Pedro 10), a seventeenth-century ducal palace that has been skillfully converted into one of Europe's most sumptuous restaurants. Choose the former library, with its crystal chandelier and the gilded plasterwork of its ceiling, or any of half a dozen showplace rooms. More important is the food. It does not take second place to the setting: the fish soup, Catalan style; the chef's pollo Puerta de Moros, the typically Spanish partridge and pheasant. Much less expensive, and even more typically Spanish, is *Sobrino de Botin* (Cuchilleros 17). Around since 1725, it can safely be called a Madrid institution. It occupies two floors, furnished as they have been for centuries, in a venerable house near the Plaza Mayor. Everything is Spanish and everything is delicious: the soups, the meats (including roast suckling pig and

roast baby lamb), the game birds (partridge stew in particular).
The service is famous, the prices so reasonable that they make
Botin Madrid's best restaurant buy. The pottery soup bowls and
wine jugs are for sale. *Xeito,* on the Castellana near the Castellana Hilton Hotel, is an attractive Galician restaurant. The specialty is seafood, as the Galicians prepare it, imaginatively and
deliciously. The *Ritz Hotel Garden* is a special Madrid treat during the warm-weather months. No restaurant in Spain offers more
classic service, a more classic Spanish-French menu, nor a more
fabulous wine list. Go for either lunch or dinner; if it's cold or
rainy, you can do worse than the *Ritz Restaurant;* same menu
and staff, but a roof over your head—and a very fancy roof, at
that. Quite as good—indeed, it is one of the very best restaurants
in town—is the *Palace Hotel Grill;* the Spanish specialties are
delicious, and the longtime waiters—pros all of them—know just
what to recommend. The *Garden Restaurant* of the *Fenix Hotel*
is a summer charmer. *El Bodegon,* on the Castellana, near the
Castellana Hilton, is modish and a source of first-rate Spanish and
continental dishes, with the former the more interesting. *Hogar
Gallego,* near the Plaza Mayor, is a well-known seafood restaurant; everything is fresh and tasty, and the service is delightful.
*El Pulpito,* Plaza Mayor 9, is fun because it is directly on the
Plaza Mayor; atmospherically old-style, and moderate-priced.
*Julian Rojo* (Ventura de la Vega 5) is a nice, old-fashioned
place—quite inexpensive, and with typical Madrid dishes. *Guria*
(Huertas 12) is excellent for Basque specialties. I have already
recommended *Cafe de Chinitas* in the To Watch section. *Gijón*
is a mellow Castellana establishment founded before the turn
of the century, and still a favored cafe-restaurant, populated by
discerning Madrileños. There are attractive, inexpensive *cafeterias*
—more cafe-restaurants than cafeterias in the American sense—
all about town. Good ones to know about are those in the *Galerias
Preciados* and *El Corte Ingles* department stores. In warm weather,
the *outdoor cafes*—along the Paseo de la Castellana, Calle

Serrano, the Gran Via—are at once Rx for sore feet, and are the
best locales in town to watch Madrid pass in review.

TO BUY

Given the slightest nudge—which they have had in the form of
a mass tourist market in the millions—Spanish handicraft producers tend to turn out lowest-common-denominator stuff. Cheap
little souvenirs—tacky dolls and five-and-ten fans and corny pottery and mass-produced Toledo jewelry junk—are all over the lot.
They do not do Spain, or its craft traditions, an iota of justice.
For a survey of what the handicrafts situation portends, have a
look at *Mercado Nacional de Artesina, 1 Floridablanca. Clothes
and shoes,* both men's and women's, are excellent buys in Spain;
both can cost half of what they would in the United States. Go
first to the two leading *department stores: El Corte Ingles* ("Eng-
lish-cut," if you want a translation) and *Galerias Preciados.* They
both have excellent men's departments, for ready-made (the style
is good *and* contemporary) *and* custom-made clothing, for which
the prices are really newsworthy. The service is excellent—they
don't see many Americans; we're still a curiosity—and the prices
are incredible. The men's shoe departments are also excellent
in both stores. There are even wider ranges in women's clothing, as
there are in all big department stores. Ladies, have a look around,
and at shoes, too. Before you leave these stores, consider other
purchases—gloves and luggage among them. Also good are Spanish *soaps* and *cologne* and *perfume*—Maja brand in particular.
These are a good deal cheaper than in the United States, are of
good quality (about the best in Europe after those of France).
The soaps can be bought in boxes of a dozen cakes. To these
downtown department stores I want to add a pair on the fashionable Calle Serrano: *Sears Roebuck* (yes, Myrtle, Sears) and
*Celso Garcia.* Sears is related to the American Sears, but do not
suppose that it is American-staffed or -stocked. The merchandise

is Spanish and the staff is essentially Spanish-speaking. Sign
language helps. *Calle Serrano* has other shops worthy of your
attention. *Loewe,* which has a branch at Avenida Jose Antonio 8,
is Spain's leading leather goods house. It is expensive but the
quality of the leather is generally good and the styling *alta;* findings
can be only fair, however. Women's handbags, men's and women's
wallets and passport cases, and luggage. *Calzados Luruena* has
handsome, high-styled, and well-priced shoes, men's and women's.
So does *Eureka. Gloria de las Medias* is for men's and women's
clothes, moderately priced. *Paneria Ingles* is a modish men's
clothing store. *Fran* is for smart women's shoes and bags. *Yusty*
is costly, but the highest-style men's shop in Madrid. *Guante
Varade* is good for gloves—another outstanding buy in Spain
for both men and women. *Santa* is for chic chocolates, no kidding.
*Kamisa* has exceptional women's handbags. *Thana Palud* has good-
looking women's clothes. But move along to other areas: *Elio
Berhanyer,* Juan de Mena 25, is a top high-style designer but
sells women's ready-to-wear in his shop at this address, along
with a fine line of smartly packaged men's and women's colognes
that make unusual gifts. *Nestares* is an old reliable leather goods
house at Avenida Jose Antonio 11. *Editorial Patrimonio Nacional*
is the publishing arm of the government organization that does a
splendid job of running museums and national monuments.
It operates a retail shop—*libraria-tienda*—at Plaza de Oriente 6,
at which are sold guidebooks to Patrimonio Nacional's museums
and monuments, as well as virtually unlimited varieties of postcards of these places. *Arce* and *Burgos,* both on the Calle
Cedaceros off the Alcalá, near Cibeles, are conservative men's
shops; both specialize in custom-made clothing. The *Rastro* is
at once Madrid's flea market and its antiques shops center, with
a separate section for each. The flea market is at its best Sunday
morning, but the antiques shops keep regular daily hours. *Pedro
Benito Blasco,* in the Ribera de Curtidores section of the Rastro,
sells nice nineteenth-century pottery and still-life paintings. *Luis
Carabe,* also in the Ribera de Curtidores section of the Rastro,

has a variety of highly decorative objects—plates, candlesticks, and much more. *Ferrari,* in the same Rastro section, has pottery, china, wood fragments, *santos,* angels, and wrought-iron fragments —many of them good. *G. Zazo,* in that same Rastro area, sells eighteenth- and nineteenth-century paintings, agreeable if not of the highest quality; ikons; and a variety of decorative pieces.

TO NOTE

**Access:** From the United States, there are direct flights New York–Madrid, via our own TWA and the Spanish national carrier, Iberia, which also connects Madrid with major European points. Additionally, a number of European airlines link the Spanish capital with their own, and there are good air services to nearby North African destinations. Domestically, Iberia is much preferred over another airline, Aviaco. Madrid's modern Barajas Airport is about seven miles from town; airport buses to the city are dirt cheap, but taxis are bargains, too, and therefore recommended. There's a minimal departure tax upon leaving the country. The best trains to and from the east are expresses—the Sud Express in particular—out of Paris; because the Spaniards, for strategic reasons, prefer their own gauge track, there are changes of trains at frontier stations; this situation obtains also with trains into Portugal, to the west. There are international bus services, and the roads—full of foreign motorists going to and from Spain— are, at long last, being improved, and substantially; it is almost essential that the premium—rather than the ordinary—gasoline be used in cars. As for domestic trains, the streamliners, usually with "TER" and "TAF" designations, and connecting major cities, are the ones to use, and then in first class. Within Madrid, the taxis—so available, so cheap, so efficiently and politely operated —solve every transport problem. They are metered, but drivers are allowed to charge five pesetas for each bag carried. Otherwise, walk; distances can be appreciable, but the geography is

not difficult and the terrain is eye-filling. **Climate:** Madrid's
two-thousand-foot elevation obviously has something to do with
the extremes of temperature it experiences. The hottest months
are July and August, when high in the eighties is not uncommon, with mid-seventies the average. June and early September
are cooler, averaging in the high sixties. Spring—April and May,
in the fifties and low sixties—can be pleasant; October—in the
fifties—is a good month too. From November through March the
temperature averages in the forties—lowest, of course, in December, January, and February. **Clothes:** Urban Spaniards, Madrileños most definitely among these, are among the most smartly
dressed of Europeans; male and female, rich, middling, poor.
The Spaniard, no matter his economic level, puts his best foot
forward when he leaves the threshold of his home. If la Señora
is going to own one good dress, or el Señor one good suit, the
chances are it will be well cut and stylish. Jackets and ties, and
dressy dresses, have not gone out of fashion, especially after dark.
**Currency:** the peseta. **Tipping:** Although most restaurant and
cafe bills include service charge, employees of these places rely
on additional tips. The economy of Spain is still such that an
overwhelming proportion of adults must moonlight with two jobs.
So add from 5 to 10 percent to food and drink tabs. Tip bellhops
5 pesetas per bag and baggage porters 10 pesetas per bag. Leave
the chambermaid a few pesetas per night if she's done a good job.
Leave something with the concierge upon departure—say, an
average of 10 pestas per day—if he has performed special services
for you. Tip theater ushers 5 pesetas. Tip taxi drivers 10 percent.
**Business hours:** Most stores are open from about 9:00 A.M. to
about 1:00 P.M., take a siesta break, reopen at about 4:00 P.M.,
and do not close until cocktail time, at about 8:00 P.M. The employees of the department stores somehow or other survive without
siestas, for these establishments stay open without a break—
9:00 A.M. to 7:00 P.M.; for all stores the hours are the same,
Monday through Saturday. **Language:** A little more than a decade
back it was not uncommon to be unable to communicate, even at

major Spanish airports, unless one spoke Spanish. The study of foreign languages has improved tremendously in recent years. One rarely has difficulty in Madrid, for if English is not understood, French is; and Italian-speaking visitors can usually make themselves understood in that language. The beautiful Spanish spoken is the authentic version of Castile—the region of central Spain of which Madrid is the chief metropolis. It is called Castilian, or—in Spanish—*Castellano,* and many Spaniards, when asking you if you speak their language, will refer to it as *Castellano* rather than as *Español.* If your Spanish has been limited to the Americas, you may find the Castilian lisp—on words like pesetas (pronounced *pethetath* in Castilian)—a novelty; but it sounds sort of nice when you get used to it. **Local literature,** in English, abounds on touristic matters; hotels distribute various *What's On* giveaways, none of them distinguished, and shops and newsstands sell local illustrated guides, in foreign languages, and of varying quality. **Further information:** Spanish National Tourist Office, 589 Fifth Avenue, New York; 180 North Michigan Avenue, Chicago; 209 Post Street, San Francisco; 338 Biscayne Boulevard, Miami; 13 Queen Street East, Toronto; Ministerio de Información y Turismo, Torre de Madrid and Medinaceli 2 (information office), Madrid, Spain; Oficina Municipal de Información de Madrid, Plaza Mayor 3, Madrid, Spain.

# *Monaco*

If you discount the remote Himalayan mountain kingdom of Sikkim, whose queen is American-born, Monaco is the only monarchy on the planet with a Yank sharing a throne. And although the area of the realm is—as we all learned from the gossip columns in 1956, when Grace Kelly of Philadelphia and Hollywood became Her Serene Highness Princess Grace—less than half the size of Manhattan's Central Park, it has other things going for it.

There is, after all, something to be said for a ruling house that has been in business since the twelfth century. At the back of the little guide book they sell at the Prince's Palace, there is a genealogical table of the House of Grimaldi, which indicates that it was founded in 1133 by one Otto Canella, whose son gave his name, Grimaldi, to the clan. Rainier III, the current reigning prince, came along thirty Grimaldis and eight centuries later, Rainier II—according to that table—having concluded his reign in 1407. Succession? Prince Rainier and Princess Grace have had three children; the youngest and eldest are girls, with a boy— Prince Albert, born in 1958—in the middle. He is the heir to this ancient if hardly impoverished throne.

**Near-bankruptcy and the Casino:** The Monaco that the world knows today as a tiny enclave surrounded on three sides by France, on the fourth by the Mediterranean, and with a solid

gold casino as its trademark, was impoverished to the point of
bankruptcy something over a century ago. It was during the
reign of Prince Charles. The principality had had to give up
territory to France—the nearby towns of Menton and Roquebrune, with the small settlement atop the rocky promontory of
Monaco constituting the bulk of the remaining territory. But Prince
Charles—a handsome, intelligent-looking man, if the portrait of
him in the palace is a guide—had an idea. Better to say he
adapted an idea—the scheme of the Duke of Baden, who had
opened a profitable casino at his German spa. Prince Charles
decided to do likewise. He did not have an overnight success,
but in 1860 he hired a pro to take over his enterprise and before
1870 there was rail service from Nice, and business at the
casino was so good that Prince Charles did away with direct
taxes, as have all of his successors. Before long, the Riviera had
its most fashionable resort. The rich English came over from
older, neighboring communities, and royalty made its way to
the gaming tables too. Although the Principality of Monaco retained its honorable and ancient name, the area of the principality
in which the new casino was situated had its name changed from
Les Spelugues to Monte Carlo, Italian for Mount Charles, in
honor of the enterprising man on the throne.

**The Grimaldis—and the French:** Until as recently as 1911,
Monaco's princes were absolute rulers. A new constitution in that
year set up a representative government. The government is run
by a Minister of State, who must—by terms of agreement with
France—be a French citizen. He has a trio of state counselors
under him, while the legislative body is the unicameral eighteen-
member national council. An even newer constitution, in 1962,
at long last gave female Monégasques the vote (an American-
born princess may have had something to do with this). In the
interim—in 1918—Monaco had signed a treaty with France in
which it agreed that the French Government would have to
approve succession to the throne, and also stipulating that with
cessation of the monarchy Monaco would become a part of

France, and its for-long-untaxed citizens would become subject to French taxation. Needless to say, there has never been a republican movement in Monaco, and so long as the Monégasques enjoy the bliss of freedom from taxes, it is not expected that there will be any moves in that direction.

Not everyone living in Monaco is a Monégasque. By no means. Of the population of about twenty-five thousand, only some three thousand are citizens. A great majority of the remainder are French, and under the terms of a 1963 agreement with Paris they must pay French taxes unless they had been Monaco residents before 1957. So, indeed, must companies doing more than a quarter of their business out of Monaco.

**Rainier versus Onassis:** But still more history was made in the sixties. As that decade progressed, a feud between Prince Rainier and his government on the one hand, and Greek shipping magnate Aristotle Onassis developed. Onassis owned 52 percent of the Société des Bains de Mer, the rather euphemistically named company formed by Prince Charles over a century ago to run the casino. SBM, as it is called, had acquired other properties over the years—a number of the leading hotels, restaurants, and recreational facilities. The prince and his advisers had come up with a scheme to expand the principality's tourist industry by attracting middle-income vacationers, instead of the very rich exclusively. This plan was opposed by Onassis, who was accused of impeding the country's tourist development. After two years of maneuvering, the Monaco Government bought out Onassis' holdings for eight million dollars.

Since then, SBM has become one of the most live-wire and expansionist of European enterprises having to do with tourism, recreation, and accommodation. It has spruced up its properties, the casino, hotels, clubs, restaurants, cafes, *boîtes*—and it has plans for brand-new construction, a pair of hotels among these. But not only SBM is preparing for the mass-tourism era ahead. Government projects include a convention center with a slew of adjacent hotels and all manner of new recreation facilities, as well as the 320-room Holiday Inn at a choice Monte Carlo beach location, and the beachfront Loew's Hotel. Monaco's friends, supporters, and *aficionados*—those who have loved it for its beauty and distinctiveness and charm—wish it well as it Goes Modern, but at the same time hope that it will move with enough prudence to preclude the transformation of a unique resort into a run-of-the-mill plastic playland. It may already be too late. A thousand U.S.-style hotel rooms plopped down in the core of a smallish traditional French-style resort may well produce an unhappy conflict of cultures, with neither side the winner.

### TO SEE

**Lay of the land:** The whole 370-acre country is called the Principality of Monaco. It is divided into three principal parts. The first has two names. It is called either *Monaco* or *The Rock,* for it is an elevated stony peninsula that juts into the Mediterranean. It overlooks the harbor, or Port of Monaco, which is flanked by a sea-level commercial and residential area known as *La Condamine.* La Condamine separates Monaco, or The Rock, from the third major area of the principality— *Monte Carlo,* which is the site of the casino, the leading hotels, and the beaches.

**Choice destinations:** Happiness in Monte Carlo is, first and fore-most, *the view,* or any one of a number of views from one elevated point or other. There is a lovely panorama from The Rock, looking down to the harbor of La Condamine and across the water to Monte Carlo. There are choice views, too, from high points in Monte Carlo—the casino terrace, for example, or a window or terrace of the Hôtel de Paris.

Then one concentrates on specifics. If it is July or August, guided tours of the State Rooms—including the Throne Room

—of the *Prince's Palace* are popular. Essentially a Renaissance
building with strong Italian overtones, the palace gained some
crenelated towers in the late nineteenth century during the rich
Prince Charles era. It is at its best in the galleried courtyard,
where there are some fine frescoes, and where concerts take
place in summer. For those ten months of the year when the
interior of the palace is off-limits to visitors, there is always the
noontime *Changing of the Guard*, whose members must surely
be the most advanced in years and the least prepossessing in all
of Europe. Even allowing for the commendable nonmilitarist
traditions of the principality, one would suppose that His Serene
Highness's government could do a mite more professional job of
recruiting. What one sees, though, is a troupe of Keystone Cops,
Mediterranean Style, that is nothing if not unintentionally amusing.

While one is up on high, atop The Rock, it is worth strolling
over to the *Cathedral*, a neo-Romanesque structure that went
up in the late nineteenth century, which would not have been a
bad thing had not a thirteenth-century church on the site been
razed in the process. Close by are the *Town Hall*, the *Government Palace*, and the neoclassic-design *Oceanography Museum*
(you might at first glance mistake it for the New York Public
Library), which was established by a turn-of-the-century prince
named Albert, and whose ace-in-the-hole is an aquarium in
the basement. Over in Monte Carlo the lure is, it need hardly
be said, the *Casino*. Its architect was the same Charles Garnier
who designed the Paris Opéra, and aside from its splendid and
recently refurbished gaming rooms (roulette, baccarat, chemin
de fer, boule, and trente-et-quarante—all starting at 10:00 A.M.
daily), it is the site of a treasure of a theater known as the
*Salle Garnier*. I hope there is a performance of *something* taking
place during your visit, so that you can see it, for it is one of the
great theater interiors of a continent not without more than its
share. And it is not only a pretty-pretty shell of a place. Bear in
mind that it was the home base of Diaghilev's Ballet Russe de
Monte Carlo and saw early performances of such classic ballets

as *L'Après-Midi d'un Faune, La Spectre de la Rose,* and *Le Sacre du Printemps.* Opera, too, has had historic Monte Carlo moments: Composers including Berlioz, Massenet, Saint-Saëns, Ravel, and Puccini presented works there. And the tradition remains, with a year-round season of high-caliber presentations.

Down below, along the sea, there are the *beaches*—Larvetto and Monte Carlo—and a mix of hotels, clubs, restaurants, and cafes. Beyond are the Monto Carlo Golf Club, with its elevated, seaview eighteen-hole course that is one of the most beautiful in the world (in my opinion, only the links at Banff National Park in the Canadian Rockies are as eye-filling), and the Monte Carlo Country Club, with its tennis courts. The Yacht Club in the harbor is one of the most renowned in the Mediterranean. And although I don't make a point, in my books, of dwelling upon social events, the Monégasques make such a point of them that some are worth mentioning. Winter remains the smartest of the four seasons, with the Opera House the site of National Orchestra of Monte Carlo concerts, opera, and ballet, and galas at the Winter Sporting Club. Summer sees an Arts Festival July through September, galas each Friday, and nightly dinnerdance with cabaret at the Summer Sporting Club; outdoor ballet, theater, and concerts in the square and courtyard of the Prince's Palace; open-air movies ("100 Films in 100 Nights") on the Casino Terrace. International tennis matches take place each Easter, and the Grand Prix auto races—with cars winding through the streets—are an annual May event.

## TO STAY

Monte Carlo has three exemplary luxury hotels—all three of the Old School, in the very best sense of the term. The most expensive, the most famous, and the most elaborate of the trio is the *Hôtel de Paris.* Almost a century old, it has seen additions, modernization, and refurbishing, all of them, though, in keeping with its original décor and its ambience of great *luxe*. The glass-roofed, crystal-chandeliered main lobby is the prototype of grand-hotel main lobbies. The restaurant and cocktail lounge, both leading off the lobby, are similar to it in design. There is a modern grill room up on the roof that relies on the panoramic views from its picture windows for dramatic interest. The bedrooms are beautifully decorated in period style, and many have terraces. The essence of Monaco, I want to tell you, is breakfast of a sunny morning on one of those terraces, with a matchless Mediterranean view as a backdrop. The location is the best in town. The casino is just across the street, as is the Café de Paris. There is an arcade of shops, barber shop, and beauty salon, and a pool in connection—the Piscine des Terrasses, which is part indoor, part outdoor. Although the hotel is billed as being open the year round, it is worth noting that its pool is closed the entire month of June—considered Monte Carlo's off month—to give its staff a holiday. The hotel has 320 rooms and suites; the latter are sumptuous. It also has an annex—the Residence—of 42 less desirable rooms. This is the queen bee of the Société des Bains de Mer, and it is beautifully operated. Still, if you would like to be attended by a staff a bit more spontaneous, a little more prone to an informal pleasantry or a smile, you might want to choose one of the other two of the top three. If you're a swimmer or a sun nut, you'll want to consider the *Hôtel Metropole*. A hop and a skip from the casino—it is almost as central as the Hôtel de Paris—the Metropole is a 300-room *grande dame* that dates to about the turn of the century and has aged gracefully. It is operated by the British Grand Metropolitan chain, a firm that has taken over some of the best hotels in Europe. The bedrooms—all with bath—are lovely. There are both indoor and outdoor (for summer) restaurants, and the outdoor pool and terrace, overlooking town and sea, is the envy of every other hotel in town. I've saved the architectural Belle Epoque treasure that is the *Hermitage Hôtel* for last. An almost next-door neighbor of the Hôtel de Paris, and a part of the SBM group, it has been restored to its original *fin-de-siècle* beauty—the famed painted-porcelain sinks in the public washrooms, the wrought-iron and glass-roofed Winter Garden, the exquisitely appointed dining room, and 200 capacious bedrooms, all of them brightly redecorated, and with super views of harbor, town, and sea. Guests have access to the Piscine des Terrasses, the same pool that Hôtel de Paris guests use; and, like Hôtel de Paris guests, they may also use the swimming pools and beaches of SBM properties of the Monte Carlo Beach and Sea Club. Without anything like the elegance or architectural beauty of the top three are a pair of SBM hotels that have as their great advantage an on-the-beach, where-the-action-is location that appeals to a younger clientele. They are generally open only from May through September, and they are named, accurately if not poetically, the *Old Beach* and the *New Beach.* The Old Beach has air conditioning in all of its rooms, all of which have private baths, and it is the more expensive of the two. The New Beach's rooms all have their own baths, but no air conditioning. Less expensive, less fashionable, but comfortable, is the *Balmoral;* the great majority of its rooms have bath or shower, and it has a restaurant. Also moderately priced, centrally located, with 28 of its 42 rooms having private bath, a restaurant that is al fresco in summer, and a nice homey feeling, is the *Hôtel d'Europe.* Agreeable too, quite central, and with a nice, comfortable ambience, is the *Hôtel de Russie.*

## TO EAT (AND DRINK)

The cuisine of Monaco is, not unsurprisingly, basically French, but, as elsewhere on the Riviera, there are Italian accents because of the nearby frontier with Italy. Fish and seafood specialties abound for the obvious geographic reason. Absolutely must-try specialties include *pan bagnat,* a hero-type sandwich with a tuna-tomato-olive-oil base, and *pissaladiera,* the regional version of pizza—usually baked (but not always) in a flat, square pan, as is pizza in Sicily, and with an onion-black olive-anchovy-to-mato-olive-oil base, more doughy than the conventional Italian pizza, and without cheese. The noted regional wines of the area —Chateauneuf du Pape, Tavel, and the other rosés of Provence —are invariably good bets, but restaurants offer wide choices, as they do throughout France. And Monégasques are proud of their local beer. The best food I have had in Monaco was at an attractive but not overly elaborate restaurant called *Le Bec Rouge*. The menu is a classic French one, strong on local fish and seafood, and with specialties including a variety of hot hors d'oeuvres, broiled lobster, and steak Charolais style with morrels. Moderately expensive. Far more elaborate, and more costly, too, is the restaurant of the *Hôtel de Paris*. Some of the captains and waiters have become patronizing with foreign guests— this is an invariable occurrence in hotel dining rooms—but food is taken very seriously indeed by the chefs, and can be first-rate if one takes one's time in ordering. The wine cellar, incidentally, is one of the biggest in Europe; it really *is* a cellar, with about 130,000 bottles in stock at any given moment. In summer, lunch and dinner are served on the casino-view terrace, for which one must book in advance. The restaurants of the *Metropole* and *Hermitage* hotels are also first-rate, as is the *Restaurant du Beach,* which is animated and smart during the summer season, particularly at lunch. In season, the *Summer Sporting Club* has dinner-dance-entertainment galas every Friday, dinner and dancing nightly, and is very festive and well dressed; the *Winter Sporting Club* is its cool-months replacement. The restaurant of the Casino is a year-round favorite, and its *Black Jack Club*—for dinner-dancing and cabaret—is very posh, very expensive, and winter only. After dark is kicky in Monte Carlo. *Maona* is a newish *boîte* with Polynesian décor, entertainment, and cuisine. *Jimmy's* is an engaging disco, and the *Sea Club* doubles as daytime swimming-sunning rendezvous and as late-hours disco. For any time of the day or evening pick-me-ups,

remember the attractive *Café de Paris,* opposite the Hôtel de
Paris, and by all means sample the delicious pastries and ice
cream at *J. Ardoin,* on Boulevard des Moulins, Monte Carlo's
main shopping street.

## TO BUY

One doesn't go to Monaco to shop (Nice, Cannes and other
Riviera towns offer smarter wares), but there are some interesting
purchases to be made. Local *handicrafts*—ceramics, jewelry, and
the like—can be found in several shops, including *Louis
Testa,* 1 Ruelle Sainte-Barbe, Monaco-Ville; *Céroc,* 1 Avenue
de la Madonne, Monte Carlo, and 2 Rue Emile de Loth, Monaco-
Ville; and *Atelier Vairel,* 3 Rue de l'Industrie in the Fontveille
sector. You might want to be the first on your block to take home
Monaco-made *perfume* or cologne; Moehr and Monaco are among
the brand names, and *parfumeries* like *de la Costa,* Avenue
de la Costa, and *Helder,* Boulevard des Moulins, stock them, as
well as French perfumes—which are, alas, more expensive than
in France.

The *Riviera Supply Store,* on the Boulevard des Moulins, is
chock-a-block full of all kinds of potable and edible treats—
wines, cookies, packaged chocolates, and the like. *Clothing*—
both men's and women's—is not a Monaco strong point; the
shops of Nice and other Riviera towns are smarter. *Lanvin*
(men and women) and *Jean Patou* (women) have boutiques
at the Place du Casino, as do the *jewelers Cartier* and *Van
Cleef and Arpels.* The Paris firm of *Hermès*—with scarves,
leather, and accessories for both men and women—has a branch
on the Avenue de Monte Carlo. *Sapjo* and *Galerie Saint Charles*
are a pair of side-by-side *antiques* shops at 16 and 17 Boulevard
des Moulins, and there is always the main post office, or *Poste
Central,* on the Place Beaumarchais, for the renowned *postage
stamps* of the principality.

TO NOTE

**Access:** This dot-on-the-map enclave on the French Riviera is quite as easy of access as neighboring Riviera points. Air travelers, coming from abroad or from within France, use the modern International Airport at Nice, which is connected with Monte Carlo by means of a regular bus service, taking about forty minutes, by considerably more expensive taxis, and by even more costly helicopters. Rail travelers use the Monaco-Monte Carlo station. There are modern highways leading eastward into Italy and westward to other Riviera destinations, with convenient bus service to Nice via Cap d'Ail, Eze, Beaulieu, and Villefranche; to Menton via La Turbie and Roquebrune, and to the Italian Riviera. And, should you be arriving on your yacht, be assured that there is a lovely harbor. Getting around locally is by means of private or rented car, taxi, the local bus company, and organized sightseeing tours. **Climate:** The average yearly temperature is given as 61° F. Summers are, of course, hot, with 78° F the average July–August maximum. Winters can be mild and sunny but are by no means swimming weather; January and February minimums are in the forties, but it can, on occasion, be damp, windy, or dry, if one is unlucky, even into early spring. Late spring (May and June are sixtyish) and autumn (September averages 70° F, October 63° F) are generally mild and delightful. **Clothes:** Resort wear—casual but smart—during the day; dressier, of course, in the evenings, with occasional Casino galas that are black-tie. **Currency:** The franc, at par with the French franc. Indeed, all the paper money is French; so are most of the coins in circulation. There are, however, Monégasque coins in the same denominations as the French ones, and with the same values. **Tipping:** As in France, restaurants and cafes invariably add service charges to bills, in which case there is no need to tip additionally. But you will do enough tipping, otherwise. Treat a franc as you would a quarter, and tip bellhops and baggage porters a franc per pag; leave something for the chambermaid (50 centimes to a franc per day); tip the concierge upon departure, but only if he's done more for you than hand you your key—a couple of francs per day is adequate if you've had special help. Tip taxi drivers, barbers, and beauticians 15 percent, less than half a franc for washroom attendants, and remember, should you go to a performance in the Opera House of the casino, that you pay the usher for your program. **Language:** The national language is, not unsurprisingly, French. But there is a good deal of English spoken. **Further information:** Monaco National Travel Office, 610 Fifth Avenue, New York; Service du Tourisme de la Principauté de Monaco, 2a Boulevard des Moulins, Monte Carlo, Monaco; Société des Bains de Mer, Place du Casino, Monte Carlo, Monaco.

# Oslo

Oslo's trouble is the western fjords, near Bergen. No other Scandinavian capital has such touristic competition. Visitors going to Denmark want to see Copenhagen, Sweden-bound travelers beeline for Stockholm, holidaymakers in Finland consider Helsinki the principal destination, and the same is certainly the case for travelers to Iceland: They gravitate to Reykjavik. Oslo in the wanderer's mind is something else again. The prevailing habit is to work it in for a day or two, going to or from the fabled western fjords of the midnight sun country on the other side of the Arctic Circle.

The result of this far-too-accepted Norwegian travel pattern is that the capital of the kingdom goes on season after season being not only underappreciated, but what is worse, patronized. Not disliked, mind you. Patronized. It would almost be better if the would-be detractors were vehement in their dislike of the place, rather than the usual reaction: "Oh, Oslo. It was nice enough . . ."

**The ideal city:** The fact of the matter is that the Norwegians have created a capital that meets every major test of the ideal city —or at least as ideal a city as we can expect in these difficult closing decades of the twentieth century. It is just the right size, with its near half-a-million population—not so big as to be unmanageable and ungovernable, not so small that it can't be taken seriously. It enjoys a distinctive Norwegian Modern architecture. (The Town Hall, perhaps ahead of its time upon completion in 1950, is more than holding its own as one of Europe's exceptional contemporary public buildings, wherein the art of the painter and the architect are combined to a point rarely attempted elsewhere other than in Mexico.) And it enjoys the unpolluted bounties of nature as do few other seats of government. The waters of Oslofjord are a perfect foil for the spanking beauty of the manmade town—or one aspect of the town, at least; for it extends in the other directions to cover a total of 175 square miles, making it one of the biggest in area of world capitals. Well over half of it is woodland, including a mountain, Holmenkollen, that was the nucleus of a Winter Olympics. Not many other cities show so versatile a face, and few others have made such an obvious point—especially in the last decade—of enriching the life of their handsome-to-look-upon environment. Oslo is today, to give you an idea of what I am talking about, perhaps the most underrated art center of modern Europe.

**The Vikings go west:** Few capitals, indeed few countries, have had a more consistently rough time over the centuries, for Norway is as devoid of such natural resources as minerals and great areas of arable soil as it is rich in physical beauty. From the earliest periods that we know about them, their naturally poor land impelled the Vikings to set sail in their graceful ships to conquer new worlds. They were not always winners, and they found themselves under foreign yokes as much of the time as not. By the time Oslo was founded, almost a millennium ago, in 1050, Norsemen had discovered Iceland and Greenland, Leif Erickson had discovered America, the classic Norwegian sagas were written, and Norwegian kings ruled an empire extending into the great New World island of Greenland. But then came an era when fellow Scandinavians became so competitive with their Norwegian cousins that their kings took to ruling jointly over Norway—a situation that was to prevail for some centuries to come, with Denmark (1380–1814) and with Sweden (1319–60, 1814–1905). There was even a period, 1397–1521, when all three countries constituted a union.

**The Danish and Swedish cousins and a sovereign Norway:**
For some four centuries, Oslo had a change of name. King Christian IV, as coruler of Denmark and Norway, decided rather immodestly in 1624 to rename Oslo after himself, after it was rebuilt following a disastrous fire. And so the town was Christiania until 1925, when the then fully sovereign Norwegians sensibly decided to revert to the original appellation; for by 1925 Norway had been a kingdom—100 percent completely on its own—for two decades. In 1905 the union with Sweden, begun in 1814, was dissolved, and the Norwegians elected as their monarch the then Prince Carl of Denmark; he sailed from Copenhagen to Oslo and his new realm with his English bride (a daughter of Edward VII) and their infant son, and they became the Norwegian Royal Family: King Haakon VII, Queen Maud, and Crown Prince Olav.

No part of Norway came to know World War II more intimately. Oslo fell to the Germans on April 9, 1940, after which the Royal Family moved to London to set up a Government-in-Exile that was to function for the duration of the war, while Free Norwegian forces fought with the Allies, and a brave, world-respected Norwegian underground fought the Nazis and the hated puppet Vidkun Quisling government by means of an ingenious network of sabotage units. (The name of the infamous Quisling became a noun—synonymous with traitor—in the English language, and other tongues as well, and Norway's fate during the Quisling years of the Occupation is movingly and graphically recounted in the Resistance Museum, in Oslo's Akershus Castle.) No Nazi-occupied people fought the enemy more valiantly than the Norwegians, and it is to their great credit that no occupied country of the West was slower to forget the Nazi barbarism after the war than the Norwegians, who were the last and most reluctant to return to a business-as-usual status with the Germans.

**Post-World War II rebirth:** Oslo celebrated its nine hundredth birthday in 1950 with the official opening of its Town Hall. Half a decade later it commemorated the first half century of its modern rebirth as a "democratic kingdom" (to quote the official government publication of the celebrations), and of Haakon's reign. Five years later the King died, to be succeeded by his son Olav, by that time a widower and the father of three children. Two of these were princesses, who gave up their rights of succession to the throne when they married commoners. The third is Crown Prince Harald, the heir. Norway takes democracy so seriously that it is the only monarchy in Western Europe without a nobility. One is either a member of the very small Royal Family or a commoner; there are no barons or dukes or counts or knights in between. The Norwegians like the institution of the monarchy, or they would vote it out of existence. (Their government has long been one of the most progressive in the world.) King Haakon was held in great affection, and his son, King Olav, enjoys great popularity. But the Norwegians keep fuss and feathers to an absolute minimum with their Royal Family, as with most aspects of their national life. Their unusual monarchy reflects their distinctive way of doing things—with respect for the traditional, but a healthy, open approach to the contemporary.

Norway, which shares an ever-so-mini frontier with the Soviet Union (some thirty miles way, way up north near Kirkeness), remains friendly with both East and West, but has cast its lot with the West since World War II, as a member of NATO, and most recently as one of the newest batch of nations affiliated with the European Common Market. The nice part about meeting these people in their capital is that they are so much gladder you have come than are residents of other so much more tourist-frequented capitals. You're not taken for granted in Oslo, and when a resident asks you to stay more than the day or two that is typical of foreign visitors, they're not kidding. They want you to remain longer, for they have a quite understandable affection for Americans: a hundred thousand of them emigrated to the United States just about a century ago, and in the first decade of this century some two hundred thousand more crossed the Atlantic. At times it seems that about as many Norwegians have American relatives as have Irishmen. It makes for a nice reception.

**Lay of the land:** The street to remember in Oslo is the broad, boulevardlike thoroughfare called *Karl Johansgate*. Its namesake was the dashing Frenchman who became Charles XIV of Sweden during the Napoleonic period, and who reigned also as King Karl Johan of Norway. Oslo's main street is named for Karl Johan because it was he who built the Royal Palace that dominates the thoroughfare, standing in a lovely public park at one end of the street. *Palace Park,* or Slottsparken, is a capacious, meticulously cared-for green that the locals—and visitors—enjoy strolling through. But an earlier walk should be from the start of Karl Johansgate in front of the palace, for within a hop and a skip of that street is the heart of the city. Directly beneath the palace is the original University of Oslo building, with the National Gallery, Historical Museum, and National Theater. Walking down the main street on the left, a block or two distant, is *Radhusplassen,* the square that sets off the twin-tower Town Hall, and the *Harbor of Oslofjord.* Ancient Akershus Castle, on an eminence of its own, as it has been for centuries, can be seen from the Town Hall. *Bygdøy,* across the waters of the fjord and quickly accessible by boat, is the museum quarter of the city. But return to Karl Johansgate from the Town Hall, continue down that thoroughfare, and one gains the mid-nineteenth-century Storting, or Parliament, with the Oslo Cathedral (and its adjacent butchers' stalls now turned into craftsmen's studio/shops) just beyond, and the East Railways Station at the street's extreme end.

**Choice destinations:** If Oslo is without the animation of Copenhagen or the sweeping grandeur of Stockholm, it is still among Europe's most engaging cities, with a congenial populace, and the

kind of don't-rush-enjoy-yourself ambience that requires—even of
time-shy Americans—a minimum of three days for a visit that
will do the place any kind of justice.

There is nothing corny about the beaten-path group of attractions. One wants to see them, and some others as well. Here are
my recommendations: The group of requisites begins with the
*Town Hall* (*Radhuset*), whose mid-twentieth-century good looks
I have paid tribute to earlier in this chapter. It is a twin-tower
red brick structure splendidly sited in its own little garden-filled,
fountain-playing park overlooking the harbor. But the silhouette
of the exterior—strong, distinctive, pleasing as it is—is but one
facet of the building. Within, forgetting the municipal offices, of
course, one finds a veritable gallery of contemporary Norwegian
art. Note the bold frescoes by Alf Rolfsen and Saage Storstein,
among others, the paintings by Reidar Aulie and Henrik Sorensen
—to name but two of the artists, the expressively strong sculpture
for which Norway has made a name for itself. *Frogner Park* is
quite as frequented as the Town Hall. It is the site of the monumental achievement of the Norwegian sculptor Gustav Vigeland—
150 groupings occupying 75 acres of a handsome city park. The
Vigeland sculpture breaks down into half a dozen main areas.
Chief among these are the playground area, with bronzes portraying the development of a child, starting with the fetus; the fountain section, embracing three-score individual reliefs and 20 additional groups, which encircle the massive fountain complex and
depict the Cycle of Life—infancy, adolescence, maturity, death;
and the monolith—nearly 60 feet high, with carving on its surface
of well over a hundred persons, surrounded by three dozen
enormous groups in granite, the lot representing Vigeland's interpretation of the business of everyday living. The wrought-iron
gate to the park is a Vigeland work, as well. More of his sculpture
may be seen in his former studio—now a museum—not far from
the park.

The *museum complex at Bygdøy,* across the fjord from downtown Oslo, and accessible by either boat or surface transportation,

offers a host of treats, each of them to be considered a requisite, the lot easily taking up the better part of a day. There is the *Folk Museum,* which comprises 150 farm structures—farmhouses and outbuildings, shops, schools, and the like—taken down at their original sites all over the country, carefully transported to Bygdøy, and painstakingly re-erected. The chef d'oeuvre is a wooden stave church one of relatively few of these purely Norwegian medieval masterpieces of architecture. There is, as well, Old Town area of eighteenth- and nineteenth-century houses and other structures, mostly all furnished in period; there's a section devoted to Lapp life, and a special surprise is Henrik Ibsen's study, quite as it was at his death. Another Bygdøy attraction is the *Fram Museum,* which is home to the ship *Fram,* the very same that took explorer Fridtjof Nansen to the North Pole way back in the early 1890s, with equally noted Roald Amundsen a later star passenger, his destination the South Pole. The *Gjøa,* on which Amundsen sailed through the Northwest Passage in 1903, was brought from San Francisco, where it had reposed well over half a century, and put on display at Bygdøy in 1972. A newer vessel, in a considerably older style, is *Kon-Tiki,* the balsa craft on which Norwegian explorer Thor Heyerdahl and five colleagues sailed five thousand miles across the Pacific from Peru to Polynesia, on a historic 1947 journey lasting over three months. Heyerdahl copied the boat after a Peruvian craft used in the sixth century, to prove that early South Americans could have settled the South Seas islands after reaching them on simple *Kon-Tiki*-type rafts. But there are still more sailing vessels at Bygdøy. The oldest, most famous, and most typically Norwegian are those in the *museum devoted to Viking ships.* Here one finds a trio of sleek beauties—the *Tune,* the *Oseberg,* and the *Gokstad*—each of which is well over a thousand years old. Still other vessels are in the Norwegian Maritime Museum. And should your visit to Bygdøy take place on a summer Sunday (the only time it is open), add *Oscarshall* to your itinerary; it is a mid-nineteenth-century souvenir of the joint Swedish-

Norwegian reign, and was used as a summer palace by its builder, King Oscar I. The *King's Farm,* another Bygdøy landmark, is the summer home of the sovereign; you'll see royal sentries at the entrance when King Olav is in residence.

Last but not least of the basic basics is *Holmenkollen.* To give you an idea that the Norwegians are anything but Johnny-come-latelies to the sport of skiing, it is worth observing here that Holmenkollen has had a ski jump since 1882. The one you see today is a far cry from the original, but it is not all that changed in essentials. A fairly recent addition that ski buffs like is the *Norwegian Ski Museum.* Holmenkollen is a magnet the year round. Norwegians (all of whom are born on skis—no joke) flock to it in winter to enjoy the countryside, as would be expected (about a hundred thousand watch annual winter jumping matches), but they come in summer as well to soak in the sun from the stands and to swim in Lake Besserud. (Norwegians are not only born on skis; they are also polar-bear swimmers. Be warned: The water is cold.)

**Other Oslo destinations:** There are two exceptional art museums. The *Munch Museum* opened in 1963 and is a repository of the collection of the works of the Norwegian-born painter Edvard Munch, who was not only a great Impressionist—one of the all-time greats, to be sure—but a prodigious worker, so disciplined and well organized that the works he bequeathed to the City of Oslo—by no means all of what he painted—included more than a thousand paintings and almost five thousand water colors and drawings, and some fifteen thousand prints. The catalogue of the museum, published shortly after it opened, termed the collection "both in its actual bulk and its value, as well as artistically, the greatest art treasure ever donated to the Norwegian people by a single citizen." And further: "Taken as a whole, the collection, with its incredible variety and diversity, vividly represents the working material which a great master has gathered around him in the course of a long and devoted life spent in the service of art." The paintings are arranged chronologically, from the first— about 1880—through to his later paintings in the early 1940s. (Munch was born in 1863 and died in 1944, less than a decade after more than eighty of his paintings in German museums were called "decadent" by the Nazis and confiscated.) More than one devotee has considered a visit to the Munch Museum reason enough for a trip to Oslo. Still more Munch works can be seen in the *National Art Gallery* (along with other Norwegian, Danish, and Swedish work, plus some French Impressionists and Post-Impressionists) and in the *Festival Hall,* or Aula, in the main building of *Oslo University,* just below the Royal Palace.

The *Sonja Henie-Niels Onstad Art Centre,* outside of town in Hovikodden, will perhaps be most appreciated by that generation that is old enough to have remembered the motion pictures of the pretty blond Norwegian-born ice skater-actress. Sonja Henie spent her later years (she died in 1969) in Norway with her husband, Niels Onstad, a shipowner and longtime art collector. The masterful building, designed by Jon Eikvar and Sven-Erik Engebretsen, a pair of young Norwegian architects, is in itself a work of art. The collection includes some 250 contemporary paintings of Impressionists and Post-Impressionists, with the abstract masters and, more recently, Expressionists, included as well. Not all of these are on display at all times, however, and there are as well temporary exhibitions, of a not necessarily high standard. A bonus in nostalgia (at least for those of us of a certain age) is a room filled with Miss Henie's trophies and medals.

But I'm not through yet. *Akershus Palace,* because it was built of stone rather than wood, is one of the few remaining structures of ancient Norway. On a dramatic cliff overlooking town and fjord, it is the very model of a medieval castle, and has been intelligently restored and furnished in period. It keeps rather erratic open hours, though; they are at their most generous in summer. Inquire when you might go. The very building itself is superb, but one should also see such parts of the interior as the chapel, the north and south scribes' rooms, and the vast reception halls, particularly the one named for Christian IV, who rebuilt the palace (and lived in it) at the same time that he reconstructed Oslo after its tragic fire and renamed it Christiania after himself. A part of the Akershus complex and in itself a worthy destination is the relatively recent *Resistance Museum.* This museum—depicting the Resistance Movement in Norway from the Nazi invasion in 1940 until the 1945 liberation—is for you regardless of age—no matter if you are old enough to have lived through World War II, or if you are too young to remember it.

The Nobel prizes are a joint Swedish-Norwegian enterprise, even though Alfred Nobel, their donor, was himself a Swede. It is the prize in the Peace category that is given annually in Norway, after determination by a committee appointed by the Norwegian Parliament and the *Nobel Institute,* the Norwegian branch of the Nobel Foundation in Stockholm; the institute is open to visitors who phone it in advance (44-36-80). The house where a Danish princess—Anne, sister of Christian IV—married no less a personage than the son of Mary Queen of Scots (James I of England and James VI of Scotland) is in Oslo. It is called *Ladegard,* and both it and the adjoining *Bishop Nicholas's Chapel* are open to the public, generally on Wednesdays and Sundays. The *Storting,* or *Parliament* (1866) is hardly one of Oslo's most beautiful buildings, but it is not without political and historic interest, as you might perceive from one of the tours offered daily in July and August. The *Museum of Applied Arts* is rich furniture, silver, ceramics, crystal, and textiles—made over a span of seven centuries, with a single room given over to the clothes worn by the late King and Queen, Haakon VII and Maud. There are several galleries of contemporary Norwegian arts. The *Oslo Art Association* occupies a treasure of a seventeenth-century house at Radhugate 19.

TO STAY

There are occasional exceptions to the rule, but generally Oslo
—as all Norway—believes in the basics of cleanliness and comfort,
rather than frills, when it comes to hotel accommodation. Service
tends to be efficient and polite, if not effusive. Rooms are frequently not as sizable as one might like them to be, and neither,
for that matter, are baths. I may be wrong, but it seems to me
that it was the Norwegians whom we may thank—if indeed, we
want to, which is doubtful—for the tiny chambers that adjoin
bedrooms and that contain, without benefit of curtain or partition
or even floor separation, all of the basic ingredients of a bath
—or rather, shower room: sink, toilet, and—protruding from
the ceiling with nothing to stop it from drenching the whole
little room—a showerhead. Showering in these baths—which
have been copied elsewhere in Scandinavia, and in other countries
as well—means removing in advance towels, pajamas/robe, and
all exposed toilet articles that would not benefit from a shower. It
is a Norwegian experience I first remember from some two decades back, am never particularly anxious to repeat, but am always
prepared for. Hardly in the category of hotels that offer such
conveniences is the *Grand,* hands down Oslo's No. 1. The location
on Karl Johansgate is perfect. The building is elderly enough to
be of the Old School, with most of its handsomely decorated
guest rooms of good proportions, and with nice old-fashioned-
*size* but otherwise thoroughly modern, baths. The ambience is the
most sophisticated in town—just peppy enough so that you know
you're in the heart of things. The Grill, with its great back-of-
the-bar mural of turn-of-century Oslo, by Per Krohg—Europe's
best competition for the Maxwell Parrish painting of Old King
Cole behind the bar of that name in New York's St. Regis-
Sheraton—is congenial from breakfast onward through closing,
and there are a number of other fine wine-dine spots that are

among the city's most exemplary. The *Bristol,* with a neo-Renaissance façade, its Gloomy Gus-lobby, its cavernous if hardly
beauteous Moorish Restaurant, and its way-down-in-the-basement
bar, has a sprightly, good-looker of a Grill in its favor, and
comfortable guest rooms. The *Continental's* big plusses are the
delightful reception and concierge service, a central locale, and
a wealth of restaurants; as a hotel it has not the luxury-ambience
of, say, the Grand. In the moderate-price category, the *Nobel,*
opposite the Grand, is updated (there are spiffy new baths) but
still with a pleasing traditional air. The *Astoria* is another spruced-
up middle-ranker that is agreeable. The *Gabelshus* is a honey of
a capacious, antique-filled onetime house in a residential quarter,
a quick train ride from the center; all rooms with bath or shower;
restaurant, bar. A nod, too, to the modern *Stefan,* an excellently
operated temperance hotel; all rooms have bath or shower; full
facilities—a bar, of course, excepted. To be noted, too, is
modern SAS's *Globetrotter,* should you need overnight accommodation at the airport in the course of a complex journey.
Coming up: an SAS-sponsored *Royal* in town, and hopefully
as fine as its namesake, also SAS-owned, in Copenhagen.

### TO EAT (AND DRINK)

You can't be everything. The Norwegians are great sailors and
explorers and architects and city planners and painters and industrial designers—and hosts. But they have never had a reputation for their cuisine. Things are improving tremendously, especially in Oslo. But it is perhaps worth knowing that the good
restaurants in the capital are *particularly* commendable for this
is a country where boiled fish or fish pudding, served with a
boiled potato, and garnished with a bit of green dill, has for long
constituted the average lunch or dinner. The Norwegians, now
that so many of them are traveling to the Continent and beyond
on holidays, are at last beginning to expand their culinary hori-

zons. But, as a general rule, they have not the deft touch of the Continent-adjoining Danes nor the finesse of the Swedes or, for that matter, the Finns. That said—and it applies far more to provincial Norway than to the capital—let me add that one may now dine very well indeed in Oslo. Fish and seafood are, it should go without saying, exceedingly popular, and when well prepared can be very tasty; crayfish, during its limited summer season, is among the leaders in this category. Reindeer steak, though never a favorite of mine, is appreciated by many visitors, and Norwegians consider it a special treat. The cheeses are good (the goat cheese, brown in color, is a national staple, which you may—or may not—like). Milk, butter, ice cream, and other dairy foods are fresh and wholesome. Beefsteaks are available everywhere. The dark breads are good, if not always as good as elsewhere in Scandinavia, but the Norwegian version of the flatbread so popular throughout Scandinavia is unique in that it is paper-thin, crisp, and delicious. (You've no doubt seen it in U.S. supermarkets under the "Ideal" label.) And Norwegian variations of the open-face sandwiches invented by the Danes are popular and tasty. Although Norwegians at home eat breakfasts no more spectacular than yours or mine, Norwegian hotels traditionally serve that meal smorgasbord style. There is invariably a buffet table chock full of a variety of fish—tinned sardines and tinned herrings of various varieties, platters full of assorted cheeses, flatbread and other species of bread and rolls, great bowls full of dry cereal for you to fill your own plates from; pitcher after pitcher of cold milk. In addition, there are fruit juices, boiled eggs to order, and, of course, coffee (which is good in Norway and is copiously consumed). After the first day or two of the buffet, you find yourself sticking to the fruit or juice, boiled egg or cereal, toast, and coffee; but the big spread is fun until the novelty wears off.

*Restaurant recommendations:* Surely the best-looking restaurant is that of the *Sonja Henie-Nels Onstad Art Centre* at Hovikodden, a few miles outside of town. The menu is classic continental, with Norwegian specialties, of course. The décor is elegant, and the setting—with a view of the fjord beyond—is one of considerable beauty. Especially good is *3 Kokker,* at Drammensvein 30, a good-looker of a place—neat and modern and welcoming, with a menu combining grills and Norwegian specialties, and with a kitchen that stays open until midnight, which is late for Oslo. (Afterward, the place becomes a bistro-cafe until the wee hours, and that too is worth knowing about.) Good also is *Holmenkollen Restaurant,* at Holmenkollen. The menu is essentially Norwegian, at its best, the restaurant attractive, and the views of Oslo and Oslofjord absolutely sublime—particularly if the sun is shining. The *Grand Hotel* offers several choices, each good. I have already enthused about the moderate-price *Grill,* full of interesting locals, with the old-Oslo mural behind its bar, breakfast-lunch-dinner service, and a late (1:00 A.M.) closing as an added asset. The main restaurant, or *Speilsalen,* is smart, and has dancing, and the basement *Bonanza* is a Norwegian Wild West fantasy; you are apt to think the décor exaggerated, but the steaks are good and there's dancing as well as a show of sorts. The *Continental Hotel's* restaurant is far better to look at than to dine in, but there is a good, inexpensive *Grill* and the atmospheric, always-humming *Theatercafeen* (populated with actors and staff of the National Theater, across the street) as well. Good to know about if you are exploring the Bygdøy area is the attractive, first-rate *Najaden Restaurant*—perfect for lunch. *Valenta* is authentically Italian, the best such in town. *La Belle Sole* is an old-time seafood house. *Grillstora,* opposite the Bristol, is a good, inexpensive place for breakfast, lunch, and snacks. And *Østmarkseteren*—away from the center—is a delightful, moderate-category restaurant, with a good Norwegian kitchen. *Statholdergaarden* (Radjusgate 11) is a moderate-price restaurant in a honey of a seventeenth-century house, and it's open for lunch through latish dinner. And *Bergfjerdingen* (Damstredet 14, Telephone 20-79-89) is a delightfully furnished cottage that goes back some three centuries and specializes in serving either morning coffee and pastries, afternoon tea, or traditional-type meals, but only if you're part of

a group of about a dozen persons. If you're not part of that large
a party, call the number above and try to work something out
anyway, with Miss Egede-Nissen, the owner. Why not the *Telle*
complex (Nansens Plass 4)? It consists of a bar, a dance hall,
*boîte,* and coffee house, and it's as good a place as any to meet
a cross section of Oslo of an evening. There are a number of
quick and cheap *cafeteria-snack bars.* Two reliable ones both
have the name *Kaffistova;* one is at Karl Johansgate 13; the
other at Storgate 28. The *Pavilion* in the Continental Hotel
is still another good one.

**Having a drink:** Alcohol in Norway has been a ticklish proposition for as long as I have known the country. There is no
need for me to go into the sad details for the whole country.
Suffice it to say that drinks by the glass, at a bar or cocktail
lounge or restaurant, are available only in Oslo and in a relative
handful of other major cities and tourist-frequented resort hotels.
Even in these places, Oslo included, no strong stuff may be
served before 3:00 P.M. or after midnight, and then only on
Monday through Friday—never on Sunday *or* Saturday *or* holidays *or* the days before holidays. So if you would like something
besides beer or wine during these dry intervals, you had better
lay in a little supply at a government liquor store; your hotel
concierge can fill you in on hours (they're limited) and locations.
The Norwegians' favorite spirit is aquavit, similar to the Danes'
(but not as good, in my view), generally consumed with a beer
chaser and—if you are prudent—with some solid food.

## TO BUY

Norwegian industrial design appears to have made greater strides
than that of any of the other Scandinavian nations. It was the last
of the lot to make a niche for itself in this area, and it has progressed by leaps and bounds. (Omit the Forum, a cooperative

display/sales venture that opened in the fifties with such high
hopes. It has stood still. Its wares remain those of its founding
period and now seem dull, dated, and stereotyped.) And while
prices have inched up in Sweden in recent years—to the point
where buying anything but the token Swedish souvenirs is big
business—and in Denmark as well, Norwegian tabs remain lower,
if not as inexpensive as Finland. Oslo, not unsurprisingly, offers
the biggest selection in the country, with sources that are nowhere else any better. Norwegian folk art, with that of Sweden,
is the most interesting in the north. Interesting smallish objects
are fashioned of carved and painted wood, reindeer bone, pewter, or brass. The Norwegians, with their climate, just have to be
good weavers—and are. The enamelware of Norway is perhaps its
most elegant specialty, with spoons, bowls, platters, and jewelry
of gold or silver beautifully layered with enamels of every hue.
Silverware, flat and hollow, and jewelry are first-rate. Look also
at stainless steel, glass and crystal, china, pottery, knitwear, and
ski equipment. Remember, too, that if you buy at least one
hundred kroner worth of merchandise, you are entitled to a tax
discount of 16.67 percent, provided the goods are sent from
the shop directly to Norwegian Customs and thence to the airline
or shipping company you will use upon departure from Norway.

Before starting your shopping, have a look at the traditional
folk and applied art in the *Museum of Applied Arts,* which I
have recommended earlier in this chapter. Look also at the
*Norwegian Design Center,* Drammensvein. It is operated by manufacturers of Norwegian products as a showplace for their wares;
the exhibits change frequently, so that you get an idea of what's
new before entering the shops. A good starter for shops is *Den
Norske Husflidsforening,* known far and wide for some eighty
years as Husfliden. This is the retail outlet of the *Norwegian Association for Home Arts and Crafts;* it is Norway's prime source for
handicrafts. There are four floors full of crafts, including the
hand-knitted ski sweaters for which Norway is noted, embroidered
and woven work, and splendid textiles, woodenware, ceramics,

articles of reindeer horn, copper, and pewter; dolls, kitchen utensils, even toys and minor souvenir-type objects that have the
virtue of being the well-designed genuine article. There are a
number of leading jewelers. My favorite is *Tostrup;* it has been
in business since 1832, and is noted for its enamelware—sets of
half a dozen coffee spoons, each enameled a different color, for
example; bowls, bracelets, brooches, and fine Norwegian silver
as well. *David-Andersen* is a major competitor. *Glasmagasinet* is
just what the name implies—a glass shop, with the glass and
crystal of the fine Norwegian firm of Hadelands its headliner,
but with other lines as well, not to mention table linen (Norway
is good at placemats), kitchenware, cutlery, pewter, toys, and the
like. *Steen and Strom* is Oslo's biggest department store. It has
spruced itself up in recent years, but you must not expect anything quite like Stockholm's NK, Helsinki's Stockmann's, or Copenhagen's Magasin du Nord. Still, like the major department stores
of major cities of every country, it quickly conveys a picture of
the standard of living of the people it serves, of their tastes and
needs as consumers. Additionally, it is strong on applied arts—
especially the Norwegian-made Porsgrunn porcelain and china,
which remains relatively little known in the United States but
certainly competes with its Scandinavian counterparts. The inexpensive and exceptionally smartly designed Plus glassware, factory-
made rather than hand-blown and comparable to Sweden's Boda
glassware, and a wide variety of other products in silver, pewter,
plastic, wood, and the like are worth checking, at *Norway
Designs.* Stenseth and Larsen specialize in old porcelain and
china. Shopper or only browser, do have a look at the delightful
group of studios and shops known collectively as *The Bazaars,*
and occupying a group of onetime butchers' stalls behind the
Cathedral. There are Weavers (*Adrienne Handvev* is a standout,
and her wool scarves are knockouts), ceramists (*Arne Nilsen,*
for one), jewelers (*Oivind Modahl,* for example), and a slew of
others. And, in the case of artisans, you'll see them creating
the wares they sell. Not a great many indigenous antiques remain

on the market today; you might browse *Kaare Berntsen* and *Hammerlunds Kunsthandel* to get an idea of what is currently available. And have a look at the street stalls and shops in the engaging, car-less *Strøget*—for pedestrians only.

TO NOTE

**Access:** Arriving by air, chances are good that you'll fly in on SAS, the remarkable multinational airline of the three Scandinavian kingdoms: Norway and neighboring Denmark and Sweden. SAS flies direct from New York, as well as from a number of other Scandinavian and continental points, not to mention London. There is first-rate service by ship, should you be coming from Copenhagen. The handsome, supermodern luxury liners of the DFDS Line—a Danish company—make daily overnight crossings both Copenhagen–Oslo and Oslo–Copenhagen. There is also good steamship service via modern ships of the Fred Olsen Line (you may take your car) and, should you be on the Continent, from Kiel, Germany to Oslo, via the crackerjack pleasure liners of the Sven Winge Simonsen Line. Train? If you are coming from Bergen, the railway linking Norway's No. 2 city on the coast with Oslo is one of the great roller coaster adventures of the globe—an unparalleled engineering feat—and is but one route on an extensive system leading out of and into Oslo. One may also travel by rail to Stockholm, and in conjunction with ships to Copenhagen and Helsinki. Within Oslo, the central sector is so relatively compact and easy to get about in that walking is my favorite means of transport. Taxis are easily secured at hotels by phoning the central taxi service, 33-03-86, at least an hour ahead. There are, of course, self-drive car-rental offices; chauffeured cars are available, too, and there is a variety of both bus and fjord-steamer tours, reasonably priced and professionally conducted. **Climate:** It is worth remembering that Norway is 1110 miles long and that Oslo is in the south, so that it must not be confused with polar bear territory.

Winters are long, to be sure—from November through April—but temperatures are rarely below the twenties, often in the thirties or maybe the low forties. There is lots of snow. Spring is brief (May and June) but surpassingly beautiful, particularly in the western fjords, where masses of fruit trees blossom in vivid unison. Summer (June, July, and August) is mostly in the high sixties and low seventies. Autumn virtually limits itself to September, in the fifties and sixties. And skiers, note: You may ski in Oslo from Christmas through April, making excursions to any number of other ski areas, both near the capital and otherwise. It is worth noting, in this connection, that all Norway takes to skis during Easter Week; if you want to join in, do so only with confirmed reservations for a roof over your head. **Clothes:** The impeccably groomed Norwegians have nothing like the clothes sense of the wealthier Swedes or the closer-to-the-Continent Danes, and tend toward the conservative, although the youngsters like to be as with-it as their counterparts everywhere. Adult gents still wear jackets and ties, particularly in the evening, with their ladies dressing accordingly. **Currency:** The *krone* (plural: *kroner*). Each krone is divided into one hundred øre. **Tipping:** Norway has never, to its great credit, been uptight about tipping. A service charge is added to hotel, restaurant, and cafe bills, and there's no need to tip additionally, except of course about a krone per bag to bellhops, and an average of a few kroner per day to whatever hotel concierges perform special services for you. Ten percent is plenty for taxi drivers (many Norwegians still don't tip cabbies). Porters in a railway station get one krone for the first bag and half a krone for each additional bag. **Business hours:** There are no lunch-hour closings in the north country. Shops are open from 8:30 A.M. to 5:00 P.M. in summer, with earlier closings on Saturdays. Offices generally open at 8:00 or 8:30 A.M. and close by 4:00 P.M., with employees eating quick sandwich lunches at their desks, the better to enjoy leisure in the late afternoons. **Language:** Norway, which has known English tourists for almost as long as Switzerland, is right up there with Denmark and Holland in that its populace is almost completely bilingual in English. Speak English to anyone—from grade-schoolers on upward—and you'll have commenced an English-language conversation. As for the national language situation, let me quote one Eric the Ruddy, identified as author of the admirable volume published some years back by the Norway Travel Association, entitled *Veni Vidi Viking:* "There are three languages in Norway: Landsmal, the official language, which no one speaks, Riksmal, which most people speak in a few varieties, and English, which everyone speaks in an amazing number of varieties, of which the best known is vi-King's English." (Riksmal, the popularly spoken Norwegian, though it *sounds* different, is similar to Danish, when written; Swedish is of the same language group, of course, but less closely related than Danish. All three languages are so closely related, however, that nationals of the three countries can usually understand each other's tongues. When in doubt, they speak what has become the Scandinavian *lingua franca:* English.) **Local literature:** *Oslo Guide,* published seasonally by the Oslo Travel Association, is obtainable without charge in the hotels, as is *This Week in Oslo.* Bookstores carry any number of books in English—some beautifully illustrated—on the capital city and other aspects of life in the kingdom. **Further information:** Norwegian National Tourist Office, 505 Fifth Avenue, New York; Scandinavian National Tourist Offices, 612 South Flower Street, Los Angeles; Norway Travel Association, H. Heyerdahlsgt, 1, Oslo, Norway; Oslo Travel Association (head office) Radmannsgarden, Radhusgate 10, Oslo, and—for information—Munkedamsveien 15 (near Oslo West Station), Oslo, Norway.

# *Paris*

So often, the trouble with the American new to Paris is that he knows so much less about it—and the country of which it is the capital—than he thinks he does. Joan of Arc and Maurice Chevalier and Chanel No. 5 and Napoleon and the Folies Bergère, of course. But we are hard put, without a little research, to distinguish between Louis XV and Louis XVI (the monarchs, not the furniture styles, although they can put us off, too). It has to do with our schools. We have been taught disproportionately much about Queen Victoria and Oliver Cromwell. We are sadly weak on, say, the Second Empire of Napoleon Bonaparte's nephew, and on King François I, who built the oldest part of the Louvre as his palace. All those Merovingians and Carolingians and Capetians: Shakespeare didn't get around to writing plays about the French dynasties, and they remain mostly beyond our pale. The only fairly early sovereign of whom we have some knowledge is Mary Queen of Scots, although I suspect many fewer of us realize that she was a Queen of France and was married to her first husband in Notre Dame de Paris, than that she was imprisoned the second half of her life by Elizabeth I in a series of drafty English castles.

It is entirely possible to have the holiday of a lifetime in Paris without the faintest idea of what transpired before Charles de Gaulle. But not every country can also boast a King Clodion The

Hairy (so called because he ordered his Frankish subjects to wear their hair long) or Queen Clotilda (who was sainted because she converted her husband, King Clovis—the sovereign who designated Paris as France's capital—to Christianity), or a King Pippin the Short (his son was Charlemagne), or a King Charles the Fat, or sovereigns of such distinctive dispositions that they are remembered as Louis the Quarreler and Charles the Affable.

**The Paris before Christ:** Early Paris goes back to the century before Christ, when Caesar conquered it, and its residents—a tribe called the Parisii, whose name gradually replaced the earlier Lutetia. But before that happened, Lutetia, with its Seine location, became a tie-up point for ships sailing past, toward Rouen, which it gradually passed in importance, thanks to the ingenuity of transplanted Romans, who cleared its swampy environs. Those same Romans built a temple to their deities on the Île de la Cité, and later the area developed as the town center. But in 451, Attila's Huns might well have taken the town had not a young woman named Genevieve inspired the people to resist, to the point where the Huns were driven away; and the young heroine of the battle is the same St. Genevieve who has been the patron saint of Paris down through the centuries.

Charlemagne, who in 800 had gone to Rome to be crowned the first Holy Roman Emperor by Pope Leo III, is known as a military-minded monarch and as a much-married one. (He does not quite measure up to England's Henry VIII, but still, four wives is a record not to be lightly dismissed.) Between wives and battles Charlemagne made Paris a seat of learning to be reckoned with. At the end of the tenth century, with the start of King Hugh Capet's Capetian dynasty, Paris had become a handsome, substantial city. Hugh Capet and his successors made it even more so. This was the era of the founding of the University of Paris, of the paving of streets, the founding of a police force, the first city wall, and the building of Notre Dame by another very military and much-married monarch, Philip Augustus. Louis IX—later to become St. Louis—embellished Paris with the exquisite Ste.-Chapelle, and by the time Philip the Fair added even more to its beauty, Paris had become the biggest and richest of medieval cities. Albertus Magnus and St. Thomas More added theological eminence to the Sorbonne's already established intellectual reputation. The rich merchants and guilds set up their own municipal government, with their provosts on an equal footing with the provost of Paris, who was the King's own man.

**Joan of Arc and the Renaissance:** The Hundred Years War— that near-interminable series of struggles waged by the French to drive the English from their shores—saw the burning of Joan of Arc at the stake two years after her unsuccessful siege of Paris— an English-occupied Paris in which the English Henry VI had been crowned king in Notre Dame. The Renaissance came in with a bang with François I, who built the Louvre, founded the College de France, set up the first royal printing press, and set the stage for continued royal patronage of architecture and the fine arts, as well. Under Louis XIII, Cardinal Richelieu made Paris the intellectual as well as the political center of Europe. The succeeding Louis—the Fourteenth—began his reign in 1643 and moved his court to the palace he built at suburban Versailles—a palace that was to be copied by monarchs all over Europe for the next two centuries.

Louis XIV reigned an astonishingly long time—seventy-two years. It was a period of tremendous cultural, political, and military accomplishment for France. It was, after all, Louis XIV who unequivocally stated, *"L'état c'est moi."* (I am the state.) The move to Versailles benefited Parisian industry immeasurably; indeed, it was from that period that Paris became a world center for luxury goods, which it remains to this day. Architects like Mansart, under Louis XIV, and Soufflot under Louis XV, created works that added to the splendor of Paris. This was the period, too, of the plays of Molière and Racine, of scientists like Lavoisier and Buffon, of brilliant salons, of Gluck operas, and of powdered wigs.

**"L'état c'est moi"—and the Revolution:** But the poor were

getting poorer. If isolating his courtiers from his people was politically expedient for Louis XIV, it was also the beginning of the
estrangement of the sovereign from the people. The succeeding
reigns of Louis XV and Louis XVI culminated in the Revolution.
The mobs forced the Royal Family from Versailles to Paris and
stormed the Bastille. One may still visit the cell in the gloomy
Conciergerie in which Marie-Antoinette, the excessively extravagant Austrian-born wife of Louis XVI, lived just before being
guillotined at a public execution on what is now the Place de la
Concorde.

Paris was a turbulent city in the years that followed. The Terror,
as the Revolutionary period was called, was followed by the First
Republic, proclaimed in 1792. In 1795 the stormy Directory
began its rule. There was a sweeping change in matters aesthetic
—from the elaborate Louis XIV, Louis XV, and Louis XVI
décor of the monarchy to a neoclassic simplicity in architecture,
furniture, and even clothes, with women in severe high-waisted
dresses, and men—the *incroyables* or "unbelievables"—in tight
trousers. Politically, the severity was equally *incroyable*. The Directorate was bankrupt and its personnel at such odds with each
other and so intrigue-laden that, on November 9, 1799—a fateful
day in French history—a bright young Corsican army officer,
who had distinguished himself in foreign engagements, played a
major role in a *coup d'état*.

**The Corsican named Bonaparte:** The Consulate had replaced
the Directorate. It was actually a dictatorship, with the Corsican
Bonaparte the No. 1 of the three consuls. In 1802 he was made
first consul "for life." In 1804 we are back in historic Notre
Dame for the coronation of Emperor Napoleon I. As he set
about conquering Europe and brilliantly reforming French domestic institutions, he found time to erect the Arch du Carrousel
in the Tuileries, the arcaded Rue de Rivoli, the splendid column
in the Place Vendôme. Most important, he expanded the collection of the recently founded Louvre with loot that his troops
had gathered in military campaigns. Those artistic spoils had to

be returned to their rightful owners after the Congress of Vienna in 1815, but no matter—the concept of great public museums had been popularized. The Congress of Vienna was, of course, the aftermath of Napoleon's earlier and final defeat by Wellington at the Battle of Waterloo.

**Little-known kings, and Louis-Philippe:** The Bourbon dynasty restored itself rather briefly after his exile, in the persons of two monarchs we hear little about these days—Louis XVIII and Charles X. (Louis XVII, if you are wondering, was the son of Louis XVI, and died in prison at the age of ten in 1795.) Charles X was forced, as a result of the so-called July Revolution, to abdicate in 1830, and in came Louis-Philippe, who was proclaimed King, in a rather complex run of affairs, by the National Assembly. His "July Monarchy" (called after the revolution that brought him to the throne) was a big-business reign. He even dressed like a businessman, walking the boulevards, umbrella in hand. He had no comprehension of the working classes' plight, though, and was attacked from both right and left. All the same, France prospered materially (the Arch of Triumph went up at this time) and the romantic movement flowered. Victor Hugo made his reputation as a writer. Delacroix painted. Berlioz composed. Still, Louis-Philippe went out as had Charles X before him, by abdicating. The Second Republic followed—but only for four years. Louis Bonaparte, an ambitious nephew of Napoleon Bonaparte, who had been elected President of the Fourth Republic, managed to get his title changed. In 1852 he was proclaimed Napoleon III. (Napoleon II, Bonaparte's son, was better known as the King of Rome and the Duke of Reichstadt; he never reigned, and died at the age of twenty-one at Schoenbrunn Palace, Vienna.)

**The later Napoleon—and Haussmann:** The eighteen-year reign of Napoleon III (who was Emperor for precisely as long as Louis-Philippe was King) proved a significant period for Paris. The Emperor appointed the Baron Eugene Haussmann to convert Paris into a modern city. With the authority of the imperial

command behind him, Haussmann was ruthless in the changes
he made. Indeed, there are students of art, architecture, and
town planning who still have not forgiven him. In order to build
the wide arterial boulevards and the great squares that typify
Paris today, he had to destroy much that dated back to medieval
times. Notre Dame, for example, was fronted by a cluster of
venerable houses, all of which were razed to make way for the
broad open space that Haussmann considered an improvement.
Much of the façade of the Paris we are so accustomed to today—
the grandiose Opera is a prime example—dates from the Second
Empire.

That epoch came to a dreary culmination with the siege of
Paris that was a consequence of the Franco-Prussian War, and
the Commune of Paris. The Third Republic saw recovery. Paris
escaped damage during World War I, after which the victorious
Allies met in the palace that Louis XIV had built at Versailles,
imposing harsh terms on the vanquished Germans, who—never
forgiving—invaded Paris, and the rest of France, in 1940.

**The two World Wars—and De Gaulle:** The government tem-
porarily left the capital for the thermal resort of Vichy, where
the quisling Pétain regime were German puppets until 1944. That
was when Paris was liberated by France's own remarkable resistance forces. American forces entered the city thereafter, and the
unbombed city—though austere and hungry in the early days of
peace—quickly regained its brilliance.

The postwar years saw Charles de Gaulle as President in 1945
and 1946, and later from 1958–69, under a new, strong-executive
constitution. France voluntarily relinquished its vast black African
empire, as well as Tunisia and Morocco, and eventually—after
much blood was shed—Algeria. The great student-worker up-
risings of 1968 alerted France to the need to update its institutions even more rapidly than had been the case. It is happening:
Beyond central Paris, in the industrial suburbs and in the cities
of the provinces, France is coming to terms with the technology of
the late twentieth century. De Gaulle saw to it that France ex-

ploded its own atomic bomb. Its young people are impatient for modernity and change. But it is not necessarily wisdom, in a country with so great a past, to make arbitrary breaks with such a rich tradition. France is not moving recklessly. Which is as it should be. Hopefully, at least another century will elapse before another Baron Haussmann bulldozes his way through this still supremely beautiful capital.

TO SEE

**Lay of the land:** No great city, New York excepted, is easier to find one's way about than Paris. We may regret that Baron Haussmann destroyed much of medieval Paris when Napoleon III commissioned him to redesign Paris—with the installation of the wide boulevards and great squares—a little over a century ago. But Haussmann's Paris is sensible and practical. And walkable —despite its considerable size.

Let me try to orient you by delineating what I consider the thoroughfares and landmarks that are essential to a basic geographical understanding of Paris. Start with the *Right Bank* circle that till recently was the *Place de l'Étoile* and is now officially the Place Charles de Gaulle. (I suspect that like New York's Avenue of the Americas—still Sixth Avenue to natives— Place Charles de Gaulle will remain "Étoile" to those who have so known it.) No less than ten streets radiate from the Étoile (thus the name *étoile*—star), whose landmark is the Arc de Triomphe. The most important of these is the *Avenue des Champs Élysées*—the broad, cafe-cinema-auto showroom boulevard that leads directly into the square that is the most beautiful in the world, and the most difficult to negotiate in traffic, the *Place de la Concorde*. Continue through, for safety's sake, *around* Concorde, and you are in the heart-of-Paris park that is the *Jardin des Tuileries,* with the *Palais du Louvre*—the onetime royal residence turned museum. The Tuileries and Louvre are bordered on the

south by the Seine River, and on the north by the arcaded Rue de
Rivoli. One may leave this Concorde-Tuileries-Louvre area for
the *Place de l'Opéra*—the heart of the Right Bank—by any one
of several routes. *The first:* From the Concorde, take the Rue
Royale directly north to the Parthenonlike Church of La Madeleine, turn right at the Madeleine on the multinamed but popularly
called Grands Boulevards and walk, for a few blocks, to the Place
de l'Opéra and the Paris Opéra landmark, for which it is named.
*Two:* Walk from the Rue de Rivoli, bordering the Tuileries, onto
the *Rue de Castiglione,* and a couple of moments later emerge
into the extraordinarily beautiful *Place Vendôme,* easily identifiable because of the column in its center—erected by Napoleon
and with a statue of none other than himself at its summit. Pass
through Vendôme to the celebrated *Rue de la Paix,* and within a
few moments, you have reached the Opéra by a second route.
*Three:* Continue walking down the Rue de Rivoli, bordering the
Louvre, until reaching the broad *Avenue de l'Opéra*. Turn left
on that thoroughfare, walking north to the Opéra at its far end.
   Now to the *Left Bank,* via the greatest landmark of them all,
Notre Dame, which is situated on an island, Île de la Cité, in the
Seine. Return to the Louvre-flanking Rue de Rivoli. Pass the
Avenue de l'Opéra, continuing east on Rivoli, beyond the en-
trance to the *Palais Royal,* until you reach *Rue du Pont Neuf*.
Turn right here; this street leads directly onto the famous bridge
for which it is named. Over the bridge, and there you are: on the
*Île de la Cité* with the twin towers of Notre Dame just beyond.
An even smaller island, *Île St.-Louis,* is directly to the rear of
Notre Dame, gained by the little Pont St. Louis. But you want to
continue from the Île de la Cité to the Left Bank. The most
direct way is to continue on the same Pont Neuf you took from
the Right Bank to the island; it continues to the Left Bank. Or,
if you would rather orient yourself on main thoroughfares, go this
way: After arriving on the Île de la Cité, walk toward Notre
Dame to the first broad thoroughfare you hit. It will be the
*Boulevard du Palais*. Turn right, across the narrow *Pont St.-*

*Michel,* and *voilà!* The Boulevard du Palais has changed names to become the *Boulevard St.-Michel*—a principal Left Bank street. The spires of Ste.-Chapelle—another landmark—are to your right. But continue south on the Boulevard St.-Michel—"*Boule-Mishe*"—to the first principal cross street. This will be *Boulevard St.-Germain.* Turn right on it, and you are in the core of the Left Bank, with the landmark *St.-Germain des Près Church,* the shops and the cafes all nearby. If you like, you may *return to the Right Bank* in roughly circular fashion. Continue along the Boulevard St.-Germain, past St.-Germain des Près and the cafes, following the boulevard's curves. Before long, you will reach the *Palais Bourbon,* the landmark that is the National Assembly, facing the Seine and the bridge that is the *Pont de la Concorde.* Before crossing, look up to your left at the Eiffel Tower. I want you to make a note of it at this point, so you will realize its Left Bank situation. Behind it is the broad green called the *Champ de Mars,* at whose other extremity is the *École Militaire,* or Military Academy. Still another Left Bank landmark—not at all far from where you are standing at the Pont de la Concorde—is the complex of the *Hôtel des Invalides,* with the domed church where Napoleon is buried. Back you go now to the Right Bank—over the Pont de la Concorde to the familiar Place de la Concorde.

**Choice destinations, or The Essential Paris:** What follows is one chronic enthusiast's Introduction to Paris, the absolute essentials. They may be taken in on a first trip, or divided into a couple of trips. Some, for me at least, are revisited trip after trip after trip. These would include the Louvre (I take in new-to-me sections each time), Notre Dame, maybe the Place des Vosges. Others are once-is-enough destinations—the Eiffel Tower, Sacré Coeur, Invalides. Still others are parts of the Paris landscape, areas through which one passes, or places one passes by, with renewed pleasure on each return: Place Vendôme, Place de la Concorde, St.-Germain des Près.

*Notre Dame,* along with Westminster Abbey in London, is the cathedral we grow up with. It is part of our life long before we ever see it. And when we do, it does not disappoint. Begun in the mid-twelfth century, it was not completed until the mid-thirteenth. It is one of the great Gothic cathedrals, with its twin bell towers (you may climb up, as did Hugo's hunchbacked *jongleur* Quasimodo), its trio of arched front doors, its exquisite rose window, the famed flying buttresses along its sides, and the needlelike spire over its transept. The apse, or altar area behind the choir, is perhaps the loveliest part of the always-crowded interior. The *Louvre* was first inhabited by King François I in the sixteenth century. All of his successors lived there up through Louis XIII, and many added and altered, most especially Catherine de Médici, who built the adjoining Tuileries Palace. There was a hiatus, commencing with Louis XIV, who built Versailles, where he lived, as did both Louis XV and Louis XVI. By the time Napoleon was emperor, the place had become a slum. He restored the Tuileries and moved in; then he went to work on the adjoining Louvre buildings. His nephew, Napoleon III, made the latest additions half a century later. It is as well to know, before going near the place, that the Louvre today is not one but half a dozen museums, all of them absolutely super. The *painting galleries* go back to François I, who brought Da Vinci's *Mona Lisa* to Paris as part of his collection. On display today is a group that is unsurpassed as representing European art at its finest. Consider Fra Angelico's *Coronation of the Virgin;* the Raphael *Madonna* and her chubby Christ; Titian's much-reproduced *Man with Glove;* Vermeer's lovely *Lace Maker,* works by France's Ingrès, David, Delacroix, and Corot. *Sculpture* is a Louvre specialty—the *Winged Victory of Samothrace* and the *Venus de Milo,* both of classical Greece, but masterworks as well, from medieval Renaissance Europe—Michelangelo's *Slave* and Goujon's *Diana of Anet* among them. Other Louvre Museum departments—you can't begin to do justice to them on one or two visits—are Ancient Egypt, Furniture, Objets d'Art, and Asian Antiquities. (These are in addition to the first-mentioned paintings, sculpture, and classical sculpture.) The *Eiffel Tower* went up in

1889, is more than a thousand feet high, and has three observation levels, two of which have restaurants; the highest platform, almost at the top, is the one to head for, picking as clear a day as you can, for the panoramic view. The *Arc de Triomphe* was begun by Napoleon and finished by Louis-Philippe. Haussmann later added seven to the three existing avenues that lead from the Place de l'Étoile, making the total a rather confusing ten. You may go upstairs in the arch. There's a little museum relating to the monument, and a marvelous view (in many ways better than that from the Eiffel Tower). If you are wondering why Napoleon is buried in a place called *Les Invalides,* it is because the church with his tomb is but a part of an enormous veterans' hospital— probably the world's first—built by Louis XIV. The *Army Museum* is now a part of the complex, but what you probably want to see is the Church of the Dome, named for its top-heavy cupola, under which, within, is the bulky stone casket containing Napoleon's remains. In great contrast to the overblown, graceless ostentation of *le Tombleau de l'Empereur* is the Gothic grace of the *Ste.-Chapelle,* after Notre Dame the most important church in Paris. This is a thirteenth-century masterwork built by Louis IX—later St. Louis. The slimness and elegance of its exterior proportions would be enough to make it a standout for the centuries, but its stained-glass windows are easily the finest in Paris, and among the finest in Europe. The *Place Vendôme,* under which in recent years has been added the indignity of a parking lot, is an almost completely enclosed square that is the work of a single architect, the noted Hardouin-Mansart. It has but two entrances, one on the Rue St.-Honoré, the other on the Rue de Castiglione. The shape is square, but with the charm of chopped-off slanted corners. The palaces of the square are all early-eighteenth-century; one is now the Hotel Ritz. The column in the center, with a statue of Napoleon atop it, replaces an earlier statue of Louis XIV, which is rather unfair to Louis XIV, as it was he who started the building on the square. The nearby *Church of the Madeleine* is an enormous, late-eighteenth-century neoclassic landmark that started out to be all manner of things, none of them a place of worship, and was almost a railroad station, before the decision to make it a church (one of the few we hear about, of the short-reigned Louis XVIII) was adhered to. It is the scene today of *haute monde* weddings. There are flower stalls in the surrounding square, whose food shops are in many ways more inviting than the church. *Sacré Coeur:* The world is full of churches built as acts of thanksgiving to God. Sacré Coeur is quite the opposite: It was conceived as an act of contrition after France's emergence as the loser in the Franco-Prussian War, which was such a disaster that it led to the abdication of Napoleon III. It was not, however, until after still another conflict, World War I, that the Sacré Coeur finally opened. There is little one can appreciate as regards its aesthetics. The best that can be said for it is that its white, domed façade and its high Montmartre elevation make it stand out, and that the view from the terrace is excellent. A visit to it can be nicely combined with a stroll through the Montmartre streets that Utrillo painted; now, alas, without the charm they once knew. We may thank Louis XV for the *Place de la Concorde,* which was begun during his reign and named for him—until the Revolutionists tore down the central statue of him, called the square for their insurrection, and proceeded to set up their guillotine in its midst. When you try to cross, today, as thousands of cars block your way, think of earlier days. Louis XVI, Marie-Antoinette, and Madame Du Barry were among those whose heads were chopped off in this beautiful spot. The palace on your left as you look inward from the Seine is the Crillon Hotel. The American Embassy is its left-hand neighbor, while the twin palace to the right of the Crillon is the Navy Ministry. The *Opéra* is the great neo-baroque structure that dominates the square that takes its name. The work of the same Charles Garnier who designed the similar but smaller theater in the Casino of Monte Carlo (see the chapter on Monaco), it is the most opulent of Paris public buildings; it behooves you to get inside for a performance of something or other. (Neither the opera nor ballet companies performing within are as exceptional as the building itself, so it doesn't make too much difference what you see.) The splendid red-and-gold auditorium is but a small part of the interior. There is an enormous backstage area (one of the biggest of any theater), and a promenade area above the very grand grand-staircase that must have been a perfect foil for classy Second Empire audiences. The *Church of St.-Germain des Près* goes all the way back to the sixth century, but is mostly much more recent; the bulk of it is eleventh-century. Within, the Gothic sanctuary and choir are particularly lovely. While you're here, amble about the neighborhood, which is the heart of the Left Bank. Visit the seventeenth-century *Luxembourg Palace*—built by Marie de Médici and now the seat of the French Senate—and its surrounding gardens, and take time, also, for the *Cluny Museum*. The museum building itself is a medieval treasure; it had been a monastery in the fifteenth century; you may see the chapel, and a couple of dozen additional chambers rich with medieval art, the most noted piece of which is the *Dame à la Licorne* tapestry. The *Place des Vosges* in the old, deteriorating, but still handsome Marais area, near the Place de la Bastille, is Paris at its most serene and beautiful. Henry IV had this square built in the early seventeenth century. The Renaissance houses are of basically uniform design. No. 6 is where Victor Hugo lived, and it is now a Hugo museum. But the Place des Vosges is at its nicest on a sunny day in late spring, when the old trees have their new leaves, and you have the time to sit back on one of the benches and relax with the neighborhood locals.

**Museums—beyond the Louvre and the Cluny:** Given the French background of a culture enriched as a result of an extensive imperialistic foreign policy, it should not come as a surprise that Paris has well over seventy museums, nor that only a few of them are lemons. The French are absolute wizards at the museum-keeping art, but because their capital tempts visitors with so

many other diversions, many of the museums are pitifully underappreciated—or, at least, underattended. Of the lot—and excluding the already-recommended Louvre and Cluny museums—
I have selected ten of my favorites. Here they are, alphabetically.
The *Musée des Arts Africains et Oceaniens* (293 Avenue Dau-
mesnil, Métro stop: Porte Dorée) is way out in the Twelfth
Arrondissement, in a not particularly appealing lower-middle-
class quarter. But it is worth the longish subway ride. Housed
in a capacious Thirties-Modern pavilion is a sumptuous collection that the French—always appreciative of exotic cultures—
acquired during the colonial period, both in Africa and in the
Pacific. The African masks, headdresses, and other ceremonial
pieces are among the finest to be seen in any museum in the
world. The *Musée National d'Art Moderne* and the *Musée d'Art
Moderne de la Ville de Paris* are next-door Avenue President-
Wilson neighbors. The National is the more important of the
two, with enviable collections of the art of this century: a Picasso
Harlequin, Bonnard's *Cliche Flammarion,* Matisse's *Le Peintre
et son Modèle,* works by Roualt, Utrillo, Bonnard, Kandinsky.
The City Museum has special shows, but a permanent collection as well—including works by Dufy, Vlaminck, Chagall,
Modigliani, Léger, and others. The *Musée des Arts Décoratifs,*
in the separately entered Marsan Pavilion of the Tuileries at 107
Rue de Rivoli, does justice to the Catherine de Médici-era palace
it occupies. There are three floors of exhibits relating to the arts
of decoration—a fifteenth-century wood-canopied bed from
Auvergne; the collapsible desk that traveled with Napoleon in the
field, with lines so clean it could have been designed at the end
of the twentieth century instead of the end of the eighteenth;
chairs of the three Louis periods, so that once and for all—if this
trio of styles confuses you—you can sort them out to your satisfaction. There are, as well, porcelains, silver, jewelry, tapestries,
sculpture, painting—and from Asia as well as Europe. The *Musée
Carnevalet* (22 Rue de Sevigne, Métro stop: St.-Paul) is, along
with the earlier-recommended Place des Vosges, a treasure of

the Marais district. To say that it depicts the history of Paris is hardly to do it justice. The main building of the museum is the sixteenth-century *hôtel*—or mansion—of no less a personality than Madame de Sévigné, and is where she wrote her famous letters of social commentary. The choicest part of the museum is a group of rooms—the Henriette Vouvier Collection—furnished in the Louis XV and Louis XVI styles of the eighteenth century. Elsewhere you see what Paris was like in earlier eras, from specimens of its citizens' clothes, their documents, etchings, paintings, and all manner of *bibelots*—even including the few personal possessions left by Louis XVI and Marie-Antoinette before they were beheaded. The *Musée Cernuschi* (7 Avenue Velasquez) occupies the mansion of a rich lawyer who bequeathed it—and his fantastic collection of Chinese art—to the City of Paris at the turn of the century. There are some spectacular screens and porcelains. The *Musée Cognacq-Jay* (25 Boulevard Capucines) occupies the upper floors of a building in the heart of the busy Grands Boulevards area. The subject matter is the art—applied and fine—of the eighteenth century; in a series of period rooms one finds some of the finest pieces of furniture and other objects of the era to be found in Paris—which is saying a great deal in this of all cities. The *Musée Guimet* (6 Place d'Iéna) is one of the relatively few really superlative museums of Asian art in the world. The exhibits come from all over the Far East—the Khmer culture of ancient Cambodia, for example, Afghanistan, Tibet, Indonesia, India, and of course China. In two words: Oh, wow! The *Musée du Jeu de Paume* (Place de la Concorde, near the Rue de Rivoli) is the branch of the Louvre whose specialty is Impressionist paintings. It occupies one of the two detached pavilions at the Place de la Concorde and Tuileries. The collection is nothing less than *sensationelle:* a Van Gogh self-portrait, Renoir's *Moulin de la Galette;* Manet's *Déjeuner sur l'herbe;* Gauguin's *L'or de leur Corps;* and paintings by Monet, Corot, Sisley, Pisarro, Toulouse-Lautrec, Degas, Mary Cassatt, Rousseau, Seurat. Watch for special exhibitions at the twin pavilion to the Jeu de Paume; it is called the

*Orangerie,* and it is just across the Tuileries. When there's a well-reviewed show, you'll see the lines extending outdoors. The *Musée Nassim de Camondo* (63 Rue de Monceau) occupies the house of the parents of a young man who died in World War I. His father and mother left the house as a museum in their son's memory. Though the structure itself is modern, the interiors are eighteenth-century, and aside from the mostly Louis XVI furniture and accessories, there are exceptional paintings, Chinese porcelains, and both Beauvais and Aubusson tapestries.

**Other Paris destinations:** The *Palais-Royal* is a tranquil oasis of striking beauty right in the heart of town. A royal palace it is not, nor was not, despite its name; rather, it is a great quadrangular mass of buildings—entered from the Rue de Rivoli, across from the Tuileries—enclosing a formal, fountain-centered garden. It was built in the mid-seventeenth century by no less a personage than Cardinal Richelieu, and has housed, successively, his art collection, his relatives, and their mistresses, and in more recent years the novelist Colette. The *Panthéon* is a good deal more recent than that of Rome—about seventeen hundred years. It is a somber, neoclassic, domed structure that Louis XV commissioned the noted architect Soufflot to design; it was finished in 1789. There is more to the building than at first meets the eye. The detail work—Corinthian columns, fine ceilings, arches, and cupolas—is superb. And down in the basement is a crypt containing the tombs of such French immortals as Zola, Hugo, Rousseau, Voltaire. You may see the crypt only in the company of a guide who takes groups as they collect. Because French civil servants have a way of staying on in their jobs, it is conceivable that you will have the same guide who has been in the crypt for years. No matter how elementary your French, his repartée results in the funniest running show in Paris. *The Conciergerie* is the one ancient building in Paris, with which I am familiar at least, that is more interesting outside than within. You cannot look at it yourself; dull guides take groups through darkish, depressing spaces of cavernous size and little interest, the only exception being the simple little cell—now a chapel—where Marie-Antoinette lived before she was carted to her death, on what is now the Place de la Concorde, in 1793. The *Palais-Bourbon* has a colonnaded neo-classic façade not dissimilar to that of the Madeleine (it was planned that way by Napoleon), but it dates to the mid-eighteenth century. Since 1832 it has been the home of the Assemblée National, which deliberates in its semicircular *Salle des Séances;* it's worth lobbying your way in. I first visited the *Jardin des Plantes* when I had time to kill before departing on a train from the nearby Gare Austerlitz. This is at once a botanical garden and a zoo, with the latter much more amusing than the former, and the whole complex a delightful way to brush elbows, on a pleasant day, with Paris at its leisure. *Maison de l'UNESCO* (Place de Fontenoy on the Left Bank near the École Militaire) is the glass-and-reinforced-concrete world headquarters of the United Nations Educational, Scientific, and Cultural Organization, and is one of the most imaginative pieces of contemporary architecture in Europe. It was a joint international collaboration, and there are works of Picasso, Mexico's Tamayo, Japan's Noguchi, and our own Alexander Calder—to name a few. *Hôtel de Sens* (1 Rue du Figuier) is not, of course, a hostelry or inn, but a onetime private mansion that is Gothic Paris at its best. You cannot, of course, go in, but it is worth passing by the *Palais de l'Élysée,* on the smart Rue du Faubourg St.-Honoré; this is, after all, the official residence of the President of the French Republic. The guards are used to people peering into the courtyard to see what they can see. The palace known as the *Quai d'Orsay,* housing the Ministry of Foreign Affairs, began admitting visitors on hour-long guided tours (for which there is a fairly steep charge) in 1972; lures are Louis-Philippe and Napoleon III-style salons, and the chamber where the Congress of Paris met and the Kellogg Pact was signed. Paris is nothing like Rome for *churches.* Here, though—aside from those earlier mentioned (Notre Dame, Ste.-Chapelle, La Madeleine, St.-Germain des Près, and Sacré Coeur),

are a quartet of lesser-known churches that I like. I mention
*St.-Roch* first, because it is in the heart of town at 269 Rue St.-
Honoré, and because its priests say masses in English. It is a
beauty of an eighteenth-century baroque church with some fine
sculpture and painting of the period of its construction. *St.-Ger-
main l'Auxerrois,* in the Place du Louvre, had been the parish
church of the French Royal Family during periods when the
Louvre was a royal residence. Although it is essentially Gothic,
there have been additions over the centuries by the royal wor-
shipers, whose religious objects are on view. *Église de la Sorbonne* (Place de la Sorbonne) is the university chapel, and the
only one of its buildings that is quite as it was when Cardinal
Richelieu had it constructed four centuries ago. It contains the
cardinal's tomb. *Val de Grace* (Place Alphonse-Laveran) had its
origins with Queen Anne, the mother of Louis XIV. She ordered it
built—it is domed baroque—after giving birth to her son, having
been unable to conceive during the first twenty-three years of her
marriage. Young Louis laid the cornerstone when he was seven,
in 1643.

Of the **excursion destinations** from Paris, *Versailles*—the residence of Louis XIV, Louis XV, and Louis XVI—is essential
for an understanding of France's—and indeed Paris's—last four
centuries. Go by train on your own, go by car, go on conducted
tours, as you will; the distance is a dozen miles. To be seen are
the opulent State Apartments, the Grand and Petit Trianons,
Marie-Antoinette's "Petit Village," and the formal gardens. Allow
the better part of a day for the works. The interiors alone—Hall
of Mirrors, Royal Chapel, Royal Opera Theater, often-imitated,
never equaled, let alone the quarters of the various kings and
queens—take time. *Fontainebleau* is the country palace that preceded Versailles, although it was used concurrently with it after
Versailles was completed. It goes all the way back to the mid-
sixteenth century of the same François I who built the Louvre.
The exterior architecture is a masterwork in itself, but within,
such rooms as the chapel, the theater, the François I Gallery,

and the ballroom (with its parquet floor to end all parquet floors)
are of unusual beauty. No soldiers could ever have clicked their
heels in a more elaborate Guard Room. There are, as well, the
rooms in which Napoleon lived—and abdicated. And the Queens'
Apartments housed such illustrious ladies as Catherine de Médici,
Mary Queen of Scots, and Marie-Antoinette. *Chartres,* though
sixty miles from the city, can be done in a fairly active day.
You go, of course, for its magnificent twelfth-century cathedral
with its matchless windows; only those of the cathedral at Bourges
and at Paris's Ste.-Chapelle are its peers in France. *Chantilly*
(twenty-three miles from town) is the site of a pair of fine
Renaissance castles, in the bigger of which are the painting
collections of the Conde family—Raphael, Titian, and Perugino
are among the artists represented. The grounds are splendid, and
there is a stable that cared for several hundred horses two
centuries ago—something you don't run across every day. The
twelfth-century cathedral in the little medieval town of *Senlis,*
nearby, can be combined with a Chantilly visit. *Malmaison,*
about ten miles west of Paris, is the country house Napoleon
built for his first empress, Josephine, who came from the Caribbean island of Martinique (her Martinique birthplace is a major
visitor attraction). There is nothing really *mal* about this elaborately furnished *maison* except its excessive expense. The
rooms on both floors are furnished as they were when Napoleon
lived there with his wife. (Josephine remained after her husband,
wanting a male heir, divorced her to marry Austrian Princess
Marie Louise). Josephine found it difficult to manage on the
more than 3½ million francs' settlement her husband gave her;
she was in debt after two years.

## TO WATCH

The earlier-recommended *Opéra* should be a requisite; its
interior is more remarkable than either the resident opera or

ballet company. The *Comédie Française,* which functions as the National Theater, performs classics and other works, all in French, of course. There are a number of other theaters presenting straight plays, comedies, musicals, ballet, and opera. They advertise daily in the press, and their schedules are in the giveaway weekly *What's On* publications, available at hotels; and hotel concierges can book. Concerts can be heard at the *Palais de Chaillot* and sometimes in the *Opéra Theater* in the palace at *Versailles,* and at *Salle Pleyel.* Some—not all—*cinemas* show imported films in their original sound tracks. Their ads and marquees say "V.O." (or *Version Originale*) if that is the case; concierges can advise. *Son et Lumière* (Sound and Light) spectacles—which were invented in France—take place at various historic locales in summer, including the *Invalides* and *Versailles.* The *Folies Bergère,* after all these years, still puts on a splashy revue with gorgeous girls, sets, and costumes. The *Casino de Paris* is a dreary second. If you are determined to see the floor show at the *Lido,* no one—certainly not I—can stop you. It will be expensive, stuffy, and predictable. It's cheaper if you stand at the bar, but the visibility, in that case, will be near zero unless you take your periscope along. The venerable *Au Lapin Agile* in Montmartre—it must go back to François I—has been packing the crowds in for generations. But the best after-dark shows are seen from the alfresco tables of cafes like the *Flore* and the *Deux Maggots* on the Boulevard St.-Germain, or if you prefer more conventional crowds of passersby, there are the cafes of the now quite tacky-touristy Champs Élysées and the Grand Hotel's *Café de la Paix*, where it is absolutely true that you'll run into *someone* you know, if not from home, then from a nearby restaurant table in Vienna, the hotel you stayed at in Oslo, or the check-in counter at O'Hare. The bars of the smart hotels are good people-watching spots at cocktail time—those at the *Prince de Galles, Crillon,* and *Plaza-Athenée* are among the choicer.

## TO STAY

The French, it must be remembered before one checks into a Parisian hotel for the first time, lead systematic, well-ordered lives. And in the case of the simpler hotels, frugal lives. Everything is done according to systems that have long been perfected. The visitor must be flexible enough to understand this. If he finds but one very tiny bar of soap in his bathroom, rather than separate bars at both bathtub and sink, he must realize that a decade ago he would have found no soap at all. If he finds writing paper—even if only two sheets of paper and two envelopes—at the desk in his room, he must realize that until a few years back he would have had to ask the concierge for that paper. (In lower-category hotels, he still must.) If, in a smaller hotel, the operator tells him, when he is trying to place a telephone call on his tippy-toes (the wall phone being just under the ceiling) that he must realize that if the operator says, *"Racrochez l'instrument, monsieur"* she means it: "Hang up, I'll call you back," she is saying, and she will. She does not make the call while you wait, because that is not the system. Many of these facets of French hotelkeeping are inexplicable. It is like toast in England—ice-cold at breakfast, warm and buttered at tea, and no one knows why. One must accept. And when one accepts, one enjoys French hotel life. Concierges, by and large, are wizards; maids, marvelous; room-service waiters prompt, and efficient. And in the bigger hotels, luxuries promised are luxuries available. Indeed, in no city are luxury hotels more luxurious. There is still the feeling, in the Old-School, *luxe* category hotels of Paris, that one is staying in a kind of palace. They remain stubbornly traditionalist. The décor is likely to be Louis XV or Louis XVI or a combination of the two. The staffs are still enormous in proportion to the size of the clientele. Individual floor waiters, rather than a central kitchen, are still the rule for room service. The reception manager remembers you when you book again—and so does the concierge, when you ask him to get you an opera seat at the last minute. In some of these places the bellhops are still likely to be wearing white gloves. There are even places where you will run into staff wearing spats. What are spats, you say? Now come on, you're not *that* young! I have known the *Ritz* since I wandered in to have a drink in 1948. It is one of the handful of great ones on the planet, and to its great credit it has not been content to rest on the laurels of a global reputation. Recent years have seen it go through a renovation program running into several million dollars. The Ritz occupies one of the original eighteenth-century Place Vendôme palaces. The Ritz is a feeling—from the moment you step into the lobby. The staff, by and large, is among the most skilled in Europe. The period décor—only the Rue Cambon bars are a bit contemporary—is sumptuous, and the bedrooms—singles, doubles, and those oh, wow suites—as well as the restaurant and grill. The quiet inner garden, on which many of the bedrooms front, is a delight at all seasons, particularly in summer, gastronomically, when it is a restaurant. The *Meurice,* with its inspired location— as beautiful as it is convenient—on the intersection of the Rue de Castiglione and the Rue de Rivoli, is quite possibly the most intrinsically Parisian of the great Paris hotels. The ambience is elegant but low-key. The lobby, bar, and intimate Louis XV-décor restaurant are handsome. And so are the accommodations, particularly those—mostly the suites—overlooking the Tuileries. They remember you here; the Meurice has a long roster of repeaters. The *George V,* on the avenue of the same name, off the Champs Élysées, is a grand hotel in the grand manner—not old, like the Ritz or the Crillon or some of the others of this category—but exquisitely furnished (and recently refurbished) in eighteenth-century style, with the genuine article—tapestries, paintings, sculpture, clocks, *boiserie*—scattered about to add to the ambience. The service—from reception to room service—is exceptional. The restaurant is one of the best hotel dining rooms in town, and goes outdoors to the terrace in summer. Bravo, Trust Houses-Forte management. The *Lancaster* at 7 Rue de Berri, just off the Champs Élysées, is surely the most charming of the luxe hotels—smallish, intimate, with impeccable personal-style management. The bedrooms are as big as the hotel is small. There is a cozy bar, and a first-rate restaurant that in summer is transferred to the patio—one of the handsomest in Paris. The *Crillon,* like the Ritz, is an intrinsic, original part of a venerable Paris square, in this case the Place de la Concorde. The interiors are almost entirely Louis XVI, under sparkling crystal chandeliers. (The sole exception to this rule is the very contemporary grill room/bar, a favorite after-hours spot for staffers from the next-door American Embassy.) Rooms overlook either a quiet interior courtyard or the glorious Concorde. The *Bristol,* on the Rue Faubourg St.-Honoré, comes closer to seeming like a palatial townhouse than any other luxe hotel. Though not small, it is just intimate enough to give you the feeling that you're the guests of a marquis rather than a hotelier. The public rooms—lobby, lounges, dining room—are authentic eighteenth-century; a rather nice touch is that one has drinks in the lobby (where there is waiter service) rather than in a separate bar. The bedrooms are big and comfortable. And the service is quite as unobtrusive, as you would expect in so quiet and elegant a setting. The *Plaza Athenée* is, not unlike the George V, a relatively modern building with an off-Champs Élysées location (in this case, Avenue Montaigne), perfectly beautiful eighteenth-century interiors (the Relais Grill and Bar Anglais are the contemporary-look exceptions), and skilled service. The *Prince de Galles* (doesn't Prince of Wales sound nice in French?) is the next-door Avenue George V neighbor of the George V. There's a crisp, smart French feeling to the place; a good restaurant, handsome guest rooms and suites, and the bar is one of the most Parisian-animated in town, come apéritif-time. The *Vendôme* occupies one of the palaces designed by Mansart, Louis XIV's noted architect, at the entrance of the Place Vendôme. The bedrooms are sumptuous, and there is an attractive bar-cafe, with meals served at its tables and in the bedrooms. *The Lotti* (7 Rue de Castiglione) is another hotel that is at once beautifully located and beautiful. Lobby, restaurant, bedrooms, suites—all are in eighteenth-century style. The service is professional, the ambience engaging. Move along now, from de luxe to *first-class category.* In this group the unique *Saint-James & d'Albany* (211 Rue St.-Honoré and 202 Rue de Rivoli) stands out. This hotel is actually two hotels combined. The Saint-James is an eighteenth-century structure that was the ducal palace where Marie-Antoinette welcomed the Marquis of Lafayette upon his return to France from America. It is connected by a lovely courtyard-garden with the newer structure that is the Hôtel d'Albany, facing onto the Rue de Rivoli and the Tuileries. The ambience of the combined hostelries is one of serenity, taste, and charm. The accommodations in both are comfortable (although not all have private bath), they are fully serviced, and they have restaurant and bar. The *Résidence du Bois* (10 Rue Chalgrin) is a smallish town-house kind of hotel on a residential street just off the fashionable Avenue Foch, which is one of the arteries leading from the Place de l'Étoile. The bedrooms (all with bath) and public rooms are period-style and handsome; you have the feeling that you are in the country. The *Scribe* (1 Rue Scribe) is in the heart of the busy Place de l'Opéra area. It's a big, comfortable old-timer that has been intelligently and sylishly refurbished by its current proprietors, the first-rate Grand Metropolitan group, out of London. The high-ceiling bedrooms—all with bath— are a highlight; restaurant, bar. The *PLM Saint-Jacques* (17 Boulevard St.-Jacques, at Place Denfert-Rochereau) is tomorrow's French hotel, today. In this, the first of Baron Elie de Rothschild's PLM group in Paris, all rooms are zingy twins with supermodern baths, radio, TV, air conditioning, built-in refrigerator, and "automatic bar" at bedside, from which you help yourself to snacks and drinks, the charges going on your bill downstairs as you do so. Facilities include restaurant, cafe, bars, shopping arcade, even a branch of Carita, the hairdresser-barber; Métro at the door. The *Victoria Palace* and the *Grand Hôtel Littré* are next-door neighbors in the Montparnasse area. The Littré is at 9 Rue Littré, its neighbor at 6 Rue Blaise Désgoffes. Both are first-class, both handsomely appointed as a result of smart and recent refurbishing, and both are under the same deft management. There's a good-looking traditional-style restaurant and contemporary-décor bar in each, and all rooms have luxurious marble baths. The *Mont-Tabor* (2–4 Rue du Mont-Tabor) is smack in the heart of things on a street that lies between the Rue de Rivoli and the Rue St.-Honoré, near the Place Vendôme. The lobby, restaurant, and bar are handsome, and the refurbished bedrooms likewise. There's a smart Franco-Spanish lilt to the place, in part because the clientele is heavily South American. English is spoken, but if you know Spanish you feel particularly at home. *Going down a category to three stars,* the *Hôtel de Calais* (4 Rue des Capucines) is at the corner of the Place Vendôme and the Rue de la Paix, and has been a favorite of mine these many years. The bigger rooms, with their own baths, are especially comfortable and attractive, and the management is astute and congenial. The *Hôtel Angleterre* is no more English than the Rue Jacob (No. 44) on which it is situated. It is a delightful middle-category, typically Parisian inn; all rooms have bath or shower, and the management is at once pleasant and efficient. The *Métropole-Opéra* (2 Rue de Gramont) has a convenient, near-Opéra location. All rooms have shower or bath and are spiffy-shiny-attractive. On to some *two-star* hotels. The *Scandinavia* (Rue de Tournon) may not sound like it from its name, which connotes functional modern, but it is a handsomely restored old inn, built during the era of Louis XIII when it was known as the Auberge des Scandinaves. It is furnished in period, with many antique pieces. There are but twenty-two rooms, all with bath, and the location is the Left Bank, between Luxembourg and St.-Germain des Près. The *Grand Hôtel de Mont-Blanc* is hardly grand, but it is attractive, and all fifteen of its rooms have bath. The location, 28 Rue de la Huchette, at Place St.-Michel, is a step from Notre Dame. The *Hôtel Brighton* (don't let that English name fool you) is a comfortable, smallish, well-located hotel at 228 Rue de Rivoli; all rooms have bath. The *Hôtel Chambiges* (8 Rue Chambiges, off the Champs Élysées, near the George V) is nicely run and well priced; restaurant on the premises. The *Hôtel de Lys* (25 Rue Serpente) is in the *one-star* category, and in a seventeenth-century Left Bank building. There's no elevator, but all rooms have bath and French Provincial furniture—a good budget buy.

## TO EAT

It is not enough to tell Americans that French cuisine, along with that of China, is the greatest in the world. They've been told that before. I have watched fellow countrymen in restaurants in France and in French restaurants at home. If they have a comfortable familiarity with the cuisine, they enjoy themselves tremendously. If not, watch out: they're on the defensive. I think it is because they have been told the greatest-in-the-world story too many times. They begin to think of themselves as un-pretentious New Worlders who don't know about all those fancy sauces and *galantines* and *chaud-froids* and *soufflés* and what have you. Just a nice meat-and-potatoes dinner, thank you, with dessert, coffee, and maybe a drink beforehand. Well, if the truth be known, the average Frenchman's average dinner is not that elaborate. He may or may not have a drink before dinner, if he is dining or lunching at home. More likely, it will be a glass of wine with his meal. The meal? There are variations, of course. But the mainstay of the French diet is *entrecôte*—steak—*pommes frites* (we call them French fries), a simple green salad, perhaps, fresh fruit, and/or cheese, and coffee. Elaborate restaurant meals are as much of an occasion for most Frenchmen as they are for us.

Now, then, *that* out of the way, what can one look forward to, gastronomically, in Paris? The capital runs a wide gamut as regards restaurant cooking. It has become, in recent years, quite simple to get a less-than-excellent restaurant meal, just as it has in the leading American restaurant cities. And restaurant tabs are no longer inexpensive. Really good meals are more consistently found in the provincial towns and the countryside, where labor is less erratic, clientele less transient, costs of restaurateurs lower, and the upkeep easier. The advantage of Paris is that there are restaurants serving the food specialties of all the provinces.

French food for the newcomer is easily described. Lunch (the Frenchman's principal meal) will start with a soup, while dinner would more usually start with hors d'oeuvres, go on to a main course of a meat (broiled, roasted, or in casserole) or a fish or seafood dish, with a green salad dressed with oil, vinegar, salt, and pepper following; thence cheese selected from a platter of several varieties with bread or crackers; fresh fruit or dessert, and coffee. If the meal is unfestive, one wine will accompany it—generally red if with red meat or poultry, or white if with fish or seafood. The French have far less aversion to the consummation of water than do, say, the British; one may always feel free to request it. French hors d'oeuvres are a special pleasure and are similar to what the Italians call *antipasto*. In France they might include fresh relishes like scallions and radishes, black and green olives, and celery. There might be, as well, eggs mayonnaise, lentils or beans, tiny shrimps, and mussels in a vinaigrette dressing. Other delicious first courses include snails—*escargots*—served piping hot in their shells, with a parsley-butter and garlic sauce; and *pâté* of goose liver (*foiegras*), sometimes flavored with hound-hunted truffles. The French, unlike the Italians, are fond of beef, and prepare it well— steaks, roasts, superb stews—*ragouts* or *daubes*. They are equally adept at veal. The *blanquette de veau* is the veal stew specialty *par excellence*. But they cook the thin *escalopes,* not unlike the

*scallopine* of Italy; as well as chops (*cotelettes*), sweetbreads
(*ris de veau,* and brains (*cervelles*). *Lamb* is another favored
meat dish. *Gigot d'agneau avec flageloets* is a superb dish. The
pork specialties are no less good, from the *charcuterie* (sausage
and specialty pork products) to ham (*jambon*) and more prosaic
roasts. Fish (*poisson*) is masterfully prepared, be it simply broiled
with a squeeze of lemon, or accompanied by an appropriate
sauce. Look for crayfish (*écrevisse*), lobster (*homard*), and
oysters (*huitres*). No people prepare poultry more imaginatively
than the French, particularly chicken (*poulet*) and duck (*canard*).
If you haven't tried frogs' legs (*grenouilles*), you are missing a
treat. Even ordinary vegetables come out well under French
auspices, and not only *petit-pois* (peas). The cheese platter in
French restaurants is worthy of serious attention; sample as you
make the restaurant rounds. You know *camembert* and *brie,*
and *roquefort,* but try *pont l'éveque, chèvre, port salut,* and
any number of others you'll be exposed to. Pastries are available
as restaurant desserts, but you might enjoy them more in midafternoon or midmorning at cafes, with coffee or tea or simply
purchased, by the bag, from bakery shops whose windows tempt.
Hot *soufflés*—chocolate, lemon, vanilla—are delightful restaurant
desserts, and so are *crêpes*—the thin, sweet pancakes the French
excel at. Coffee always follows lunch or dinner; it is served in a
pot, by the cup, and also *filtre* (filter) style, with its individual
little drip apparatus over the cup. Sugar is served with coffee but
not milk or cream—not, at least, after lunch or dinner. With
breakfast the usual hot beverage is *café-au-lait,* a pot of coffee
served with an equal-size jug of hot milk, the idea being that
you mix the two, more or less half and half. Accompanying
the *café-au-lait* with a typical French breakfast is a *petit pain*
(crusty roll) and a *brioche* or a *croissant,* along with butter
and jam. This is the *café-complet* or continental breakfast. Fruit
juice, eggs, or what have you may be ordered additionally, at
least in the better hotels. (If a Frenchman ever has anything
more than *café-complet* it is a single boiled egg, served *à-la-coq*

—in the shell—with salt, but rarely pepper, which must be specially ordered.)

Regional specialties are a glory of French food. Look for *bouillabaise,* the fish stew from Provence; *cassoulet*—a bean and goose-sausage casserole out of Languedoc; *friture de la Loire,* a fried fish dish from the Chateau country; *sole Normande,* the fish specialty of coastal Normandy; *gratin Dauphinois,* the potato extravaganza from the Alps; *quiche Lorraine,* the classic custard tart you already know; the varied dishes with truffled flavorings from gastronomically splendid Perigord.

Meal hours in France are moderately late: lunch from 1:00 P.M. to 2:00 P.M.; dinner from about 8:00 P.M. to 10:00 P.M. *And let me emphasize a final food point:* Ask waiters, captains, *patrons* about their menus, specialties, ways of preparation. It is worth emphasizing how important food is in the French culture. One is not considered pesty by asking questions before ordering. On the contrary, the interest shown is appreciated. So, for that matter, will any comment—and, hopefully, compliment—after finishing the meal.

*About wines:* They are not to be made too big a fuss of. Nor, it would seem, should one slough them off as of no consequence. The French have, after all, put a great deal into their vineyards, and over the centuries the whole world, or at least the whole wet world, has come to regard French wines as the finest extant. On the other hand, one can go too far. There is no need, it seems to me, to carry a chart of the good vintage years in one's pocket —or head, for that matter. Basically, red wines go with meat and poultry; whites with fish and seafood. Rosés go with light meats and seafood both—*if you like* rosés. French reds are of two principal types: Bordeaux (the British call these clarets) and Burgundies. Bordeaux are the lighter-bodied and more versatile of the two, and the more complicated as regards categorization. They break down into the four major areas of the Bordeaux region from which they originated: Graves, St.-Émilion, Médoc, and Pomerol. From each of these areas are the individual brands, or châteaux, so named for the region around the château of its grower and bottler. Red Burgundies are fuller bodied than Bordeaux—good with a roast goose or duck, or a roast of beef. The classification of Burgundies is simpler than that of Bordeaux, and they are not marketed by individual vintners, but rather by groups of growers who collaborate on marketing and shipping— such as Calvet, B & G, Moreau, Jadot, to name a few. There are white Bordeaux (Chateau d'Yquem is tops) and Burgundies (Montrachet is a top one) as well as red. And there are other good French wines too. Vouvray is a famous Loire white. Château Grillet is a good white Rhone. Riesling is the famous white Alsatian wine. Additionally, many restaurants in France serve inexpensive wines that they buy by the barrel and take to the table in carafes; they are the *vin ordinaires* that can be very good and are always inexpensive. A good general rule: Ask the waiter or, in restaurants where there is one, the wine waiter (*sommelier*) for his suggestions. But don't let him do *all* the work. Ask to see the wine list; read it over. You learn a lot from these carefully prepared compilations as you go from restaurant to restaurant. Other French drinks? The cognacs are the best in the world. So are the champagnes. French liqueurs are unsurpassed. Bottled mineral waters—Perrier, Évian—are excellent. Coca-Cola has made inroads in France. Only the beers could stand improvement.

The *de luxe restaurants* of Paris are in themselves reason enough for a visit to this city. At least one per Paris trip is a good rule. Here are some that I like. *Taillevent* (15 Rue Lamennais) occupies a handsome, onetime embassy in the attractive quarter off the Avenue de Friedland, near the Étoile. In a setting of paneled walls and Louis XVI furniture, the ambience is engaging but not gimmicky. Food is taken seriously, and is nowhere better prepared in Paris. Try eggs Benedict as a starter and you may never be happy with them again, at home. Fish are well prepared (a specialty is *Supreme de Turbot*). The *carré d'agneau roti Claude Deligne,* for two, is a masterful lamb specialty.

Taillevent's desserts are renowned, particularly the *soufflés*. And
if wines interest you, ask if you may carry off the wine card;
it lists the vintages of one of the great Paris cellars. *Maxim's*
(3 Rue Royale) deserves commendation for carrying on to beat
the band, despite the burden of a global reputation. The Art
Nouveau look of the place is an inspired foil for the *fin-de-siècle*
service, the dressy and loquacious clientele, and—most important
—the food. It is very good indeed. Consider *quiche Lorraine*
or *crêpes Maxim's* to set the mood, the duck with peaches
specialty—*caneton Nantais aux pêches*—or maybe *cailles de
Bombes au raisins de Muscat;* why not quail for a festive change?
The seafood menu is delicious and extensive. Likewise that of
the sweets. The *Ritz Hotel's Restaurant and Espadon Grill*
are each distinctive-looking, but both with the esteemed Ritz cooking and the masterful Ritz service. In summer, lunch in the
garden is the essence of Paris; try *salade Nicoise* or *Crudités*
as hors d'oeuvres. The menus are classic—an excellent chicken
dish, *poularde de bresse Riviera,* for example; *filet de sole
Joinville, steak Marchand de vin.* And I'll tell you what's delicious: bread-butter pudding. *Lassèrre* (17 Avenue Franklin-
Roosevelt) puts on a great show and puts out a fine meal. The
setting is a sumptuous townhouse. You have a drink in one of
the ground-floor lounges. When your table is ready, poof! You
are escorted upstairs to the dining room whose roof—in summer
at least—slides open to reveal the stars. The food can be anti-
climactic after all this drama. It is still top-drawer, with
*poussin Viroflay* (a chicken preparation) and *rognons aux Xérès*
(kidneys with sherry) among the specialties. The *middle-level*
restaurant group—neither budget nor moneybags—is, of course,
the biggest in Paris. Here are some recommendations: *La
Bourgogne* (6 Avenue Bosquet) obviously specializes in the rich
dishes of Burgundy—and does so to perfection. *Jambon persillé
de Bourgogne* (a ham dish) and *fricassée de petits gris aux
croutons* (snails as you may not have had them) are fine appetizers. The *coq au Chambertin* is chicken at its most sublime.

The *estouffade de boeuf au Pommard aux Fettucines* is beef as you would expect the Burgundians to prepare it. The wines, it should go without saying, are superb. And so are the oversize Burgundy glasses; you may buy them, if you like. *Le Bistrot de Paris* (33 Rue de Lille) is the bourgeois bistro at its smartest, most convivial, and most delicious: no-nonsense stick-to-the-ribs dishes of Burgundy—and does so to perfection. *Jambon persillé casses,* for example. So are the *pâtés.* The *sauté de veau a l'estragon*—sauteed veal with tarragon—is first-rate, and the *boeuf Bourguignon* is superlative. Desserts run to favorites like apple tarte and *mousse au chocolat. Chez Michel* (10 Rue Belzunce in the Tenth Arrondissement, should the taxi driver want to know) is an unpretentious destination when what is desired is an excellent meal, in the company of knowing Parisians with the same aim. The stuffed mussels—*moules farci en cocotte* —are a specialty of merit, and so is the delicious *coq au vin. Côte de veau Florentine*—veal with spinach—is offbeat and excellent. The pastries—especially strawberry tart with whipped cream—have helped make this house's reputation. *La Truffière* (4 Rue Blainville near the Panthéon), as you might perceive from its name, specializes in truffled dishes, and these come mostly from the Périgord—as do this restaurant's owners. The *escargots* stuffed with truffles and ham are a fine opener, as is the more traditional Périgordine specialty, *foie d'oie frais à la gelée*—fresh goose liver in aspic. *Brochette de truffes*—shish kebab with truffles—is a novelty. And in winter, the cassoulet is an ideal choice. The *Hotel Lancaster Restaurant* (7 Rue de Berri) is, to first-timers trying it, a surprise package of great charm, what with its setting in the most delightful of the better, smaller, quieter hotels. The cuisine is classic, well prepared, and beautifully served. There is a good cellar, too. And if it is summer, tables are set in one of the most eye-filling little courtyards in town. The attractively decorated *Cau-Camaou* (14 Rue Pascal) serves what has to be the most imaginative, tasty, and value-packed lunch in Paris. You begin (and if you are not

careful you end) at a buffet heavily laden with dishes in great
variety (I counted—and then sampled—four different kinds of
pâté alone). A hot main dish follows, and desserts are super,
too. (The hot apple pie called *tarte de pommes Catalan* is recommended.) And included are pitchers of as much red and
rosé wine as you would like. *Bas-Bréau* is the inn-restaurant in a
lovely Barbizon, outside of Paris—a perfect lunch destination on
a balmy day; the food is as choice as the eighteenth-century
ambience. *Ferme St.-Simeon,* in the little harbor town of Hon-
fleur, is another perfect country-dining spot. *Ambassade d'Auvergne & du Rouergue* (22 Rue du Grenier Saint-Lazare) is
rather a mouthful, but this is an offbeat restaurant, offering the
specialties of the Auvergne, which are so rarely encountered in
Paris that you see the Parisian customers asking for menu ex-
planations. There is a special *prix-fixe* dinner that is comprised of
specialties. These include *soupe aux choux* (a cabbage *potage*);
*petit sale aux lentilles* (an interesting pork dish); and the difficult-
to-describe but delicious *aligot. L'Alsacienne* (54 Boulevard St.-
Michel) is for the hearty foods of Alsace, most especially the
sauerkraut-sausage favorite that is *choucroute garni.* The *pâté
maison* is good, and so are the desserts. Service is slow, but the
tabs are relatively low. *Au Charbon de Bois* (16 Rue du Dragon,
near St.-Germain des Près) is for grills—steaks and chops, char-
coal-broiled, and very good indeed. *Some good, budget restaurants: Madame Faure* (40 Rue du Mont Thabor), *Panorama* (14
Quai du Louvre), *Le Petit Tonneau* (20 Rue sur Couf, near Les Invalides, *La Rive d'Ott* (38 Avenue de Suffoen, near the Eiffel
Tower), *Café Procope* (13 Rue de l'Ancienne-Comédie in the
St.-Germain des Près area). *Brasserie de l'Île Saint-Louis* (55
Quai de Bourbon), and *La Pergola* (144 Avenue des Champs
Élysées). *Le Pub* (48 Boulevard Haussmann) is a good-to-
know-about restaurant-cafe in the Galeries Lafayette Department
Store—breakfast, snacks, lunch, hot plates, drinks—alcoholic and
otherwise—in an attractive pub setting that includes a counter, if
you're alone or in a hurry. *Angelina,* 226 Rue de Rivoli, is

for afternoon tea *de luxe*. The china is fine Limoges. The waitress
will bring tea or coffee, but another lady—*la patissière*—comes
with trays of irresistible pastry, including those meringue con-
coctions known as Mont-Blanc. And the clientele is authentic
*ancien régime*. To satisfy visitors from across the Channel, *W. H.
Smith & Son,* near the Concorde end of the Rue de Rivoli, have
a tearoom on the upstairs level of the bookshop that is a branch
of their United Kingdom chain. The staff is French, but the
goodies served with tea could not be more authentically British.
And for the hopelessly homesick, there's a counter at the cashier's
desk selling tins of biscuits and jars of jams from the mother
country.

## TO BUY

Perfumes, colognes, soaps, and such remain the best French
bargains and, for that matter, as typically French as any gift
can be. Women's accessories—scarves, bags, gloves, lingerie, shoes,
blouses, hats, costume jewelry, compacts—can be very smart
indeed, although they are not cheap. Men's clothes, in the better
places, are attractive but not inexpensive, and by and large
without the style of those to be obtained in Rome and London.
Ties can be good-looking and are about the same price as those
of the United States or England, but are not cut to tie as well,
and the silk is often quite thin. Housewares—kitchen equipment,
china, gadgets—are sensible buys in this most gastronomic of
capitals. Antiques can be superb, for Paris remains one of the
great world markets for them. And last, foods and wines. In no
city are they more temptingly merchandised. What follows is a
selective group of suggestions, by category.

Of the **department stores,** *Galeries Lafayette,* on Boulevard
Haussmann, is my favorite. It occupies three buildings, one a
separate—and very good—men's store. I purchased a suede jacket
there almost a decade ago and it has worn beautifully. Pick up a

leaflet at the main-floor information desk in the main building; it will tell you where to buy what. The gift shop upstairs—La Maitresse—is a requisite for the classic white-with-orange-stripe Auteuil china and other wares; there's a super Monoprix supermarket on the premises at which you may obtain envelopes of French powdered soups; they're lightweight, cheap, and delicious, for yourself or as gifts. Housewares is another excellent department. So is children's clothing. Women's clothing is found in a number of locales, including "Club 20 Ans"—twenty-five boutiques of well-known designers' clothes, including Ted Lapidus, Daniel Hechter, and Mic-Mac. *Monoprix* and *Prisunic* are nationwide cheapie chains, often interesting to case. The Prisunic at 60 Avenue des Champs Élysées had just what I needed a trip or two back. It started to pour and I was without a raincoat; I found one for about fifteen dollars, that I wore for the rest of my rainy stay— and am still wearing. **Perfume:** *Catherine* (6 Rue de Castiglione): Petite, attractive Madame Catherine knows her scents, stocks only those from among the leading makes that she has confidence in (no gimmicky, unheard-of labels, in other words), publishes an annual catalog so that you may re-order by mail, carries beaded evening bags, compacts, and the like that you won't see coming and going, all over town. And don't worry about buying more perfume, cologne, and soap than you can carry; Catherine will give you one of her own pale-gray flight bags. Now, how about *that* for a status symbol? *Guerlain* (Place Vendôme, Avenue des Champs Élysées and Avenue de Passy.) The clever Guerlian folks see to it that there's nowhere else in town that you can buy their fragrances, soaps, talc, or cosmetics, except in their very own trio of shops. So if you hanker after Shalimar, Chant d'Arôme, or Sapoceti soap, this is where you're going to buy it. **Food** is at its fanciest at *Fauchon,* 26 Place de la Madeleine—*pâtés,* olives, mustards, *cornichon* pickles, *flageolet* beans, wines, tinned cookies, crackers, candies, and—worth knowing about—a cafe that vends delicious ice cream cones, among other things. *Hédiard,* a Place de la Madeleine neighbor of Fauchon, is a smaller and more old-fashioned grocery store; it gift-wraps beautifully. *Caviar Kaspia* and *Maison de la Truffe* (the former for caviar, the latter for truffles and other delicacies) are additional Place de la Madeleine sources. **Children's clothes and toys:** The *Baby Dior* shop at the Dior Boutique, 30 Avenue Montaigne, is expensive and as *haute* kids' couture as you are likely to want to get. *Jones*—yes, just plain Jones—at 39 Avenue Victor Hugo is another smart kids' toggery. *Au Nain Bleu,* 406 Avenue Faubourg St.-Honoré, is expensive but the biggest and oldest toy shop in town. **Crystal:** *Baccarat* (30 bis Rue de Paradis) sells its own classic designs more cheaply than in the United States, but they are hardly Mono-prix. *Lalique* is globally noted for its distinctive pieces, amusingly reminiscent of the thirties. **Silver:** *Christophle* (12 Rue Royale, 34 Boulevard des Italiens, and 95 Rue de Passy) is the most esteemed and renowned of French silversmiths. And prices are not all that steep. **Porcelain, ceramics:** *Talma* (Rue des Saints-Pères) specializes in white porcelain of all kinds, particularly Limoges. *Le Petit Depot* (2, Rue de Provence) is for seconds of porcelain and china as well as crystal. Often you can't even tell. **Kitchen- and tableware:** *Verrerie des Halles* (15 Rue du Louvre)—soup tureens (which the French are very big on) and *bistrot*-style wine glasses. *Delcherein* is an institution that was for long in the Old Halles area. The lure is kitchenware—copper pots and pans, casseroles, and other uniquely French cooking implements; pack-ing and shipping. **Luggage:** *Morabito* (1 Place Vendôme)—de luxe, beautifully designed and manufactured. *Peau de Porc* (67 Rue du Faubourg St.-Honoré)—pigskin in every imaginable mani-festation, and very smart. *Aux États-Unis* (229 Rue St.-Honoré) —American in name only; the luggage selection is first-rate, and a specialty is dog collars as well as dog bowls with French legends; these last for your Fido only *s'il comprend le français*. **Women's handbags:** *Franck et Fils,* 80 Rue de Passy—a huge and hand-some selection. *Hermès* (24 Rue du Faubourg St.-Honoré)—the estimable Paris institution that is as good for scarves and belts and gloves and accessories as for bags. **Women's shoes:** *Adige* (53

Avenue Victor Hugo, 27 Rue Cambon and 6 Rue Royale)—exact copies of famous couture design, at about a third less than original price. *Christian Dior* (32 Avenue Montaigne, 15 Rue François Ier)—high style, of course, and expensive; made to measure if you like. *Charles Jourdan* (5 Boulevard de la Madeleine, 86 Champs Élysées, other locations)—moderate-priced, up-to-the-minute, with a Fifth Avenue branch in New York. *Roger Vivier* (24 Rue François Ier, 11 Rue du Faubourg St.-Honoré)— the most famous name in French shoes; somewhat cheaper than at Saks Fifth Avenue in New York. **Jewelry:** *Cartier, Van Cleef and Arpels,* of course. Consider also *Au Vieux Cadeau* (59 Rue Bonaparte)—old jewelry and watches dating from the Renaissance; *Jane Beaucaire* (29 Rue Marboeuf)—jewelry used by couturiers in their collections and sold at half price. *H. Stern* (3 Rue de Castiglione)—the Paris outpost of the justifiably famed Rio de Janeiro jeweler, featuring gems from Brazil (amethysts, tourmalines, topazes) splendidly embedded in Paris-designed settings. **Men's and women's gloves:** Department stores and boutiques sell gloves, but here are a couple of glove shops, in addition, for French gloves (invariably very well made) that remain good buys. *Roger Faré* (31 Rue Tronchet) has been making gloves for the hands of royalty as well as for commoners these many years. *Gants Perrin* (22 Rue Royale) is equally renowned. **Stationery:** *Armorial* (98 Rue du Faubourg St.-Honoré, opposite Élysée Palace) is where you go if you're loaded, and you want to knock 'em dead back home with engraved writing paper, calling cards—or invitations to your wedding. **Chinese clothes and doodads:** *Compagnie Française de l'Orient et de la Chine* (24 Rue St.-Roch, 167 Boulevard St.-Germain) was the first firm in the West to import the unisex blue cotton workers' suits—and all manner of other objects—from mainland China. Not quite as browseworthy as it was before these goods were allowed into the United States, but still interesting. **Men's clothing:** *Roger & Gallet,* the perfume, cologne, and soap people, have a separate men's department in their boutique at 62 Rue du Faubourg St.-Honoré that I consider the fairest-priced, most courteously staffed, and most interestingly stocked of all fancy men's boutiques in town. (Besides the clothes and accessories, note the suede flight bags.) *Dorian Gray* (36 Avenue George V) has smart, quality clothes. *Renoma,* 129 bis Rue de la Pompe, has audacious clothes with lots of color. *St.-Germain des Près* (37 Rue du Four) with a Madison Avenue branch in New York—stylishly avant-garde. *McDouglas* (23 Rue St. Sulpice, 155 Faubourg St.-Honoré)— high-style suede and leather jackets, coats, trousers, other handsome accessories. *Ted Lapidus* (1 Place St.-Germain des Près, 6 Place Victor Hugo, other locations)—inventive, amusing, sometimes way out; ties are a good buy. **Women's clothes:** *Amie* (6 Rue Pierre Charon)—superstylish sportswear. *Castillo* (76 Rue du Faubourg St.-Honoré)—clothes that are at once contemporary and subdued; moderate to expensive. *Cynthia* (44 Rue du Passy) —a recognized leader. *Loris Azzaro* (65 Rue du Faubourg St.-Honoré)—way, way out, attractive. *Korrigan* (14 Avenue Victor Hugo, 11 Rue Faubourg St.-Honoré, and other locations)— noted for knitwear. **Old etchings and prints:** *Sartoni and Gervaux* (Rue de Seine) and *F. Girard,* on the same street, are both good sources. **Books:** *W. H. Smith & Son* on the Rue de Rivoli; and *Brentano's* on the Avenue de l'Opéra, are the leading English-language bookstores. Check the *Hachette* and *Larousse* stores all around town, as well, and of course the *bouquinistes,* at their Seine-side stalls, selling used books, prints, posters, and elderly— if not antique—postcards that make amusing souvenirs and gifts. **Antiques:** *Swiss Village* (Avenue de Suffren at Avenue de la Motte-Piqué, near the Eiffel Tower), an antiques shopping center, with shops of varying quality and price-levels. Good dealers include *Michel Prost* for seventeenth- and eighteenth-century provincial furniture, and *Michel d'Istra*—excellent Spanish, French, and Italian furniture, religious statues, fragments. *Marche aux Puces* (Flea Market) opens Saturday, Sunday, and Monday each week, from 9:00 A.M. to 6:00 P.M. It's a long Métro ride; get off at Porte de Clignancourt, and allow a good half day, as the

market is quite sprawling, there being some three thousand
dealers. Much of the stuff is elderly rather than antique, or just
plain used, for that matter. You must search diligently for anything of value: even then, there are no really fine antiques. *Hotel
Drouot* (6 Rue Rossini) is Paris's famous and enormous auction
house; excellent buys are possible; sales Monday through Friday,
2:00 P.M. to 6:00 P.M., but you may inspect merchandise daily
from 10:00 A.M. to 11:00 A.M. *Jean Rouge* (265 Rue St.-Honoré)
sells fine furniture and objects, mostly French eighteenth-century.
*Jacques Kugel* (269 Rue St.-Honoré) is a major dealer, with large
stocks of furniture and other objects. Left Bank streets with concentrations of antiques shops include Rue du Bac, Rue Bonaparte,
Rue des Saints-Pères, and Rue de la Boettie (this last for tapestries, the others for furniture and other objects).

TO NOTE

**Access:** The international airline that does *not* fly to Paris is
the exception to the rule. There is transatlantic service by Air
France, as well as TWA and Pan Am. Intra-European service is
extensive. Air France links Paris with virtually every country of
the Continent, and conversely those nations' carriers link their
capitals with Paris. There is frequent service, as well, between
Paris and Africa, Asia, and other distant parts. Air Inter is
France's domestic carrier. Orly International Airport is used for
intercontinental flights; it is about eleven miles from Paris. There
are cheap airport buses between Orly and the Aérogare, on the Left
Bank, near Les Invalides. But taxis are only moderately expensive,
and recommended. Le Bourget is used for many intra-European
flights; it is a few miles closer to town than Orly. (A third Paris
airport—Roissy-en-France—is abuilding.) There are airport departure taxis; they vary, according to destination. As for trains,
Paris is Europe's be-all, end-all rail terminus. The celebrated expresses going in every direction either begin, terminate, or pass

through one of Paris's great railway stations—Gare du Nord, Gare de l'Est, Gare St.-Lazare, Gare de Lyon, or Gare Austerlitz. You may go by train from Paris north to the Scottish Highlands or Finnish Lapland; south to France's own Riviera (taking a crack train like the *Mistral*); southwest all the way to Lisbon; and easterly to Istanbul, Eastern European capitals, or Moscow. French National Railroads (SNCF—Société National Chemins de Fer Français) is one of the world's best—excellently operated, and with some superb trains; consider it for excursions out of Paris to anywhere in France you would like to visit; you'll be surprised at the number of places you can cover in a day, returning to your Paris hotel the same evening. The major European international bus services serve Paris, and there are modern highways connecting the capital with every corner of France and the Continent. Within Paris, the taxi is the most used means of conveyance among foreign visitors. Most drivers are nice. Many have good ears for foreign-accented French. But if you don't think you can pronounce your destination well enough to be comprehended, simply write it out for the driver. Most, but not all, Paris cabs are metered. Often unmetered ones will congregate around big hotels and other tourist-frequented places. At such locales, look for a meter; if there is none, settle on a fee before entering. Note, too, that after 11:00 P.M., rates increase by 50 percent. In all the years I have been visiting Paris I have not figured out the complex bus system; however, I highly recommend the Métro. Maps of this super subway system are easily obtained. Get hold of one and keep it with you; you'll find the Métro easy to use, cheap, quick, and convenient. There are about fifteen different routes, each distinguished by its two terminus stations. If you want to go, for example, from the Place de la Concorde to the Place de l'Étoile, you enter the Concorde station and buy a ticket specifying (a) the class—first or second (the difference in both cost and comfort is minimal), and (b) the station at which you will exit—in your case, Étoile. Having studied your pocket map, or the wall map of the system on display in every station, you know that you are to proceed to the platform of the Neuilly-Vincennes line; you will have noted on your map that your stop —Étoile—is en route to the Neuilly end of the line, so you look for the track marked *"Direction Neuilly,"* board the appropriate train, and exit at your station. All Métro cars are equipped with easy-to-read maps of the route they travel, and stations are well marked. The example I have given above is for a direct trip. Others may be more complicated, involving a change of trains, or transfer. The French word you want here is *"Correspondance";* ask the ticket agent for directions when you buy your ticket. If your Paris visit will be at all lengthy, buy a copy of the little red book known as the Guide Taride (*geed-tah-reed*); it has Métro and bus-route maps, and an index of streets with nearest Métro stations plus a separate section that the editors immodestly, albeit accurately, entitle *"Renseignements Indispensables"*—Indispensable Information—purchasable at news kiosks or bookshops in Paris, and a selected few in the United States, including Librairie Française at Rockefeller Center, New York. For indoctrination purposes one has a wide choice of sightseeing tours, via the buses of several companies, and boats that ply the Seine (the *Bateaux-Mouches* and the competing *Védettes Pont-Neuf* and *Védettes Paris-Tour Eiffel*). There is also a service called "Meet the French" that employs English-speaking university students who drive from one to four customers about, in their own cars, to wherever the customers want to go, day or evening, city or country, or combinations thereof. The trick is in getting a bright, reasonably put-together kid as your guide-chauffeur; some are super, some are not; address: 39 Rue Godot-de-Mauroy, Paris 9, or through hotel concierges, or French Line, the U.S. representatives. Remaining are one's own *deux pieds*—use them as frequently as possible, in this greatest of walking cities. **Climate** is not necessarily what one is fondest of in Paris, particularly in summer, when it can be gray-nasty-rainy or sweltering dripping-humid, with relatively little air conditioning to compensate. On the other hand, I have had glorious, crystal-clear sunny days in midwinter, and there is no denying that spring in Paris, if one is lucky, can be sublime; autumn likewise. Winter (late November through March) averages in the thirties and low forties, with January and February the coldest months. Spring (April and May) is likely to be in the fifties. Summer (June through early September) averages in the sixties, with July and August the hottest months, averaging in the mid-seventies, but capable of being much hotter. Fall (late September through October) is apt to be fiftyish. Rain is more commonplace throughout the year than you might imagine. **Clothes:** Like every major world city, Paris is surprised at nothing with respect to personal adornment. It runs a wide, wide gamut. The Left Bank cafes and cheaper restaurants are as way out as one likes. The smarter places, on both banks, regard jacket and tie as essential in the evening, many being square enough to still prefer a dark suit to a sports jacket or blazer and slacks; female attire is correspondingly dressy. High-style in Paris is generally restricted to the upper-middle and upper classes. Your ordinary gal or guy in the street is not nearly as interested in clothes as her or his Rome or London counterparts. Food—which runs high—comes first in French budgets, and not all that much is left for clothes, which also run high. **Language:** It is true that many Parisians are impatient with the less-than-perfect French spoken by foreign visitors. But it is increasingly true that these same Parisians, as they themselves study foreign languages more than they used to, realize that speaking a strange tongue is no easy matter. There is, as a consequence, more tolerance with your pronunciation of, say, the earlier-mentioned Métro station, Neuilly, than there was a decade back. What is important in Franco-foreign relationships are the polite niceties of conversation. To say simply "Thank you" to a lady is enough in English. In French, it is not. One says, *"Merci, madame"* or *"Merci, mademoiselle."* And, with a man, *"Merci, monsieur."* It is the same with a *bonjour,* or an *au revoir;* you tack on *madame, mademoiselle,* or *monsieur*—no matter how impersonal or brief the exchange has been, and no matter the occupation or station in life of the person with whom you are speaking. It helps. Honest. And one more point: By no means everyone in Paris speaks even *un petit peu d'Anglais.* Your French will be very useful with this majority; don't be bashful about using it. **Local literature:** One of the nicest things about a visit to Paris is the International Edition of the New York *Herald Tribune,* even though there has not been a New York edition of that estimable newspaper in many years. And the Paris edition's owners (the New York *Times* and the Washington *Post*) have wisely kept the great *Trib* format. Air mail editions of the London papers are everywhere to be purchased. And so are quantities of local guides and picture books of varying quality. Newsstands, and concierges in some hotels carry *Cette Semaine* or *Allo Paris,* weekly what's-on summaries —all in French but easily understood regardless of one's fluency in that language. And if you know some French, for heaven's sake, pick up the Paris papers—*Le Monde, Le Figaro,* and *Le Canard Enchainé,* of course, but the more popular papers, too. Reading them is excellent practice, and their entertainment pages are useful. The *Life*-style picture magazine, *Paris-Match,* is good reading, and so are the ravishingly beautiful magazines devoted to the arts such as *Conaissance des Arts* and *Plaisir de France.* **Currency:** The franc is divided into one hundred centimes. *Check on current regulations regarding discounts on appreciable-size purchases if made with travelers checks.* **Tipping:** Hotels and most restaurants and cafes add a service charge to bills—usually 15 percent in restaurants and cafes. You may—but only if you want, and naturally only if the service has been good—add 5 percent additional to this. Bills with service added say *"Service compris";* if they say *"Service* non-*compris,"* the service is not added. If they say neither, inquire before tipping. In hotels, tip bellhops a franc per bag, doormen who get cabs half a franc to a franc; concierges who have rendered special services an average of a couple of francs per day; chambermaids a quarter franc to a half franc per day, if the room has been nicely taken care of; half a franc to a franc to the room-service waiter for breakfast or whatever; a franc or two to the wine waiter—or sommelier—if you've ordered your restaurant bottle through him; half a franc to the ubiquitous washroom attendant, and the same for theater usherettes, irrespective of the cost of the theater program—usually purchased from someone other than the usherette who seats you. (The program seller gets only the program price—no tip.) Tip taxi drivers, barbers, and beauticians 15 percent. Insist on small change whenever you change money: you need it at all times. **Business hours:** Most shops are open Monday through Friday from 9:00 A.M. to about noon, and from about 2:00 P.M. until about 6:00 P.M.—sometimes half-past six. Generally, they close Saturdays, at least if they are among the better shops selling the sort of things of interest to visitors. Department stores have different hours: They're open Tuesday through Saturday, except in the summer, when they have the good business sense to be open Monday as well as Saturday; they also have the good business sense not to close for lunch. Barbers and beauty salons close Monday the year round to compensate for remaining open Saturday. **Further information:** French Government Tourist Office, 610 Fifth Avenue, New York; 111 North Wabash Avenue, Chicago; 9418 Wilshire Boulevard, Beverly Hills; 323 Geary Street, San Francisco; 1170 Drummond Street, Montreal. Commissariat Général au Tourisme, 8 Avenue de l'Opéra, and—for tourist information—127 Avenue des Champs Élysées, Paris, France; Comité de Tourisme de Paris, 7 Rue Balzac, Paris, France. At any of the foregoing addresses, you may pick up the current edition of the free map of Paris that the Commissariat Général au Tourisme has published these many years. It is a work of genius, the clearest, easiest-to-read map of any major world city that I know. And published on its reverse are maps of the Paris Métro and bus systems.

# Reykjavik

A sophisticated Scandinavian capital on an island just below the Arctic Circle, and but two hundred miles from Greenland? Of course I'm not kidding. That's Reykjavik. And there's nothing new about it, as relatively unknown as it remains to so many otherwise experienced globetrotters. A Norwegian tourist by the name of Ingolfur Arnarson, though not the first to explore Iceland (a band of Irish monks are believed to have had that distinction) was the first to settle there, in what is now Reykjavik. That was some time back—in the late ninth century. Other Norse settlers, unhappy with their oppressive king back in the old country, followed, as did some Scots and Irishmen.

They lost little time in organizing themselves—and well. In 930, in an alfresco assembly at a place called Thingvellir, not far from Reykjavik (and a popular visitor destination to this day), they sent representatives to a legislative body they named the Althing. It has been sitting for all but forty-three of the intervening years (indoors, to be sure, a good bit of this time) and celebrated its thousandth anniversary in 1930.

**Grandaddy of parliaments:** At the time, of course, the Icelanders did not know they were creating what is now the world's oldest parliament. Less than a century after the Althing was formed, Christianity was introduced, gradually replacing the old Norse obeisance to such mythological Viking gods as Odin and

Thor. All this while Icelandic authors were producing a great body of writing. It is surely a fact worth pondering that virtually no medieval literature emanated from Norway, Sweden, or Denmark. It came, instead, from Scandinavia's mid-Atlantic outpost of Iceland. Old Norse literature, as the scholars term it, had its zenith in the early eleventh century—about when Christianity was introduced—and remained at a high level for a century and a half. Best known and, say the experts, most readable of these works are the Sagas, which chronicled the adventures of the warrior chiefs of the time, both Icelandic and foreign. But if the Sagas were readable, the Eddas—poems of the period—were complex. Still more Icelandic works of consequence were written through the twelfth century, the best by the memorably named Snorri Sturluson, who was a chieftain/politician/historian as well. His work was among the last of a period that scholars concede developed a conscious, clear prose style earlier than any other modern European literature, the Gaelic excepted.

**Norway-dominated Iceland and later Danish rule:** That very same Snorri Sturluson attempted to bring Iceland under the aegis of Norway, and in the mid-thirteenth century this came about. A century or so later, both Norway and Iceland were taken over by the Danes, during which time both the printing press (1528) and Lutheranism (1539) were to make their first appearances on the island. Although Norway loosed its bonds with Denmark, Iceland was to stay Danish-governed for half a millennium. It became nominally independent in 1918, but the Danish king ruled also—from Copenhagen, of course—as the King of Iceland, with foreign affairs, still Danish-controlled. World War II was to change this. When the Nazis invaded Denmark in 1940, the Icelandic Althing took over the Crown's functions and the control of foreign affairs. Washington and London formally recognized Reykjavik, and the former (1940) followed by the latter (1941) sent forces to defend the island from the Nazis. Before the war was even over—in 1944—the Icelanders had conducted a referendum that resulted in their terminating the union with Denmark. On

June 17, 1944, the Kingdom of Iceland became the Republic of Iceland. The first President moved into the white frame mansion outside of Reykjavik that had long been the home of the Danish governor. Probably no other dependent territory has ever made a smoother transition to complete sovereignty.

**The young republic:** At war's end, Iceland plunged right into participation in international affairs. Though without an army (as it still is), it joined the North Atlantic Treaty Organization, and in lieu of troop commitments its contribution was permission for NATO, through the United States, to man an air base at Keflavik, outside of the capital. The Icelanders came, by and large, to dislike the base, not for political or military reasons necessarily, but primarily because the presence of well-paid young men in a country so small constituted a threat to the maintenance of the distinctive Icelandic culture. To prevent Yanks with paychecks to spend from taking over the supply of young Icelandic womanhood, it became necessary to largely restrict them to the base, with the result that Keflavik became an officially designated "hardship" post (with a bonus added to regular salaries, and one-year duty maximum for single men). By the time of the 1971 Icelandic elections, with East-West cold war antagonisms happily subsiding (it would be unfair to term the 1972 Reykjavik-based world championship chess match between the USSR's Boris Spassky, and the USA's Bobby Fischer a cold war manifestation, although the going was at times rough), the left-wing Progressive party came out victors, with a consequence the government announcement—later withdrawn during a visit of U. S. Secretary of State William P. Rogers—that the NATO base at Keflavik would be gradually dismantled over a four-year period, even though Iceland would continue its NATO affiliation.

Simultaneously, the doughty Icelanders made it known that they would extend fishing limits from twelve miles offshore to fifty. (They had, earlier, won a "codfish war" with Britain, extending the five-mile limit to twelve.) The new fifty-mile limit was considered necessary to protect the fish and fish-related industries that constitute a whopping 90 percent of Icelandic exports. After all, not even the world's most literate country—there is nary an Icelander who doesn't read or write in this land of the ancient Sagas and Eddas—can go without eating. And Icelanders, with so much of their volcanic-origin island a moonscape kind of unfarmable wasteland, must catch and sell an awful lot of fish.

TO SEE

**Lay of the land:** When you consider that the population of the entire Republic of Iceland is little more than two hundred thousand—the size of, say, Syracuse, New York—it should not be surprising that the capital is in proportion. Some eighty thousand Icelanders call Reykjavik home. There are, to be sure, many smaller seats of government on the planet. Still, Reykjavik is small, knows and accepts the fact, and its architects wisely build everything to scale. Downtown is set against a pretty boat- and bird-dotted *harbor* (it is pleasant to watch the swans, geese, ducks, and Arctic terns swim about its waters). Just a couple of blocks inland is the main street, *Austurstroeti,* with shops, banks, office buildings, and the like. The little square known as *Austurvöllur* skirts the similarly named thoroughfare, and is perhaps the most important bit of territory in the city. Fronting it is the current home of the *Althing,* small but dignified, and compared to the Althing's advanced age (it turned 1000 in 1930), brand new, having gone up only in 1881. If it's not in session, look for some official or other to have a peek; there are two chambers. The Althing's next-door neighbor is the *Lutheran Cathedral,* or Domkirkjan, a few decades older than the Althing, and with more charm, perhaps, than beauty. The elderly *Borg Hotel,* my Reykjavik home on my first visit a couple of decades back, is also on the main square. Nearby and an agreeable stroll away are other downtown landmarks, including the *National Theater* and its next-door neighbor, the *National Library;* the *Government*

*Office Building* on Laekjartorg Square; and the modern *University of Reykjavik* and its next-door neighbor, the *National Museum*, which front the capital's surprisingly central lake. The museum is worth some time, embracing as it does an art gallery largely devoted to Icelandic artists, a well-done historical section, and still another area devoted to natural history, including Iceland's own. Two other museums of interest: *Arbaer*, a collection of venerable—and typical—old houses transported from around the country and furnished in period style, and the *City Museum*, depicting the history of the capital.

Beyond the central downtown area, one does well to have a look at *Sundlaug Vesturbaejar*, one of the new outdoor swimming pools that are heated from the hot springs of which Iceland has more than its share. (The springs are used to heat buildings as well as swimming pools, throughout the country.) If you can get a boat to take you out, have a look at *Vilbey Island*, just off the coast. The eighteenth-century house and adjacent chapel, which had been home to the Danish governors, have been well preserved. *Bessastaoir*, on a scenic peninsula about ten miles south of Reykjavik, was the later home of the Danish governors, and is now the President's official residence.

**Excursions:** Iceland is some three hundred miles wide by as much as nearly two hundred miles north to south, so that you can't take it in as effortlessly as you might imagine. Still, it is small and unusual enough to inspect at least partially, while you are in Reykjavik. I would include as requisites the following: The *Great Geysir* is the spouting hot spring that gave its name to all such phenomena. If it's not performing, there are others in the area to make a visit worthwhile. The splendid waterfall known as *Gullfoss* is not far from the Great Geysir. Some fifty yards high, and in a still completely natural setting, it is surely one of the most beautiful in the world. Nothing like Niagara or Victoria or Iguassu in size, of course, but not to be missed if one is in Iceland.

*Skalholt* has historic prominence (the first bishopric was established there about a millennium ago) and is now the site of what is probably the handsomest contemporary church in Iceland. *Thingvellir,* site of the first Parliament, which I describe earlier in this chapter, is now little more than a natural site, but the guides usually on hand in summer can describe things as they are believed to have been in the old days. The *Whaling Station* at Hvalfjorour is fascinating. Whales caught between Iceland and Greenland are cut up and processed there. The *Westmann Islands,* believed to have been named for the "west men"—Irish slaves who fled their Norse masters on Iceland proper (the "mainland") are a half-hour's flight from the capital. Only *Heimaey,* the principal island, is inhabited. There's a simple hotel in the neat little town on the island, beyond which—on steep cliffs—live a colony of those remarkable-looking, great-beaked, primary-colored birds called puffins. The locals like to collect their eggs. It is a rather precarious business, involving dangling from long ropes; I have watched, without participating. You may make arrangements to do either or both. I have saved for last Iceland's No. 2 city, *Akureyri.* It's just below the Arctic Circle on its own idyllic fjord, with a snow-capped mountain for a backdrop, a fine little hotel-restaurant (the *Kea*), and an ambience of extraordinary charm and beauty, the likes of which you'll not experience anywhere this side of Norway. And I should add, also, that if you allow yourself enough time you may golf, hunt, ride Icelandic ponies, fish for Icelandic salmon, and of course swim (swimming in heated pools is the Icelandic national sport) during your Icelandic sojourn. And because there is always a wind (Iceland is distinguished by two natural phenomena that take getting used to: a constant wind and a virtual lack of trees), gliding is a popular pastime. And if I went up with a glider pilot in the second seat of the two-seat craft, so can you! And bear in mind: there are inexpensive air excursions to Iceland's neighbor island—Danish-governed Greenland.

## TO STAY

Reykjavik's leading hotels are indeed leaders—modern, attractive, with a wide range of facilities and services and professionally staffed, with good service. One, called the *Loftleider,* is named for Loftleider Icelandic Airlines, its owner, and adjoins the local airport, which is but a hop and skip from downtown. It's very Scandinavian Modern with indoor swimming pool, first-class restaurant, and bar-lounges. It's big competitor is the *Saga,* in the Hagatorag Square section west of downtown; ninety-eight attractive rooms with bath, a pair of restaurants, cocktail lounges, and in the same building, should you want a good book to read, is the American Library, operated by the U. S. Information Service. (Don't take me too seriously in that regard; these libraries our government runs abroad are for the locals, not us. And when it comes to books, Icelanders read more per capita than any other people in the world—mostly, of course, in winter, when there's not a good deal of daylight.) Also in the top league is the capacious, modern, and full-facility *Esja* Hotel. Though no longer new, the *Hotel Borg,* sharing Austurvöllur Square with the Althing and the cathedral, remains attractive, atmospheric, and of course central, and about half of its rooms have baths. The modern *Holt* is reasonable, central, and with a good restaurant.

## TO EAT (AND DRINK)

Given its Scandinavian profile, it should follow—and does—that the Icelandic cuisine is Scandinavian. Despite some five centuries of association with Denmark, though, it is not as good as Denmark's. I would rate it closer to that of the Scandinavian nation whose people first settled it—Norway. There is considerable fish, frequently steamed, considerable lamb, and considerable boiled potatoes. One must not, of course, be under the impression that such is standard fare in the better places. They are adept at steaks and at tasty ways of preparing the local seafood and fish. Breads are good; as elsewhere in Scandinavia, the dark varieties are the best. Open-face sandwiches or smørrebrød, out of Denmark originally, are tasty. And there's *skyr,* a form of yogurt usually served with sugar and cream. Table settings— again the Danish influence is at work here—are frequently handsome and imaginative. Mealtimes are earlier than in most of continental Europe—lunch from noon to one, dinner between seven and eight, to give you an idea. Only the very top hotel dining rooms and cocktail lounges, and the leading restaurants, are licensed to sell anything containing alcohol, and then only between noon and 2:30 P.M., and from 7 P.M. until closing time—which is usually 11:30 P.M. And (shades of another capital, India's New Delhi) Wednesday is a semidry day, with restaurants and hotels serving only wine and beer. The national beverage is *brennivin,* an Icelandic variation of the aquavit so beloved of continental Scandinavians. (It might be mentioned here that despite these government restrictions on public drinking, Iceland continues to have an alcohol problem of some magnitude. Living on an isolated island in the North Atlantic, particularly through the long dark winters that typify Iceland, obviously takes its toll. The visitor must, therefore, be prepared to come upon more than the usual number of drunks, of an evening, in public places, or on the streets, for that matter. It is my experience that they are invariably good-natured.)

The handsomest and most perfectly situated restaurant in town is the *Grillroom of the Hotel Saga.* It's a capacious chamber on the roof of the hotel, and the panoramas are all that restaurant panoramas should be. The continental-style cuisine is delicious and artfully served; and there's dancing. Also very good indeed is the *Garden Restaurant of the Loftleider Hotel*—stylish

Scandinavian Modern appointments, a varied menu of local and international dishes, first-class service, entertainment, and dancing. The rooftop *Grillroom of the Hotel Esja* is another favorite. Of the independent restaurants one is obligatory for either lunch or dinner (when there's dancing). It is *Naust,* with a hearty, hefty nautical décor, a menu with Icelandic specialties, and the more familiar steaks as well. Good downtown coffee stops are the *Borg Hotel* (particularly in the morning if you'd like to sip yours with the local gentry), and the *Mokka-Espresso cafes.*

### TO WATCH

Plays in Icelandic are not of much interest to foreigners—they are the principal fare of the *National Theater.* But there are symphony and other concerts at the *University Concert Hall,* and a number of *movie houses.*

### TO BUY

As in so many other areas, Iceland's Scandinavian culture manifests itself in the area of handicrafts. Especially good buys are wool products—hand-knitted ski sweaters with motifs similar to those Norway is noted for; knitted scarves and caps. Sheepskin, calfskin, and ponyskin rugs are well priced. There is some production of silver and ceramics, with the latter often pleasing. *Icelandic Handicraft* at Laufasvegur 2, downtown, has a wide selection, as does the shop operated by the *Iceland Tourist Bureau,* Laekjargata 3. There is a duty-free shop at *Keflavik Airport* that sells the usual liquor, French perfume, Swiss watches, and Japanese cameras; *Icemart,* also at Keflavik Airport, sells Icelandic knitwear and other specialties; one that I warn you to keep your distance from is something called Icelandic caviar.

TO NOTE

**Access:** Icelandic Airlines has daily bargain-rate pure-jet service to Reykjavik from New York, with the planes continuing, after a stop, across the Atlantic to Luxembourg. Passengers with New York–Luxembourg tickets may buy special layover tour packages of Iceland, or even without these packages make a layover stop on their own before continuing to Europe. Similar layover privileges are, of course, allowed on the westbound flights from Luxembourg to New York. **Getting about:** There are no railroads but Icelandair, another airline, flies to points throughout the country. There are roads, as well, with regular bus services. Self-drive cars are for hire in Reykjavik. Reykjavik has a modern bus system, and of course taxis. **Climate:** Not as cold—or icy —as you may think. The best season, not unsurprisingly, is summer, meaning June, July and August, when the thermometer goes as high as the mid- or upper fifties. Spring (May) and autumn (September) can be as warm as the low fifties. The rest of the year is mostly winter, with temperatures hovering between the mid-to-upper twenties and the mid-to-upper thirties. It's the Gulf Stream that makes the climate so moderate. Bear in mind that the midnight sun months are June and July, and that one sees the Aurora Borealis, or Northern Lights, in late August. **Clothes:** Dress in Reykjavik as you would in any American or European city—informally for daytime sightseeing, jacket and tie in the evening. The attractive Icelandic women are as clothes-savvy as their counterparts in both America and the European Continent. The men tend to dress conservatively. **Currency:** The krona, or crown (plural: kronur). There are one hundred aurar to a krona. **Tipping:** Steep service charges (combined with taxes) are added to restaurant and hotel bills—between 20 and 25 percent, so that no additional tips are expected in this refreshingly un-tip-happy land. You may tip a bellhop or baggage porter the equivalent in kronur of a quarter, if you like, but as for taxi drivers, barbers, hairdressers, hatcheck girls—none expect tips. **Business hours:** Shops are generally open from 9:00 A.M. to 6:00 P.M., and on Fridays till 7:00 P.M. Most close on Saturday at noon (in summer) or 1:00 P.M., and many close an hour for lunch on weekdays. **Language:** Icelandic is the national language, and a most interesting one. It is essentially the tongue of the ancient Norsemen who settled Iceland, and has changed virtually not at all for some eight centuries; Icelanders can read their ancient Sagas without any difficulty. But if they want to converse with Norwegians or Danes they must learn their languages—or the *lingua franca* that is English. English is the No. 2 language of the country; all students study it in school, and virtually everyone—particularly in Reykjavik—speaks it well. **Local literature:** *Iceland in a Nutshell* by Peter Kidson (Reykjavik: Iceland Travel Books) is excellent for both background and for getting about. **Further information:** Icelandic National Tourist Office, Scandinavia House, 505 Fifth Avenue, New York; Scandinavian National Tourist Offices, 612 South Flower Street, Los Angeles; Iceland Tourist Council, Skolavoroustigur 12, Reykjavik, Iceland.

# Rome

For the generation I have known it, Rome has been the most changeless of the capitals. Return when you will, and the skyline as seen from the Pincio, in the Borghese Gardens, is quite as you have always remembered it, with the dome of St. Peter's dominating, as it has for centuries, and as surely it will for many centuries more. The municipal authorities—whose oft-seen symbol, "SPQR" (*Senatus Populusque Romanus*) dates back to a Senate that met twenty-five hundred years ago—may not have had the success they would like in restricting the automobile from the core of the city. But they have kept the skyscraper out in the newer peripheral sectors. Central Rome remains, rather miraculously, the Rome of the Caesars, of the great Renaissance-era *quattrocento,* of the beautiful baroque centuries, even of the later nationalists' *Risorgimento* that resulted in the city becoming capital of a modern, united Italy.

It is not necessary in Rome, as in other cities, to make special excursions to an "old town." You are already there. Your hotel is within walking distance of where your Roman hosts' ancestors lived more than half a millennium before Christ was born. The gruesome Romulus and Remus legend having to do with the founding of Rome is no more than that: legend. You may remember that these twins were brought up at first by a female wolf on whose breasts they fed, later by a shepherd, and that Romulus, after doing in his sibling twin, set about founding the town that took its name from his, populating it with local passersby whom he mated with ladies of the neighboring Sabine tribe, these last having nothing to say in the matter.

**The Etruscans' Rome:** There is more sense in the historians' reports to the effect that it was the ancient Etruscans who gave the settlement its name—the very same *Roma* it is called today —in the seventh century B.C. The Roman Republic was formed in 509 B.C., and by 272 B.C. Rome had the whole Italian peninsula under its control; then came Carthage, whose ruins still are to be seen on the Tunisia coast, across the Mediterranean. All of the Hellenistic states fell to Rome. Asia Minor, Egypt, Greece, Spain, and Gaul followed, so that, by the time Julius Caesar (102–44 B.C.) took over as dictator, Rome controlled the entire Mediterranean world. Caesar intelligently reformed what had become a strife-ridden state, with a program that ranged from the granting of citizenship rights to the Spaniards and Gauls to intensified public building on the home front. But his good works ended with his assassination, and within decades the republic had become the empire.

Its first emperor, Octavian Augustus, was extraordinarily competent; he set a course of peace and prosperity that lasted for two centuries. Rome, despite the stigma of the institution of slavery, had long since accepted the culture of the Greeks whom it had conquered, and had continued to extend its frontiers. This was the period of such emperors as the high-living but nonetheless efficient Nero, whose reign ended with his suicide; of Hadrian, the sophisticated administrator and reorganizer; of Marcus Aurelius, at once a fine ruler and a philosopher-teacher.

**The splendor of imperial Rome:** Imperial Rome—visualized today from its remarkable remains—was a luxurious and architecturally splendid city of a million population whose life revolved around the market center that was the forum, and the entertainment center that was the Colosseum, and whose upper classes knew central heating, efficient sanitation, and running water. Both republic and empire were studded with immortals—Lucretius (poetry), Caesar (history), Cicero (author of the first Latin prose, with his *Orations*), Virgil (poetry as exemplified by the *Aeneid*), Horace (poetry and satire), Livy (history), and Pliny the Younger (prose).

It ended in 476—the fateful year when a barbarian upstart named Odoacer was able to dethrone Romulus Augustulus—for a variety of reasons, the barbarians' strength but one of them. Politically, Rome was overlarge and overwieldy. Spiritually, there was the conflict of the new Christianity with the old Roman religion. Morally, there was the spectacle of a slave-dependent society, sloppy-rich at the top, and with morale-poor masses.

Which is not to write classical Rome off as a decadent bust. We are still, a couple of millennia later, greatly in its debt. We learned from the enormous empire Rome administered for centuries how sophisticated governments are organized and run. We inherited legal codes that were the first to espouse the principle that better a guilty man go free than an innocent man be adjudged guilty. The Latin language, from which all of the Romance languages sprung—not to mention other languages with Romance connections, like our own—is a major Roman legacy. And so, for that matter, was the rich culture—embodying art, architecture, philosophy, and literature—that the Romans adopted from the Greeks and passed along to posterity.

**The Rome of the Great Popes:** Rome, as an empire, moved east to the Byzantium that the Emperor Constantine renamed Constantinople. But within the city itself the power that was increasingly to be reckoned with was that of the leaders—or pontiffs—of the rapidly growing Christian Church, who gave Rome an eminence in the area of religion that it had lost in matters political. Still, the early medieval centuries saw tremendous decline. Gregory I, the sixth-century pope who was one of the greatest Romans of them all, started the city back on the road to greatness. The later establishment of the Holy Roman Empire, with the German emperors assuming their crowns in

Rome, gave the city a renewed prestige, if not the political power it once knew. But the Middle Ages were not Rome's proudest. There were incessant squabbles between factions vying for the papacy that resulted in periodic turmoil and a variety of types of government. Coincident with the arrival of the fifteenth century, moral standards in the papal court sunk to a level that made easy the appeal of the Reformation.

Withal, this period of the *quattrocento* was the Golden Age of the arts in Italy, of popes like Sixtus IV, Innocent VIII, Leo X, Clement VIII—whose patronage of the arts, possibly not always with spiritual motivations, resulted in the employment of such geniuses as Michelangelo and Raphael in the papal courts. They created much of the Rome that we know today; and their successors, in the baroque period of the seventeenth and early eighteenth centuries—Bernini, for example—added to the city's still-evident splendor.

**Kingdom of the Savoys and Mussolini:** By the time Napoleon invaded Rome at the end of the eighteenth century, its papal rulers had made of it one of the great cities of the world. Intervening decades saw popes in and popes out. At one point Mazzini—one of the three great leaders of the *Risorgimento* movement for Italian unity, along with Garibaldi and Cavour— headed a short-lived Italian republic. But in 1870, Rome became the capital of a united Italian kingdom under the House of Savoy. King Victor Emmanuel II that year moved into the Quirinale Palace, displacing Pope Pius IX, who retreated to the Vatican Palace to complete the longest pontificate in history.

From that year until 1929, the Vatican and the Italian Government were angry with each other, the popes not recognizing during all that period the loss of their temporal sovereignty. (With the 1929 Lateran Treaty, they agreed to sovereignty only over Vatican City.)

Fascism marched into Rome—and Italy—in 1922 in the person of Benito Mussolini, who promptly took over the government (leaving the little King Victor Emmanuel a puppet and creating for himself the title of *Il Duce*). Mussolini became at once an imperialist (snatching Ethiopia in the face of the League of Nations' condemnation), racist (emulating the anti-Semitism of fellow dictator Hitler), Axis partner (with his admired Hitler), and supplier of troops to Francisco Franco's insurgent Spanish Civil War troops. Italy joined Germany in World War II, to suffer losses so severe that Mussolini's own people overthrew him, executed him in 1945 at Lake Como, and ended the war on the Allied side. At war's end King Victor Emmanuel III fled the country for Egypt (where he died a few years later), leaving the throne to his son Umberto. Umberto's reign was not long—from May 19 to June 13, 1946. A referendum voted the monarchy out of existence. Umberto packed up and went off to a villa in Estoril, the beach resort outside Lisbon; he lives there still, the kingpin in a little community of ex-monarchs.

**Today's republic:** Republican Italy, in the north at least, has made remarkable economic progress. The long-impoverished south remains way, way behind the rest of the country in many economic and social areas. The seventies saw the beginning of a southern development fund, and reforms in education and housing. But the same decade saw agitation in the city that is the seat of the worldwide Roman Catholic Church, for divorce, birth control, and legal abortions. Added to that was a commendable experiment—the first in the world, and may it spread!—of free, no-fare public transport, the sensible idea being to get Romans to leave their street-clogging, air-polluting cars at home. Contemporary Romans are as partial to strikes as their ancestors were to circuses. They have even spread to places like hotels, to the point where tourism—the leading source of foreign revenue—has begun to feel a slight pinch. All the while, though, governments change with a frequency not unlike that of pre-de Gaulle France.

But this is a city that has known Octavian Augustus and Julius Caesar, Virgil and Horace, Napoleon and Mazzini, the Victor Emmanuels and Mussolini, Gregory I and John XXIII, Michelangelo and Bernini. It can take these work-stoppages and challenges to spiritual dogma, and the comings and goings of late-twentieth-century premiers. For Rome *is,* after all, the Eternal City.

TO SEE

**Lay of the land:** The wise visitor to Rome walks until his feet kill him and he can go no farther. He then relaxes over an *espresso* in a cafe, and resumes. There is always the door of a newly discovered church to open, with who knows what great art or architecture within. Or a newly noticed shop to case. Or a cafe in a previously unexplored quarter. Or a restaurant that looks inviting. Rome is at once the Romans themselves—attractive, animated, amusing—and the Rome they and their ancestors have created. The combination is unbeatable and unsurpassed anywhere on the planet.

Nowhere have I come across a map of Rome as good as the map of Paris that the French Government Tourist Offices have for years distributed free to all who ask. The map of the Ente Provinciale Per Il Turismo di Roma is adequate, though, and one comes across others with certain advantages. Take a look at whatever map you have and find the north–south thoroughfare called *Via del Corso.* It is Rome's principal street, and its extremities are both easy-to-remember landmarks. At the north is the *Piazza del Popolo,* with a central obelisk and a pair of churches, and a situation just beneath the *Pincio Hill* of the *Borghese Gardens.* The southern extremity of the Via del Corso is the *Piazza Venezia.* You cannot miss it because it is dominated by the massive nineteenth-century wedding cake that is the *Vittorio Emmanuel Monument.* The *Palazzo Venezia,* onetime home of Mussolini and now a museum, is opposite the monument, and *ancient Rome*—or what is left of ancient Rome—is just behind it: the *Forum, Capitoline Hill,* and, more distant, the *Colosseum.* Retrace your steps on the Via del Corso about two-thirds of the way back to the Piazza del Popolo, until you come to the *Via Condotti,* on your right. It is at once the heart of the smartest shopping area in town, and leads to the *Piazza di Spagna*—the Spanish Steps area —which is where you're likely to bump into Cousin Jane or your college classmate or the couple you sat with on a bus your first day in London. There are flower vendors in the lovely plaza, and the splendid steps leading up to the *Church of Sta. Trinita dei Monti* are congested the summer long with hirsute, incense-burning, candle-selling youngsters from throughout the Western world.

From the Piazza di Spagna, you may proceed to the Piazza del Popolo via the *Via del Babuino,* the main antiques-shop street of Rome, or via the *Via Margutta,* another fashionable thoroughfare running parallel with Babuino. You are wondering, about now, how to get from the Piazza di Spagna to the *Via Vittorio Veneto,* another street of which you've heard. You're close. Walk up the Spanish Steps to the *Via Sistina,* on which the earlier-mentioned Church of Trinita dei Monti faces. Take *Sistina* (another interesting shopping street) downhill a bit to *Via Francesco Crespi,* turning left on that street until you reach *Via Ludovisi* and the Eden Hotel on its corner. Walk down Via Ludovisi a couple of short blocks, and you've reached Via Veneto. Walk to its summit, and you bump smack into the *Borghese Gardens.* Walk downhill and you pass a number of hotels as well as the palazzo that serves as the *American Embassy;* follow Via Veneto's curve and you are at *Piazza Barberini*—which for some reason or other has become Japanese tourist headquarters in Rome— with its lovely *Triton fountain* by Bernini. Just beyond is the capacious *Palazzo Barberini* that houses one of the city's great museums. From Piazza Barberini, you may take the shop-lined *Via del Tritone* westward to the Via del Corso—where you began. Or you may walk south on the *Via Quattro Fontani* to the Basilica of *Santa Maria Maggiore,* thence a few blocks to its right and the *Stazione Termini,* the main railroad station that is perhaps the finest example of modern architecture in the city (the British Embassy is another). St. Peter's and the Vatican? They are across the Tiber. You may take either of two bridges, one leading directly to the circular fortress-landmark that is the *Castel San Angelo*. The other is closer to the *Via dell Conciliazione* that leads directly to the *Piazza San Pietro* and the basilica, with the *Vatican Museums* to the right of St. Peter's, as you approach it. On this same side of the river, but considerably below St. Peter's and the Vatican, is the mellow *Trastevere* quarter, which you will want to amble about, perhaps in connection with a lunch or dinner.

**Choice destinations:** *St. Peter's and the Vatican Museums* are where every visitor beelines for, and why not? St. Peter's— from whose main altar only the Pope may officiate at mass— is the masterwork that took a number of artists well over a century to complete. By the time it was consecrated by Pope Urban VIII in 1626, its collaborators had included Michelangelo (the dome and the marble Pietà—the Virgin Mary with Christ descended from the Cross in her lap, which you may have seen at the 1964–65 New York World's Fair and which was tragically damaged by a Hungarian fanatic in 1972), Bernini (the brilliant altar canopy, or baldachin), and Rafael, the Carlo Maderno (the façade). I am not much for statistics, but some of St. Peter's are worth noting. The dome is 390 feet high. The basilica proper is 610 feet long. The canopy is almost 100 feet wide. There's a lot to take in; wander about slowly. And come again. The *Vatican Museums* include the *Sistine Chapel,* whose great ceiling Michelangelo began decorating in 1508. If your visit is a summer one, you had better prepare yourself for a mob scene in the chapel. Indeed, every part of it except the ceiling will be occupied. Have a good look around. The end wall is Michelangelo's interpretation of the *Last Judgment,* while the ceiling embraces his *Creation* and *Prophets* and other themes. The right and left walls are by other artists—Botticelli most especially. The *Pinacoteca* is the Vatican's picture gallery—a room of Raphael tapestries, and works by Caravaggio, Da Vinci, Giotto, and even, as a surprise, some French Impressionists. The *Pio-Clementino Museum* is devoted to classical sculpture. There are busts of the

Roman emperors that you may enjoy seeing in the *Chiaramonti Museum*. The *Raphael Rooms* are not as well known as the Sistine Chapel, but are quite as magnificent. They house a series of frescoes on various themes—mostly biblical and classical. The adjacent *Rafael Loggias* are a gallery full of religious-theme paintings based on designs by Raphael but executed by his students. The *Library* is beautifully decorated, full of old manuscripts and globes. Ask how you may reach the *papal chapel* decorated by Fra Angelico and note that in 1972, the *Vatican Gardens* were opened to the public for the first time in centuries. *Papal audiences* —by and large the Wednesday morning audiences, rather than the rare private ones—are arranged for Americans through the American Visitors' Office, on Via dell' Umilita in downtown Rome, in conjunction with the Prefecture of the Apostolic Household.

**Ancient Rome:** The *Colosseum* is the subject of so many framed prints in the elementary schools of America that we all feel as though we've been there. It dates to the first century before Christ and had a seating capacity of some fifty thousand —which was not all that large, if you consider that ancient Rome had a population of about a million. This is where the action was: gladiators vs. lions, other fun and games. The *Forum* was Downtown Rome, where the toga-clad locals promenaded, shopped, and gossiped. It has been in ruins for centuries, during most of which time it was neglected and ignored, except by grazing cattle. Besides the Roman Forum proper, there are the nearby forums of Trajan, with a noted hundred-foot-high column remaining; Augusta, and Nerva. This is an area for a leisurely stroll, to note what remains of temples and arches and shops, even the Curia, or Senate chamber. The *Palatine Hill* was aristocratic imperial Rome—where the rich, and later, the emperors, lived; it is now a cluster of somber ruins, including that of Domus Augustiana, the imperial palace. The *Arch of Constantine* is named after the same Constantine for whom Byzantium was renamed Constantinople—the first Christian emperor. It was last restored in 1804—and a very good job of it. It is difficult to believe that work was begun on the *Pantheon* almost three decades before Christ was born. It is the only 100 percent shipshape ancient Roman building. Its domed, colonnaded exterior is in such good shape that it could be *neo*classic. But it's the real thing. The unusual proportions of the dome are not fully appreciated until one steps inside. The Pantheon is now a Roman Catholic Church, and contains the tombs of the painter Rafael and of the kings of the House of Savoy.

**Selected museums:** The Vatican Museums are only the beginning. Rome's museums—because of the deserved fame of those in the Vatican—are among the most undervisited of any capital in Europe. They are also among its very best. The *National Gallery in Palazzo Barberini* is nothing less than sublime. The eighteenth-century palace itself—a work of one of the great builder popes, Urban VIII—is in itself a work of art. Indeed, the ceiling of its immense and sumptuous ballroom, *Il Trionfo della Gloria,* painted by Pietro da Cortono, is a glorious triumph, and surely the No. 2 ceiling in town after that of Michelangelo in the Sistine Chapel. The paintings? Tintoretto's *Jesus and the Adulterous Woman,* a Holbein *Henry VIII,* Lotto's *Portrait of a Young Man,* Raphael's beautiful lady, *La Fornarina;* Piero di Cosimo's exquisite *La Maddalena*—just for starters. The *Borghese Gallery* houses a remarkable group of paintings and sculpture collected by Cardinal Borghese in the seventeenth century—not long after most of these works were created. The beautiful gallery was designed for the purpose for which it is still being used, except that when it went up the Borghese Gardens were vineyards rather than a public park. The cardinal knew how to pick painters whose works and whose fame would last through the centuries—Raphael's *Deposition from the Cross,* Titian's *Sacred and Profane Love,* Caravaggio's *Madonna dei Paladrenieri,* Botticelli's detail of *Three Angels Singing,* Bernini's *Youthful Self-Portrait,* Raphael's *Maddalena Strozzi.* The *Roman National Museum and Baths of Diocletian* comprise the baths themselves, built seventeen centuries ago, and a splendid collection of ancient Roman art—mosaics, frescoes, sarcophagi, and sculpture, both busts and full figures, ranging from a *Satyr Looking at His Tail* to an *Amazon Leaping on a Fallen Gaul.* The *Palazzo Doria* (2a Piazza del Collegio Romano) has some fine paintings —most especially a Velazquez of Pope Innocent X—but is of even more interest because of the setting itself—a gem of a rococo palace with, among other appurtenances, a chapel and a hall of mirrors. *Villa Giulia National Museum* is of dual interest, too. The lovely house itself had been the sixteenth-century summer retreat of Pope Julius III. The exhibits, on the other hand, are of quite another era—mostly pottery from the pre-Roman Etruscan period, but including a reconstructed temple in the garden. The *Palazzo Venezia,* on the piazza of that name, opposite the wedding-cake Vittorio Emmanuel monument, is possibly the most bypassed major museum in Rome. It is pointed out as a fine specimen of fifteenth-century architecture (the cross-shaped windows of the second floor are exceptional) and as a former home not only of some Renaissance popes and later Venetian ambassadors, but of this century's Benito Mussolini—who harangued the Romans from a balcony. Within, though (once you find the entrance) is one of Europe's best museums of the decorative arts: furniture, paintings, tapestries, ceramics, metalwork, sculpture, and armor, mostly all from the great Italian late and middle Renaissance periods. The *Farnesina Gallery* occupies an exemplary early-sixteenth-century mansion whose interior decorators included Raphael and Il Sodoma (both of whom painted frescoes), not to mention other works. The *National Gallery of Modern Art* is capacious and with a well-hung collection of Italian moderns with whom you may or may not be familiar, and their foreign contemporaries. *National Museum of Castel San Angelo* is another Roman surprise package, at least to the many visitors who believe that the ancient circular mausoleum-*cum*-fortress-*cum*-papal palace on the right bank of the Tiber near the Vatican is today no more than an historic landmark, to be admired for its exterior façade. Well, step inside. Up you go on the ramps that connect the various levels, in which are housed exhibits ranging from armor, guns, and swords to Renaissance paintings and frescoes, with a series of papal apartments the real treats, most especially the so-called Cupid and Psyche Room, with its del Vaga frieze and carved and gilded ceiling of unusual beauty.

**Palaces**—*palazzi,* if you would like the Italian plural—are not to be ignored, in Rome of all cities. I have already, in the preceding section, recommended some palaces that are dominantly museums. Here are some others, to be regarded principally for their architecture and decoration, although hardly without significant works of art. *Palazzo Farnese* is one of the greatest townhouses in the world. It has for a long time served as the residence of the lucky French ambassadors to Italy, and we are greatly in their debt for allowing us one hour each Sunday (11:00 A.M. until noon—unless a new ambassador changes the schedule) to see some of the interior. Even with the place out of bounds the rest of the week, the Piazza Farnese, on which the palace fronts, is in itself a major Roman destination. The building itself was begun in 1514 by Antonio Sangallo the Younger—using building material from the Colosseum, of all places. But it was completed by Michelangelo. The French think enough of the building to have commissioned Jean Cocteau to write a preface to the French-language guidebook to the palace and to the illustrious Farnese family, which they sell at the entrance. The entire building is a work of genius—the architectural proportions, arched entrance vestibule, superhigh ceilings, immense frescoed-and-tapestried reception rooms. It may not be shown, but one room, the White Room, was where Sweden's Queen Christina (see the chapter on Stockholm) lived after her abdication. In connection with your visit to the palace, do not fail to look in at the *Church of Santa Brigida,* on the Piazza Farnese; its blue ceiling is dotted with gold stars, and there is a gilded sunburst over the altar. Then pop around the corner, on Via di Monserrato, to see the equally sumptuous *Church of*

*San Girolamo della Carita.* The *Palazzo Quirinale* is open to visitors only an hour or two a week (your hotel concierge can advise you as to specifics). Work it in if you can. It is the history of Rome for the last five centuries—all in one building. It went up originally in 1574 as a papal summer palace, and remained so until about a century ago, when Rome became the capital of the unified Kingdom of Italy. At that point, the popes withdrew to the Vatican, and the kings moved in. They stayed until after World War II, when the current republic replaced the Savoyard monarchs. Today, the palace is the official residence of the President of Italy. Bernini designed the main gate, fronting on the Piazza del Quirinale. The interiors—completed over a period of several centuries—are, not surprisingly, magnificent, most particularly the high-ceilinged, fresco-walled Sala Regia. Across the square is the newer (eighteenth-century) *Palazzo della Consulta.* It has been a papal ministry, as well as the headquarters of the Foreign Ministry, and the Ministry of African Affairs, during the period when Italy controlled Ethiopia, part of Somalia, and Libya. It is now a law court, worth peeping at, if you can gain, or plead a case, for admittance. *Palazzo Borghese* (not to be confused with the earlier-mentioned Borghese Gallery) is a seventeenth-century palace in the Borghese Gardens, with fine interiors and an especially impressive courtyard. The *Palazzo Madama* was the Rome outpost of the powerful Florentine Medicis, who rarely stinted with building budgets. It is seventeenth-century outside, eighteenth- within, and it is now the seat of the Senate of Italy.

**Churches:** Where, after St. Peter's, does one begin in this city of great churches? To begin, it is worth remembering that Roman Catholic churches—which these all are—are open most of every day, unlike Protestant churches, which are so often locked, except on Sundays. Second, simple exteriors can conceal opulent interiors. Pop into whatever churches you pass by. Few of the hundreds in central Rome disappoint; more often than not they are exemplary on architectural lines, with art treasures as well. You may enter when masses are being said, but *quietly*. At other times, don't hesitate to query priests or sacristans for details; they are usually happy to answer questions. The *major churches,* or basilicas—aside from St. Peter's—are requisites. *Santa Maria Maggiore* (St. Mary Major) goes back nineteen centuries, but has been remodeled several times. It is impressive because of its elaborate Renaissance ceiling, its mosaics, and its several chapels. *San Giovanni in Laterano* (St. John Lateran) dates to the first Christian emperor—Constantine. It is the core of an impressive complex that includes the palace (now a museum with ecclesiastical and classical exhibits) wherein was signed the 1929 Lateran Treaty between the Vatican State and the Italian Government. The church itself was the very seat of the papacy and remains the Cathedral of Rome. The gilded wood ceiling and the mosaic-decorated apse highlight the interior. *San Pietro in Vincoli* (St. Peter in Chains) is so named because it is the repository of the chains of St. Peter's Jerusalem and Roman imprisonments; they are contained in a glass-walled bronze casket in front of the main altar. The pewless, multiperiod sanctuary is severely handsome, and dominated by Michelangelo's powerful statue of a stern, long-bearded Moses. *San Pablo Fuori le Mura* (St. Paul's Outside the Walls) is the loveliest of this basilica group, thanks to its Romanesque cloisters, and a sanctuary within of considerable splendor, and with a mosaic frieze of portraits of all the popes from St. Peter to John XXIII.

Of the *other churches,* let me offer this handful of personal favorites. *Il Gesu di Roma* (Church of Jesus in Rome) is the world headquarters church of the Society of Jesus. It is a masterful sixteenth-century work that has served as a prototype for Jesuit churches around the world. The baroque interior is one of the most elaborate—and beautiful—in Rome. *San Clemente* (St. Clement's) embraces a beauty of a twelfth-century street-level basilica, and a fresco-decorated fourth-century subterranean basilica as well. The gifted mystery novelist Ngaio Marsh barely disguised it as the setting for her 1972 Inspector Alleyn thriller,

*When in Rome.* It has been operated by Irish Dominicans for almost three centuries; sure and it's nice to hear their brogues when you greet them. *Santa Maria in Cosmedin* (St. Mary in Cosmedin) has a superb medieval exterior and an essentially Byzantine interior. The combination is winning. *Quattro Coronati* (Four Crowned Saints) is an away-from-the-center combination church-convent that sees few visitors. One enters as callers have since medieval times. You knock at the entrance of the little convent. A revolving metal box—as old as the church itself —is silently turned outward to meet your gaze. You open it, and bending to look within, find an equally venerable key, with the veiled face of a silent nun in the darkened background. The key opens the door to the church, which in turn leads to a serene garden-cloister that is in itself one of the most memorable of Roman destinations. On leaving, one returns the key in the same way. *Santa Pudenziana* is a charmer of an old Byzantine church, with a towering medieval campanile. And pop into these beauties as you pass by: *Trinita* (Via Condotti), *San Carlo al Corso, Gesu e Maria, Santa Maria, San Marcello*—all Renaissance-era, and all on the Via del Corso; *San Teodor,* near the Arch of Velabbro; *San Andrea al Quirinale,* near the Quirinale Palace; *Santa Maria del Popolo,* with a fine chapel and paintings by Caravaggio and Pinturicchio; and the handsome Romanesque-style *Santa Maria in Trastevere.*

**Other Roman treats:** The *Piazza Navona* is the most beautiful in a city full of beautiful piazzas. Bernini's glorious *Fontana dei Fiumi* dominates, but there are fine seventeenth-century palaces and churches (including *Sant' Agnese in Agone*), good restaurants, and relaxing cafes. Until a little over a century ago, the square was flooded on summer Sundays, becoming Rome's—if not all Europe's—No. 1 swimming pool. The *Fontana di Trevi* is the richest fountain in the world, ever since the world learned from the film *Three Coins in the Fountain*—back in the fifties —that if you threw a coin into the Trevi you were bound to return to Rome. On my last visit, I happened by about ten in the morning. The water had been turned off and the fountain's pool drained, while sanitation men (bank tellers, they should be called) gathered up the previous day's haul. There appeared to be enough to keep a visitor in Rome for an entire season. Coins or no, the fountain is Rome's most dramatic, with its sculpted, chariot-drawn Neptune surrounded by the playing gusts of water. The *Fontana di Paola* is a Renaissance monument, one of the biggest in town, with eagles and dragons—from the Borghese family crest—surmounting the quintet of arches through which the waters flow into a communal basin. The *Piazza Esedra* (on maps as the Piazza della Republica) is dominated by the high-spraying jets that encircle the nymphs of its formal fountain. *Tivoli* is a Roman excursion requisite. It is an elevated town of venerable mansions, the most celebrated of which is *Villa d'Este,* a onetime cardinal's retreat set amid terraced, fountain-filled formal gardens. Its neighbor is *Hadrian's Villa,* the well-restored home of Emperor Hadrian, in the second century A.D., and the site of summer Sound and Light performances.

## TO WATCH

In Rome, what one wants most to watch is the most sublime Roman treat of all, the original and all-time-champ beautiful people—the Romans themselves. But there are other diversions of note. The *Rome Opera*—without the international repute of Milan's La Scala, but still hardly to be despised—performs from late November through May at its beautiful, late-nineteenth-century home base, the *Teatro dell' Opera,* Via del Viminale. Note, though, that in July and August the opera company moves to the *Baths of Caracalla* (Termi di Caracalla), a major monument of ancient Rome, and an inspired setting for opera. There is, as well, a kind of supplementary opera season, in June and September, at the *Teatro Eliseo,* Via Nazionale 183. *Concerts*—symphonic and chamber—take place fall through spring, in a number of halls, on which hotel concierges can advise. *Vaudeville,* Italian style, is presented at the *Teatro Sistina,* Via Sistina 129. The above-mentioned *Eliseo, Quirino* (Via Marco Minghetti 1), and *Valle* (Via del Téatro Valle) are among the top legitimate theaters; plays are, of course, performed in Italian. Rome is the headquarters for Italy's celebrated movie industry, and has no dearth of cinemas; some fifty are first-run houses, but at almost all, the sound tracks are dubbed into Italian. Two exceptions —where imported movies are shown with the original sound tracks (and with printed Italian titles) are the *Archimede* and *Fiammetta* cinemas. In summer there are Sound and Light shows at the *Roman Forum* and, out of town, at *Hadrian's Villa,* Tivoli.

## TO STAY

A well-run Roman hotel is as pleasurable a home away from home as one could ask. Italy has, after all, been hosting tourists for centuries; it knows what hotelkeeping is all about. Of the hundreds of acceptable hotels in Rome, here is a *selected, centrally located* group that I like. All have either full or partial air conditioning. The conveniently located *Grand,* an elderly beauty that has always been a leader, stands out even more now, as a result of an extensive and expensive refurbishing. The result is the most stylish hotel in town, with the details of the traditional-style décor accented to perfection. It would be difficult to find hotel interiors where color has been more imaginatively used. The bedrooms and suites are absolute beauties, and I do not know of a more elegant restaurant in Rome. The lobbies and lounges could easily rank with some of the palazzi as sightseers' attractions. This is one of the CIGA group, with gifted management and skilled staff. The *Eden* is among the smaller of the luxe-category hotels; its ambience is intimate and relaxing. There are a pair of fine restaurants, including the newer rooftop one affording fine Borghese Gardens vistas, as well as a cosy bar. Bedrooms and suites are charmers; the location, on Via Ludovisi midway between the Via Veneto and the Piazza di Spagna, is inspired. The *Hassler-Villa Medici,* at the head of the Spanish Steps, next door to the twin-tower Trinita dei Monti church, is a Rome landmark—which is not to say that it should be regarded as either venerable or stuffy. On the contrary, there is a low-key but perky air to the place. The luxury is smart, never overblown. Guest rooms are handsome, and there are both rooftop-*cum*-view and garden restaurants in summer. Service is super. The *Ambasciatori Palace* has a smart Via Veneto location, just opposite the American Embassy. The lobby is among the more beautiful in town; the restaurant moves to a canopied terrace in summer. The level of luxury is such that fully a fifth of the bedrooms have *two* baths; all are provided with refrigerators, and, if you please, cookies for nibbling. How about that? The *Flora* is at the Borghese Gardens end of the Via Veneto, a dignified old-timer that has been handsomely refurbished, with high-ceilinged public areas and comfortable guest rooms. The *Bernini Bristol* is on the close-to-everything Piazza Barberini just behind Bernini's Triton fountain, from which it take the first half of its name. The rooms are luxuriously updated, and the top two floors consist of kitchenette-equipped suites. There's a summer roof restaurant with a socko view, and an agreeable bar. The *Quirinale* (Via Nazionale 7) is just off Piazza Esedra, and a hop and a skip from the Teatro dell' Opera, with which it is connected by both tradition *and* a tunnel—heavily trafficked, after performances, by patrons en route to the Quirinale for refreshment. The hotel, dating back to 1865, is graced with a quiet inner garden where lunch is served in summer, and has for some years been the sole foreign property of the generally first-rate Stiegenberger chain of Germany. The *Parco dei Principi* is quite the most imaginatively designed of Roman hotels—mid-sixties Italian Modern at its severe, understated best. The dominant color is green, and the setting is a capacious green garden—with a lovely terrace and outdoor pool—on the Via Mercadante side of the Borghese Gardens, which is a fairish walk to the Via Veneto but is close enough so that it *can* be walked. One whole window wall of the restaurant overlooks the garden and pool. We move now from the de luxe to the *first-class category.* The *Hotel de la Ville,* on the central Via Sistina, almost next door to the earlier-mentioned Hassler, is quiet, luxurious, and traditional-style beautiful, and by that I mean spacious lobbies, restaurant (it moves to the garden in summer), bar, and guest rooms, some of which have absolutely panoramic views. The *Savoy,* with its Via Veneto-corner-of-the-Via Ludovisi location, and a completely refurbished plant, is a winner: good-looking, high-ceilinged, red-accented public spaces, inviting guest rooms, alert management. The *Grand Hotel Plaza* was built in 1860 with what must then have been the most knock-'em-dead public rooms in Rome, and it has maintained them well ever since. The lobby-lounge, with its great crystal chandeliers and neo-Renaissance ceiling, sets the pace for the whole hotel. And what a location: on the Via del Corso, but yards from the Via Condotti and, just beyond, the Spanish Steps. The *Regina-Carlton* is diagonally opposite the American Embassy on the Via Veneto, and has been skillfully refurbished; the updated bedrooms are among the most desirable in Rome, and there's a welcoming high-ceilinged lobby. The *Majestic* is another Via Veneto charmer, with a quietly stylish ambience. The lobby with its frescoed ceiling is handsome, and there is a summer terrace-restaurant. The *Boston,* at 47 Via Lombardia, in the Veneto area, has been completely updated, and its management can be—and is—particularly proud of the bedrooms. I have been unable to learn the precise reason for the name, although the Roman executive who showed me about on my last visit, studied, coincidentally, at Boston University. The *Imperiale,* 24 Via Veneto, has been tastefully renovated; a number of its bedrooms are particularly spacious—and handsome. The *Eliseo* on Via Porte Pinciana, just off the Via Veneto and overlooking the Borghese Garden, is smallish and smart, with a notable roof restaurant. Down a mite, to the *top second-class category,* is the *Alexandre,* next-door neighbor to the

Imperiale on the Via Veneto, and a delight, with a nifty green-and-yellow lobby, and comfortable rooms. The second-class *Inghilterra,* on Via Bocca di Leone, just off Via Condotti and a step from the Spanish Steps, an early Roman home of mine, has been refurbished in recent years, to the point where all rooms now have bath; there's a bar, but breakfast only—no restaurant. The *Dinesen*—if its name didn't give you a clue—is Danish-owned (Izak Dinesen was a Danish writer who chronicled Kenya, where she lived), and with an agreeable Porta Pinciana location. It is elderly and comfortable, attracting a loyal English clientele; half of its rooms have bath; breakfast only. You will have noticed that all of the foregoing hotels are in the Via Veneto-Spanish Steps area, simply because I consider that the most convenient, heart-of-things part of Rome for the visitor to live in. Should you prefer the area around the Stazione Termini, the five Bettoja hotels should not be overlooked. They are well run and offer good value, particularly the one de luxe hotel of the group, the *Mediterraneo.* The *Massimo d'Azeglio* follows, and the others are the *Atlantico, San Giorgio,* and *Nord.*

## TO EAT (AND DRINK)

Italian food is the European cuisine many Americans think they know the most about. Some do, of course. Many, though, go to Italy and content themselves with samplings of the relatively few Italian dishes they have known at home—minestrone, spaghetti with meat balls, ravioli, and naturally the late-twentieth-century competitor to the hot dog: pizza. To make maters worse, some Italian hotels rope clients into staying with them on a full- or demi-pension basis (which means that either lunch and dinner or lunch *or* dinner are included in the room rate) so that they don't have an opportunity to get out into restaurants and sample food as Italians eat it. Far too many hotels—particularly in Italy

—believe their foreign clients want bland, nondescript continental food rather than the local specialties.

It is surely worth noting at this point that cuisine was a major part of the ancient Roman culture. Food again came to play a major role in Italian life with the advent of the Renaissance—in Venice and Florence and Rome, as well. In the mid-sixteenth century, Catherine de Medici left her native Florence to become wife of the future Henry II of France, and instead of taking her hairdresser, which is currently the fashion when ladies of state travel, she very sensibily took her cook. He taught the then gastronomically inferior French a thing or two, and so did other Italian cooks who followed him. As time went on, the French altered and created. But the fact remains that the Italians were the first great cooks of Europe, and they remain among the greatest. Their cuisine is far more sophisticated and diverse than we have been allowed to believe on this side of the Atlantic. They eat a great deal more than pasta. Indeed, in Italy, pasta is an introductory course to a lunch or dinner—not the principal course. And it is created in vast variety. Italian *antipasto* is the most imaginative of any European cuisine's hors d'oeuvres. The Italian green salad is simple, always simple—just greens with oil and vinegar and perhaps a touch of garlic, and it is unsurpassed. Italians are wizards with rice (mostly in the north) as well as with cheese (not only parmesan) and with herbs—basil, marjoram, oregano, rosemary, parsley, tarragon. They have known spices since the days of the Imperial Roman and Renaissance eras, when they traded in them with merchants of the Far East. Of the meats, they are most skilled with veal—and their veal is the tenderest in the world. But their ham (the dried *prosciutto* especially) is good, and so is their lamb. One of their sausages—*salami* —gave its name to the world, but there are many delicious species. They eat fewer hot vegetables than we do, perhaps, but when they do they are separate courses, and they are festively and deliciously prepared. Italian cheeses are globally celebrated, and, with fruit, are the usual dessert, followed by a cup of strong *espresso.* Pastries can be oversweet, when made with rum. But some—*zuppa inglese* ("English soup," a variation of the English trifle)—when expertly prepared, surpass it. Italian sherbets and often ice cream are delicious, and so, as a matter of fact, is Italian bread. Rome has a number of its own specialties. Here are a few: *gnocchi alla Romana*—semolina-base dumplings; *spaghetti alla carbonara, all' Amatricana,* or *alla carrettiera; cannelloni* —wide, canal-shaped pasta with appropriate sauce and melted cheese topping; roast lamb, chicken, either *alla diavola* or *alla cacciatore;* roast suckling pig; *saltimbocca*—braised veal knuckle; vegetables, including broccoli with lemon and artichokes prepared various ways.

Italians have never bothered with an elaborate vintage ritual in connection with their wines. Which is not to say that their wines are not good, and frequently exceptional. Their reputation suffers in the United States. To many Americans, Italian wine means a bottle of coarse Chianti in a fat straw-wrapped bottle. There are many varieties of Chianti, some of them not coarse, and not all are put up in straw-wrapped bottles. But there are many other wines to be sampled, particularly among the reds, at which Italy excels. These would include Barolo, Frascati, and Valpolicella. Verdicchio and Soave are among the fine whites. I have never gotten the message of rosé, even in France, where it is at its best, let alone Italy, where it is not. The Italian dry champagnes can be very good. The vermouth-type apéritifs are the preferred pre-dinner and pre-lunch drinks—Martini (that's a brand name of vermouth—not to be confused with our dry martini cocktail), Cinzano, Campari. These are good with ice and soda, taken by themselves as you would a glass of sherry, or on the rocks. The Italians' most masterful liqueurs are Galiano and Strega; their brandies are not as good as the Spaniards' (let alone, of course, the cognac of France), but the brand called Vecchia Romagna is good. Of course, imported whiskies and gins are easily come by, and the barmen of leading hotels know how to mix non-Italian drinks expertly.

It is harder in Rome than in Paris to order a poor meal. That said, here are some restaurants that I like. *Passeto,* Via Zanardelli, is an old-timer that has, happily, never gone out of fashion. You enter on Via Zanardelli, but if it's summer, aim for a table at the rear on the covered terrace overlooking Piazza Sant' Appolinare. *Spaghetti All' Amatriciana*—with bacon, tomato, and white wine sauce—is a specialty. So is the *tacchina novella* in casserole *con cipolline*—a turkey dish. *Abbachio d'Aruzzi* is a baby lamb preparation. *Ranieri* (Via Mario de Fiori 26) is a step from the Via Condotti, near the Spanish Steps. It's another old-timer—smallish, intimate, and with a history that goes back to the middle of the last century. The place is named for a onetime chef of Queen Victoria who took over the restaurant only after his subsequent employer, Queen Carlotta of Mexico, lost her husband to a firing squad—and her own reason. The *Canellone all' Casaalinga*—the house's own—is four-star; so is the veal dish called *Costoletta di Vitella all' Imperiale,* and the chicken, *Massimiliano* style. *Torta deliziosa,* a cake enveloped with chocolate creme and bitter chocolate shavings, is indeed *deliziosa. Flavia* (Via Flavia 9) draws as smart a crowd as you are likely to see in Rome, unpretentious décor notwithstanding. The lure is the absolutely super food—the vegetable soup called *zuppa verdura,* and *saltimbocca Romano,* a variety of excellent meat dishes. And note the Italian bread transformed via the grill into hot toast. *Piccolo Mondo* (Via Aurora 39), just off the Via Veneto, is no-nonsense delicious. The pasta known as *tortellini* is a house specialty. So is veal *scaloppine* and spaghetti with clam sauce. The roast lamb is good, too. In summer, you lunch or dine under a canopy on the sidewalk; it's delightful. *Cesarina* (Via Sicilia 209) is a big, busy, noisy, immediately likable place, minutely and expertly supervised by Mama Cesarina. A delectable house specialty is a tripartite pasta plate—*tortellini, lasagna,* and *ravioli verde.* The *Misto Cesarina*—deep-fried *fritto misto* of vegetables and hot stuffed tomatoes—is inspired. So is the simple sautéed veal *piccata* with lemon butter sauce.

Mama is bigger on desserts than many Roman restaurateurs; her *Semifreddo Cesarina* embraces soft vanilla ice cream, *zuppa inglese* (trifle), and chocolate sauce. Oh, wow! *Al Chianti* (Via Ancona 19) dishes up such relative rarities as *Pappardelle sulla Lepre*—a pasta concoction with hare sauce, out of Tuscany; *vitello tonnato*—the cold veal-tuna specialty that is so good on a hot summer day, and a variety of Tuscan dishes. *Trattoria Geleassi* (Piazza Santa Maria in Trastevere) is smack in the heart of Trastevere, on its finest square, facing its finest church. In summer, you eat under canvas on the piazza, and you eat well. Consider such unusual pasta dishes as *penne all arabbiata* or *agnolotti,* house-style fish specialties like *spigola orata,* or fried *calamari*—the squid so beloved of Rome. *Casino Valadier* (Pincio, Borghese Gardens) neither is nor was a casino. It was, rather, a little palazzo built expressly for l'Aiglon, the son of Napoleon designated by his imperial father as King of Rome. The son never lived in the palace; instead it remained a private villa until about half a century ago when it turned restaurant— and a smart restaurant, to be sure. It still is. In winter, one lunches or dines in elegant, turn-of-the-century salons. In warm weather the terrace affords a splendid city view. The pastas— *spaghetti all' Cozze* (with tomatoes and mussels) or *alla Carbonara* (with eggs and bacon) are commendable. So are the veal dishes. One goes to the *Hostaria dell' Orso* (Via Monte Brianzo 93) because of the Hostaria dell' Orso, neither for the food, which is pedestrian, nor the service, which can be patronizing. (Affluent steak-and-baked-potato Americans have a way of demoralizing restaurant staffs.) Tabs are high, but one looks upon a dinner as an expensive evening, with something to eat and drink, at a magnificent antique of a medieval house. The Hostaria dell' Orso, or Inn of the Bear, goes back more than half a millennium and embraces three sumptuously furnished levels—bar-lounge as you go in; restaurant, up a flight; and *boîte,* topside. Inspect the furnishings, objects, and paintings of all three. *Hotel cooking* in Rome can vary. The danger is not that it is bad, but that, in far too many places, it is dull and nondescript continental rather than distinctive Roman-Italian—which it could so easily be. The *Roof Garden Restaurant of the Hotel Eliseo* is moderate-priced, attractive, and as Italian as you'll find in the hotels; it has a substantial Roman clientele. Its own *Risotto Eliseo* is worthy; so are the *tournedos Rossini*. The *Roof Terrace* of the *Hassler* is a happy choice for lunch of a sunny day in late spring or summer. The fare is Franco-Italian, and of high caliber. The *Hotel Mediterraneo Restaurant* is one to remember if you are in the Stazione Termini area; forget the continental dishes and concentrate on Italian ones—they are as good as you'll find in town. The *Grand Hotel Restaurant* is one of the most beautiful to look upon in Europe. Its chef makes a specialty of pasta, offering an astonishing variety of sizes, shapes, and sauces. (You may order a combination plate, to give you an idea.) The rest of the menu is equally professional, and so is the service. Of the drop-in-for-*espresso cafes*, *Caffe Greco* (Via Condotti 80), which had passed its sixteenth birthday the year our Declaration of Independence was signed, remains, decade in and decade out, the most convenient locale in town for the study and observation of cream-of-the-crop Romans. I have saved *Allemagna,* on the Via del Corso, for last. It is a great big cafe-bakery-confectionery-caterer restaurant run by the people who make the *pannetone* bread widely exported to the United States at Christmas. The species of *gelati* (ice cream and *sorbets* [sherbet]) are limitless and magnificent. They are candies boxed as only Italians can box them, tiny frosted cakes, little sandwiches and minipizzas, and great counters of *antipasti*. And, best of all, there is the drink called *frullati di frutta:* strawberries, peaches, bananas, pears, apples, apricots, lemon, oranges, and grapefruit are combined in a blender with milk, sugar, and maraschino liqueur. Think of me when you order one.

TO BUY

One does not shop in Rome for bargains—although there are still some good buys to be had. One shops for style and design. That is the way it always has been in this most stylish of all the European capitals. Here is a selective list of shops I like. **Glass and china:** *Richard Ginori* (177 Via del Tritone, with a smaller Via Condotti branch) is Italy's leading designer-manufacturer of porcelain; tremendous variety of dinner services, with prices high but still much lower than in Ginori stores in the United States and other countries. *Arte 70* (Via Sistina 19) is smart Italian Modern—plastics, china, pottery, housewares. Expensive. *Venini* (Via Condotti 59) is the fine old Venetian glass house; steep-tabbed except for some kicky little gifts—paperweights, ashtrays, and the like. **Prints and etchings:** *Plinio Narcecchia* (Piazza Navona 25) is a treasure trove, with both elderly etchings and new reproductions in stock; some antiques, too. Fair prices. *Slam* (Via Babuino 153) is still another well-stocked source for etchings and prints. **Art books:** *Rizzoli,* which has a Fifth Avenue outlet in New York, carries a big stock of art books, which the Italians print beautifully; prices are excellent; other books, too, of course. **Silver and jewelry:** *Bulgari,* on the Via Condotti, is perhaps Rome's best-known jeweler—expensive, but high-style. *Mario Buccellatti,* which has a New York branch, specializes in the hammered Florentine-style silver—heavy, ornate, and often handsome; old pieces, too. **Linens-embroidery:** *Mamma Galassi* (Via Condotti) has a big selection; fine quality. **Children's Clothes:** *Ida Simonelli* (Via Sistina) has what is perhaps the most imaginative kids' togs in town. **Tassels and fringe**—an Italian specialty for centuries—are sold in a wide array at *Giuseppe Mici,* Via Fratina 57-A. **Gloves:** for both men and women remain one of Italy's best bargains. Three good sources are *Barra* on both Vias Sistina and Condotti, *Hass* (Via Condotti), and *The Glove*

*Shop* (Via Veneto 106)—which is reasonable. **Leather:** is not cheap, but is less costly than in the United States, and often beautifully designed and of superb quality. *Gucci* with its big two-story main Italian store on the Via Condotti and a branch out at the Cavalieri Hilton Hotel, is where you want to look for luggage, wallets, briefcases, men's and women's shoes; women's handbags, men's shoulder-strap bags; the prices are appreciably lower than at the Gucci shops in New York. *Metius* (Via del Tritone 195) has attractively styled and priced luggage and handbags; *Val Corso* (Via del Corso 151) does, too. **Candy:** *Perugina* (Via Condotti and other locations) and *Allemagna* (Via del Corso) are both excellent sources. Perugina is an oldtime Perugina candymaker whose wares—particularly the chewy chocolate-almond *bacci,* or kisses—you see all around the world, including their own New York shop. *Allemagna* (of which more in the To Eat and Drink section) vends all manner of delicious comestibles. **Shoes** out of Italy are the world's most beautiful. And they are quite good buys. Retail outlets are virtually limitless. *Gucci,* earlier mentioned in connection with leather goods, has fine shoes for both men and women. Here are some more. *For women—Petrocchi* (Via Sistina), *Silvia of Fiorentina* (Via Sistina), *Salvatore Ferragamo* (Via Condotti), *Fragiacomo* (Via Condotti). And for entirely *hand-made* shoes, for both men and women: *Michele di Ceglie* (Via Sistina 83). **Women's clothing and accessories:** On the Via Condotti, there are *Fabiani* (haute couture), *Schubert* (a conservative boutique), and *Gucci* (this time for sportswear and scarves). *Luisa Spagnoli,* on the Via Veneto, has beautiful knitwear and sweaters. On the Via Sistina, consider *Marcella Pucci* for high-style fashions; *Pannani*—an amusing, camp boutique; *Eleanora Garnett*—still selling her own quiet but lovely, albeit costly, clothes; and *Batilocchi,* with boutique clothes and costume jewelry. **Men's clothing and furnishings:** Among the high-style shops are *Emilio* (Via dei Crociferi 30, near the Fontana di Trevi); *G. Battistoni* (Via Condotti 61-A—courtyard); *Costa* (Via di Cappuccini 15), particularly good for custom-made suits; *Ibbas* (Via Barberini 16) especially for conservative, custom-made shirts; *Angelo Sermonetti* (Via Fratina), very smart, very mod suits, custom-made quickly— overnight if you insist; *Testa* (Via Fratina), offbeat, inventive resort and casual wear. *Tomassini* and *Avenia* are two inexpensive Via del Corso men's shops. *Cucci*—that's spelled with a capital *C*—is a conservative Via Condotti haberdasher; *Piatelli,* on the Via Condotti but with Via del Corso and Via Nazionale branches, is similar in concept, and a good source of men's ties; these last—as has for long been the case in Italy—*look* better than they tie. Italians still consider **Department stores** as sources of relatively inexpensive merchandise. There is nothing like a Harrods or Galeries Lafayette or NK. *Rinascente,* at the Piazza Colonna, off the Via del Corso, is as good as any; you can often find buys in clothing and accessories—men's, women's, and children's. **Antiques:** Unless you know this field, it is well to make the rounds with someone who does, for there are many ingeniously executed copies of Italian antique furniture, not to mention paintings; have whatever you buy authenticated by means of a written notation from the seller. (You will want this for U.S. customs, in any event, to qualify your purchases of anything more than a century old, for duty exemption.) No matter how fancy the shop, it is always wise to *ask if the price quoted is indeed the final price.* It also pays to ask questions about age, origin, workmanship, and the like. Good dealers are glad to answer, and you learn a lot in the process. The main antiques-shopping areas are Via del Babuino, Via Giulia, and Via Margutta. Here is a selection. There are several *Di Castro* shops: *Alberto,* at Via del Babuino 102; *Amadeo,* at Via del Babuino 72; and *Leone,* at Piazza di Spagna 94; they're all worth exploring for antique furniture and decorations; Alberto also has paintings. *Fallani,* Via del Babuino 58-A, specializes in ancient Roman and Greek coins, and Italian medieval coins, too; objects of archaeological interest as well. *Gasparini* (Via Fontanella di Borghese 56) is known for old paintings, tapestries, and furniture. *Marcello and Carlo Sestieri* (Piazza di Spagna 81) sell old paintings and antique decorative

objects. *V. and L. Veneziana* (Via Fratina 15) specialize in
Italian faience and antiques. *Antiquaria* (Palazzo Massimo, Corso
Vittorio Emmanuel 141) deals in eighteenth-century Italian furniture, Italian paintings, and *boiseries*—antique wood paneling.
Rome's *flea market* takes place Sunday mornings at Portese—
lots of junk, of course, but if you know what you're about,
you may find something worthwhile.

TO NOTE

**Access:** There is excellent air service from U.S. points to Rome,
via the Italians' own Alitalia, as well as TWA and Pan Am.
Intra-European air services are equally good; Alitalia and the
lines of foreign carriers link Rome with major continental points,
not to mention Africa and Asia. Leonardo da Vinci Intercontinental Airport is at Fiumicino—twenty-two miles from town;
the inexpensive airport-to-town buses are recommended. Ciam-
pino, the older airport, is still used for certain shorter flights.
As for trains, one is advised to travel first-class on the major,
crack, very-best-available expresses in and out of Rome, *always
booking seats in advance—or risk standing, even in first class.*
Driving into and out of Rome is not the problem that driving
*within* the traffic-clogged city presents; there are modern *auto-
stradas,* the north–south Highway of the Sun in particular. There
are good bus services, including that of the Italians' own CIAT,
which combine sightseeing with getting there. Within Rome, taxis
are metered and plentiful (except at rush hours) and cheap;
drivers are entitled to a post-10:00 P.M. surcharge, and fees for
baggage, and for being summoned by telephone. There are, as
well, buses, trams, and a subway—the Metropolitana—if you
are staying long enough to get the hang of them. But never
underestimate the pleasure of walking within central Rome.
**Currency:** The lira. **Climate:** Spring and autumn are the months I
would recommend, with winter following, and summer—at least

July and August—last of all. The peak summer months can be excessively hot and humid. There is not all that much air conditioning outside the hotels in Rome, and there are hordes of tourists. In spring (April and May) the temperature averages in the high fifties and low sixties. In autumn (October and November) the thermometer ranges, roughly, from the low sixties to the low fifties. December through February sees days averaging in the forties; March is low-fifties, and it can be rainy in winter. Summer runs from June through much of September; the first and last months can be lovely—averaging in the seventies. July and August, as I have mentioned, are often sizzling, in the eighties. **Clothes:** Roman clothes-sense, both male and female, is unequaled. This is the best-dressed capital in Europe. Be as informal as you like during the day, but dressy—in better places, at least—after dark. **Tipping:** One has the feeling that this is where it all began, and where it will never end; keep pocketsful of change handy at all hours. Although restaurants add a 15 percent service charge, waiters expect 5 percent—or more—in addition. Hotel bellhops expect 100 lire per bag (150 lire to station baggage porters); chambermaids look forward to 75 to 100 lire per day, and the waiter who brings your breakfast should get about the same. Hotel concierges, if they have been of special service, should get 300 or 400 lire per day. Service is included at cafes, but leave a bit extra, anyway. Washroom ladies—they are inescapable—get 50 lire ransom; bootblacks the same. I could go on and on, but suffice it to say that taxi drivers get 15 percent of the metered fare. **Business hours:** Shops open at about 9:00 or 9:30 A.M., close at about 1:00 P.M., and reopen from 4:00 to 7:30 P.M., in winter, and from 4:30 to 8:00 P.M. in summer; these are Monday-through-Saturday hours. Hairdressers and barbers are usually closed Monday. **Language:** Italian, of course, but the English-language fluency rate is high; French is a popular foreign language, too. And Spanish-speaking visitors manage to make themselves understood with little difficulty. The Italians are the most encouraging language teachers in Europe.

Speak only a word or two of their language and they call you bilingual, and encourage you to go right on—which is precisely what you do, enjoying every broken sentence of it. **Further information:** Italian Government Travel Office, 630 Fifth Avenue, New York; 500 North Michigan Avenue, Chicago; St. Francis Hotel, Union Square, San Francisco; 3 Place Ville Marie, Montreal; head office: Via Marghera 2, Rome, Italy. Ente Provinciale per il Turismo di Roma, Via Parigi 11, Rome, Italy.

# *Stockholm*

Sweden—and consequently its capital, Stockholm—appears never to have had the fair shake it deserves in the United States. It is not for lack of positive images and connections. The little colony of New Sweden that is now Delaware, for starters. Hundreds of thousands of settlers from Sweden in the last century. Greta Garbo and Ingrid Bergman. Ingemar Johansson's boxing and Ingmar Bergman's movies. Smorgasbord and Strindberg and sculpture by Milles. Jenny Lind and Jussi Björling. The Nobel awards. And, until a couple of decades back, the octogenarian tennis-playing king who was a newsreel favorite and reigned longer than any other in Sweden's history.

**The Sweden nobody knows:** These have had to be weighed against Sweden's World War II neutrality. (We don't hear much about humanitarian efforts during that period, or the agonizing soul-searching of many Swedes at the time their government decided, for better or for worse, that it had no choice but not to resist the Nazis.) The tales of long cold winters, and of wildly permissive sex, exaggerated in the telling. A thoughtful, independent foreign policy that so angered our government that the President of the United States ignored the gifted young Prime Minister of Sweden when he visited America in 1970. The reports of American military deserters from Vietnam lonely and unhappy in their Swedish haven.

The Sweden of the real world lies somewhere in between. Although it may be the most introverted, the most difficult to know, and the most complex of the Scandinavian nations, it is also the biggest, the richest, the most innovative, and the most brilliant, with an additional asset that is of immediate concern to us here: the most beautiful of the Scandinavian capitals.

Stockholm is by no means as venerable as the Sweden of the Goths and the Svears (from whom it took its name). It had not yet been established during the wide-ranging Viking period of the ninth through the twelfth centuries, during which time the swash-buckling Swedes had made their weight felt as far east as the Russian-bordered Black Sea, and—in the company of fellow Danish and Norwegian Vikings—as far west as Ireland. By the time Erik IX conquered Finland in the twelfth century, Sweden had become Christian. Stockholm emerged the following century, thriving as a mercantile center under the business acumen of the Hanseatic League.

**Gustavus Vasa's Stockholm, and the reign of Christina:** Ever since, Stockholm has been the center of the action. It was to Stockholm in 1520 that Danish King Christian II journeyed with the express purpose of declaring himself ruler of Sweden as well as of his homeland. At a gathering of Swedish nobility in a square of what is now called the Old Town, he staged not only a coronation but a bloody mass execution of the anti-Danish peers who were present. The horrendous event has gone down in history as the Stockholm Massacre. Its immediate effect was to generate an intense nationalism whose first major manifestation was an uprising against the Danes led by Gustavus Vasa, who soon became King Gustavus I of Sweden, and who lost no time implementing a Sweden-for-the-Swedes policy, which meant the ousting of the unloved Hanseatic merchants from Stockholm.

It was only a century or so later that Stockholm began to flower under the aegis of the kingdom's most eccentric monarch, Queen Christina. Christina's reign saw a period of intensive building.

But her greatest service to her country came during the earlier years of her reign, when she developed what amounted to almost a passion for matters of the intellect. The kingdom gained because she attracted a rather dazzling circle of artists and scholars —Descartes the most noted among them—to her court. She rewarded them and other favorites heavily, though; so heavily that by the end of her reign half of the Crown lands had been given away. As confirmed a spinster as Greta Garbo—who a few centuries later portrayed her in a film (Christina, alas, had not the beauty of Garbo, if portraits of the monarch are accurate) —she appointed a cousin as her successor, rather than produce an heir. Not long after, these things happened: (1) She became bored with her job as queen; (2) her subjects were unhappy with the way she was running things; (3) the Protestant monarch of a Protestant country, she became attracted to Catholicism; there was nothing for her to do but to (4) abdicate, which she did in 1654, slipping out of Stockholm disguised as a man, becoming a Catholic in Innsbruck, traveling the Continent, settling in Rome in the *palazzo* that is now the French Embassy, and trying—in vain—years later to regain her throne, on one occasion, and admittance to her country (which was refused on religious grounds) on still another. Christina died in Rome and was buried at St. Peter's. Just as she had established Sweden's reputation intellectually, so had her predecessor, Gustavus II, established the country as a military power to be reckoned with.

**Gustav III's Versailleslike reign, the Bernadottes, and neutrality:** There was a late-eighteenth-century period of brilliance and flamboyance marked by intellectual vigor, military aggressiveness, and Versailleslike extravagance; this occurred during the reign of the gifted Gustav III. But, by and large, Sweden had at least as many downs as ups between the seventeenth century and the early nineteenth century. It fought its last war, rather ironically, against Napoleon, with its army led by the ex-Napoleonic marshal named Jean Bernadotte, who thereafter became the founder of a new Swedish dynasty (it remains the dynasty of the realm today) as King Charles XIV (Karl Johan). Karl Johan, after forcing Denmark to cede Norway to Sweden (with whom it was united until 1905), set Sweden on the course of neutrality it has never abandoned.

From the time of its first Social Democratic government in 1920, it has managed to thrive as a constitutional monarchy that is at the same time remarkably progressive. The eight million Swedes, in their thousand-mile-long land—Sweden is the biggest and most populous of the Scandinavian countries—enjoy the highest standard of living in Europe. The remarkably long period of peace has helped make this possible, as has the government-private enterprise cooperative blend that constitutes modern Sweden. Something like 90 percent of industry is privately owned, with only about 5 percent state-controlled, and the rest the province of the highly successful Swedish cooperatives. Social welfare is expensive (it takes about a third of the annual budget), but it includes national health insurance, pensions that equal two-thirds of one's average annual earnings during his period of highest salary, prenatal and maternity care, child-bonus allowances to mothers of children up to the age of sixteen, tuition-free schools and universities, and unemployment insurance.

**Socialist kingdom:** Although Swedes complain, much like people everywhere, the government must have reason to believe that it has been doing something right. A single Social Democrat—Taage Erlander—remained Prime Minister for almost a quarter century; he was succeeded by his secretary, Olaf Palme, in 1969. The Palme period has seen Sweden recognize North Vietnam and change its Parliament from a two-chamber to a unicameral house, which moved into a spanking new building in 1970. King Gustav VI Adolph—a noted archaeologist in his own right, and the widower of British-born Queen Louise—did not ascend the throne until 1950, when he was sixty-eight, after the death of his athletic father, Gustav V, who died at the age of ninety-two, ending a popular reign that had begun in 1907. (Gustav VI Adolph is the father of Queen Mother Ingrid of next-door Denmark.)

Although it is likely that the already limited functions of the monarchy will be phased out, there remains the king's young (born 1946) grandson, heir to the throne, Prince Carl Gustav, whose father, Prince Gustav Adolph, was killed in a 1947 accident. The crown prince, one of five children, has four pretty sisters, as glamorous as their names: Princess Margaretha, Princess Birgitta, Princess Christina, and Princess Désirée—namesake of the French-born Désirée who broke her engagement to Napoleon and became the queen of the first Bernadotte king—Karl Johan—in the early nineteenth century.

TO SEE

**Lay of the land:** The reigning beauty of the Baltic, Stockholm is built on a maze of bridge-connected islands at an evergreen junction of the sea itself, and Lake Malaren. The city's islands number a dozen; they are linked by some forty bridges, but there is no need to go into all the specifics. Suffice it to say that the heart of mainland Stockholm embraces two contiguous districts: *Ostermalm* and *Norrmalm.* (Consider the Royal Opera as a landmark.) Directly south of this area is the small island known simply as the *Old Town,* which is a major destination for every visitor. (Consider the Royal Palace as a landmark.) The Old Town is connected to a much larger and more southerly island called *Sodermalm* by means of a complex cloverleaf traffic circle that was considered revolutionary when it went up, and is called *Slussen* (which consider a landmark). (Sodermalm is without any major visitor incentive save possibly the Katarina Elevator near Slussen; this alfresco lift is attached to an office building, and you may ascend it to get a good bird's-eye view of town.) Still another major island is directly west of "mainland" downtown; it is called *Kungsholmen,* and its landmark is the tower of the Town Hall; and last, there is *Djurgarden* (*Deer Garden*), the big easterly island that is full of visitor treats.

(Use the neo-Renaissance pile that is the Nordiska Museum as a landmark.)

Lest this mite of geography has confused you, let me take another tack: main drags, squares, and parks worth remembering. For me, the Royal Opera on *Gustav Adolf Torg* (*torg* means square in Swedish) is the focal point of town. The square gives onto a handsome little park, *Kungstradgarden,* with cafes and stands selling delicious sausage and glass cases full of ceramics, china, silver, and the like. This park's northern frontier is the principal street known as *Hamngatan.* It has two distinguishing characteristics. One is Sweden House (Sverigehuset), the Stockholm Tourist Traffic Association's hotel-booking and guide-hire center/lounge/cafe/restaurant/shop complex. And the other is Nordiska Kompaniet, which the locals know as NK (*N-Koh*) and us gringos as *NKay.* This is one of the great department stores of the planet (see the To Buy section on later pages) and is also a good landmark with its revolving "NK" electric sign. Follow Hamngatan west a couple of blocks, passing still another landmark—a row of five identical next-to-each-other skyscraping office buildings—to *Drottninggatan,* running perpendicular to it. A block or so north of Drottninggatan is PUB, No. 2 of the department stores and another good landmark. But go back to Hamngatan and NK and walk east on the street. Proceed a couple of blocks and you'll almost bump into the Royal Dramatic Theater. Turn left at that building and you're on *Birger Jarlsgatan,* full of smart, browsable shops like Georg Jensen and showrooms of the Rorstrand and Gustavsberg china factories. Now recross your steps back to the showcase-lined Kungstradgarden and adjacent Karl XII Torg. Cross the square onto the bridge before you, and poof, you're in the Old Town, with the Royal Palace dead ahead. The Old Town is full of venerable narrow streets, but the water-bordering main thoroughfare is *Skeppsbron;* it leads all the way to the cloverleaf Slussen that connects it with Sodermalm, the big island to the south. To walk to Kungsholmen, the westernmost island containing the Town Hall, take *Hamngatan—*

the street with NK—as far west as you can. It becomes *Klara-bergsgatan* just before you cross a bridge to the other island. To get to the easternmost island, Djurgarden, walk east from the Royal Opera on *Arsenalsgatan.* You pass a little green called *Berzeli Park* (landmark: Berns Restaurant), and continue onto the water-straddling *Strandvagen,* until you reach a bridge across which are the unmistakable Renaissance towers of the Nordiska Museum.

**Choice destinations:** There's a lot that is very worthwhile to see in Stockholm. Just strolling about is satisfaction in itself— the smart shops of the mainland business area, the far more Bohemian ambience—students and guitars, coffee shops and antiques shops—on the narrow streets of the Old Town. But let me make some specific suggestions.

As regards public buildings and churches, leaving the Royal Palace for the museum category, I would place the *Town Hall* No. 1. With its graceful triple crown-topped tower overlooking Lake Malaren—indeed, overlooking the whole city—it is quite possibly the most timeless major structure of any major city to have emerged in the 1920s. The red brick exterior and gardens are in themselves extraordinary, but the interiors—especially reception chambers like the Blue and Golden rooms, with their mosaics and other art—are among the city's aesthetic highlights. (The nearby *Law Courts,* about a decade older, are visitworthy, too.)

The Old Town's major monuments, the Palace excepted, are the *Storkyrkan,* the thirteenth-century church where Sweden's monarchs are crowned, with the choicest art within, the sculpture of St. George and the Dragon, the silver altar, a painting of the city—the oldest extant—done in 1535, and the royal pews. Although kings are crowned in Storkyrkan, they are buried in still another Old Town church—*Ridderholm,* richly medieval and with crypts of kings through the centuries. The *Stock Exchange* is the home of the Swedish Academy, the very same that awards the Nobel Prizes for every category except Peace (these are given in Oslo). There is the *Riddarhuset,* the Old House of the Nobility. And each day at noon the spit-and-polish *Royal Guard* changes in front of the palace.

If I appear to emphasize *museums* in the paragraphs that follow, it is because Stockholm is an exceptional museum city. The Swedes, for reasons they may know better than I, are absolute wizards at organizing and operating museums with dash and verve and fun and imagination. Stockholm has no less than forty-seven such institutions. I am hardly about to recommend them all. But my favorites follow.

Because it is more fun than a barrel of monkeys—something amusing seems always to be going on—I give the *Museum of Modern Art* first play. On the little island called Skeppsholmen (in what appears to have been nothing so much as an enormous warehouse), this is the baby of one Pontus Hulten, the curator who, small budget be damned, has made this a prototype of what MOMAs should be the world over. Quite as unusual— eccentric is surely the word here—is the *Hallwyl Museum,* the 1898 mansion of the late Countess Wilhelmina von Hallwyl, with *all* of her belongings—inventoried, they fill seventy-nine good-size volumes—left quite as they were when she died in 1930. The collection ranges from the conventionally important— the main drawing room built around the Countess's sixteenth- century Belgian tapestries, as well as paintings by such masters as Hals, Brueghel, Rembrandt, and Steen—to toothbrushes, clothes, pots and pans, and *objets* collected on endless travels to innumerable countries. As in the case of the Isabella Stewart Gardner Museum in Boston, none of the exhibits—and they total some fifty thousand—may be touched (except, one supposes, for dusting), according to the terms of the will setting up the museum. We revert, then, to the real world, and the series of museums that are a part of the five-hundred-room, eighteenth- century *Royal Palace*—the largest extant still serving as a royal residence and, so far as I can tell, the only inhabited capital-city home of a European monarch that is open the year round to the public. To see those sections of the palace that are open takes concerted effort. You must first obtain an up-to-date schedule of what sections are open and when, for the hours for each section vary, and in no case is any section open for a nice, solid, all-day nine-to-five stretch; that would be too easy. Having ascertained this intelligence, you must find your way to the entrances of these various parts of the enormous palace. There are occasional guards to inquire of, and pleasant elderly ladies—most speak French and German, some English—are in charge of the various sections. I go into all this detail because the efforts (you will have to make several distinct trips to see the lot) are worthwhile. Open sections include the State, Guest, and Bernadotte Apartments, the Throne Room (a gold-and-blue chamber with Queen Christina's silver throne, and that just has to be the throne room to end all throne rooms), the rococo Royal Chapel, and the relatively recent Treasury in the palace cellars (wherein are displayed the magnificent regalia and treasures of the realm dating to the sixteenth century). (The security precautions, please be advised, are very much twentieth-century. To quote the catalog: "Do not touch the show cases. Otherwise you may set off a burglar alarm. The exhibition is monitored via closed-circuit television.") The *National Museum* is the most crowded of the conventional museums because it is the most conveniently located, just a hop and a skip from the Opera and Karl XII Torg. This is an excellent survey-museum. It is the central museum for the kingdom's collections of paintings, sculpture, applied arts, prints, and drawings, both Swedish and foreign. Buy a printed guide and you can cover the highlights of the three floors of galleries in minimum time. The *Museum of Far Eastern Antiquities* is special because it is so handsome. NK department store did the décor and design for it in the late fifties, and King Gustav VI Adolph took a personal interest, contributing to the collections from his own acquisitions. The *Nordiska Museum* is a superb compendium of Swedish culture from the Renaissance onward. The *National Historical Museum* looks at Sweden historically as the Nordiska does culturally. The *Royal Library* is full of priceless ancient manuscripts. There are a trio of very personal art galleries. One, *Milles Garden,* was the home and studio of Carl Milles, and contains a good bit of his work and of ancient Roman sculpture as well. (Note Milles' Orpheus Fountain in front of the downtown Concert Hall on Kungsgatan.) Another, *Waldmarsudde,* was the residence of Prince Eugen (1865–1947). On exhibit are many of the prince's own paintings and a number of other contemporary Swedish works. The *Thiel Gallery* had been the house of a rich Stockholmer and is now a repository of Swedish art of the late nineteenth and twentieth centuries, as well as some paintings by French Impressionists and the Norwegian genius, Edvard Munch. As for the warship *Wasa,* it sounds too preposterous to be true. What happened is that a seventeenth-century vessel capsized in Stockholm Harbor on its maiden journey a few centuries ago, and a few years ago—well, in 1961, to be precise—some Swedish scientists tried to recover it. They succeeded. Almost all of the contents of the ship were intact—the crew's clothes, eating utensils, furniture, coins, tools, guns, and ammunition. But you *must* have a look for yourself. I've saved *Skansen* for last. It is one of the great open-air museums. Swedish novelist Selma Lagerlof was at the opening in 1891, and it's been going strong ever since. There are country dances before the old farmsteads. Rural musicians accompany them. Native Scandinavian animals are in residence. There are restaurants [see the To Eat (and Drink) section], concerts, and special exhibits. And the interiors—from those of elegant manor houses to simple country places—are superbly done.

There are several *excursions from Stockholm* that should be considered requisites. The eighteenth-century *Drottningholm Palace* and the *Court Theater* of that era, on its grounds, are first and foremost. The interior of the palace (built from designs of Nicholas Tessin the Elder) is one gemlike room after another, with Queen Hedvig Eleonara's bedroom the one to knock you dead—tapestries from Delft, considerable Swedish furniture and mirrors of the great Gustavian era, and earlier; frescoed ceiling, Savonnerie screen with portrait of Gustav III. The theater, at which one may—indeed, should—see at least one or two summer performances of period opera and ballet by casts from the Royal Opera in town, who still sing in the ingenious original sets, with candle footlights and other period equipment. It is furnished quite as it was when Gustav III went to hear Handel, Gluck, and others of his favorites, which still constitute the current repertoire. *Gripsholm Castle* is a turreted Renaissance masterwork straddling Lake Malaren, furnished quite as it was during the centuries it served as a royal residence, and with an astonishingly immense collection of royal portraits. *Haga*, restored only in recent years, is a graceful Gustav III palace that is now used by the Swedish Government much as Washington uses Blair House—as a residence for visiting bigwigs from abroad. It was from Haga that Gustav III, in fancy dress, took off on an evening in 1792 for the gala at the Opera House he had just built in town, only to be assassinated. But you know all about it if you know Verdi's opera, *Un Ballo in Mascara.*

## TO WATCH

If there are performances, be it opera or ballet or both, during your visit, beeline for the *Royal Opera.* This late-nineteenth-century neo-baroque pile is not only all that an opera house should be aesthetically, it houses first-rate opera and ballet companies. In 1971, you will remember, the director of the Royal Opera, Goeran Gentele, departed Stockholm for New York's Lincoln Center to replace Sir Rudolph Bing as director of what was widely hoped would finally become a dynamic, contemporary, and alive Metropolitan Opera; he died in a tragic 1972 auto crash, before his first Met season had begun. But Gentele was by no means the first distinguished name to emerge from the Stockholm Opera. Jussi Bjoerling, surely one of the greatest of tenors, was of that company. (His son, Rolf, following in dad's footsteps, is a current tenor star at the opera.) Birgit Nilsson, Nicolai Gedda, and Elizabeth Söderström are other Stockholm Opera luminaries; and also choreographer Birgit Cullberg. The *Stockholm Concert Hall,* behind the earlier-mentioned Carl Milles-designed Orpheus Fountain (and with wide steps on which Stockholmers sun themselves at the least provocation), is an agreeable 1920s structure that is home to the Stockholm Symphony and a variety of visiting attractions. The *Royal Dramatic Theater's* only handicap for the non-Swedish-speaking visitor is that its performances are, of course, in Swedish. But if you feel that you can get an idea of what's going on anyhow, plunge right in. The place has a star-studded history, heaven knows—Garbo, Ingrid Bergman, Viveca Lindfors, Signe Hasso, Mai Zetterling, Max von Sydow, O'Neill's last plays before we got them in America, and Ingmar Bergman, as a former director. The *Drottningholm Court Theater,* earlier recommended, is a summer requisite for seventeenth- and eighteenth-century opera and ballet as performed by casts from the Royal Opera, in costumes of the period, utilizing the theater's ancient sets, candle footlights, and backstage equipment. And then there is *Berns,* the venerable Stockholm cabaret-restaurant that offers a variety of diversions in a variety of *fin-de-siècle-*décor rooms, the most noted of which has a big-name show. And the *movies;* there are a lot of foreign ones, all of which are shown with their original soundtracks (no dubbing) and Swedish printed subtitles. Performances are usually at 7:00 P.M. and 9:00 P.M.

## TO STAY

The Swedes have never been the hoteliers they could be if they set their minds to it. One continues to have the feeling, over a two-decade period, that they are frequently ambivalent in their concepts of what hotels should be (no frills, roofs over the head—or something else again) and that their staffs are not

always as comfortable working with guests—at least foreign
guests—as they might be. This is changing, for Swedes are
traveling abroad more, learning foreign languages, and coming
more in contact with strangers. But Swedish hotelkeeping, like
Soviet plumbing, has not yet been perfected. A splendid city
like Stockholm, for example, should have half a dozen traditional-style hotels of the caliber of the celebrated *Grand*—
or better. But it doesn't. And even the Grand—invariably so
fully booked that it can slough off on service, and with those
glorious views only from the limited number of front bedrooms—
has limitations. A nearby hotel that I've enjoyed a stay at very
much is the *Reisen.* The views from its front rooms are quite
as smashing as the Grand's, for it is located just over the bridge
in the Old Town, on the waterfront thoroughfare called Skeppsbron. The Reisen comprises three seventeenth-century houses
that have been thoroughly refurbished and modernized. There are
126 rooms, all with radio and TV, and most with at least one
wall of original brick. The small lobby is a mistake, but the
waterfront restaurant upstairs is a nice one (with good fare),
and the service throughout is as pleasant as the location is
inspired. Also new is the 13-million-dollar, 476-room *Sheraton-
Stockholm,* only a block from the Central Railway Station in the
"mainland" part of downtown. Part-owned by SAS, the hotel is
Swedish-designed, -decorated, and -furnished and fully air conditioned (not that Stockholm has more than its share of heat waves),
a pair of restaurants (one is a coffee shop), and a cocktail lounge.
And you're close enough to the center of things to be able to
walk. The modern, good-looking *Continental* is another wise
choice, well operated, well located, and with a variety of services
(including three restaurants) and facilities. The *Stockholm* has
the great advantage of being about as central as you can get. It
occupies the top floors of an office building, serves breakfast but
no other meals, and is nothing fancy; all rooms have bath,
though, and I have found the service good.

## TO EAT (AND DRINK)

The Swedes are better at restaurants than they are at hotels. They eat very well. The world-copied smorgasbord was, after all, their invention, and when one encounters the real thing the diverse attributes of the Swedish cuisine are immediately apparent. These people are good, as well they might be, with the fish and sea-food of which they have so much. Like the Finns, they make a big fuss over the summer-only crayfish, which they down with aquavit and beer. But they treat the vegetable with the care it warrants, both in salads and as hot dishes. They know what to do with good red beef, with pork and lamb. Their soups (the pea with pork is a specialty) are commendable, as are their delicate dessert pancakes, served with cream and the delicious native lingonberries. Like their fellow Scandinavians, they bake well—pastries (not as famous as the Danes', but very good indeed), dark breads, and the Swedish variation of the crackerlike flat bread; of the Scandinavian species, the Swedes' are more like the copycat American Rye Krisp. But to get back to smorgasbord. Imitation is, of course, the sincerest form of flattery, but the Swedes' masterwork is frequently distorted in translation, so that one might recap the principles at this point. Go around as often as you like, naturally picking up a fresh plate each time. The order of battle is eminently logical. One starts with the cold seafoods—herrings in great variety, sardines, smoked whitefish, and the like. These may be combined with cold salads. Cold meats—beef, ham, tongue, turkey, or chicken, perhaps, would follow. Then come the hot dishes. Most smorgasbord tables have at least one or two—the inimitable Swedish meatballs are invariably one of these. There are usually a selection of cheeses, which may be taken with the salads, or after the hot dishes in lieu of, or in addition to, desserts, of which there are usually a variety. Liquor has not been a problem— the ordering of it in public places, that is—for some years now.

It is not served until noon (1 P.M. on Sundays). There are bars and cocktail lounges in the better hotels, and most restaurants are licensed to serve both hard stuff and wine and beer; some may serve only wine and beer; whichever, they may serve until as late as 2:30 A.M., with final closings set at 3:00 A.M.

No international capital has a more obvious No. 1 restaurant choice than Stockholm. It is the *Operakälleren.* To miss it is like missing the Lincoln Memorial in Washington. Restored to its turn-of-the-century opulence in the 1960s, with the Swedish Government contributing some three million dollars toward the restoration, this is quite the most magnificent eatery in Scandinavia, and one of the extraordinary restaurants of Europe. The oak-paneled, mural-decorated main dining room is a national treasure; there are, as well, a handsome grill room, and a bar that is quite the poshest drinking palace in town. The *Operakälleren* smorgasbord is a daily lunch (not dinner)-time tradition in Stockholm (it's served through 8:00 P.M. on Sundays). The *Grand Hotel's terrace restaurant* is smart, good, and with the panorama of the water and the Royal Palace that the hotel is famous for. The Old Town offers a number of atmospheric restaurants in venerable houses. Two that I like very much are *Aurora,* where a dinner in its brick-walled cellar is a Stockholm gustatory adventure of the first order; food, service, ambience— all rate honors. Good, too, is *Fem Sma Hus,* which utilizes the cellars of five-in-a-row houses of considerable vintage. *Solliden* is as famous a name to Stockholmers as Skansen, the open-air museum-park of which it is an integral part. This is a very big, very authentically Swedish, and very attractive place; moderate-priced. You might not think it, what with its location opposite NK and in conjunction with the Sweden House information center, but the *Cosmopolite Restaurant* offers two good dining rooms—a moderate-price main-floor one, and a more informal and cheaper place in the basement. *NK* itself, as earlier mentioned, has a rooftop restaurant that's a summer delight, a year-round indoor restaurant, and a tearoom. I have already recommended *Berns*

in the To Watch section. But I shall add here that there are a
number of discos (*Alexandra* at Biblioteksgata 5, is probably the
smallest, and it serves food) and places that are more dance spots
than restaurants, or that have entertainment as well, and sometimes even roulette. I mention *Ambassadeur,* Kungsgatan 18,
because it is bits and pieces of all these ingredients; you may
or may not like it. *Baldakinen,* in the City Theater (Stadsteatern),
Barnhusgatan 12, is popular after-theater, drawing an interesting
crowd. There are some *pubs,* too; *Engelen,* on Kornhammnstorg,
in the Old Town, is congenial and is above a basement night club
called *Kolingen.* A never-close sandwich shop, should you require
one, is *Cafe Auto,* Kungstensgatan 14.

## TO BUY

The only difficulty relating to shopping in Sweden is that almost
everything is damned expensive. Take that high standard of
living and combine it with inflation, and you think you're back
home in the good old U.S.A. No bargains unless—accidentally
—you hit a humdinger of a sale. Still, you'll want to have a
look around because the Swedes were pioneers not only of the
contemporary applied arts—furniture, ceramics, china, glass,
lighting fixtures, stainless steel tableware and flatware, kitchen
utensils, textiles, *rya* rugs—but of interior design as well. Indeed,
they rank with the Americans and the Britons as the Westerners
who can put together the rooms of a house or apartment most
successfully.

Names like Bruno Matthsson, Carl Malmsten (furniture),
Stig Lindberg and Wilhelm Kage (ceramics and china), Erik
Fleming (silver), and Viola Grasten (rugs), are but a few of the
modern classicists in this area. And manufacturers like Gustavsberg and Rorstrand (china), Kosta, Orrefors and Strombergshyttan
(glass), and Gense (stainless steel) are equally blue-chip internationally.

To start, *NK,* the earlier-mentioned Nordiska Kompaniet that is both a Stockholm institution and department store, on Hamngatan, in the heart of town. Most of the departments that will interest visitors are in the basement—glass, ceramics and china, silverware, kitchenware, stainless steel. The information desk, on the main floor, will give you an all-department shopping card, allowing you to pay for all you buy at expedition's end, having it shipped abroad (probably saving you taxes), and paid for all in one fell swoop, at the basement shipping office. Other NK conveniences: a main-floor tearoom, a fourth-floor restaurant (with a rooftop eatery in summer), and fourth-floor rest rooms. Furniture (third floor) is interesting, as are the various men's, women's and children's clothing departments. Also noteworthy: beauty parlor (seventh floor) and barber shop (second floor). *PUB* (which stands for Paul U. Bergstrom) is a less-smart department store than NK, but certainly browseworthy. On Birgar Jarlsgatan you will want to have a look at the display and sales of *Gustavsberg* at No. 2 and *Rorstrand* at No. 16, at the Stockholm branch of *Georg Jensen* (No. 13), which features the noted Jensen silver (including jewelry), the equally noted Royal Copenhagen porcelains, and a boutique full of both men's and women's fashions and accessories, mostly imported. *Helmslojdsforening* (don't try to pronounce it; just *go* there) at Hornsgatan 82-B is to Stockholm what Husfliden is to Oslo, the national center for traditional handicrafts and a place where you invariably find inexpensive little objects that make welcome gifts—or decorations for your own Christmas tree, for that matter; ditto for the excellent *Svensk Hemslöjd* (Sveavägen 44). *Libraria* has two locations, at Storkyrkobrinkenl, near the Storkyrk, and at Jakobsbergsgatan 15; the subject is gifts—stylish glass, stainless, wood, textiles, with some handsome inexpensive souvenirs scattered among them. The furniture of *Carl Malmsten,* the earlier-mentioned pioneer furniture designer, is available at the Malmsten shop, Strandvagen 5B. *Nordiska Kristallmagasinet* (Kungsgatan) specializes in glass. The narrow streets of the Old Town are full of

interesting antiques shops. The *T-Centralen subway station* typifies the many attractively decorated terminals of the system and
contains clustered shops (including groceries) worth noting because they are open to 10:00 P.M. every evening.

TO NOTE

**Access:** The most obvious way of arriving is by plane, SAS
having the most direct service from New York, and a number
of other North American gateways, via Copenhagen or Bergen.
Pan Am also flies from New York via Copenhagen. SAS, the
national airline of the three Scandinavian kingdoms, Sweden and
neighboring Denmark and Norway, has an extensive intra-
Scandinavian route (including summer midnight sun flights to
Kiruna in the Swedish Arctic), as well as a dense all-European
network. Additional domestic flights are operated by a line called
LIN. The Stockholm airport for international flights is Arlanda,
a longish twenty-four miles north of town; there are cheap airport
buses to the air terminal in Stockholm; cabs are costly. There's
no departure tax for intercontinental flights. The airport for
domestic flights is Bromma, only six miles from the city; both
airport buses and taxis will take you to town. Upon departure, if
you're flying to the Swedish city of Malmo, or Copenhagen, there's
a small departure tax. Rail? There are direct overland trains if
you're coming from Oslo or Lapland, or from Helsinki via
Lapland. Coming from the Continent, the most direct routing
would be via Copenhagen, from which you would take a boat
(hydrofoil is the quickest) across The Sound to Malmo, in Sweden,
thence proceeding north by direct train (taking about six hours) to
Stockholm. There is modern bus service, and roads—particularly
from Stockholm southward—are very good. Within Stockholm,
there is extensive public transport, including a clean, modern
subway; taxis, some of whose drivers are English-speaking, and
are trained as guides (phone 22-04-00 to book them in advance),

and an excellent selection of sightseeing tours not only by bus
but, especially enjoyable, by boat. Bear in mind that not all
hotels are central, and that if you are not staying in the heart of
town, getting about can be bothersome. There are a number
of car-hire firms. **Climate:** Late spring, summer, and the very
brief autumn are the ideal months for a visit. By late spring I
mean May, when it should be mostly in the fifties. June, July,
and August constitute summer, with highs in the upper sixties,
maybe seventy. September, like May, is fiftyish, and the coldest
months—November through April—range from the twenties to
the forties. Be prepared for light nights all summer long, and note
that the midnight sun shines above the Arctic Circle from mid-
May to mid-July; if you are in Stockholm at that time, make it
a point to fly up to the Arctic, if only for a day or two. Note,
too, that although Sweden, even in the far north, has nothing like
the rugged mountain terrain of Norway, the Swedes do indeed
ski a great deal; up north the season usually lasts into early
June. **Clothes:** Although the Danes are catching up with them,
the Swedes are the smartest-dressed of Scandinavians. Stockholmers, both men and women, deck themselves out modishly,
supporting a sophisticated Swedish couture. Although any kind of
dress goes in pubs and cafes, discos and informal restaurants—as
in London, Paris, or New York—jacket and tie is a good rule after
dark in better places. **Currency:** The Swedish *krona,* or crown
(pural: *kronor*). It is divided into one hundred *öre.* **Tipping:** Hotels add a 15 percent service charge and restaurants add 12½ percent, so that no additional tipping is necessary, although you may
round out the bill to the nearest krona, if you like. Bellhops and
baggage porters expect a krona per bag, hatcheck ladies a krona
per coat, cabbies 10 to 15 percent, barbers and hairdressers
likewise. **Business hours:** Most shops are open from 9:00 A.M.
to 6:00 P.M., Monday through Friday, closing earlier (the times
vary) on Saturdays and the days before holidays. Bigger stores,
including department stores, usually remain open until 8:00 P.M.
Monday *or* Friday, except in June and July. **Language:** Swedish

is, of course, the national language. It is similar enough to Danish and Norwegian so that nationals of the three countries can communicate with each other. Often, though, they speak in the Scandinavian *lingua franca,* English, which is widely spoken in Sweden—not to the extent that it is in Denmark, Norway, and the Netherlands, but much more so, on the other hand, than in Finland. There is considerable German spoken, particularly among older people, and an appreciable amount of French. **Local literature:** *This Week in Stockholm* is a well-prepared weekly giveaway found in the hotels. There are a number of good free maps of the town, but one eminently worthy of mention here is that published by the Stockholm Enskilda Bank; someone should give it a prize. NK department store, at its main floor information desk, passes out a helpful folder on the city, with maps and tips. Because there is such a variety of bus and boat tours of the city, the brochure of Tourist Sightseeing AB is worth obtaining. **Further information:** Swedish National Tourist Office, Scandinavia House, 505 Fifth Avenue, New York; Scandinavian National Tourist Offices, 612 South Flower Street, Los Angeles, California; Stockholm Turisttrafikforbund (Stockholm Tourist Traffic Association), Sverigehuset, Hamngatan 27, Stockholm, Sweden.

# *Vaduz*

Vaduz is Europe's Curiosity Capital. One visits it for much the same reason that Tensing and Hillary ascended Everest: because it is there—the seat of government of the anachronistic, but ever so solvent, Principality of Liechtenstein. It is difficult to divorce the capital from the realm, which itself is only about the size of the District of Columbia—some sixty square miles, and with a population of about twenty thousand. Vaduzers comprise about a fifth of the national total; there are about four thousand of them. And although the principality at first glance—even second and third glances—may seem little more than pastoral with a touch of tourism added, there's more there than meets the eye. Recent years have seen a veritable boom in small industry, to the tune of some eighty million dollars in exports annually, and that's not including the revenue from those famous postage stamps.

**Tiny principality:** There is little doubt but that Liechtenstein's diminutive size has aided in the retention of its sovereignty. Actually, though the castle of its reigning prince is some eight centuries old, the principality was not created until the early eighteenth century, when the Holy Roman Empire welcomed it as a fief created by the welding of the County of Vaduz and the Barony of Schellenburg, both of which had been acquired from previous owners by a rich Austrian family, name of Liechtenstein. The French invaded during the Napoleonic era, after which

Liechtenstein joined the Germanic Confederation. In 1866, though that entity was dissolved, and Liechtenstein was on its very own, albeit linked to Austria in an economic union that lasted until after World War I, when Switzerland took over, in such areas as currency, customs, and foreign affairs, including representation abroad.

The number of reigning princes has been relatively few, thanks to the excessively lengthy period that one ruler—Johan II—remained on the throne: from 1858 to 1929. That's seventy-one years, a near-record. It's only a year less than Louis XIV's seventy-two years, but it easily beats Victoria, whose reign lasted sixty-four years. Johan II did such a commendable job of keeping the principality sovereign that his subjects think of him as Johan the Good. He was succeeded by Franz I, who remained on the throne less than a decade, abdicating in 1938 in favor of his nephew, Franz Joseph II, who was born in 1906 and who has the distinction of being the first Prince of Liechtenstein to make his permanent home in Liechtenstein; his predecessors preferred the family estates—many times larger than their principality—in Austria and, earlier, in Czechoslovakia.

**Voteless women, profitable factories:** Graustarkian as it may sound, and despite its lack of a railroad, airline, radio or television stations, or even a daily newspaper, Liechtenstein has a two-party system and a fifteen-man Parliament, control of which was gained in 1970—a single vote did it—by the minority Patriotic Union, taking over after forty-two years of Progressive Citizens' party control. You will notice that I termed the Parliament a fifteen-"man" body. I meant just that. Unlike the neighboring Swiss, who finally gave women the vote in federal elections in 1971, the Liechtensteiners, in a referendum of their own that same year on that same subject, voted to keep the ladies ballotless. Of course, a good number of other residents—a good third —are without the vote also; they are mostly foreigners—Austrians and Swiss—who have come to help man the profitable little factories that turn out more dentures than any other country in Europe, and a variety of precision instruments of the kind that Switzerland also excels at. Liechtensteiners are known for happy dispositions. And why not? Taxes are so low as to be almost nil, not only for people but for companies as well, which explains why a substantial number of international firms have their headquarters there—on paper, anyway.

## TO SEE

Sightseeing in Vaduz does not take a long time. This is an agreeable enough little Rhine River valley town. The snowy peaks (Liechtenstein has a couple of dozen of them) are a picture-postcard backdrop. The originally medieval *castle* wherein reside Prince Franz Joseph II, Princess Gina, and their son Prince Johann—the heir apparent—is on an eminence affording a panorama of not only the town but virtually the whole realm. It is not open to the public, but upon payment of a fee, the Prince invites you to inspect *paintings* from the brilliant collection —valued at something like 150 million dollars—that he inherited from his ancestors. The sixteenth- and seventeenth-century Flemish paintings—including works by Hals, Brueghel, Van Dyck, and Rubens—constitute the cream of what is without question a costly crop—one of the great private holdings of art in the world. The pictures are on view in a building at once known as the *Englanderbau* and the *National Tourist Office*. To see, also, are a *museum* devoted to those postage stamps that bring the principality so much of its wealth, and an interesting little *historical museum*. There are a number of shops, none distinguished, along the main street.

Of course, you will want to drive into the mountains. The *Malbun Valley,* with a number of hotels, is pretty in summer and snowy and skier-populated in winter. But look over the map obtainable at the National Tourist Office and plan your own itinerary; serviceable roads lead to a surprising number of Alpine points.

### TO STAY

The Prince's castle excepted—and you must have a personal invitation to stay there—there are no de luxe places of accommodation. The *Real Hotel,* small to be sure, but central and the site of the principality's most distinguished restaurant, is a good bet. The *Engel,* also in the heart of things, is somewhat bigger, and action-packed—at least by Liechtenstein standards. The *Sonnenhof* is good, but you have to want a restful away-from-town location; this one is on a mountain slope with a view. Aside from the flicks and leisurely dinners—the top hotels all have restaurants, with the Real's (see above) the leader—there is dancing at hotels like the *Wald* and *Vaduzerhof,* and a bit of after-dinner levity at the Engel. The food has Austro-Swiss overtones, and there is a local red wine, a few glasses of which will impel you to dreamland, obviating any desire for the kind of night life that Vaduz is not prepared to offer.

### TO BUY

Predictable souvenir-type souvenirs are to be seen in the shops; nothing to write home—or write here—about.

### TO NOTE

**Access:** Look at a map and you'll see that Liechtenstein is tucked between Switzerland (on the west) and Austria (on the east). Vaduz has no airport. The nearest major one is at Zurich, which is about a two-hour drive away. There is no railway

station, either. Going by train, the destination you want is Buchs,
Switzerland, from which there is Swiss Postal Bus service to
nearby Vaduz. If you are motoring, note that the roads are good
and that other nearby points, so that you may orient yourself,
are Chur and Bad-Ragaz in Switzerland, and Innsbruck, in
Austria. Because of a customs union between Liechtenstein and
Switzerland, there are no customs or immigration formalities for
travelers going between the two countries. **Getting about:** Taxis,
hired cars, guided tours. **Climate:** Similar to Switzerland's (see
the chapter on Berne), with cold snowy winters, sunny but not
overly hot summers, mild springs and autumns. **Clothes:** Dress
as you would in smallish northern towns elsewhere in Europe, or at
home. Informality is the keynote during the day in Vaduz or the
countryside, with jackets and ties usually the rule after dark. **Currency:** The Swiss franc is legal tender. **Tipping:** A service charge
of 10 or 15 percent is added to bills, and is adequate. A franc per
bag to porters and bellhops is more than enough. **Language:** The
national language is German; there's a good bit of English spoken,
though. French, too. **Further information:** Swiss National Tourist
Office, 608 Fifth Avenue, New York; 661 Market Street, San
Francisco; Liechtenstein National Tourist Office, Vaduz, Liechtenstein.

# Vienna

You don't have to be a monarchist to appreciate the Hapsburgs. Not, at any rate, if you appreciate Vienna. Say all you want about the Austrian republic with its democratic government—and I say three cheers. The fact remains that the Hapsburgs continue to be as integral a part of Vienna as the spire of St. Stephen's, even though they gave up their throne more than half a century ago.

There were good Hapsburgs and less-good Hapsburgs. Even at their least prepossessing, though, they had a brand of resilience that enabled their dynasty to span six centuries and, at its peak, embrace an area extending from the Balkans clear across Europe and the Atlantic into Spanish America.

**The resilience of the Hapsburgs:** It is gone now, that unbelievably gargantuan realm. Vienna is today capital of an Austria smaller than Maine. But the Hapsburgs built for keeps—which, of course, is why Vienna will always feel their presence. When they came on the scene, their capital had not a good deal more than its name, which it had taken from *Vindobona,* the name the Romans had given to the place when they settled in. In the ninth century Charlemagne took over the region as a province of his empire; later, it became a part of the Holy Roman Empire. The crown of *that* empire is to be seen in the Treasury of Vienna's Hofburg. The Hapsburgs displaced a local ruling dynasty called the Babensbergs, under whom it must be admitted there

were several relatively progressive and placid medieval centuries.
But it was the Hapsburgs who put Austria on the map. Or, it
might almost be said, it was the Hapsburgs who jammed almost
the whole map into Austria. They were expansionist. They had
an ingenious knack for carrying off marriages of political brilliance.
Long before the British were saying that the sun never set on the
Union Jack, the Hapsburgs' version of that slogan had become their
motto. They began their acquisitions in the fourteenth century
—taking over such areas as the Tyrol and Trieste.

At the close of the fifteenth century the family pulled off a
pair of its most consequential marriages. Maximilian I married
Mary of Burgundy, so that Burgundy and Burgundy-controlled
Flanders came into the empire; and Philip of Hapsburg married
Johanna of Castile, thereby becoming occupant of the throne of
Spain, and bringing that important land and its New World
dominions under Hapsburg domination. But the east remained as
important as the west to these monarchs. In 1683—a date every
Austrian knows as well as Americans know 1776—the Austrians
decisively defeated a force of several hundred thousands of
Turks at the gates of Vienna, thereby securing not only their
own country but all of Europe to the west, from Ottoman advances.

**Defeat of the Turks—and Maria Theresa's elegant era:** All
along, the political and military process of the clan was matched
by an extraordinary aptitude for, and interest in, the arts, beginning with such fourteenth-century highlights as the establishment of Vienna University and the building of that city's St.
Stephen's Cathedral. Almost every emperor, up to but not including Franz Joseph in the mid-nineteenth century, was an avid
collector. A number of others were exceptional, buying up the
paintings of the masters in every major continental art center.
The defeat of the Turks was more than a major military-political
event. The victory inspired the Hapsburgs and their Austrian
subjects to commence their baroque era, which was nowhere
more brilliant and inspired than in Vienna.

By the time the strong-willed Maria Theresa ascended the throne in the mid-eighteenth century, Vienna had become a city of considerable elegance. Maria Theresa, in between battles with her keen adversary, Prussia's Frederick the Great, made her capital even more splendid than she found it (she loved elaborate parties in opulent settings), the while introducing reforms that her unusually enlightened son and successor, Joseph II, improved upon. It was Joseph II who abolished serfdom and instituted complete religious toleration. And it was the same Joseph who gathered together the enormous collection of paintings that had been amassed by his ancestors and installed them in the lovely baroque Belvedere Palace built earlier by the adored Prince Eugene, who led the victorious battle over the Turks. Emperor Joseph did not simply have the paintings hung as elements of the palace décor. He had them framed uniformly and, moreover, arranged so as to depict chronologically the history of art, a then unheard-of concept. Moreover, he opened the palace galleries to his subjects, making the pictures available to the public for the first time. This was another virtually unknown concept. (During the Napoleonic wars, several hundred of the paintings were seized by the French and taken to Paris; a number were returned, however.)

**The musicians' Vienna—and Metternich's Congress:** Joseph II's reign was notable in still another respect. It saw Vienna begin to develop as one of the most significant music centers the world has known, with such entrants upon the scene as Gluck, Mozart, Haydn, Schubert, and Beethoven. Napoleon's early-nineteenth-century defeat led to the all-Europe deliberations that every schoolchild on both sides of the Atlantic studies: the Metternich-masterminded Congress of Vienna, which took place in Schoenbrunn Palace (Maria Theresa's heavy-handed answer to Versailles) in 1815. This was followed, not too much later, by the early waltzes for which the city was to become celebrated, these by Joseph Lanner and the Strauss family.

The year 1848 saw Franz Joseph ascend the throne for a re-

markably long reign that was to last for sixty-eight years—right
into World War I. The beginning of his reign coincided with the
beginning of European nationalism; the subject peoples of the
empire were unhappy.

To placate one group, the Magyars, the dual Austro-Hun-
garian monarchy was established in 1867, with Vienna and
Budapest designated as cocapitals. Franz Joseph tore down
the old ramparts of Vienna's inner city and had them replaced
with the Ringstrasse; there followed a succession of public buildings, parks, and gardens—the neoclassic Parliament, the neo-
Gothic City Hall, the pair of domed neo-Renaissance museums,
the hallowed Opera—that were to form the nucleus of the modern
city.

**Franz Joseph, Mayerling, the end of the empire:** While he
built, and while the city knew commercial prosperity and cultural
eminence, Franz Joseph himself suffered personal tragedy. His
beautiful empress, Elizabeth, absented herself from the stiff
formality of the court for Corfu holidays. Franz Joseph lived
very simply and ate very sparingly. His restless brother, Maximilian, who had accepted a bid to become Emperor of Mexico,
was killed in a battle in that country. His only son, Crown Prince
Rudolf, was found dead at the out-of-town hunting lodge called
Mayerling, along with his mistress, Baroness Maria Vetsera, and
the ever-mysterious deaths were officially declared a double suicide. Mayerling, for that reason, remains a tourist magnet.

The early years of the twentieth century brought with them
increasing dissatisfaction with the crown from the empire's various
national groups, the Slavs most particularly. On June 28, 1914,
a Serbian nationalist assassinated the heir to the throne, Franz
Joseph's nephew, Archduke Franz Ferdinand, on a state visit to
Sarajevo, in what is now Yugoslavia. It was the spark that
kindled World War I. Austria fought with Germany, and lost not
only a war but an empire. With the Armistice of 1918 came the
dissolution of the dual monarchy and the secession of Czecho-
slavakia, Yugoslavia, Poland, and Romania. Franz Joseph had

died two years earlier. His successor, eager young Charles I, who had tried in a number of ways to save the throne, reluctantly abdicated as Emperor of Austria on November 11, 1918, and as King of Hungary two days later. Even though he tried twice afterward to regain the Hungarian throne—going to Hungary from his place of exile on both occasions—he was unsuccessful, and died of pneumonia on Madeira, the site of his final exile, in 1922, at the age of thirty-five. Although his son, Otto, carried on as pretender, Charles was the last of the Hapsburgs to reign on the throne his family had occupied for precisely 636 years. Monarchist or not, it shakes you up.

**Stormy republic, Hitlerian occupation:** The infant Republic of Austria had a baptism of fire. Vienna found itself capital of a tiny state with all of the raw material and export markets of its big empire taken away from it simultaneously. Additionally, the country's two big neighbors drew increasingly toward fascism; little Austria found itself doing likewise. The years between the wars were neither its proudest nor its happiest. Vienna became a city of riots, hunger, unemployment, and inflation—all helping to contribute toward the growth of the National Socialist movement, which, feeding on anti-Semitism, attracted a large following. The only major opposition to the fascism of National Socialism—which was allied to that of Germany's Hitler—was an indigenous species led by Engelbert Dollfuss, who became chancellor in 1932, fighting the idea of *Anschluss,* or union with Germany, with the support of Mussolini's fascist Italy. His suppression of Socialist resistance in 1934 resulted in a revolt that the army put down ruthlessly. The National Socialists later assassinated Dollfuss. His successor, Kurt Schuschnigg, continued to oppose the Austrian-born Hitler's desired *Anschluss,* but in March 1938, the inevitable happened: Hitler marched his troops into Austria and absorbed the country.

**Post-World War II renewal:** At war's end, each of the four Allies occupied different regions of the country—and of Vienna, as well. The U.S.-offered Marshall Plan aid helped tremendously

toward economic recovery. Finally, on May 15, 1955, in a ceremony at Belvedere, the earlier-mentioned Vienna palace built
by military hero Prince Eugene, the Allies and Austria signed a
"state" treaty, rather than the usual "peace" treaty reached with
defeated enemies—in recognition of Austria's having been forced
to acquiesce to Hitler's 1938 occupation. The new republic—
called the Second Republic—determined from the outset to observe strict neutrality. It became a member of the UN shortly
thereafter, and of the Council of Europe, as well. And, in the
process, Vienna has been restored to its striking prewar splendor,
surely the Hapsburgs' greatest gift to it; indeed, a gift to all of us.
The Viennese, with their hallowed Opera House rebuilt, argue
the pros and cons of its presentations, over outrageously rich
*schlag*-embellished pastry and cups of the coffee the Turks introduced them to, centuries ago. They debate other matters, too
—the merits of the *taffelspitz* in their various restaurants might
be a topic. And—in white tie and flowing ballgown, beneath
baroque crystal chandeliers—they waltz away at the slightest
provocation.

## TO SEE

**Lay of the land:** Central Vienna is baroque, it is Gothic, it is
mid-to-late-nineteenth-century neoclassic. It is just about everything but late-twentieth-century glass-plastic-concrete. It is a delight. Hapsburgs began building it six centuries ago with St.
Stephen's Cathedral, and Hapsburgs were still abuilding in the
early years of this century. Perhaps the most inventive of their
monuments is the series of boulevards—the names vary, but they
all end in "ring," which enclose, horseshoelike (the open end
is the Danube Canal) the core of the city, occupying the site of
the ancient town battlements.

Starting at the Opera House—the focal point of the entire city
—and going clockwise, the *ring* is variously known as *Opernring,*

*Burgring, Dr. K. Renner-Ring, Dr. Karl Lueger-Ring, Schotten-ring.* The *Danube Canal* intervenes, and then the rings continue as *Stubenring, Parkring, Schubertring,* and return to where we began at *Opernring* and *Kartnerring.* This last—Kartnerring—touches Opernring and is also at the intersection of the major shopping street, *Kartnerstrasse.* Kartnerstrasse extends smack into the heart of town—in the direction of the Danube Canal. It ends before one is anywhere near the canal, however, after about eight or nine short and lively blocks, at an intersection with two names—*Singerstrasse* to the right, and *Graben* (yes, just plain Graben) to the left. St. Stephen's Cathedral is dead ahead —Vienna has no more distinctive landmark—but one does well at this point to continue to the left on Graben—a major part of the shopping area—until it leads in a block or so to *Kohlmarkt.* This last-mentioned runs parallel with Kartnerstrasse. Take it to its terminus, *Michaelplatz*—named for St. Michael's Church —and then move along, over the square, to *Augustinerstrasse* (named for still another landmark—St. Augustine's Church), which, taken to its terminus, will lead past the massive *Hofburg* complex, right back to the Opera and the Ring. All of this ring-surrounded area—which embraces the oldest part of the town—is walking territory. The narrow side streets yield many an architectural and historic surprise—relatively modest old dwelling houses, palaces, churches, shops, cafes. During the warm-weather months the more important of the monuments are identified with the red-and-white Austrian flag and identify-ing markers.

**Choice destinations:** Schoenbrunn, the suburban summer palace built by Maria Theresa, is obviously so romantic a spot in most visitors' minds that it gets considerably more attention than the Hapsburgs' town palace, the *Hofburg.* This, to my mind, is un-fortunate. There are variations of Schoenbrunn—itself a rather heavy variation of Versailles—all over Europe. But there is only one Hofburg. What keeps visitors from evincing more interest in it than they do is its astonishing complexity. The state apartments of Franz Joseph and Elizabeth draw their share of visitors; others take in the Vienna Choir Boys and the Spanish Riding School, frequently without realizing that they are within the Hofburg when so doing. Not all of this vast agglomeration of structures is open to the public. It has almost a score of distinct subdivisions, totaling some twenty-six hundred rooms, in which some five thousand persons, including the President of Austria, live and work. The whole town-within-a-town is under the aegis of an official called the Chief Warden of the Hofburg; his title was created more than four centuries ago.

The complex breaks down into two broad parts: the *Alte Burg* (or Old Castle) and the *Neue* (or new) *Burg*. The *Schweitzerhof*—named Swiss House because Swiss guards protected it during Maria Theresa's reign—is the original Hofburg. It was begun in the early thirteenth century by Babensbergs, the dynasty that preceded the Hapsburgs; its stellar features are a Gothic chapel, the Treasury museum, and the apartments occupied by the same Crown Prince Rudolf who killed himself at Mayerling. The *Amalienhof* is sixteenth-century, and knew many imperial occupants (Empress Elizabeth—Franz Joseph's wife—was the last); it is partially open to visitors. The *Leopoldine* wing, mostly seventeenth-century, was, like the adjacent Amalienhof, redecorated by Maria Theresa. It is probably the most opulent link in the Hofburg chain, so that one cannot blame the government for reserving it as the official residence of the presidents of the republic; it is not open to visitors. The Court Library, now a part of the *Austrian National Library,* is an eighteenth-century triumph that constitutes one of the great interiors of the planet, what with its fresco-embellished cupola, its superb proportions, and its ingenious mix of decorative elements. The library is open to the public and is in the same building as another magnificent chamber, the *Redoutensale,* originally a ballroom and now used for special meetings and occasional operas; worth bribing an attendant, shamelessly, to have a look. The *Albertina* will be dealt with in the museum section, later on in this chapter. Its neighbor, *St. Augustine's Church,* was the Imperial Family's parish church, and goes back to the fourteenth century. It had been modernized over the centuries, but when Joseph II became emperor in the late eighteenth century he had the church restored to its original Gothic, and the urn-enclosed hearts of his ancestors (there are now more than half a hundred of these) moved to an adjoining chapel. A number of marriages took place there. Napoleon—after divorcing Josephine—was married by proxy to his second wife, Marie Louise, with a view to fathering an heir with royal blood; Marie Louise was the daughter of Emperor Francis I. Other brides include Maria Theresa, and the moody, albeit beautiful Bavarian princess who was to become Empress Elizabeth, the oft-absent wife of Franz Joseph, stabbed to death on a Geneva pier forty-five years after her marriage, in 1898. The eighteenth-century *Reichskanzleitrakt,* the Hofburg wing, contains Franz Joseph's open-to-the-public apartments. The *Spanish Riding School* building, whose perfect proportions rival those of the National Library, is early-eighteenth-century and has housed the Spanish-origin, almost balletlike equestrian activity of the court (and since the court, the republic) from the time of its founding, with people replacing the horses on occasion; as, for example, during the Congress of Vienna. The *Neue Burg,* if one wants to be logical, has no business co-existing with the Alte Burg. But it does. And it works. It is late-nineteenth-early-twentieth-century neoclassic on the grand scale, with its colonnaded façade fronting the broad green that is called *Heldenplatz,* or heroes' square, with the lovely park that is the *Volksgarten* extending from it. The Neue Burg's immense interiors house ballrooms, museums, the newer part of the National Library, and a remarkably handsome and up-to-the-minute *Congress Center.*

*Belvedere,* the eye-filling baroque palace built by Prince Eugene, the hero of the decisive victory over the Turks, is beautifully sited on an elevated plateau overlooking the old part of the city. Its principal hall was the site of the 1955 ceremonies at which the occupying Allied powers—the United States, the Soviet Union, Britain, and France—granted Austria a state treaty, setting it free as a republic for the second time in its history. *Schoenbrunn,* built as Maria Theresa's suburban summer palace, is at times excessively elaborate, graceless, and heavy (as, indeed, are the Hofburg's state apartments). But the setting is agreeable, and there are some especial gems among the interiors, most particularly the happily still-used theater and the reception room known as the Great Gallery (Austrian presidents entertain there). Without, in the surrounding park, there remain the Maria Theresa-established zoo, as baroque as a zoo can be in the late twentieth century, and Roman ruin-embellished formal gardens. Allow half a day for the whole show.

*The Town Hall,* (*Rathaus*), one of Franz Joseph's "ring" structures, is among the greatest and grandest of neo-Gothic structures. You might well expect to run into King Arthur in the Banqueting Hall. There are tours of the public rooms and, in summer, concerts in the courtyard. The *Theresianum* was a seventeenth-century summer house, and has had other functions since; it's now the home of the Austrian Academy of Diplomats; diplomatically, you might ask to have a look around. *Schwarzenburg Palace* is a sumptuous baroque pile, about half of which is now a hotel (see the To Stay section later in this chapter). But you want to have a look at the interiors of the nonhotel sector. And just in case, heaven forbid, you don't get to at least one performance (see the To Watch section on later pages), there are guided tours of the *Opera House* (*Staatsoper*). It was originally built in the 1860s, but was virtually destroyed in World War II. Rebuilding was completed in 1955. Unfortunately, the auditorium—capacious and attractive, to be sure—is neither fish nor fowl as regards décor. Its designers did not reproduce the original, and were obviously hesitant about going all the way with a contemporary hall. The result is aesthetically mediocre. The promenade salon and refreshment rooms are in period style, however—and sumptuous.

You would expect Vienna to be a *church* city; it does not disappoint. If the earlier-mentioned *St. Augustine's Church* is perhaps the most history-rich, it has competition in matters æsthetic. *St. Charles Church* (*Karlskirche*), for example, is the finest baroque house of worship in town, an imperial gesture of thanksgiving for the victory over the Turks, and the first major specimen of the postvictory Austrian baroque period. The dome is a landmark. The *Burgkapelle,* a link in the Hofburg chain, is a Gothic-Baroque meld celebrated as home base for the *Vienna Choir Boys,* who sing virtually every Sunday morning (and on Church holidays) at the 9:25 A.M. mass. The *Franciscan Church* (*Franziskanerkirche*) and its cloister are late Gothic/early Renaissance on a square named for them in the heart of town. *St. Peter's* (*Peterskirche*) is said to have been around when Charlemagne was—in the eighth century. It is, however, mostly baroque, and art-filled. The *Votive Church* (*Votivkirche*) is good neo-Gothic—a mid-nineteenth-century work put up by Franz Joseph as part of his "ring" group. I've saved until last the church you will surely look at first: *St. Stephen's Cathedral* (*Stepheansdom*), as much an Austrian national monument as a place of worship, dating in part to the twelfth century, with the most recent work done after World War II—restorations after extensive bomb damage paid for by contributions from every Austrian province. Highlights include the spire, the beautifully designed slate roof, and a Gothic interior as ever-populated as Paris's Notre Dame and London's Westminster Abbey.

*Composers' houses* are a rather unusual Vienna attraction. There are several for Bonn-born *Beethoven.* (See the chapter on Bonn.) One is the so-called *Eroica House,* where he wrote the *Eroica Symphony.* The city owns the house and has recently restored it; address Doblinger Hauptstrasse 92. Another, at Pfarrplatz 2, is where he lived during 1808, when he composed *Pastorale.* The house where Johan Strauss composed "The Blue Danube," just over a century ago, is at Praterstrasse 54. *Mozart,* between 1784–87, lived in a house now known as *Figarohaus,* at Schulerstrasse 8; it is, needless to say, where he composed *The Marriage of Figaro.*

*Museums,* after you get into them, are memorable. Before even attempting entrance, get hold of a schedule of open-hours from the Vienna Tourist Office. Study it carefully; the hours are the most erratic and confusing of museums in any city, *anywhere.* The Viennese blame this on strong labor unions in a full-employment economy. Regardless of whose fault it is, it is shocking that the leading museum—the *Kunsthistoriches*—is closed all day Monday, open Tuesday through Saturday only from ten to three, and on Sunday only from ten to one. That, of course, is virtually round-the-clock, in contrast to the *Museum of Austrian Culture,* which keeps hours from ten to three two days a week, and nine to one on a third. Period. Well, that gives you an idea. The *Museum of Fine Arts* (*Kunsthistoriches*) is one of the two massive-domed "ring" museums (its twin is Natural History, which you may skip without pangs of guilt, unless you're a buff in that area). It is one of Europe's greatest, packed with works collected over the years by the Hapsburgs. (The greatest Hapsburg collector was Archduke Leopold Wilhelm, while he was governor of the Netherlands in the mid-seventeenth century. He amassed so many pictures that he hired the painter David Teniers the Younger to serve as his curator and catalog the lot in a gallery. Teniers did as he was bidden by creating several paintings of the gallery, with the prince's pictures reproduced in miniature on the painting's gallery walls.) You will have heard of Cellini's exquisite gold salt cellar, with its tiny statues of Tellus and Neptune. But there is a good deal of rather larger proportioned sculpture, and paintings by such artists as Velazquez, Titian, Rubens, Raphael, Rembrandt, Dürer, Holbein, Cranach, Tintoretto, and Correggio—to name some. *Arrive in advance of half an hour before closing* or you won't get in. The *Treasury* (*Schatzkammer*) is a glittering Hofburg requisite—priceless mementoes of the Hapsburgs and of the Holy Roman Empire. The *Albertina* is that part of the Hofburg that serves as a remarkable repository of prints, drawings, and engravings—many from Renaissance masters—that constitutes one of the finest such in the world. *Belvedere Palace* houses three museums: modern Austrian Art in the palace proper; baroque Austrian art in the lower pavilion; and medieval Austrian art in the Orangery. The *Museum of Applied Art* is a treasure trove of lovely things—goldwork, furniture, and porcelain; the *Bundessammlung after Stilmodel* has more of the same—in this case, Hapsburg furniture through the centuries. The *National Library* in the Hofburg, earlier recommended simply for its interior décor and architecture, contains magnificent globes, maps, and manuscripts. The *Portrait Academy* (Akademie der bildenen Kunste), Schillerplatz 3, is a sort of Kunsthistoriches annex—in subject matter, at any rate. It's full of fine paintings by such as Botticelli, Guardi, Titian, and Bosch. The *Stallburg Gallery,* Reitschulgasse 2, is Vienna's Impressionist center, with works by such greats as Munch, Cézanne, van Gogh, Renoir, and Toulouse-Lautrec. The *Folk Art Museum* (*Osterreichisches Museum for Volkshunde*), Laudongasse 15, is what its name suggests, with excellent collections not only from the modern republic, but from the lands of the earlier empire as well. And for a rich portrayal of the history of Vienna, there is the *Historisches Museum der Stadt Wien,* Karlsplatz.

## TO WATCH

The earlier-described *Opera* (*Staatsoper*), of course. Buy tickets at the opera house booking office (English is spoken) or, if there's no time for that, from your hotel concierge, to whom you will pay an additional fee, of course. Additionally, there are the *Volksoper,* where light operas, operettas, and musicals are performed; the beautiful *Redoutensaal* of the Hofburg, where there are occasional operas and other presentations; the historic and handsomely restored *Theater an der Wien,* with ballet, operettas, and musicals; and for plays—in German, of course —the *Burgtheater,* with its versatile and globally known repertory company; the *Volkstheater* (mostly contemporary plays); and the *Theater der Courage* (experimental avant-garde). The *Vienna Philharmonic,* one of the handful of truly great symphony orchestras, performs regularly in the *Musikverein.* There is also the younger but also excellent *Vienna Symphony,* which usually plays in the elderly, barnlike, but acoustically excellent *Konzerthaus.* And, if you have a chance to hear it, the *Vienna Orchestra of the Austrian Radio.* I have earlier recommended concerts of the globe-girdling *Vienna Choir Boys* (Wiener Sanger-knaben) Sundays and religious holidays at 9:25 A.M. in the *Burgkapelle of the Hofburg;* tickets are required. The historic *Spanish Riding School* occupies a masterfully proportioned and decorated hall of its own, in which performances of its uniquely precision-trained Lipizzaner horses are regularly presented. Morning training-sessions may be observed at certain times, and there are tours of the stables, too. *Son et Lumière* (Sound and Light) performances are presented at the floodlighted Belvedere Palace, usually from mid-May through September; the performance is in German, but English synopses are provided.

TO STAY

Crossroads Vienna knows what hotelkeeping is all about. The very best hotels are among the very best in the world. There are some good lesser hostelries, too, although the city could do with more of these. Every room in town is booked well in advance for the annual mid-May/mid-June Vienna Festival. The *Sacher* is described in a single word: Vienna. All that we associate with Vienna, at least for the last century. It went up in 1876, opposite the Opera, and it has been going full steam ever since, even during World War II—and through to 1951—when it housed British officers. A thorough renovation followed that period, so that the hotel one sees today is as much like the pre-war article as can be. There are more beautiful hotels. The charm of the Sacher is its solid, bourgeois quality. Sophisticated interior designers putting a hotel together today might not, to give one example, fill the main lounge with *quite* so many conflicting patterns in the furniture, rugs, and tapestries. Some of the bedrooms are busier than they might be if outfitted by a firm of contemporary budget-watchers. But that is what makes the Sacher the Sacher. A collection of some two thousand paintings—most of the nineteenth century and none of them quite deserving of space in the Kunsthistoriches Museum—line the walls not only of the public rooms but of the corridors on each floor *and* of each and every bedroom. Whereas a contemporary hotel room might have a single piece of art on the wall, and that rarely original, a Sacher bedroom will easily have half a dozen. And although I don't need to—because you already know— I will elaborate on its restaurant-cafe-bar situation on a later page. The *Bristol* has quite as enviable a location as the Sacher —just opposite the Opera. It is a onetime nobleman's palace, enlarged over the years, of course, and recently thoroughly refurbished, with the result a modern-as-tomorrow hostelry in flawless period style. Bedrooms are big beauties; baths likewise. The atmosphere of the public rooms—the cocktail lounge is the most relaxing in Vienna and the restaurant one of the best in town—is without the stiffness that is sometimes typical of de luxe hotels. The *Imperial* was built a little over a century ago as a townhouse for the Duke of Wurttemberg, but within a few years was converted into a hotel. In pre-World War I days, it was accorded the rare distinction of an Imperial Court "By Appointment" warrant. During the post-World War II Occupation it was a home-away-from-home for Soviet officers, and before returning to civilian life it was given a skilled refurbishing, emerging as quite the most elaborate hostelry in Central Europe. Looked at from a distance, with its distinctive neoclassic façade, one expects very grand marble halls within—and gets them. In-

deed, there is a marble staircase with a great crystal chandelier
illuminating it that few monarchs' palaces could improve upon.
The bedrooms and suites are a dream, the restaurants and cafes
worthy of extended comment on a later page. *Hotel im Palais
Schwarzenberg* is just what its title leads you to believe: a
hotel in a palace—the right wing of the earlier-mentioned baroque
palace that is one of the most historic in Vienna. Baroque or not,
every bedroom has a modern bath—they vary in size, shape, and
décor, much of it old. The smartly understated public rooms are
antique-filled. There is a handsome restaurant overlooking the
broad garden, with its own cafe, original fountain, and view of
the Belvedere Palace beyond. And the location is just off the
"ring" area. The *Vienna Inter•Continental,* overlooking the Stadt
(City) Park, almost next door to the Konzerthaus, and a ten-
minute walk from the Opera, is a modern five-hundred-room
full-facility structure. Bedrooms and baths are a generous size,
as they usually are in IHC hotels, and often with fine views of the
heart of town. There is a big late-hours coffee shop—the Viennese
patronize it heavily—as well as a restaurant that is one of
Vienna's top rankers. There are several pleasant moderate-
category hotels. The *Hotel Astoria* is heart-of-town right on
Kartnerstrasse, and thoroughly modernized; many of the attractive
rooms have bath, and there's a good restaurant. The *Kaiserin
Elizabeth,* where I stayed in Vienna on my very first visit—
during the Occupation days, when you still needed a "gray
card" permit from the Russians to get through on the train—
remains among the leaders in the middle group. It is old (the
building was originally thirteenth-century), charming, and now
fifty-eight of its seventy-six rooms have baths of their own. The
dining room is so good-looking that it's a pity it serves only
breakfast. *The Royal* is so well run, so basically comfortable (all
rooms have bath, and there's a restaurant), so nicely located
(a stone's throw from St. Stephen's), and with such eager-beaver
management that you overlook its aesthetics. It is a perfect

example of why the Austrians are better off sticking to traditional décor rather than modern.

## TO EAT (AND DRINK)

When one considers the diversity of the area of which Vienna was once the capital, it is not surprising that its food is such a cosmopolitan mix. From the Hungarians—whose inventive, distinctive cuisine is one of Europe's most underrated—came *strudel* (*retes,* if you want the Hungarian word) and *gulyas*—to name but two specialties. And from other countries—Czechoslovakia, Yugoslavia, Poland, Holland, Spain—come still other dishes. The Turks left countless bags of coffee beans at the gates of Vienna when they were defeated in the late seventeenth century, and the thrifty waste-not-want-not Viennese made use of them, and have never gotten over their passion for the beverage made from them. Younger, waistline-conscious Vienna watches its calories, but the older generation continues with the five-meal day, bless them! First there is continental breakfast—coffee with rolls, butter, and jam. By 10:00 A.M. it's time for *gabelfruhstuck,* or fork breakfast, a kind of cold buffet. (The briefcases of office-bound Viennese often contain the ingredients.) Lunch is usually the main meal—soup, entrée, dessert, coffee. *Jause* is the beloved midafternoon consummation—pastry and coffee usually. Supper follows—soup or an omelette; it is relatively light. Aside from coffee—the Viennese prepare it in many ways, all of them available in the coffee houses—there are specialties worth knowing about. Schnitzels are veal cutlets, breaded, if you insist, or *natur*—plainly sautéed and delicious. There are perhaps a dozen varieties. The *tafelspitz* is Vienna gastronomy carried to high art, at least when well prepared, even though it doesn't sound like much—boiled rump of beef served with a special apple-and-horseradish sauce called *apfelkren. Leberknoedelsuppe*—liver dumpling soup—is, as far as I am concerned, one of the great culi-

nary inventions; *kartoffelsuppe*—potato soup—is good, too. There
are many imaginative warm desserts, such as *Kaiserschmarn.*
*Topfenknoedel* is a sweet cream cheese dumpling; the coffee cake
known as *gugelhupf* is a classic, and so is the rich chocolate cake
known as *Sachertorte.* As any Viennese will explain, that cake
was the subject of a seven-year court battle. The Sacher Hotel
people, claiming they were the inventors of the cake, sued the
owners of the Demel Cafe, who called their product *Sachertorte* also. Finally, in 1962, the hotel won the case. Its product
is now designated as the "original" *Sachertorte;* anyone else
making the product may call it "Sacher" but *not* "official." To
note, too, are the outdoor sausage stands or *wurstelstand;* they
sell a variety of species, each with roll and mustard on the side,
and their snacks, including stuffed peppers and herring and
onions, known as *rollmopse.* In winter, the *maronbrater*—hot
chestnut roaster—is seen on street corners. The favored Austrian
drinks, along with coffee, are beer and wine. Of the former,
Schwechater—a Vienna brew—is good. Austrian wines are at
their best when white. Klosterneuburger is the best known, but
there are a number of other good ones, not to mention the new
wine of the *heurigen* (wine houses) in suburban Grinzig. Prices
are quite moderate; let waiters or captains recommend.

The major gastronomic disappointment in Vienna is the lack
of good restaurants. For a city with so distinguished a cuisine—
one that its citizens quite understandably brag about and take
very seriously indeed—the dearth of first-rank places is extraordinary. There are any number of cheap, poor-to-mediocre places.
But Vienna deserves far, far better. The very best in town are
to be found in the leading hotels. No other entrepreneurs seem
to have the wherewithal to equip really good places and to
operate them professionally. There appears to be an element of
chintziness and skimpiness among the middle-category restaurant
owners that is not worthy of a city with one of the best cuisines
on the Continent. The good hotels, on the other hand, do anything
but stint. The *Sacher's* restaurant gained fame during the latter

Franz Josef period. The emperor was a very fast and very small eater. Courtiers invited to dine at the Hofburg had to keep up with him, and left the palace still hungry. They would retire to the nearby Sacher, and they made its fare famous. The Sacher's dining room is really a number of disparate rooms: the main dining room, an annex to it, the so-called Red Bar, and an upstairs place that is more informal and offers zither music. No matter where one is seated, the food is excellent Viennese and continental, and the service is professional. The hotel's cafe, particularly for afternoon coffee with a piece of melt-in-your-mouth strudel, is equally as high caliber. The *Bristol's* restaurant is the very best-looking in town. Ask for the specialties of the day, or the à la carte regulars; all are invariably delicious and impeccably served. The *Imperial* has a smart, paneled main restaurant, and a popular, informal cafe with the same menu as the restaurant at lunch and dinner. Service is super, fare superb. The *Inter•Continental's Quatre Saisons,* that French name notwithstanding, is authentically Viennese; I challenge you to find a better *taffelspitz* in town. And in Vienna, what with the reputation of restaurants like that of the Sacher, them's fightin' words. The *Schloss Laudon* is an ancient Vienna Woods castle— or, more accurately, a country resort. But if you would like a posh evening in the country, this makes a perfect dinner destination. Of the city's nonhotel restaurants, the leader, as it has been for some years, is *Zu Den Drei Husaren,* Weihburggasse 4. The setting is attractive, the service good, and the food very good indeed, with Austrian dishes featured. Mind, though, that it's not open for lunch, and it closes in the height of summer— August, usually—when the town is full of tourists who would like to patronize it. *Am Franziskanerplatz,* on Franziskaner Platz, near the earlier-described Franciscan church, occupies a couple of floors—the second, mostly—of a six-hundred-year-old house that for a period was the home of Countess Fuchs, a dear friend of whose was Empress Maria Theresa. A lot of the furnishings and accessories from that period remain, and the menu is classic Viennese and good. The restaurants of the earlier described neo-Gothic Town Hall, collectively the *Rathauskeller*, are as recommendable as any moderate-price places in town. There are three of them, one of which stays open until 1:00 A.M., which is worth remembering. *Demel's* remains the leading cafe, or *conditerei*. Go at any time: midmorning for coffee and pastry; midday for sandwiches and salads; afternoon for *jause*. Go to the counter and have a look at what's available before ordering. The chocolates are delicious and are artfully packaged, making fine gifts. Demel's has two competitors of consequence: *Lehmann*, on Graben (particularly noted for its marzipan confections) and *Heiner*, on Kartnerstrasse. *Hawelka* is among the more typical of the old coffee-only coffee houses—with a regular clientele of talky journalists, artists, and writers. There are a number of wine cellers or *caves*, some with music, all with snack-type food. They're usually three to five floors below ground, very, very old, and more congenial than elegant. *Hofkeller* has zither music, a Vienna trademark, while *Esterhazy* has a good cross section of the populace as its clientele.

## TO BUY

Austria's folk arts and crafts are charming, but best purchased outside of the capital, in towns like Salzburg and Innsbruck, closer to where they are made, in the Tyrol. A shop called *Trachten Tostmann*, on Kartnerstrasse, sells some; *Lanz* is traditional dirndl headquarters. The *petit point* is made a good deal of, by the locals, and a lot of by visitors; you see it everywhere you turn in and about Kartnerstrasse. Jewelry is also considered to be a good buy; *Heldwein* is recommended in this regard. *Lobmeyer* sells the best of the Austrian-made crystal and glass, and will engrave monograms on whatever you purchase, overnight. There may be some traditional china patterns you will like at *Augarten*, one of the oldest manufacturers in Europe

after Meissen. *Muhlbauer* sells Austrian-made skis and other
sports equipment, and amusing Austrian toys. The state-owned
*Dorotheum* is an antique auction-showroom; ask the Vienna
Tourist Office how it works, if it interests you. There are a
number of antiques shops; *Reinhold Hofstatter,* on Braunenstrasse,
is a shop that I like. Vienna has not yet accepted the concept
of the department store; its best is *Steffl* on Kartnerstrasse.

### TO NOTE

**Access:** By air, there is one-stop service from New York, usually
via Brussels—should one be coming from the United States. The
well-run national carrier, Austrian Airlines, and a number of
other carriers, connect Vienna with all of Europe, both Eastern
and Western. Vienna's Schwechat Airport is about twelve miles
from town. There is cheap airport bus service; taxis are moderately
expensive; and there's a departure tax. Vienna is on the route
of crack trains—the *Orient Express,* of course, but also the
streamlined *Wiener Walzer,* and a number of others less famed
but no less efficient, which link Western and Eastern Europe
from all directions. Coming by car means a scenic drive through
the Alps; there is good international bus service, too. Within
Vienna, taxis are one's best bet; they're modern, metered, cheap,
and frequently operated by English-speaking drivers. The central
part of town is plateau-flat and wonderful for walking. **Climate:**
Vienna, it must be remembered, is not Alpine, even though so
much else of Austria is; its elevation is only 554 feet. There are
rarely temperature extremes. For example, summer (from June
through August) averages in the mid-sixties, with highs in the low
seventies. Autumn (September and October) is fiftyish. Winter
(from November through March) is in the thirties for the most
part, sometimes dipping a bit lower in January and February.
**Clothes:** Vienna remains an essentially conservative city in this,
as in other respects. Many of the men still wear the lodencloth

suits typical of their region of the country. Dress, generally, is not so much smart as proper. The black tie—indeed, even the white tie with tails—is probably seen more than in any other capital, particularly during the winter, when the schmaltzy waltzy ball is a commonplace. The Viennese are very big, not only on jackets and ties, but on dark suits, for the opera and theater and the better evening spots, and their ladies dress accordingly. During the day, and for lesser places, dress as casually as you like. **Currency:** The schilling, divided into one hundred groschen. **Tipping:** Generally, there is a 10 percent service charge added to hotel, restaurant, and cafe bills; if the service has been efficient and gracious, you might want to add, say, 5 percent to this. Bellhops and baggage porters average five schillings per bag. Taxi drivers expect 10 percent. You will probably be going to the theater, opera, or concerts; ushers get a couple of schillings when seating you, plus the cost of the program. **Business hours:** Generally, stores are open Monday through Friday from between 8:00 A.M. and 9:00 A.M. through to 6:00 P.M., with no lunch-hour closings; they close Saturdays from between noon and 1:00 P.M. **Language:** Viennese German, of course, but there is considerable English spoken in hotels, shops, theater ticket offices, and other places patronized by tourists. **Further information:** Austrian National Tourist Office, 545 Fifth Avenue, New York; 332 South Michigan Avenue, Chicago; 3440 Wilshire Boulevard, Los Angeles; 2433 Northwest Lovejoy Street, Portland, Oregon; City of Vienna Tourist Office, Stadiongasse 6–8 (head office), and Opernpassage (information bureau), Vienna, Austria.

*Acknowledgments*

Without help, support, and encouragement from his friends, the writer of a book as complex as this is in for heavy going. I am very fortunate to have had cooperation, beyond the call of duty, from colleagues both in the United States and Europe, in connection with the series of recent research trips that preceded the writing of the book. For the chapters on *Amsterdam and The Hague,* I am indebted to Director John Bertram and Publicity Manager Hank Fisher of the Netherlands National Tourist Office in New York, my old friend Evelyn Ritchie of E. J. Ritchie Associates in Amsterdam, and Jim Reed of KLM Royal Dutch Airlines, New York. The *Athens* chapter would have been more difficult to write without the kind help of Lambros Eustaxias, of that city, and Miss Elly Economopolous, of the Athens Hilton. Rudolf W. Muenster, crackerjack manager of Berlin's Hotel Kempinski, Willi Vogler of British European Airways' Berlin office, and Howard Watson, representing BEA in New York, were most helpful in connection with the *Berlin* chapter. Godi Egli, now retired as director of the Swiss National Tourist Office in New York; Max Lehmann, that office's public relations director; genial Walter Rosli, of the Berne Tourist Office, and Bob Black, Swissair's public relations director in New York, all helped considerably with the chapter on *Berne.* Claus J. Born, director of the German National Tourist Office in New York, assisted with the chapter on *Bonn.* For the chapter on *Brussels,* I am indebted to Peter A. De Maerel, director of the Official Belgian Tourist Bureau in New York; Jean Gyory, press officer of that bureau's head office in Brussels, and the ball-of-fire Madame Lindekens, of Monsieur Gyory's staff. Axel Dessau, director of the Danish National Travel Office in New York; S. Ralph Cohen, public relations chief of SAS in New York, and his aide, Ray Chambers, made reresearching *Copenhagen* a pleasure, as did Georg Haack and Kurt Nielsen, of the Danish Tourist Board in Copenhagen; Anders Møen, formerly assistant director of Den Permanente and now manager of Georg Jensen's Copenhagen store; Karl Schaefer, manager of the Sheraton-Copenhagen Hotel, and Eigil Hummelgaard, manager of the D'Angleterre Hotel. For the chapter on *Dublin,* I am especially thankful to these Irish friends: Sean Carberry, public relations head of the Irish Tourist Board in New York; his ace colleague, John Kennedy, of Bord Failte, Dublin; Miss Maeve FitzGibbon, Shannon Free Airport's representative in New York; Sean White, ex-Irish Tourist Board New York, and currently public relations director of C.I.E. in Dublin; Alpho O'Reilly, of Irish Television, Dublin, and Miss Eve Murray of the Hotel Inter•Continental, Dublin, Iain (cq) Brown, press officer of the Scottish Tourist Board, and Charles Nicholas, press officer of the Edinburgh Festival, both extended cooperation in connection with the chapter on *Edinburgh.* Goran Hoving, director of the Finnish National Travel Office in New York; Herman Ramo, his predecessor, and Mrs. Eva Ramo; Mr. and Mrs. Bengt Pihlstrom, of the Finnish Tourist Board's head office, and Carl Nyberg, North American manager of Finnair, made the *Helsinki* chapter easier to write. Adnan Ozaktas, director of the Turkish Tourism and Information Office in New York, and Mrs. Hande Surmelioglu, assistant director, helped pave the way for a return visit to *Istanbul* to research the chapter on that city. Mrs. Evelyn Heyward of Heyward Associates, New York, was her usual helpful self, with the chapter on *Lisbon.* Thanks, here, too, to Walter Menke, on the staff of Gordon Gilmore, TWA's vice president-public relations. Many were of assistance with the chapter on

*London:* James Turbayne, O.B.E., Edmund Antrobus and Andrew Glaze, of the British Tourist Authority in New York, and Peter ffrench-Hodges (cq!) of the Authority's London headquarters; Miss Ida Payne and Gabor Denes, of Trust Houses-Forte; Miss Jean Hadow of Westminster Hotels; B. H. Griffin, manager of the Savoy Hotel; Jonathan Dale Roberts, manager of the Hyde Park Hotel, and Robin Oldland, manager of Dorchester Hotel. For assistance with the chapter on *Luxembourg,* I thank Miss Anne Bastian, tourism attaché at the Luxembourg Consulate General in New York, and Georges Hausemer, knowledgeable director of the Luxembourg National Tourist Office in Luxembourg City. Enrique Garcia-Herraiz, former director of the Spanish National Tourist Office in New York, was helpful in connection with the chapter on *Madrid,* as was his colleague, Antonio Alonso, and, in Madrid, Alfonso Font, manager of both the Palace and Ritz Hotels, and for long the most helpful friend of the travel press in the Spanish capital. For the chapter on *Monaco,* gracious cooperation was extended by Mrs. Caroline Cushing, directrice of the Monaco National Tourist Office in New York; E. J. Rochetin, director of the Monaco Government Tourist Department, in Monte Carlo; and Madame Josiane Merino, chargée des rélations extérieures, Société des Bains de Mer, Monte Carlo. *Oslo:* Per Prag, director of the Norwegian National Travel Office in New York (not to mention his predecessors, Sven Winge Simonsen, and Henning Koefoed, who introduced me to Oslo); Just Muus-Falck, crackerjack managing director of the Norway National Travel Association in Oslo, and Miss Nanna Lynneberg, publicity director *par excellence* of the Oslo Tourist Board, all made reresearching the Norwegian capital an especial pleasure. For help with the chapter on *Paris,* grateful thanks to Jacques Detrie, director, and George Hern, public relations director, of the French National Tourist Office in New York; Mademoiselle Nicole Garnier, of the Commissariat Général au Tourisme, in Paris; Myron Clement, long with the French National Tourist Office in New York and now with Clement-Petrocik,

Inc., representing PLM Hotels of France in New York; Madame
Nichole de Bussière, of PLM Hotels of France, Paris; R. C. Ver-
nay, triple-threat director of the Meurice, Prince de Galles, and
Grand Hotels; Charles Ritz, chairman, and B. Penche, manager
of the Ritz Hotel; and John Iversen, manager of the Lancaster
Hotel. *Reykjavik:* George C. McGrath, vice president of Clinton
E. Frank Inc., New York, has handled Icelandic Airlines' U.S.
public relations for years and, until Miss Ingun Ingulfsdottir
came to head the new Icelandic National Travel Office in New
York in 1972, was Mr. Iceland to the American travel press.
They have both been helpful with the Reykjavik chapter, as has
Sigurdur Magnusson, of Icelandic Airlines' head office. For as-
sistance with the chapter on *Rome,* I am indebted to Dr. Emelio
Tommasi, the Italian Travel Commissioner in New York; to
Count Sigmund Fago-Golfarelli, veteran public relations chief of
Ente Nazionale Italiano per il Turismo, in Rome; Natale Rusconi,
direttore, Grand Hotel, and Pennsylvania-born Signora Rusconi;
Gian Francesco Ciaceri, direttore, Eden Hotel; and Bernard
Lovell, Alitalia's publicity officer in New York. The *Stockholm*
chapter is a result of help received from Per Axén, director of the
Swedish National Tourist Office in New York; Ake Gille, his
predecessor; and Miss Madeleine Guleckers, formerly of the
Swedish Tourist Traffic Association's head office. Dr. Heinz Pat-
zak, director of the Austrian National Tourist Office in New York,
cooperated with the chapter on *Vienna,* as did the delightful Dr.
Johanna Kral, press officer of the City of Vienna Tourist Board;
Gerhard Paul, manager of the Hotel Bristol, Otto Heinke, recep-
tion manager of the Hotel Imperial, and Rudolf Palla, manager
of the Sacher Hotel. Other travel industry friends have been
helpful, most especially Mrs. Lis Brewer, public relations director,
Hilton Hotels International; Tom Gerst, public relations director,
Inter•Continental Hotels; Miss Marguerite Allen, vice president,
Robert F. Warner, Inc.; Miss Mary Homi, president, Mary Homi
Public Relations; Phillip D. Shea, vice president-public relations,
Sheraton Hotels; Jacques Meinnier, assistant general manager-

publicity, French National Railroads, New York; and A. William
Plenge, sales manager, Thos. Cook & Son, Inc., New York. My
thanks, as well, to Max Drechsler, for assistance with on-the-spot
research, particularly in the area of antiques, at which he is expert;
to my ever-encouraging, ever-patient, and ever-enthusiastic editor
at Doubleday, Lawrence P. Ashmead; to his pert minidynamo of
an assistant, Miss Michele Tempesta; to William D. Drennan, who
has expertly copy edited five of the seven volumes of this series;
and to Rafael Palacios, for the handsome endpaper map. Whatever errors crop up are mine, as, of course, are the opinions ex-
pressed.

R.S.K.

# INDEX

# Index